American Indian Politics and the American Political System

THE SPECTRUM SERIES
Race and Ethnicity in National and Global Politics

Series Editors: Paula D. McClain and Joseph Stewart, Jr.

The sociopolitical dynamics of race and ethnicity are apparent everywhere. In the United States, racial politics underlie everything from representation to affirmative action to welfare policymaking. Early in the twenty-first century, Anglos in America will become only a plurality, as Latino and Asian American populations continue to grow. Issues of racial/ethnic conflict and cooperation are prominent across the globe. Diversity, identity, and cultural plurality are watchwords of empowerment as well as of injustice.

This series offers textbook supplements, readers, and core texts addressing various aspects of race and ethnicity in politics, broadly defined. Meant to be useful in a wide range of courses in all kinds of academic programs, these books will be multidisciplinary as well as multiracial/ethnic in their appeal.

Titles in the Series

American Indian Politics and the American Political System, Third Edition, by David E. Wilkins and Heidi Kiiwetinepinesiik Stark

Latino Politics by John A. Garcia

Asian American Politics: Law, Participation, and Policy edited by Don T. Nakanishi and James L. Lai

Media & Minorities by Stephanie Greco Larson

Muted Voices: Latinos and the 2000 Elections edited by Rodolfo O. de la Garza and Louis DeSipio. Introduction by Robert Y. Shapiro

The Navajo Political Experience by David E. Wilkins

American Indian Politics and the American Political System

THIRD EDITION

David E. Wilkins and Heidi Kiiwetinepinesiik Stark

ROWMAN & LITTLEFIELD PUBLISHERS, INC.
Lanham • Boulder • New York • Toronto • Plymouth, UK

Published by Rowman & Littlefield Publishers, Inc.
A wholly owned subsidiary of The Rowman & Littlefield Publishing Group, Inc.
4501 Forbes Boulevard, Suite 200, Lanham, Maryland 20706
www.rowmanlittlefield.com

Estover Road, Plymouth PL6 7PY, United Kingdom

British Library Cataloguing in Publication Information Available

Library of Congress Cataloging-in-Publication Data
Wilkins, David E. (David Eugene), 1954–
    American Indian politics and the American political system / David E. Wilkins and Heidi Kiiwetinepinesiik Stark. — 3rd ed.
        p. cm.
    Includes bibliographical references and index.
    ISBN 978-1-4422-0387-7 (cloth : alk. paper) — ISBN 978-1-4422-0388-4 (pbk. : alk. paper) — ISBN 978-1-4422-0389-1 (electronic)
    1. Indians of North America—Politics and government. 2. Indians of North America—Government relations. 3. Indians of North America—Civil rights. 4. Self-determination, National—United States. 5. United States—Politics and government. 6. United States—Race relations. 7. United States—Social policy. I. Title.
    E98.T77W545 2010
    323.1197—dc22   2010021368

∞™ The paper used in this publication meets the minimum requirements of American National Standard for Information Sciences—Permanence of Paper for Printed Library Materials, ANSI/NISO Z39.48-1992.

Printed in the United States of America

Contents

List of Illustrations and Photographs

Maps

Figures

Photographs

List of Tables

Acronyms

AIM	American Indian Movement
ANB/S	Alaska Native Brotherhood and Sisterhood
ANCSA	Alaska Native Claims Settlement Act
BAR	Branch of Acknowledgment and Research
BIA	Bureau of Indian Affairs
CDIB	certificate of degree of Indian blood
CENA	Coalition of Eastern Native Americans
CERT	Council of Energy Resource Tribes
CFR	Code of Federal Regulations
CIA	Committee on Indian Affairs
D.N.A.	Dinébeiina Nahiilna Be Agaditahe
DOF	Department of Fisheries
EDA	Economic Development Administration
ICRA	Indian Civil Rights Act
IGRA	Indian Gaming Regulatory Act
IIM	individual Indian money accounts
IITC	International Indian Treaty Council
IRA	Indian Reorganization Act of 1934
ITBC	InterTribal Bison Cooperative
NAC	Native American Church
NAGPRA	Native American Graves Protection and Repatriation Act
NAICJA	National American Indian Court Judges Association
NAJA	Native American Journalists Association
NAPT	Native American Public Telecommunications

NARF	Native American Rights Fund
NBC	National Broadcasting Company
NCAI	National Congress of American Indians
NECONA	National Environmental Coalition of Native Americans
NIGC	National Indian Gaming Commission
NIYC	National Indian Youth Council
NTCA	National Tribal Chairmen's Association
NWIFC	Northwest Indian Fisheries Commission
OEO	Office of Economic Opportunity
OFA	Office of Federal Acknowledgment
OPEC	Organization of Petroleum Exporting Countries
RAR	recognition/acknowledgment and restoration
RRM	religious revitalization movements
SRM	social revitalization movements
TFW	Timber-Fish-Wildlife agreement
TTF	tribal trust funds

Preface to the Third Edition

THIS BOOK has been germinating in my heart and mind since the mid-1980s, when I began my academic career as an instructor at Navajo Community College (now Diné College), located within the Navajo Nation reservation. I began my work there teaching a course in Navajo history, about which there was plenty of material—not all of which was particularly good, though there was enough available to craft a solid course.

I soon saw a need to teach courses on Navajo government and contemporary Indian politics. I learned very quickly that, unlike Navajo or Indian history, there were no texts on Navajo government. With the college's support, I was able to write a short text titled *Handbook of Navajo Government*. Material on Indian politics was, fortunately, somewhat less sparse, thanks in large part to the work of Vine Deloria Jr. From his seminal polemic, *Custer Died for Your Sins,* in 1969, Deloria crafted a number of books, including *Behind the Trail of Broken Treaties* (1974), *American Indians, American Justice* (1983, with Clifford Lytle), *The Nations Within: The Past and Future of American Indian Sovereignty* (1984, also with Clifford Lytle), and *Documents of American Indian Diplomacy: Treaties, Agreements, and Conventions, 1775–1979* (1999, with Raymond J. DeMallie). He was a prolific chronicler of Indian political issues and Indian social, religious, and legal change, and a brilliant and sometimes caustic analyzer of the tribal-federal relationship.

Deloria was trained in law and theology and was a political activist; his eclectic works cut across disciplinary lines. But even with his works, I still saw a need for texts on tribal governments (their forms, functions, and intergovernmental relations), Indians who have three layers of citizenship (tribal, state, and federal), and Indians' distinctive relationship to the American political system. I had considered writing such a textbook for use in my courses at Navajo Community College but instead returned to graduate school in pursuit of a Ph.D. in political science.

When I joined the faculty at the University of Arizona in the fall of 1990, I was dismayed to learn that there was still very little published information by political scientists (or other social scientists) about indigenous governments—about either their internal dynamics or their relations with other governments and organizations, although there had been some improvement.

But, despite the growing quantity and quality of the literature in the aforementioned topical areas, there remains a severe dearth of information written by political scientists for college-age students that examines the state of political affairs in Indian country and between indigenous peoples and the federal and state governments that is written from a perspective that recognizes the sovereignty—the separate political status—of native nations.[1] McCulloch believes this paucity of scholarship can be explained because the very paradigms (i.e., pluralism, elitism, Marxism, and institutionalism) by which most political scientists structure their analyses are unable to cope with the distinctive status of tribal peoples and their governments.

Wilmer, Melody, and Murdock observed in a follow-up article in 1994 that:

[I]n political science we have largely left the study of native peoples and their political systems to sociologists and anthropologists and have, therefore, denied the role that indigenous people have played in the development of the American political system as well as the role they continue to play in the political and economic processes of this country. This neglect has even led us to ignore the existence of tribal governments as autonomous entities in intergovernmental relationships within the American political system.[2]

Thus I was elated when Paula McClain, Joe Stewart, and Jennifer Knerr approached me in 1997 with the idea of writing a general text about indigenous politics for the "Spectrum Politics" series that Paula and Joe were editing. The publication of such texts on tribal nations is crucial for alleviating prevalent and often pernicious stereotypes about indigenous nations who, despite their ongoing governmental status as separate nations, as landowners, and as holders of important treaty rights, are often inaccurately depicted as small and impoverished minority groups distinguishable from other peoples of color solely by their cultural traits and tribal languages.

This book, now in its third edition, is designed to increase the knowledge of students and other interested readers, increase civic discourse, provide evidence that might aid in interracial and intergovernmental problem solving, and educate readers to the fact that native nations—their lands, governments, and unique rights—are not anachronistic just because of their longevity in the Americas, but are the legitimate and ongoing expressions of the sovereign wills of distinctive peoples who desire to be the determiners of their own fates, although tribal fates are inexorably linked to those of their non-Indian neighbors.

The task before us is no easy one, considering, for instance, the sheer number of indigenous communities populating the United States—565 at last count—each with its own political, economic, social, and cultural systems and differential relationships with the states and the federal government. But my load, now shared with a co-author, Heidi Kiiwetinepinesiik Stark, has been lightened considerably by the support we have received from a number of individuals and organizations.

First, we express continued appreciation to Paula McClain and Joe Stewart. Their own individual and coauthored scholarship on racial and ethnic minorities has been a great inspiration and pool of knowledge and has played an important role in prying open views in the discipline of political science about the status of minorities in America.

Jennifer Knerr, then acquisitions editor at Rowman & Littlefield, was the key contact person initially. Jennifer's role is now occupied by Niels Aaboe, who reached out to us for this third edition.

A number of colleagues, good friends all, read early drafts of the proposal and gave outstanding comments and suggestions as I wrestled with how to prepare a book outline that adequately covered within a limited space the politics of so many indigenous groups and their political dance with one another, the states, and the United States. Tsianina Lomawaima (Creek), professor of American Indian studies at the University of Arizona; John Garcia and David Gibbs, professors of political science at Arizona; Jim White, a professor of political science at the University of North Carolina, Chapel Hill; and Franke Wilmer, professor of political science at Montana State University all provided keen insights and suggestions on what to add, what to cut, and what to merge. Their combined comments helped with the general thematic framework the book still loosely follows.

The first edition was written while Wilkins was a fellow at the Udall Center for Public Policy at the University of Arizona in the fall of 1998. He owes a debt of gratitude to Stephen Cornell, the director; Bob Varady, the associate director; the other fellows; and the excellent staff, many of whom were graduate students, for providing an environment that enabled him to get the first edition published. The second edition was called for because the book at least partially filled a niche in scholarship about indigenous politics since, as one reviewer said, it was the "first general study of contemporary Indians in the U.S. from the disciplinary standpoint of political science."

More importantly, although written broadly from a political science perspective, I sought, heeding the good counsel of my friend and mentor, Vine Deloria Jr., to write from an even broader interdisciplinary perspective that incorporated history, law, culture, economics, and communication, among others. Thus, students and faculty alike generally agreed that the first edition was a comprehensive yet concise work that addressed the critical and often complicated political issues in a way that helped them gain a deeper understanding of tribal governments and their internal and external political and diplomatic relationships with local, state, and federal governments.

Readers also welcomed the various appendices—especially the time line, Internet sources, federal laws, and so forth—and the short case histories of specific First Nations or particular issues that added detail and realism to otherwise abstract topics.

The second edition also benefited from the insights and suggestions of a number of additional individuals, tribal nations, and institutions. Thanks especially to the late Vine Deloria Jr., Patricia Albers, Deron Marquez, and the many students and faculty colleagues with whom I had the pleasure of working.

When Niels Aaboe contacted me in the summer of 2009 about doing a third edition, I was thrilled with the opportunity to update the study. Niels said the book was still selling well—thanks to all those who have adopted it for their courses and the suggestions offered on how to improve it—but given the dynamic pace and ever-volatile nature of indigenous politics, he encouraged me to revise it again.

The most important structural and perceptual change for this edition is the addition of a coauthor, Heidi Kiiwetinepinesiik Stark, a talented Anishinaabe scholar, who brings youth, knowledge, and a much-needed female perspective that will deepen and broaden the book in fundamentally important ways. I was elated when she agreed to join me in this enterprise.

And, of course, native politics has witnessed several major developments that are covered in the third edition: President Obama's election and the attendant changes he has wrought in native politics and the intergovernmental relationship; the tentative settlement of the landmark *Cobell* litigation that has been a persistent stain on the national character; the appointment of Associate Justice Sonia Sotomayor to the U.S. Supreme Court, and the implications of her decisions in federal Indian law, among other things.

This new edition features discussion of these important developments, but also contains a more developed perspective on native women's issues, updated photographs and tables, and new appendices as well.

The authors express their appreciation to Niels Aaboe for his patience and ongoing support of the project and Elisa Weeks, editorial assistant, who helped throughout this third edition.

Wilkins thanks his mother, Thedis R. Wilkins, his siblings and Lumbee relatives, his Diné in-laws, and close friends George Whitewolf (Monacan/Sioux), Danny Bell (Coharie), and June Lowery (Lumbee) who fight to remind their respective native governments and the federal and state governments that they must be accountable to the people. Last, he thanks his wife, Evelyn, and their three children, Sion, Niltooli, and Nazhone.

Stark, first and foremost, thanks her coauthor for his generous invitation to contribute to this third edition and for his unwavering support and guidance over the years. She also expresses her gratitude to the faculty, staff, and fellows at the Institute for Advanced Study who not only provided a much-needed release from teaching, but also created a welcoming and supportive working environment. Special thanks to Ann Waltner, Susannah Smith, Phyllis Messenger, Karen Kinoshita, and Angie Hoffmann-Walter, to the Ford Foundation for the Diversity Postdoctoral Fellowship received, especially Christine O'Brien and Pamela Tyler for their continued support, and Elizabeth M. Fandry for her assistance typing and formatting several of the charts and appendices. She also thanks her colleagues in the department of American Indians Studies, interim dean Olaf Kuhlke, associate dean Gerald Pepper, and close friends Jill Doerfler and Nalo Johnson. Last, she thanks her family, especially niizhote Jodi Drews and nisaye Kekek Jason Stark.

The trek continues.

Note on Terminology

THROUGHOUT THE book several terms are used interchangeably in referring to indigenous peoples in a collective sense—*tribal nations, tribes, Alaskan Natives, native nations, indigenous nations,* and *indigenous peoples.* But when we refer to individual indigenous persons, we generally use only *Indian* or *American Indian.* Of all the terms most used, Indian is easily the most problematic (though some argue that the term *tribe* is pejorative and hints strongly of colonialism), and we use it with some hesitation for two reasons: first, because of its obvious geographical inaccuracy, and second, because it erroneously generalizes and completely ignores the cultural diversity evident in the hundreds of distinctive indigenous nations in North America, each with its own name for itself. One could thus argue that continued usage of the term attests to surviving vestiges of colonialism.

Nevertheless, the terms *Indian* and *American Indian* remain the most common appellations used by indigenous and nonindigenous persons and institutions, and so it is frequently used in the text when no tribal name is specified. We have, moreover, intentionally avoided using the phrase *Native American,* despite that term's popularity among mainstream academics in recent decades, since it creates more confusion than the one it purports to replace, as it can be applied literally to any person born in the Americas. The expressions *native peoples* and *native nations* are less confusing, and these terms and the intriguing phrase *First Nations,* which are all popular in Canada and among some Alaskan indigenous groups, are just catching on in the United States among indigenous nations or policymakers.

What complicates matters, of course, is that there is no single term that is acceptable by all indigenous people all the time, and even people within specific native communities sometimes disagree vigorously on which name they prefer (e.g., Navajo or Diné; Chippewa, Ojibwe, or Anishinabe; Iroquois or Haudenosaunee), and on whether they would rather be identified as tribal communities (which emphasizes their kinship affiliation) or as national entities (which, while not discounting kinship ties, tends to place greater emphasis on an independent political character and a right to engage in diplomatic relations with other nations or states, like the United States or other polities).

Of course, federal law and policy have vacillated on these terms as well. But we shall see that despite assimilative efforts, federal lawmakers continue to recognize the sovereign character of indigenous communities regardless of whether they are called *tribes, nations,* or *peoples.*

Timeline of American Indian Peoples: All Nations and Regions

1000   This is the approximate date of the formation of the Iroquois League, the oldest political alliance in North America.

1638   The first reservation, for the remaining members of the Quinnipiac Tribe, is established in Connecticut.

1775   American colonists declare war against Great Britain. The colonies' provisional government—the Continental Congress—establishes three Indian commissions (northern, middle, and southern); each commission is charged with preserving amiable relations with indigenous tribes and keeping them out of the violence. However, many Indians ally themselves with the British, and many join forces with the American colonists.

1777   The Articles of Confederation organize the new government of the United States. The articles assume authority over Indian affairs except when the "legislative right of any State within its own limits [is] infringed or violated."

1778   The United States signs its first Indian treaty, with the Delaware Nation; in exchange for access to that nation's land by U.S. troops, the United States promises to defend and admit the Delaware Nation as a state.

1789   The U.S. Constitution is adopted. Article I, section 8, grants Congress power to regulate commerce among foreign nations and Indian tribes.

1789   Congress places Indian affairs under the War Department.

1802   Congress appropriates over $10,000 for the "civilization" of Indians.

1803   As part of the Louisiana Purchase, the United States acquires lands on which numerous Indian tribes reside.

1815   The United States begins the process of removing Indians to western lands.

1816   Congress restricts licenses for trade with Indians to America citizens.

1824   The Bureau of Indian Affairs (BIA) is created within the War Department.

1827   John Ross is elected president of the Cherokee Nation; he is the first president since the adoption of the nation's new constitution that year in New Echota, Georgia.

1830	President Andrew Jackson successfully pushes his Indian Removal Bill through Congress.
1831	The U.S. Supreme Court, in *Cherokee Nation v. Georgia,* holds that Indian tribes are domestic dependent nations, not foreign nations.
1832	In *Worcester v. Georgia,* the U.S. Supreme Court, in an opinion written by Chief Justice John Marshall, ensures the sovereignty of the Cherokees; however, President Andrew Jackson refuses to follow the decision and initiates the westward removal of the Five Civilized Tribes (Cherokee, Chickasaw, Choctaw, Creek, and Seminole). The term *Five Civilized Tribes* originated because these five tribes modeled their governments after federal and state institutions and had assimilated key aspects of white culture.
1835	The Treaty of New Echota is signed. Cherokees agree to westward removal.
1838	The Trail of Tears begins. Cherokee Indians are forced to travel almost thirteen hundred miles without sufficient food, water, and medicine; almost one quarter of the Cherokees do not survive the journey. The Potawatomies in Indiana experience similar hardships on their Trail of Death.
1847	Pueblos in Taos, New Mexico, ally with Latinos to overthrow the newly established U.S. rule.
1848	The Treaty of Guadalupe Hidalgo is signed, bringing the Mexican-American War to an end. As a result of the vast amount of land ceded to the United States, many new Indian tribes fall under U.S. jurisdiction.
1849	The Department of the Interior is created, and the BIA is shuffled from the War Department to the Interior Department.
1853	The Gadsden Purchase is completed. More tribes come under the jurisdiction of the United States.
1854	Several southeast U.S. tribes (Cherokee, Chickasaw, Choctaw, Muskogee, and Seminole) form an alliance.
1861	The Civil War begins. Various Indian tribes fight on both sides. Stand Watie, a Cherokee, becomes the only Indian brigadier general in the Confederate Army; he leads two Cherokee regiments in the Southwest.
1864	Approximately eight thousand Navajos are forcibly marched to Fort Sumner, New Mexico, on the Navajo Longest Walk; after three years of harsh imprisonment, the survivors are released.
1865	Confederate general Robert E. Lee surrenders to Union general Ulysses S. Grant at Appomattox; at General Grant's side is Colonel Ely S. Parker, a full-blooded Seneca.
1867	The Indian Peace Commission finalizes treaty making between the United States and Indian tribes.
1869	President Ulysses S. Grant appoints Brigadier General Ely S. Parker to head the BIA; Parker is the first Indian to fill this position.
1871	Congress passes legislation that ends treaty making with Indian tribes.
1884	In *Elk v. Wilkins,* the U.S. Supreme Court holds that the Fourteenth Amendment's guarantee of citizenship to all persons born in the United States does not apply to Indians, even those born within the geographical confines of the United States.
1901	Congress passes the Citizenship Act of 1901, which formally grants U.S. citizenship to members of the Five Civilized Tribes.

1921   Congress passes the Snyder Act, which for the first time appropriates money for Indians under a broad authority given to the secretary of the interior, regardless of the amount of Indian blood or residence. This act greatly expands the moneys available for Indians because it releases the federal government from a strict adherence to treaty provisions.

1924   Congress passes the Indian Citizenship Act, conferring citizenship on all American Indians.

1934   Congress passes the Indian Reorganization Act (IRA), which allows for tribal self-government, and begins the Indian Credit Program; concurrently, the Johnson-O'Malley Act provides for general assistance to Indians.

1939   Chief Henry Standing Bear and other Sioux leaders appeal to Korczak Ziolkowski, who worked on the presidential sculptures at Mount Rushmore in former Sioux territory, to create a similar monument to Crazy Horse. Ziolkowski begins work in 1947. In 2010, his wife, Ruth, and several children continue to work on the movement.

1944   In Denver, Colorado, the National Congress of American Indians is founded.

1948   Through judicial means, Indians in Arizona and New Mexico win the right to vote in state elections.

1949   The Hoover Commission recommends "termination," which would mandate that Congress no longer recognize Indian sovereignty, thus eliminating all special rights and benefits.

1953   Congress passes a law—introduced by Wyoming Representative William Henry Harrison—that gives California, Minnesota, Nebraska, Oregon, and Wisconsin legal jurisdiction over Indian reservations, thus initiating the termination process.

1958   Secretary of the Interior Fred Seaton begins to retract the termination policy.

1961   More than 210 tribes meet at the American Indian Chicago Conference, where the Declaration of Indian Purpose is drafted for presentation to the U.S. Congress.

1968   Congress passes the American Indian Civil Rights Act, providing individual Indians with some statutory protection against their tribal governments. This protection is loosely modeled on the protection the U.S. Constitution provides against state and local governments.

1968   The American Indian Movement (AIM) is founded; it is a protest movement based on the model of the black civil rights protest groups.

1969   Indian activists occupy Alcatraz Island near San Francisco in addition to staging sit-ins at the BIA.

1960s– From the late 1960s to early 1970s, tribes begin to create tribal colleges to ease
1970s the transition from reservation life to mainstream schools. Twenty-seven such colleges are created.

1971   The Alaska Native Claims Settlement Act is passed, eliminating 90 percent of Alaska Natives' land claims in exchange for a guarantee of forty-four million acres and almost $1 billion.

1972   In protest of a history of broken promises to Indian tribes, two hundred Indians participate in the Trail of Broken Treaties march and ultimately occupy the Washington, D.C., office of the BIA.

1973   AIM organizes an occupation of Wounded Knee on the Pine Ridge Reservation in South Dakota, near the Nebraska border; the occupation ends with an armed confrontation with the FBI. AIM member Leonard Peltier is still (as of 2010) held in federal prison for the murder of two FBI agents, despite evidence that his trial was unconstitutional and unfair.

1975   The Indian Self-Determination and Education Act is passed, giving Indian tribal governments more control over their tribal affairs and appropriating more money for education assistance.

1979   The U.S. Supreme Court awards the Lakota Nation $122.5 million in compensation for the U.S. government's illegal appropriation of the Black Hills in South Dakota.

1980   The Penobscots and Passamaquoddies accept monetary compensation from the U.S. government for their lands (now the state of Maine), which the Massachusetts government took illegally in 1790.

1986   Congress amends the Indian Civil Rights Act and grants tribal courts the power to impose criminal penalties.

1988   The Alaska Native Claims Settlement Act is amended, giving Alaska Native corporations the option to sell their stock after 1991.

1988   Congress officially repeals the thirty-five-year-old termination policy.

1992   U.S. Representative Ben Nighthorse Campbell, a Cheyenne from Colorado, is elected to the U.S. Senate.

1993   Ada Deer is appointed assistant secretary for Indian affairs by President Clinton. She is the first Indian woman to hold the position.

1994   Three hundred representatives from the 556 federally recognized Indian tribes meet with President Bill Clinton, the first time since 1822 that Indians have been invited to meet officially with a U.S. president to discuss issues of concern to Indian peoples.

1994   Clinton signs a law that provides Indians with federal protection in the use of peyote in religious ceremonies.

1996   Laguna Pueblo faces a legal challenge regarding its long-standing tradition of allowing only men on the ballot for tribal office.

1996   The University of Arizona creates the first Ph.D. program in American Indian studies.

1996   Skeletal remains of an ancient person (nine to ten thousand years old, estimated), dubbed "The Ancient One" by native peoples and "Kennewick Man" by scientists, are found on the banks of the Columbia River, setting up an intense conflict between the First Nations and the scientists over what is to be done with the skeleton.

1997   For the first time in history, American Indians are included in the presidential inaugural festivities as special and individual participants. American Indians are in the parade and have an American Indian ball.

1997   Alaska Natives take a case to the Supreme Court regarding their right to tax others on their land (forty-four million acres). The question posed: Does "Indian Country" exist in Alaska as a result of the 1971 Alaska Native Claims Settlement Act?

1998   Four thousand Alaska Natives march in Anchorage in protest of Alaska legislative and legal attacks on tribal governments and native hunting and fishing traditions.

1998   In a unanimous decision, the Supreme Court rules that, in the absence of a reservation, the Venetie Tribe of Alaska does not have the right to tax others on land conveyed under the 1971 Alaska Native Claims Settlement Act. In essence, the Court decrees that "Indian Country" does not exist in Alaska.

1998   Clinton issues Executive Order No. 13084, "Consultation and Coordination with Indian Tribal Governments," in which he pledges that the federal government will establish and engage in meaningful consultation and collaboration with Indian tribal governments in matters that will significantly impact their communities.

1998   Interior Secretary Bruce Babbitt is investigated in an Indian casino scandal under claims that he denied a gaming license to several Wisconsin tribes because of White House pressure to satisfy competing Minnesota tribes who made large contributions to the Democratic National Committee.

1998   The Makah Nation of Washington State renews its traditional practice of whaling after a respite of seventy years, despite protests from many environmental and other groups.

1999   A federal judge holds Secretary of the Interior Babbitt and Secretary of the Treasury Rubin in contempt for failure to provide documents related to the Indian trust funds class action lawsuit.

1999   Clinton visits the Pine Ridge Sioux Reservation in South Dakota on a swing through some of the most impoverished communities in America. He is the first sitting president since Calvin Coolidge in 1927 to make an official visit to an Indian reservation.

2000   Brad Rogers Carson, an enrolled member of the Cherokee Nation of Oklahoma, is elected as the Congressman for the Second District of Oklahoma. He is the only enrolled tribal member in the House of Representatives at the time.

2000   In *Rice v. Cayetano,* the U.S. Supreme Court strikes down a restriction that had allowed only persons with Native Hawaiian blood to vote for the trustees of the Office of Hawaiian Affairs.

2000   Assistant Secretary of the Interior Kevin Gover (Pawnee) issues a startling apology to Native peoples on behalf of the BIA, decrying the poor treatment Indians have experienced from his agency.

2000   The U.S. Supreme Court declines to review a religious freedom case centering around the use of Devils Tower, a site sacred to several Indian nations. This decision upholds a federal court ruling that supported the religious rights of Indians against challenges from recreational rock climbers.

2001   The U.S. Supreme Court, reversing a Court of Appeals judgment, unanimously rules on May 29 that the Navajo Nation's Hotel Occupancy Tax on nonmembers on non-Indian fee land is invalid.

2001   A federal Court of Appeals rules that tribal trust funds had been mismanaged by the government.

2002   In a blow to the Makah Nation, the Ninth U.S. Circuit Court of Appeals rules in *Anderson v. Evans,* in a case brought by animal advocacy groups, that the government violated the National Environmental Policy Act by failing to prepare an environmental impact statement prior to approving the whaling quota and also held that the Marine Mammal Protection Act applied to the tribe's proposed whale hunt.

2002   President Bush signs an executive order reaffirming the federal government's commitment to tribally-controlled colleges and universities.

2002   Interior Secretary Gale Norton and Assistant Secretary Neal McCaleb are placed in contempt of court by federal judge Royce Lamberth for ongoing problems associated with the Indian trust fund lawsuit.

2002   The New Mexico Supreme Court, in a first-ever development, adds federal Indian law as a subject on the state's bar exam.

2003   Senators Ben Nighthorse Campbell and Daniel Inouye, co-chairs of the Committee on Indian Affairs, send a letter to the parties in *Cobell v. Norton* (the Indian trust fund litigation) urging them to settle the lawsuit without delay.

2004   Dave Anderson (Choctaw/Chippewa), founder of Famous Dave's barbecue, is selected by President Bush to serve as assistant secretary of Indian affairs. Anderson resigned in 2005 after less than a year on the job, citing the difficulties he faced trying to serve tribes as a Washington bureaucrat.

2004   The National Museum of the American Indian opens on the mall in Washington, D.C.

2004   Ben Nighthorse Campbell, the only American Indian in the U.S. Senate, leaves office at the end of his term.

2004   The BIA formally acknowledges the Schaghticoke Tribal Nation of northwestern Connecticut.

2004   In *United States v. Lara,* the Supreme Court holds that tribal courts had the inherent sovereign power to criminally prosecute nonmember Indians, and that such power did not violate the double-jeopardy clause of the U.S. Constitution's Fifth Amendment.

2004   Congress passes a controversial law, the Western Shoshone Claims Distribution Act. This law will distribute $138 million under the Western Shoshone Claims Commission Judgment Fund to tribal members for the millions of acres of land owned by the tribe. Many Shoshone, including the noted Dann Sisters, fought to defeat this bill as they maintain that they retain a treaty right to the lands in question.

2004   Governor Arnold Schwarzenegger vetoes a bill that would have prohibited five California high schools from using the name "Redskins," a word long considered derogatory by most Native communities.

2004   In *Boneshirt v. Hazeltine,* a federal district court rules that South Dakota violated the 1965 federal Voting Rights Act when it approved a statewide redistricting plan that had the effect of diluting the voting power of Indians in two districts.

2004   President Bush signs into law the American Indian Probate Reform Act. This measure is designed to limit the fractionation of Indian trust land.

2004   The U.S. Senate Committee on Indian Affairs holds hearings in an effort to sort out the financial relationship between six tribes and two Washington lobbyists, Jack Abramoff and Michael S. Scanlon, who charged the tribes over $66 million in less than four years for a minimal amount of work.

2005   Two Connecticut tribes, the Eastern Pequot Tribal Nation and the Schaghticoke Tribal Nation, recently granted federal recognition, have their federal status rejected by the Interior Department's Board of Indian Appeals after the tribes were challenged by the state's congressional delegation. Their cases are sent back to the BIA for further review.

2005   President Bush's fiscal year 2006 budget proposes cuts of more than $200 million for education, housing, health, and other Indian programs.

2005   In July, and over the objections of several Columbia River Basin tribal nations, a team of scientists spends ten days examining the nine- to ten-thousand-year-old skeletal remains of "The Ancient One."

2005   In July Elouise Cobell and other plaintiffs propose that the nine-year-old class action lawsuit involving Indian trust funds could be ended if Congress provided $27.5 billion for a settlement and agreed to other principles.

2005   Jeffrey Weise, a Red Lake Chippewa teenager, kills ten people, most of whom are Indian high school students, in an unprecedented rampage on the Red Lake Reservation in Minnesota.

2005   In *City of Sherrill, New York v. Oneida Indian Nation of New York,* the Supreme Court rules in an 8–1 decision that, despite an existing principle of Indian law that holds that tribal nations enjoy immunity from state and local taxation of reservation lands until that immunity has been unequivocally revoked by Congress, the City of Sherrill had the right to impose property taxes on land that had been repurchased by the Oneida Nation within the Nation's historical territorial boundaries.

2005   The Oneida Nation, among other tribal nations, independently pledges $1 million to efforts to help survivors of the Indian Ocean tsunami and earthquake.

2005   The Navajo Nation Council unanimously enacts a law that outlaws same-sex marriages—the Cherokee National Tribal Council in Oklahoma had passed a similar measure in 2004. Navajo President Joe Shirley Jr. vetoes this law, but the Council, by a vote of 62–14, overrides the president's veto.

2005   The National Collegiate Athletic Association (NCAA) bans the use of "hostile and abusive" American Indian mascots from postseason tournaments.

2006   Recognizing that many states, counties, and cities continue to erect barriers to Native voters, Congress renews the special provisions of the Voting Rights Act of 1965.

2006   Jack Abramoff, the Republican lobbyist who financially exploited several tribal leaders, pleads guilty to charges of conspiracy, fraud, and tax evasion.

2006   The Cherokee Nation's highest court, the Judicial Appeals Tribunal, rules that freedmen are full citizens of the Cherokee nation, retaining citizenship and voting rights, among other privileges.

2006   Congress enacted the Esther Martinez Native American Languages Preservation Act of 2006 (PL 109-394) to ensure the survival and continuing vitality of Native American languages.

2006   The Seminole Tribe purchase the Hard Rock International for $965 million.

2007   After losing their appeal of the NCAA mascot ban and being placed on the list of schools prohibited from hosting postseason tournaments, the University of Illinois Board of Trustees decides to retire the University's former mascot—Chief Illiniwek—in name, performance, and symbol.

2007   Cherokees amend their Constitution, removing 2,800 freedmen descendants from tribal roles.

2007   The Mashpee Wampanoag tribe, composed of 1,453 members located on Cape Cod in Massachusetts, receives federal recognition.

2007   Diane J. Humetewa (Hopi) becomes the first Native American woman to serve as a U.S. Attorney in Arizona.

2007   The United Nations adopts the Declaration on the Rights of Indigenous Peoples. The United States, Canada, New Zealand, and Australia voted against the declaration's adoption.

2008   The Supreme Court in *Plains Commerce Bank v. Long Family Land & Cattle Company, Inc.* held that tribal courts lack jurisdiction to decide a discrimination claim concerning a non-Indian bank's sale of fee land that it owned within a reservation.

2009   The Department of Interior announces it has negotiated a $3.4 billion settlement to the *Cobell v. Salazar* litigation.

2009   The Supreme Court in *United States v. Navajo Nation (Navajo II)* dismissed the Nation's assertion of a breach of trust (fiduciary duty) by the secretary of the interior who failed to promptly approve a royalty rate increase under a coal lease the Nation executed in 1964.

2009   The federal government reestablished relations with the Wilton Rancheria and the Delaware Tribe of Indians.

2009   President Obama nominated Judge Sonia Sotomayor, the first Latina, to replace Supreme Court Justice David Souter.

2009   In *Carcieri v. Salazar* the High Court, limiting the authority of the secretary of the interior, ruled that the Narragansett Tribe, who had received formal recognition in 1983, were not eligible to place land into trust because they were not under federal jurisdiction in 1934, when the IRA was passed.

2009   The U.S. Supreme Court holds that a 1993 congressional apology resolution acknowledging the United States' involvement in the overthrow of the Hawaiian Kingdom did not require the state of Hawaii to reach a political settlement with native Hawaiians before transferring 1.2 million acres of land.

2009   President Obama signs a presidential memorandum seeking to renew and enhance the spirit of tribal consultation and collaboration previously outlined by the Clinton administration.

2010   President Obama signs into law the Patient Protection and Affordable Care Act, which includes the permanent reauthorization of the Indian Health Care Improvement Act, aiding in efforts to improve Indian health services

2010   The North Dakota Supreme Court supports a Board of Higher Education decision to retire the University of North Dakota's Fighting Sioux nickname and logo, which will remain until the 2011–2012 school year.

2010   Wilma Mankiller, a revered leader of the Cherokee Nation of Oklahoma, walks on.

2010   Congress enacts the Tribal Law and Order Act to address the law enforcement crisis in Indian Country

2010   The Department of Interior issues final determination to acknowledge the Shinnecock Indian Nation of Long Island, New York.

Source: Modified from Paula D. McClain and Joseph Stewart Jr., *"Can We All Get Along?" Racial and Ethnic Minorities in American Politics,* 5th ed. (Boulder, CO: Westview, 2010), 251–257.

Introduction

This conference will serve as part of the ongoing and important consultation process that I value, and further strengthen the nation-to-nation relationship.

—President Barack Obama, 2009[1]

ON NOVEMBER 5, 2009, President Barack Obama welcomed nearly four hundred tribal leaders to the White House Tribal Nations Conference, the largest and most widely attended gathering in U.S. history. In inviting leaders of the 564 tribal nations to Washington, Obama appeared to be making good on campaign promises to give native nations a voice in his administration and to shape more appropriate federal policies regarding Indian Country. Obama assured tribal leaders that he would uphold the nation-to-nation relationship. Acknowledging past grievances, he stated,

> We know the history that we share. It's a history marked by violence and disease and deprivation. Treaties were violated. Promises were broken. You were told your lands, your religion, your cultures, your languages were not yours to keep. And that's a history that we've got to acknowledge if we are to move forward. We also know our more recent history; one in which, too often, Washington thought it knew what was best for you. There was too little consultation between governments.[2]

President Obama apparently acknowledged this history and sought to forge a new relationship with tribal nations.

President Clinton had issued an executive order in 1998 that sought to establish regular and meaningful consultation and collaboration between native nations and the federal government. Yet only a few agencies executed that order. Obama sought to invigorate the intergovernmental relationship, signing a presidential memorandum that directed every Cabinet agency to provide a detailed plan within ninety days. He delivered additional opening remarks and then engaged in an interactive dialogue with tribal leaders. The conference also included discussions between native leaders and high-level federal officials covering the areas of economic development and natural resources, public safety and housing, education, health, and labor.

Indian Country had emotionally and emphatically embraced Obama during his presidential campaign. Making history as the first African American president of the United States, Obama noted in his victory speech that much of his triumph could be attributed to the support of native voters. More then one hundred tribal leaders and numerous tribal nations and organizations had endorsed Obama.[3] Indeed, the Crow Nation honored him with the name "One Who Helps People Throughout the Land" and Hartford and Mary Black Eagle adopted him into their family. Much of this support may have been attributed to Obama's detailed principles for stronger indigenous communities. His campaign in Indian Country focused on sovereignty, tribal-federal relations, and the trust responsibility. He emphasized the importance of consultation and said he would include American Indian advisors in his administration.

The Obama administration has already shown some of its commitment to strengthening the nation-to-nation relationship and improving conditions across Indian Country. The $787 billion stimulus package, entitled the American Recovery and Reinvestment Act of 2009 "included $100 million for job creation within tribal communities, $500 million for the Indian Health Service, and nearly $500 million for various education, college, and school construction programs."[4] In addition, Obama has also made good on his promise to give native peoples a voice in his administration by appointing Larry EchoHawk (Pawnee tribe of Oklahoma) assistant interior secretary for Indian Affairs, Kimberly Teehee (Cherokee) senior advisor for Indian Issues, and deputy associate director of the office of intergovernmental affairs Jodi Gillette (Standing Rock Sioux), to name a few. Obama's broad campaign slogan, "Change We Can Believe In," may perhaps, at least for Indian Country, prove true.

To me, it is now a question of sovereignty.

—Cecelia Fire Thunder, 2006[5]

Indian Country is often a microcosm reflecting the struggles that divide the United States. Several of the critical issues that continually arise during important elections and conflict voters at the polls have also proven difficult to solve in Indian Country, such as economic development, health care, and women's reproductive rights. As varied as Indian nations are, so too are their responses to these increasingly difficult issues. This was evident when, in March 2006, South Dakota governor Mike Rounds (R) signed into law House Bill 1215, the nation's most restrictive ban on abortions. In a clear attempt to challenge the 1973 Supreme Court ruling known as *Roe v. Wade,* the bill provided no exceptions for rape or incest, and only limited protection for the woman's life.

Oglala Sioux Tribal President Cecelia Fire Thunder garnered national attention when, in response to South Dakota's statewide ban, she vowed to build a clinic on Lakota lands that would preserve women's rights, stating, "I will personally establish a Planned Parenthood clinic on my own land which is within the boundaries of the Pine Ridge Reservation where the State of South Dakota has absolutely no jurisdiction."[6] Fire Thunder's declaration to build a clinic challenged the state's jurisdiction both over Indian lands and women's bodies. She remarked, "I'll continue pushing the envelope and exerting our sovereignty." She noted that in Lakota history, "You didn't have people passing laws to control a woman's body."[7]

Fire Thunder, the tribe's first female president, was a former nurse who had spent years pressing for American Indian health clinics in California. After returning to Pine Ridge, she worked as a community organizer against domestic violence. Fire Thunder had seen first-hand how Indian women were experiencing disproportionate rates of violence coupled with 85-percent unemployment rates on the reservation. Nationally, American Indians maintained single-parent households at a higher percentage and had a higher ratio of the population living in poverty than the national average. While one in six American women are the victim of a rape or attempted rape, American Indian women suffer from sexual assault and rape at three and a half times the national average.[8] Though much of the initial media focus centered on abortion, Fire Thunder pointed out that the issues went beyond this primary conception. She believed a clinic could also serve as a safe haven for victims of sexual assault as well as a venue for educating both men and women about reproductive health, planned parenting, and contraception. Fire Thunder noted that the state ban had national implications, arguing, "Ultimately, this is a much bigger issue than just abortion. The women of America should be outraged that policies and decisions about their bodies are being made by male politicians and clergy. It's time for women to reclaim their bodies."[9]

This strong assertion of tribal sovereignty was met with varied responses. Indeed, there were many native and non-native people alike who supported the building of a clinic at Pine Ridge. In fact, in November 2006, South Dakota citizens rejected the state abortion ban at a voter referendum, with citizens in the two counties that make up the Pine Ridge reservation voting against the ban by a substantial majority. Yet many also wondered whether the proposed clinic would resonate with Lakota views that recognize children as sacred beings. In addition, many tribal citizens questioned whether Cecelia Fire Thunder had overstepped her position as president of the Oglala Sioux Tribe. While she spoke as a woman, she had also solicited funds on behalf of the tribe for building the clinic, an action that had not been sanctioned by the tribal council. Fire Thunder had already faced threats of removal from her fellow councilmen who voted to impeach her in 2005 "after complaints that she had disrespected elders and improperly sought a multimillion-dollar loan to keep the tribal government from shutting down."[10] On May 30, 2006, the Oglala Sioux Tribal Council banned abortions on the Pine Ridge Indian Reservation and suspended Fire Thunder, pending an impeachment hearing. She was impeached June 29, 2006.[11]

Some questioned whether Fire Thunder's presidency was met with so many challenges because she was the first female to serve in this capacity in a community famous for its historic male counterparts, such as Red Cloud and Crazy Horse. Indigenous politics has seen a major transformation in tribal leadership along gender lines during the twenty-first century. A 1981 study showed that sixty-nine of the more than five hundred federally recognized tribes were led by women. By 2006, 133 women were in head leadership positions among the more then 560 federally recognized tribes.[12] Native women have historically served in prominent positions in their communities, as leadership was often divided across various roles and actors. As many of these positions have been consolidated in modern tribal governments, the primary roles were often filled by men. However, in recent decades there has been a growth in women serving in these capacities due to an increase in access to education and a shifting perception of female leadership nationally.

This shift in leadership has also brought a transformation in tribal policy priorities. For decades, tribes had struggled with how to codify kinship systems into law and policy. Tribal leaders strive to blend their traditional values and practices with ever-shifting social circumstances to meet community needs. Women's activism and leadership in varied capacities have brought much needed focus to the relationship between kinship and law, such as child welfare, tribal citizenship, same-sex couples, and elders programs. These issues remain as complicated and contested in Indian Country as they are across the larger state.

> The right of taking fish and of whaling or sealing at usual and accustomed grounds and stations is further secured to said Indians.
>
> —Treaty with the Makah, 1855[13]

On May 17, 1999, several members of the Makah Nation, a small tribe inhabiting lands near the Olympic Peninsula in Washington State, conducted the first legal killing of a gray whale in over seventy-five years. Whaling had been prohibited on the northwest coast since the early part of the twentieth century because global commercial whaling had driven the gray whale population nearly to extinction. The United States banned all hunting of the gray whale in 1937. The Makah had voluntarily stopped hunting gray whales in the 1920s because "whaling had begun to lose its social prestige and subsistence importance as the tribes were pulled into the global market economy."[14]

After the successful hunt, as excited Makah feasted on the blubber and raw meat from the thirty-ton, thirty-and-one-half-foot-long female whale, tribal leaders expressed pride in the resurrection of their nation's seafaring tradition, a tradition reserved by the Makah in their land cession treaty with the United States in 1855. As Ben Johnson Jr., chairman of the tribe's council, put it: "It's a great day, a historic day for the Makah, but there are a lot of other hurdles we still have to jump over, many things to work on."[15] The Makah, in fact, are the only indigenous nation that expressly reserved the right to whale in a treaty agreement with the federal government.

One of the major hurdles for the Makah centered on how the tribe intended to cope with the firestorm of anger, resentment, and oftentimes racist discourse the hunt aroused among many non-Indians, particularly environmental groups. Protesters fit into three categories: those distraught by the whale killing; those who disapproved of how the whale was killed (the Makah used steel harpoons and a shot from a .50-caliber assault rifle); and those who exhibited a deep resentment, even hatred, toward the Makah in particular and Indians in general. Protesters rained death threats and bomb threats on the Makah, and radio stations, newsletters, editorial pages, and Internet chat rooms carried anti-Indian statements that outnumbered statements supporting the Makah by a ten-to-one margin. Comments like "Save a whale, harpoon a Makah" and "shoot an Indian, bomb them, harpoon them" were rampant.[16]

All of this despite the fact that the Clinton administration supported the Makah's treaty right to whale, that the gray whale was no longer an endangered species (worldwide nearly two thousand gray whales are killed annually by hunters from a dozen countries), and that the International Whaling Commission had twice given its support to the Makah to harvest for subsistence purposes up to twenty whales between 1998–2002 and 2003–2007.

Photo I.1
Makah Indians paddle their thirty-two foot canoe *Hummingbird* into the open waters of the Pacific Ocean during a practice on August 28, 1998, in Neah Bay, Washington. The Makah tribe legally hunted and killed its first gray whale in over seventy-five years on May 17, 1999. They have since been denied the opportunity to continue their tradition by the federal courts.
Source: AP/WIDE WORLD PHOTOS

Despite the initial protests, the Makah refused at first to be stifled in exercising one of their most culturally significant rites. As Wayne Johnson, the captain of the whaling team, said,

> Some people have criticized us for this celebration [standing on the whale and raising their paddles and weapons in a triumphant manner], saying that it should have been a somber event and that we should have mourned the whale in the way they imagine to be proper. I am so tired of non-Indians pushing their values on the Makah people and telling us how and how not to be Makah.[17]

However, the firestorm unleashed in the non-Indian community by the Makah's exercise of their cultural and treaty right would not subside, and in less than a year the first of a series of legal setbacks in 2000,[18] 2002,[19] 2003,[20] and 2004[21] against the Makah arrived, fueled by the antipathy of an alliance of environmental and animal advocacy groups with the support of some congresspersons. The most damaging ruling occurred in 2002, where the Ninth Circuit Court of Appeals held that the federal government had violated the National Environmental Policy Act by having failed to prepare an environmental impact statement prior to approving the Makah's whaling quota. The court also noted that the 1972 Marine Mammal Protection Act, which prohibits anyone in the United States from harming gray whales or other sea mammals, also applied to the Makah's whale hunt.

As a result of this and the other decisions, the Makah have been stymied in their efforts to pursue another whale. In 2003 the tribal government drastically reduced their whaling budget and terminated the tribe's whaling commission.

Tribal leaders and members continue to explore their options. In 2004, the tribe applied for a waiver from the federal Marine Mammal Protection Act of 1972, but the process has been slow. Many tribal members are deeply frustrated that their treaty right is being denied. Non-Indian tensions increased when Wayne Johnson and four other tribal members killed a forty-foot gray whale off Neah Bay. In a public statement, Johnson explained "We've been waiting eight years since our last whale hunt for the United States to hold up its end of our treaty that guarantees our right to hunt whales. They have yet to carry out the legal procedures they claim to need. . . . The Makah Tribe never conceded that our treaty rights were subject to all these conditions."[22] Johnson and the others were charged in tribal court with conducting an unauthorized whale hunt and in federal court for violating the Marine Mammal Protection Act. The Makah continue to fight for the ability to exercise their treaty rights. Micah McCarty, who assumed a senior post in the Makah Tribe in January 2008, was hopeful that the tribe would be whaling again sometime in 2010. Michael Lawrence, the Makah's vice-chair in 2003, reflecting on the court's rulings and the history of Indian treaty fragility and frequent abrogation of treaty rights, observed that "this isn't the end for us. We are going to continue to protect our treaty rights."[23] The fight continues.

> In carrying out its treaty obligations with the Indian tribes, the Government is something more than a mere contracting party. Under a humane and self-imposed policy which has found expression in many acts of Congress, and numerous decisions of this Court, it has charged itself with moral obligations of the highest responsibility and trust. Its conduct . . . should therefore be judged by the most exacting fiduciary standards.
>
> —Justice Frank Murphy, *Seminole v. United States,* 1942[24]

> I have never seen more egregious misconduct by the federal government. In my own experience, government lawyers always strived to set the example by following the highest ethical standards that were then a model for the rest of the legal profession. . . . Justice has not been done to these Indian beneficiaries. Moreover, justice delayed is justice denied. The Court cannot tolerate more empty promises to these Indian plaintiffs.
>
> —Judge Royce C. Lamberth, *Cobell v. Babbitt,* 1999[25]

These statements center on the historically rooted trust relationship that dates back to fifteenth-century Europe, but saw its earliest expression in the United States during the formative years of the republic. Policymakers were pledged to carry out treaty obligations made to tribes but also assumed a protectorate role for tribal peoples, their lands, and their resources. By the late nineteenth century Congress began to enact more forceful and unilateral policies, like the General Allotment Act of 1887 that aimed to absorb Indians into American society by individualizing and then patenting Indian lands into parcels of 160, 80, and 40 acres. Federal policymakers by this time perceived

Indians and tribes as incompetent to manage their own affairs or resources. Therefore, the federal government, acting more like a "guardian" of the now "ward-like tribes," took complete charge of the Indians' lands and resources.

Typically, the Department of the Interior, the lead trust agent, leased the Indian allotments to oil, gas, timber, grazing, and mining interests for a small fee. The income generated from these leases was then processed by the Bureau of Indian Affairs (BIA) and deposited in the U.S. Treasury, where checks were supposed to be sent to the Indians and tribal nations holding interests in trust resources.[26] However, Indians have never received all the money due to them for lands sold to the United States and from various lease arrangements made by the federal government, despite constant Indian complaints and numerous investigations. As John Echohawk, executive director of the Native American Rights Fund (NARF), who led the class-action lawsuit filed in 1996 on behalf of over five hundred thousand individual trust beneficiaries, stated, "The BIA has spent more than 100 years mismanaging, diverting and losing money that belongs to Indians."[27]

The Indian trust funds have two major components: tribal trust funds and individual Indian money (IIM) accounts. There are 1,450 tribal accounts owned by over 250 tribes worth about $2.9 billion.[28] This money includes lease revenues, royalties, and court settlements. The accounts vary widely, with some worth only a few dollars, while others, like the Sioux Black Hills court award (based on the federal government's taking of the Black Hills in South Dakota), are valued at over $400 million. The Department of the Interior currently manages about fifty-six million acres of Indian trust land throughout Indian country. They administer more than one hundred thousand leases and $3.5 billion in trust funds. For example, in 2009 the Interior collected about $298 million for more than 384,000 open IIM accounts. In addition, $566 million was collected for about 2,700 tribal accounts for more than 250 tribes.[29] Untold billions have flowed through both accounts since the 1880s, and neither individual Indians nor tribal governments have ever received a thorough accounting of their monies. In fact, the Indian plaintiffs assert that they have lost upwards of $137.5 billion since 1887. Attorney General Alberto Gonzales, in March 2005 testimony, estimated the government's liability for tribal trust claims could be over $200 billion.[30]

Paul Homan was appointed as special trustee for American Indians in 1994 and was charged with remedying the government's mismanagement of Indian trust accounts. Homan, who had a wealth of experience in trust management and with failing financial institutions, engaged in a thorough investigation of the BIA's accounting system and found that "the record-keeping system [for the IIM accounts] is the worst that I have seen in my entire life."[31]

In particular, Homan found that there was $2.4 billion (32,319 transactions) for which no documents could be located; there was about $694 million in unreconciled disbursements; there were 54,921 IIM accounts totaling $44.9 million for individuals with no address or an incorrect address; and there were 15,230 IIM accounts worth $21.8 million for individuals who were formerly minors, the majority of which should have been disbursed when the minors came of age. It was also discovered that the government could not even account for fifty thousand of the active trusts. One estimate says that the government's efforts to pay out lost money to IIM account holders could reach as high as $10 billion.[32]

Because the Department of the Interior failed to assist the special trustee and because Congress failed to allocate adequate funds to implement the 1994 American

Indian Trust Management Reform Act, the NARF filed a class-action lawsuit on behalf of the IIM holders on January 10, 1996, against Secretary Babbitt and Secretary of the Treasury Robert Rubin. NARF sought to force the Interior Department to carry out its duties and obligations as trustee regarding the IIM accounts. Such obligations included maintaining an accounting system that is reliable and accurate, investing the accounts wisely, and reporting to the beneficiaries in a timely fashion.

When the federal government said that it would respond by producing all documents requested, but then refused to do so, U.S. District Court judge Royce C. Lamberth, of the District Court of Columbia, in February 1999 held then–secretaries Babbitt and Rubin and Kevin Gover, assistant secretary of the interior, in civil contempt of court. This was the first time two cabinet officers had been held in contempt simultaneously.

Eloise Cobell, a Blackfeet Indian and the chief plaintiff in the lawsuit, stated, "I think this is the beginning of justice for the victims who have had years and years of abuse at the hands of the U.S. Government."[33] On December 22, 1999, Judge Lamberth issued what he called a "stunning victory" for the Indians, when he ruled that the government had indeed violated its duty to safeguard the Indians' trust accounts. He said the federal government had engaged in "fiscal and governmental irresponsibility in its purest form." But rather than seek an independent body to rectify the problems, which the NARF and Homan had requested, the judge simply ordered the Interior and Treasury Departments to correct the situation. He gave the federal officials five years to repair the massive accounting problems and said he would personally oversee the government's efforts.[34] A federal appeals court upheld Lamberth's decision in a unanimous ruling on February 23, 2001.

Despite this string of early litigation victories, the individual Indian plaintiffs, the NARF, and Judge Lamberth continued to fight the BIA and the Department of Interior over how best to resolve this long-standing conflict. In December 2001, Judge Lamberth, fearing that the Interior Department's accounting system that handles Indian monies could be vulnerable to computer hacking, took the unusual step of ordering the shutdown of virtually all the department's computer communications, including e-mail, web service to national parks, and payments to almost forty thousand Indians. The BIA's website remained offline for several years, but it is now fully operational.[35]

As the litigation continued, Mr. Alan Balaran, who had been appointed in 1999 by Judge Lamberth to investigate the financial situation of the Indian trust fund, abruptly resigned his position in April 2004. In his resignation letter to Lamberth, Balaran accused the department of a persistent effort to block his work and said he had found a "systemic failure to properly monitor" the activities of the various energy companies that routinely underpaid Indians on royalties from oil, gas, timber, and other leases.[36] The department, for its part, accused Mr. Balaran of "concocting preposterous charges of a government conspiring against him" and denied Balaran's charges that it had "destroyed valuable trust information."[37]

Judge Lamberth on July 12, 2005, issued a devastating rebuke of the federal government, and particularly, the Department of Interior's treatment of American Indians and the Indian plaintiffs. In *Cobell v. Norton*,[38] Lamberth ordered the Interior to include a notice containing information about this litigation to the entire plaintiff class of five hundred thousand Indians. The notice was to serve as a warning to the Indians that the government's information might not be credible. But Lamberth also took this as an opportunity to graphically express his views about the disrespectful manner in which the government had and, in his opinion, continues to treat Native people, their resources, and their monies:

> But when one strips away the convoluted statutes, the technical legal complexities, the elaborate collateral proceedings, and the layers upon layers of interrelated orders and opinions from this Court and the Court of Appeals, what remains is the raw, shocking, humiliating truth at the bottom: After all these years, our government still treats Native American Indians as if they were somehow less than deserving of the respect that should be afforded to everyone in a society where all people are supposed to be equal.
>
> For those harboring hope that the stories of murder, dispossession, forced marches, assimilationist policy programs, and other incidents of cultural genocide against the Indians are merely the echoes of a horrible, bigoted government-past that has been sanitized by the good deeds of more recent history, this case serves as an appalling reminder of the evils that result when large numbers of the politically powerless are placed at the mercy of institutions engendered and controlled by a politically powerful few. It reminds us that even today our great democratic enterprise remains unfinished. And it reminds us, finally, that the terrible power of government, and the frailty of the restraints on the exercise of that power, are never fully revealed until government turns against the people.[39]

In 2006, Judge Lamberth was removed from this case after the Bush administration complained of bias. He was replaced by Judge James Robertson. Robertson pushed both parties to negotiate as continued litigation proved costly and prolonged the resolution of trust mismanagement. One example illustrated that "one 40-acre-parcel today has 439 owners, most of whom receive less than $1 a year in income from it. . . . The parcel is valued at about $20,000, but it costs the government more than $40,000 a year to administer those trusts."[40]

By December 2009, this thirteen-year lawsuit had spanned three presidencies, resulted in seven trials, produced twenty-two published judicial opinions, and went before a federal appeals court ten times. To resolve claims that the federal government had mismanaged the revenue in American Indian trust funds, the Obama administration announced on December 8, 2009, a $3.4-billion settlement of the Cobell class-action lawsuit. President Obama said, "With this announcement, we take an important step towards a sincere reconciliation between the trust beneficiaries and the federal government and lay the foundation for more effective management of Indian trust assets in the future."[41]

This settlement contained three main components. First, $1.4 billion dollars will be utilized to settle accounting and mismanagement claims. From this fund, each account holder will receive $1,000 for historical accounting claims. Second, the remaining $2 billion from the settlement offer will be used to purchase small, fractionated interests from Indian landowners on a voluntary basis. Under terms of the Indian Land Consolidation Act, consolidated lands will be turned over to the tribes. Third, the settlement calls for the creation of a five-member Secretarial Commission on Indian Trust to provide recommendations for long-term trust reform. Ken Salazar, secretary of the

Photo I.2
Department of the Interior Secretary Ken Salazar greets Elouise Cobell, a member of the Black-feet Tribe from Montana who was the lead plaintiff in the class-action lawsuit regarding the U.S. government's trust management and accounting of over three hundred thousand individual American Indian trust accounts following an announcement on the settlement of the Cobell lawsuit on December 8, 2009.
Source: AP/WIDE WORLD PHOTOS

interior, in a statement to the Committee on Indian Affairs noted, "With this settlement we will turn the page on a dark chapter in Indian Country and begin to move forward, together, towards our common goals."[42] Congress must still enact legislation and the federal courts must sign off on it for the agreement to become final, which has not occurred as this edition went to press.

Elouise Cobell noted that, though the settlement was "no doubt" significantly less than the amount to which class members are entitled, "We are compelled to settle by the sobering realization that our class grows smaller each day as our elders die and are forever prevented from receiving just compensation."[43]

> In marked contrast to traditional Western religions, the belief systems of Native Americans do not rely on doctrines, creeds, or dogmas. Established or universal truths—the mainstay of Western religions—play no part in Indian faith. Ceremonies are communal efforts undertaken for specific purposes in accordance with instructions handed down from generation to generation. . . . Where dogma lies at the heart of Western religion, Native American faith is inextricably bound

to the use of land. The site-specific nature of Indian religious practice derives
from the Native American perception that land is itself a sacred, living being.

—Justice William Brennan, dissenting,
Lyng V. Northwestern Cemetery Protective Association, 1988[44]

The United States' ambivalence toward the religious rights of indigenous peoples was exemplified by two notable events in 1996. First, President Clinton recognized the religious rights of Indians when, on May 24, he issued an executive order to promote accommodation of access to sites considered holy by Indian religious practitioners, and to provide additional security for the physical integrity of these sacred sites.[45]

However, two and a half weeks later, on June 8, a federal district court decision, *Bear Lodge Multiple Use Association v. Babbitt,* undermined these same religious rights when it ruled that the National Park Service could not "voluntarily" ban rock climbers during the month of June to accommodate the religious rights of several tribes who hold ceremonies at Devils Tower, Wyoming, a sacred site to the Indians and a national monument.

A comparative review of these two events and their historical context reveals the ongoing tension in American society and among federal policymakers toward Indian religious traditions. Clinton, for his part, was not acting hastily in the issuance of his order recognizing the importance of sacred sites to Indians. In fact, he was exercising authority derived from several constitutional provisions (including one that requires the president to "take care that the laws be faithfully executed"), the commander-in-chief clause, and the express powers vested in him by congressional statutes. He was acting, in his own words, "in furtherance of Federal treaties."

This executive order was a companion measure to an earlier Clinton order issued April 29, 1994, that required federal agencies and departments to accommodate American Indians in their need and use of eagle feathers and body parts. The sacred site order mandated that all federal agencies with any responsibility for the management of federal lands implement practices which would oblige and aid tribal members with access to and ceremonial use of sacred sites, and required those agencies to avoid activities that might negatively affect the "physical integrity of such sacred sites." The agencies were given a year to prepare a report for the president on how they were going to implement his order.

Indigenous peoples, who have historically viewed the president as both the symbolic and substantive embodiment of the federal government's treaty and trust obligations toward their nations, were doubtless pleased to receive news of this executive order, especially in light of the massive sacred site losses, desecrations, and interference Indians have experienced as a result of direct federal action or complicity. Moreover, there are dozens, if not hundreds, of spiritual sites located within land claimed by the federal government, but that once belonged to tribes, that are now threatened or imperiled by either federal, corporate, or private action.

The tribal sense of joy after Clinton's order, however, was shattered just fifteen days later when Judge William Downes, a federal district judge in Casper, Wyoming, ruled in *Bear Lodge* that the National Park Service had violated the First Amendment rights of a nonprofit corporation, some of whose members also owned a commercial rock-climbing guide service. The Park Service had developed a comprehensive management plan that was sensitive to the spiritual needs of local Indians who consider the Devils Tower a holy site, but that still allowed non–Indian-related activities. "In respect for the reverence many American Indians hold for Devils Tower as a sacred site," said the Park Service, "rock climbers will be asked to voluntarily refrain from climbing on Devils Tower during the culturally significant month of June."

However, according to Judge Downes, this "voluntary closure" of Devils Tower to commercial and recreational climbing solely for the purpose of supporting Indian religious rights violated the First Amendment's establishment clause. The climbers' motion to enjoin the National Park Service from imposing a ban on climbing was granted.

In closing, Downes did note that the Park Service's voluntary plan was both "laudable and constitutionally permissible." In December, the Park Service issued a decision revoking the commercial climbing ban. In other words, the court found that the government could not constitutionally enforce a climbing closure but that it could promote a program asking climbers to voluntarily abstain from climbing on the tower in June, when most of the important Indian ceremonies took place.

Bear Lodge Multiple Use Association was not happy with Judge Downes's compromise ruling and appealed. They alleged that the Park Service's voluntary ban was still wrong, and that the government's interpretive program promoted the religion of American Indians in violation of the establishment clause and amounted to the proselytizing of schoolchildren who visit the national monument "under the guise of educating children about the heritage surrounding the memorial."[46]

In a subsequent decision, Judge Downes ruled in favor of the government and the Indians, declaring that the Park Service's management plan was a sound policy aimed at balancing the competing needs of individuals using Devils Tower while at the same time upholding the Constitution. This ruling was then appealed to the Tenth Circuit Court of Appeals, which found that the climbers had suffered no real injury and lacked standing to sue.[47] The U.S. Supreme Court upheld that ruling in March 2000 by declining to review the case.

While the federal government was ambivalent in 1996, its actions proved downright schizophrenic in 2008. Congress, in that year, passed the Food, Conservation, and Energy Act, also known as the Farm Bill, in an apparent attempt to strengthen the Forest Service's commitment to native peoples. The law contained three sections addressing critical issues that American Indians face in exercising their religious beliefs: the reburial of human remains and cultural items, access to forest products for traditional and cultural purposes, and the temporary closure of forest lands from public access "to protect the privacy of tribal activities for traditional and cultural purposes."[48] Nonetheless, even as this act was winding its way through the legislative process, the Forest Service was simultaneously supporting enhancements to the Snowbowl Ski Resort in the San Francisco Peaks, an area deemed sacred by at least thirteen native nations in the Southwest, including the Navajo, Havasupai, White Mountain Apache, Yavapai-Apache, Haulapai, and the Hopi. These nations, and their environmental allies, had fought to prevent the Snowbowl Ski Resort from making artificial snow using treated sewage effluent as this would desecrate the mountain and demean their religious ceremonies. The ski resort, though a private, for-profit entity, operates on federal land under a special use permit issued by the United States Forest Service.

In 2007, the Ninth Circuit Court of Appeals had ruled favorably for the tribes and their litigation partners and held in *Navajo Nation v. U.S. Forest Service* (479 F.

3d 1024) that the proposed use of treated sewage water would impose a substantial burden on the exercise of religion for the native nations. This positive ruling was appealed and on August 8, 2008, an en banc panel (the entire bench) of the Ninth Circuit ruled that the use of recycled sewage water was not a "substantial burden" on the religious freedom of American Indians, which the court argued only occurred if an individual was (1) forced to choose between following the tenets of his or her religious beliefs or receiving a government benefit, or (2) coerced to act contrary to his or her religious beliefs by the threat of civil or criminal sanctions. This narrow interpretation virtually rendered the Religious Freedom Restoration Act (RFRA) of 1993 unavailable to protect sacred sites and left Native peoples with one last hope—the U.S. Supreme Court.[49]

However, in June 2009 the High Court denied the tribes' petition for certiorari, thus upholding the Ninth Circuit Court's decision. The response of Howard Shanker, an attorney for several of the tribes, was reflective of the deep concern many in Indian Country felt as a result of these latest rulings: "The Court's denial serves to perpetuate injustice and the application of bad law regarding the rights of Native Americans to protect sacred and holy sites. It is, however safe to say that as long as the San Francisco Peaks remain, there will be people willing to continue the struggle to protect the Peaks and to honor the beliefs and cultures of those peoples who hold them sacred."[50]

These five issues—intergovernmental relations, tribal leadership, treaty rights, the trust fund debacle, and religious freedom —are but a sample of topics that entail several distinctive dimensions of the American Indian political situation. First is the fact of the preexisting status of indigenous communities as separate and sovereign peoples with histories that long predate the American republic. This preexisting status meant that tribal nations had original and unencumbered claims to territory and sovereignty that would then be disputed and sometimes recognized by invading European governments and their peoples and later by the United States.

Second is the subsequent historical development of unique political, legal, economic, cultural, and moral rights and powers exercised by tribal nations—rights and powers that the United States subsequently attempted to unilaterally change in its efforts to take tribal resources and assimilate and civilize Indian peoples. With the U.S. Constitution vesting in the Congress authority to regulate trade and intercourse with tribes, states, at least in constitutional theory, were reduced to peripheral entities in this relationship. States, of course, have not been silent partners and have frequently challenged the federal government's constitutional role in administering the nation's Indian policy. Thus, the doctrine of federalism itself has been implicated because of indigenous peoples and their rights and resources.

Third, there persists a fundamental ambivalence on the part of the federal government and the American people in the history and contemporary treatment of America's indigenous nations. On one hand, the federal government supports the right of tribes to be self-determined sovereigns and promulgates policies and laws that affirm their rights as separate yet connected nations. On the other hand, the federal government has produced a bevy of laws, cases, and policies that have dramatically weakened and disrupted the sovereignty of tribes and placed them and their institutions in an inferior position vis-à-vis the federal government and, increasingly, the states. This ambivalence continues at both the state and societal levels, and fluctuations in what American citizens and policymakers envision for indigenous peoples continue to plague the efforts of tribal governments to attain any real stability in their relationship to the public, the states, or the federal government.

In this book we engage in a focused analysis of the internal dynamics of indigenous governments and their politics, and we examine the distinctive relationship between indigenous peoples (at the individual and collective levels) and the states, the federal government, and other pertinent actors.

We proceed in the following manner. Chapter 1 defines and describes some of the most important concepts in the study of Indian politics—what are tribal nations, who are Indians, what constitutes "Indian Country"—and concludes with some demographic and socioeconomic data. Chapter 2 provides an analysis of the distinctive status of indigenous peoples, examines the issue of citizenship for native individuals, and draws out and discusses in detail the two central themes of the book: tribal sovereignty and the ambivalence of federal policymakers toward native nations. We also discuss how the ambiguous status of tribal nations came into being and how it manifests itself in American politics and law.

Chapter 3 includes a general historical and contemporary description and analysis of tribal governments and Alaska Native communities, concluding with some comments on the major issues confronting indigenous nations. Chapter 4 examines tribes in their intergovernmental relations with the federal government's three branches, including a section on the important role of the BIA. Chapter 5 includes an overview of federal Indian policy from the formation of the American republic to the present day. Chapter 6 focuses on the political economy of Indian Country, including an analysis of Indian gaming.

Chapter 7 examines native political participation and focuses on patriotism, suffrage, and partisanship. Chapter 8 focuses on interest-group activity within and without Indian Country and the key role that indigenous social activism played in facilitating improved conditions for tribes in the 1960s, the 1970s, and beyond. Chapter 9 addresses the important topic of the media, images of indigenous persons and nations, and how they affect the social, political, and legal status of indigenous peoples.

We conclude in chapter 10 by reexamining the central issues that continue to animate indigenous politics, both internally and intergovernmentally. Finally, we make a number of recommendations that might help alleviate some of the problems in this dynamic set of relationships.

CHAPTER 1

A Tour of Native Peoples and Native Lands

One of the greatest obstacles faced by the Indian today in his desire for self-determination . . . [and] the American public's ignorance of the historical relationship of the United States with Indian tribes and the lack of general awareness of the status of the American Indian in our society today.

—American Indian Policy Review Commission, 1977[1]

THIS CHAPTER PROVIDES descriptions, definitions, and analysis of the most important concepts necessary for a solid foundation for the study of Indian politics. We attempt to clarify how indigenous peoples, variously grouped, are defined, and discuss why such definitions are necessary. We then analyze how the term *Indian* is defined and discuss what constitutes a reservation and Indian Country. Finally, we conclude the chapter with a description of the basic demographic facts and socioeconomic data that applies throughout Indian lands.

Who Are Indigenous Peoples?

American Indians, tribal nations, Indian tribes, native nations, indigenous nations, Fourth World Peoples, Native American Peoples, Aboriginal Peoples, First Nations, and *Native Peoples*—these are just a sample of current terms that are used to refer to indigenous peoples in the continental United States in a collective sense. Alaska Natives, including Aleuts, Inuit, and Indians, and Native Hawaiians are the indigenous peoples of those respective territories. While we provide some descriptive details about Alaska Natives, we will have less to say about Native Hawaiians because their legal status is unique among aboriginal peoples of the United States.[2]

This was brought to light in the Supreme Court's 2000 ruling in *Rice v. Cayetano*.[3] In that case, the Court struck down restrictions that had allowed only persons with Native Hawaiian blood to vote for the trustees of the Office of Hawaiian Affairs, a state agency created to better the lives of Hawaii's aboriginal people. While Cayetano did

1

not specifically address the political relationship of Native Hawaiians to the federal government, it called into question the status of the more than 150 federal statutes that recognize that Hawaii's native peoples do, in fact, have a unique legal status.

The departments of the Interior and Justice issued a preliminary report on August 23, 2000, that recommended that Congress "enact further legislation to clarify Native Hawaiians' political status and to create a framework for recognizing a government-to-government relationship with a representative Native Hawaiian governing body."[4] Senator Daniel K. Akaka (D-HI), later joined by his senate colleague, Daniel K. Inouye (D-HI), began introducing legislation in 2000, but as of July 2010 the bill had not been enacted. The most recent version of the bill, titled the *Native Hawaiian Government Reorganization Act* but commonly referred to as the Akaka bill, would provide Native Hawaiians with a legal status and political relationship with the federal government similar to that of federally-recognized tribes. It would also create a governing body that would have decision-making authority on behalf of the estimated four hundred thousand Native Hawaiians throughout the country.

The Senate Committee on Indian Affairs passed a newly amended version of the Akaka bill December 17, 2009. The House Committee on Natural Resources considered the same heavily amended version of this legislation the prior day, but after letters of opposition, instead passed an unamended version. The house bill, H.R. 2314, is more restrictive than the senate version, limiting the powers of the Native Hawaiian Governing Entity (NHGE) by clarifying that certain laws applicable to federally recognized tribes do not apply to the NHGE, primarily laws that have benefited tribes. The senate bill, S. 1011, does not guarantee any governing powers but instead leaves these areas open to negotiation between the NHGE, the state, and the federal government, such as the ability to place land in trust and questions surrounding civil and criminal jurisdiction.[5] In attempting to address the state's concerns and satisfy opponents of the bill, Hawaii's congressional delegation released what it called the final text of the Akaka bill on February 22, 2010. This new version makes clear that the bill would (1) recognize Native Hawaiians' inherent governing powers, with the exception of the right to conduct gambling; (2) would not preempt federal and state jurisdiction over individual Native Hawaiians or their property; and (3) preserves the NHGE's sovereign immunity.

Although the bill, in its various iterations, has wide support, it has a number of detractors as well. Many conservative Republicans argue that it promotes racial balkanization and would "provide a new vehicle for Hawaiian secessionists groups and spawn endless litigation by people seeking redress against the federal government."[6] Though the House voted in favor of the bill and President Obama reaffirmed his support, the Senate has yet to pass this most recent version.

More importantly, such a measure is rejected by a number of Hawaiian sovereignty groups who argue that the bill, as well intentioned as it is, would be a diminution of their original sovereignty. J. Kehaulani Kauanui, a Hawaiian scholar, summarized the positions of those in opposition to the bill:

> [T]he proposal for federal recognition is extremely controversial for several reasons. For one, it was initiated by a U.S. federal representative, not the Native Hawaiian people, as a remedy against new political developments in the courts

that threaten current U.S. federal funding and programs for Native Hawaiians. Second, numerous Hawaiian political organizations oppose what they see as an effort to contain Hawai'i's independence claim under international law. Third, there is local opposition, on the part of non-Hawaiian residents of Hawai'i, to this form of recognition. And fourth, there is rampant opposition in the U.S. Senate from Republicans who condemn this proposal because it would extend to Native Hawaiians distinct rights. However, their conservative antagonism is slowly shifting to qualified support.[7]

Indigenous communities expect to be referred to by their own names—Navajo or Diné, Ojibwe or Anishinaabe, Sioux or Lakota, Suquamish or Tohono O'odham—since they constitute separate political, legal, and cultural entities. In fact, before Europeans arrived in the Americas, it is highly doubtful whether any tribes held a "conception of that racial character which today we categorize as 'Indian.' People recognized their neighbors as co-owners of the lands given to them by the Great Spirit and saw themselves sharing a basic status within creation as a life form."[8] However, when discussing Indian peoples generically, *American Indian tribes* and *Native Americans* remain the most widely used terms despite the inherent problems associated with both. For instance, America's indigenous people are not from India, and the term Native American was "used during the nativist (anti-immigration, anti-foreign) movement (1860s–1925) and the anti-black, anti-Catholic, and anti-Jewish Ku Klux Klan resurgence during the early 1900s."[9]

There is no universally agreed-upon definition of what constitutes a native nation, in part because each community defines itself differently and because the U.S. government in its relations with tribes has operated from conflicting sets of cultural and political premises across time. Although no universal definition exists, many statutes give definitions for purposes of particular laws, federal agencies like the Bureau of Indian Affairs (BIA) generate their own definitions, numerous courts have crafted definitions, and the term *tribe* is found—though not defined—in the Constitution's commerce clause.

For example, the Indian Self-Determination Act of 1975 (as amended) defines an Indian tribe as "any Indian tribe, band, nation, or other organized group or community . . . which is recognized as eligible for the special programs and services provided by the United States to Indians because of their status as Indians." By contrast, the Supreme Court in *Montoya v. United States* (1901) even more ambiguously said that "by a 'tribe' we understand a body of Indians of the same or a similar race, united in a community under one leadership or government, and inhabiting a particular though sometimes ill-defined territory."[10]

Broadly, the term *tribe* can be defined from two perspectives—ethnological and political-legal.[11] From an ethnological perspective, a *tribe* may be defined as a group of indigenous people connected by biology or blood, kinship, cultural and spiritual values, language, political authority, and a territorial land base. But for our purposes, it is the political-legal definition (since there is no single definitive legal definition) of *tribe*, especially by the federal government, that is crucial since whether or not a tribal group is recognized as a tribe by the federal government has important political, cultural, and economic consequences, as we shall see shortly.

Federally Recognized Tribal and Alaska Native Entities

The extension of federal recognition by the United States to a tribal nation is the formal diplomatic acknowledgment by the federal government of a tribe's legal status as a sovereign. This is comparable to when the United States extended "recognition" to the former republics of the Soviet Union after that state's political disintegration. It is the beginning point of a government-to-government relationship between an indigenous people and the U.S. government.[12] The reality is that an American Indian tribe is not a legally recognized entity in the eyes of the federal government unless some explicit action by an arm of the government (i.e., congressional statute, administrative ruling by the BIA, presidential executive order, or a judicial opinion) decides that it exists in a formal manner.

Federal recognition has historically had two distinctive meanings. Before the 1870s, *recognize* or *recognition* was used in the cognitive sense. In other words, federal officials simply acknowledged that a tribe existed, usually by negotiating treaties with them or

Photo 1.1
Senator Hillary Rodham Clinton accompanied by Randy Teton of Lincoln Creek, Idaho, who modeled for the Sacagawea dollar coin, points to an enlarged version of the coin during an introduction ceremony for it at the White House. Research at the Washington State University suggests the Lenhi Tribe of Idaho Indians (of which Sacagawea was a member) was improperly stripped of formal tribal recognition by the United States government. Honoring Sacagawea is thus ironic as well as iconically inflammatory.
Source: AP/WIDE WORLD PHOTOS

enacting specific laws to fulfill specific treaty pledges.[13] During the 1870s, however, *recognition,* or more accurately, *acknowledgment,* began to be used in a formal jurisdictional sense. It is this later usage that the federal government most often employs to describe its relationship to tribes. In short, federal acknowledgment is a formal act that establishes a political relationship between a tribe and the United States. It affirms a tribe's sovereign status. Simultaneously, it outlines the federal government's responsibilities to the tribe.

More specifically, federal acknowledgment means that a tribe is not only entitled to the immunities and privileges available to other tribes, but is also subject to the same federal powers, limitations, and other obligations of recognized tribes. What this means, particularly the "limitations" term, is that "acknowledgment shall subject the Indian tribe to the same authority of Congress and the United States to which other federally acknowledged tribes are subjected."[14] In other words, tribes are informed that they are now subject to federal plenary power and may, ironically, benefit from the virtually unlimited and still largely unreviewable authority of the federal government. For example, recognized tribes have exemptions from most state tax laws, enjoy sovereign immunity, and are not subject to the same constitutional constraints as are the federal and state governments.

Until 1978, federal recognition or acknowledgment was usually bestowed by congressional act or presidential action. But in 1978 the BIA, the agency within the Department of the Interior primarily responsible for carrying out the federal government's treaty and trust obligations to tribal nations, published regulations that contained specific criteria that unacknowledged or nonrecognized tribal groups had to meet in order to be formally recognized by the United States. This set of guidelines was based mainly on confirmation by individuals and groups outside the petitioning tribe that members of the group were Indians. The mandatory criteria were the following: the identification of the petitioners "from historical times until the present on a substantially continuous basis, as 'American Indian' or 'Aboriginal'" by the federal, state or local governments, scholars, or other Indian tribes; the habitation of the tribe on land identified as Indian; a functioning government that had authority over its members; a constitution; a roll of members based on criteria acceptable to the secretary of the interior; not being a terminated tribe; and members not belonging to other tribes.[15]

These criteria largely were designed to fit the "aboriginal" or "mythic" image of the western and already recognized tribes. They were problematic for many eastern tribes who sought recognition, since they paid little heed to the massive historical, cultural, economic, and legal barriers those tribes had to endure merely to survive as tribes into the late twentieth century, lacking any semblance of federal support or protection.

Since the late 1970s there has been tension between those who support BIA or administrative recognition versus those who believe that only the Congress has authority to recognize tribes. The debate over administrative versus legislative recognition rages on, with some advocates from each camp asserting their exclusive right to extend or withhold recognition. This raises an important question: Is there a qualitative difference between the two types of recognition? There are two important differences. First, tribes that opt for the administrative variety must meet the formalized set of criteria mentioned earlier. Tribes that pursue congressional recognition, provided they can muster enough proof that they are a legitimate group composed of people of Indian ancestry, have only to make a compelling case to the congressional representatives of the state they reside in. The congressional sponsors then make the case for the tribe via legislation.

The second major difference involves the administrative law component known as *subordinate delegation.* The major grant of authority the Congress has delegated to the secretary of the interior is located in Title 25—Indians—of the U.S. Code. Section 1 states that the head of Indian affairs, formerly the commissioner of Indian affairs, today the assistant secretary of Indian affairs, is "appointed by the President, by and with the advice and consent of the Senate."[16] In section 2, the head is authorized to "have the management of all Indian affairs and of all matters arising out of Indian relations."[17] As William Quinn states, this law "would arguably not authorize the Secretary or Commissioner to establish a perpetual government-to-government relationship via federal acknowledgment with an Indian group not already under the Department's aegis."[18] Nevertheless, Quinn asserts that the secretary of the interior, with the U.S. Supreme Court's approval, has historically exercised the authority to "recognize" tribes "when a vacuum of responsibility existed over decades, resulting in a gradual and unchallenged accretion of this authority."[19]

The problem, however, is not that the secretary is usurping unused congressional authority; instead, it is the manner and degree to which secretarial discretion and interpretation of federal laws have been discharged by BIA officials. As Felix Cohen said more than fifty years ago, "Indians for some decades have had neither armies nor lawyers to oppose increasingly broad interpretations of the power of the Commissioner of Indian Affairs, and so little by little 'the management of all Indian affairs' has come to be read as 'the management of all the affairs of Indians.'"[20] This statement has relevance today, notwithstanding the federal government's policy of Indian self-determination and the more recent policy of tribal self-governance.

The Congress's track record is problematic as well. Generally speaking, however, native nations with explicit congressional acknowledgment have found their status less subject to the whims of BIA officials, though even that is no guarantee of smooth affairs, because BIA oversees and administers most of the government's political relationship with tribes.

A prime example involves the Pascua Yaqui tribe of southern Arizona. The Yaqui were legislatively recognized in 1978. However, in the late 1980s, when they solicited the approval of the BIA on some changes in their constitution, they were informed by bureau officials that they were limited in what governmental powers they could exercise because they were not a "historic tribe," but were instead merely a "created adult Indian community":

> A historic tribe has existed since time immemorial. Its powers derive from its unextinguished, inherent sovereignty. Such a tribe has the full range of governmental powers except where it has been removed by Federal law in favor of either the United States or the state in which the tribe is located. By contrast, a community of adult Indians is composed simply of Indian people who reside together on trust land. A community of adult Indians may have a certain status which entitles it to certain privileges and immunities. . . . However, that status is derived as a necessary scheme to benefit Indians, not from some historical inherent sovereignty.[21]

The bureau's attempt to create two categories of recognized tribes, a novel and disturbing approach to determining tribal identity, was halted by Congress, which declared that no department or agency of the government could develop regulations that negated or diminished the privileges and immunities of any federally recognized tribes, including the Yaqui.[22] The Congress has, moreover, in recent years tried to reassert its constitutional authority in the field by introducing legislation that would transfer administrative and congressional consideration of applications for federal recognition to an independent commission.[23]

Congress's actions, along with the increasing politicization of the administrative recognition process because of Indian gaming operations and state concerns, compelled Kevin Gover, the assistant secretary of Indian affairs (head of the BIA), in May 2000 to testify before Congress that his agency was no longer able to do the job of recognizing tribes. Gover admitted that he had been unable to streamline the recognition process, which in some cases had taken years to resolve, but he placed larger blame on the fact that Indian gaming revenues had enabled some groups to wage protracted legal battles that often involved nonrecognized tribes, non-Indian citizens and towns, and recognized tribes.[24] In 2001, BIA officials estimated that the evaluation process, which should take two years, could take up to fifteen years to resolve all completed petitions. The U.S. Government Accountability Office in 2005 reported, "While Interior's Office of Federal Acknowledgement has taken a number of actions during the past 3 years to improve the timeliness of the process, it will still take years to work through the existing backlog of tribal recognition petitions."[25] Nonetheless, the process of recognition continues. In 2007 the Mashpee Wampanoag Tribe was formally acknowledged and, in 2009, the federal government reestablished relations with the Wilton Rancheria and the Delaware Tribe of Indians.

As of 2010, the Department of the Interior officially recognizes 565 indigenous entities—335 are Indian nations, tribes, bands, organized communities, or pueblos in the lower forty-eight states; 230 are Alaska Native villages or corporations—on a list annually prepared by the BIA. These constitute the indigenous peoples eligible for the special programs and services provided by the United States to indigenous communities because of their status as Indians or Alaska Natives. See maps 1.1, 1.2, 1.3, and 1.4.

The situation of Alaska Native villages and corporations is complicated not only by distinctive ethnological differences but also by their unique political and legal status. Although Alaska Natives are eligible to receive services from the BIA, their political sovereignty as self-governing bodies has been questioned and at times constrained by the federal government. A 1998 Supreme Court case, *Alaska v. Native Village of Venetie Tribal Government*,[26] cast some doubts on the sovereign status of Alaskan villages. *Venetie* dealt with the jurisdictional status of Alaska Native villages and whether or not lands owned in fee simple by these communities—a type of ownership defined by the Alaska Native Claims Settlement Act of 1971—constituted "Indian Country."

In a major victory for Alaskan state authorities and a blow to the sovereignty of the village of Venetie, an Athabaskan community of some 350 people, Justice Clarence Thomas for a unanimous court held that Venetie's 1.8 million acres of fee-simple lands did not qualify as "Indian Country" because they had not been set aside by the federal government for tribal use and were not "under federal supervision." Thus, the tribal government lacked inherent authority to impose a 5-percent business tax on a contractor building a state-funded school in the village. In denying Venetie, and by extension every other Alaskan village, the power to tax, this ruling called into question what the actual political status of these villages was.

In addition, the indigenous people of Hawaii, who prefer to be called *Hawaiians, Hawaiian Natives,* or *Native Hawaiians,* although they are treated as Native Americans for some legal purposes, are not on the Department of the Interior's list of federally recognized tribal entities and have a unique status under federal law.[27]

But there are other indigenous people in the United States who are not federally recognized, who had their recognized status terminated by the federal government, or who have state recognition only. We discuss these three categories briefly.

Nonrecognized or Unacknowledged Groups

Nonrecognized and unacknowledged groups exhibit a tremendous degree of racial, ethnic, and cultural diversity. In some cases, they are descendants of tribes who never fought the United States, had no resources desired by the federal government, or lived in geographic isolation and were simply ignored, and hence may never have participated in a treaty or benefited from the trust relationship that forms the basis of most contemporary recognized tribes' status. Despite these circumstances, some of these groups retain their aboriginal language, hold some lands in common, and in some cases have retained some degree of traditional structures of governance. These groups feel entitled to recognition status and have petitioned the United States to be so recognized.[28]

In other cases, groups have questionable genealogical connections to legitimate historical tribes but, for varying reasons, have chosen to self-identify as particular tribes and desire to be recognized by the federal government.[29] In the case of the more questionable groups, the potential of substantial gambling revenue plays a powerful, if variable, role in which "groups" come forward in pursuit of recognition, which is supported by casino operators, and which may ultimately succeed in being recognized.[30] Since 1978, the BIA has received a total of 332 letters of intent and petitions for federal recognition. Forty-three of these petitions are from the original groups who had filed when formal procedures for acknowledgment were first established and became effective. The additional 289 are new petitions since October 1978 (table 1.1). The acknowledgment process, established in 1978 and administered by the Branch of Acknowledgment and Research in the BIA, has proven to be an extremely slow, expensive, and politicized process that requires excessive historical documentation and is greatly influenced by already recognized tribes who are reluctant to let other groups, regardless of their historical legitimacy, gain politically recognized status.[31] Because of these and other problems, the bureau has been besieged by those looking for a fairer and more expeditious process. Between 1978 and 2008, eighty-two tribal groups have submitted complete petitions. Of these, the BIA officially recognized only sixteen tribes (e.g., Grand Traverse Band of Ottawa and Chippewa, and Jamestown S'Klallam) and denied the petitions of twenty-eight groups (e.g., Lower Muscogee Creek Tribe east of the Mississippi, Kaweah Indian Nation, Southeastern Cherokee Confederacy).[32] The Little Shell Tribe of Chippewa Indians of Montana and the Brothertown Indian Nation in Wisconsin were both awaiting final determination and in 2009 were denied federal recognition, bringing the number to thirty. Nine tribes have found success though legislative restoration and recognition as of 2008.[33]

Two other Connecticut tribal groups, each with long-standing, state-recognized status, were recently recognized: the Eastern Pequot in 2002 and the Schaghticoke in 2004. But in May 2005 the Interior Department's Board of Indian Appeals, in a deeply politicized process, rejected the final determinations of recognized status of both groups. The BIA must now reconsider both groups and address the issues raised by the appeals board. As of July 2010 neither group has received formal recognition.

Table 1.1 A

Letters of Intent Received by the Office of Federal Acknowledgment (OFA) as of September 22, 2008

1978	43
1979	24
1980	10
1981	7
1982	5
1983	7
1984	7
1985	5
1986	0
1987	2
1988	5
1989	6
1990	7
1991	5
1992	8
1993	7
1994	9
1995	17
1996	14
1997	9
1998	21
1999	17
2000	15
2001	13
2002	19
2003	11
2004	9
2005	11
2006	10
2007	7
2008	2
Total – to – Date	332

www.bia.gov/idc/groups/public/documents/text/idc-001211.pdf

Terminated Tribes

From 1953 to the mid-1960s, the federal government's Indian policy was called *termination* because the United States wanted to sever the trust relationship and end federal benefits and support services to as many tribes, bands, and California *rancherias* as was feasible in an effort to expedite Indian assimilation and to lift discriminatory practices and policies that negatively affected indigenous peoples.[34] This policy was exemplified by House Concurrent Resolution No. 108, passed in 1953. This measure declared,

> Whereas it is the policy of Congress, as rapidly as possible, to make the Indians within the territorial limits of the United States subject to the same laws and entitled to the same privileges and responsibilities as are applicable to other

Table 1.1. B

Numbers of Petitions by State as of September 22, 2008

Alabama	12	Alaska	5
Arizona	1	Arkansas	9
California	74	Colorado	2
Connecticut	17	Delaware	1
Florida	10	Georgia	8
Hawaii	0	Idaho	1
Illinois	1	Indiana	5
Iowa	0	Kansas	3
Kentucky	1	Louisiana	14
Maine	2	Maryland	3
Massachusetts	9	Michigan	21
Minnesota	2	Mississippi	1
Missouri	10	Montana	2
Nebraska	0	Nevada	1
New Hampshire	0	New Jersey	5
New Mexico	3	New York	7
North Carolina	21	North Dakota	2
Ohio	12	Oklahoma	3
Oregon	5	Pennsylvania	1
Rhode Island	6	South Carolina	11
South Dakota	0	Tennessee	3
Texas	11	Utah	0
Vermont	2	Virginia	12
Washington	9	West Virginia	2
Wisconsin	2	Wyoming	0

www.bia.gov/idc/groups/public/documents/text/idc-001212.pdf

citizens of the United States, to end their status as wards of the United States, and to grant them all of the rights and prerogatives pertaining to American citizenship; and Whereas the Indians within the territorial limits of the United States should assume their full responsibilities as American citizens: Now, therefore, be it resolved . . . that it is declared to be the sense of Congress that, at the earliest possible time, all of the Indian tribes and the individual members thereof located within the States of California, Florida, [and] New York . . . should be freed from Federal supervision and control and from all disabilities and limitations specially applicable to Indians.[35]

Over one hundred tribes, bands, and California *rancherias*—totaling a little more than eleven thousand Indians—were "terminated" and lost their status as "recognized" and sovereign Indian communities. Termination thus subjected the tribes and their members to state law, their trust assets were usually individualized and either sold or held by banks, and they were no longer eligible for the other benefits and exemptions recognized tribes enjoy.

The terminated tribes, other tribes faced with termination, and Indian and non-Indian interest groups began to lobby Congress to end this disastrous policy because of the economic and political hardships it was causing. By the mid-1960s, the policy was stifled. Gradually, terminated tribes began to push for "restoration" of their recognized status. The first tribe terminated, the Menominee of Wisconsin (terminated in 1954), was also the first tribe to be legislatively "restored" in 1973.

Although discredited as policy by the mid-1960s, and rejected by Presidents Nixon and Reagan in their Indian policy statements, termination was not officially rejected by Congress until 1988 in a largely symbolic gesture that declared that "the Congress hereby repudiates and rejects HCR 108 of the 83rd Congress and any policy of unilateral termination of federal relations with any Indian nation."[36]

State-Recognized Tribes

Some Indian tribes have been recognized by their host states since the colonial era (e.g., Pamunkey Tribe of Virginia), although others have been recognized by state decrees (governor's action or state statute) in contemporary times. There are currently over sixty state-recognized tribes in Alabama, California, Connecticut, Georgia, Louisiana, Michigan, Montana, New Jersey, North Carolina, New York, Oklahoma, Virginia, Washington, and West Virginia. See table 1.2 for a list of these tribes. Depending on the policy established by the individual state, state recognition may or may not depend on prior federal recognition. Importantly, state recognition is not a prerequisite for federal recognition, although a long-standing relationship with a state is one factor in the federal recognition criteria that the BIA weighs in its determination of whether a group has historical longevity in a particular place.

For example, the Lumbee Tribe of North Carolina was legislatively recognized by the state in 1953.[37] Confident, the Lumbee leadership two years later asked Representative Frank Carlyle (D-NC) to introduce a bill before Congress that would extend federal recognition to the Lumbee. On June 7, 1956, the Congress passed an act that provided a measure of recognition to the Lumbee Nation,[38] without giving them the full range of benefits and services other federally recognized tribes received because federal policy at the time was focused on terminating the unique trust relationship between tribes and the United States. To date, the Lumbee Tribe is still not considered a federally recognized tribe by the BIA or the Indian Health Service, though they qualify for and receive other federal services as a recognized tribe.[39]

Who is an American Indian?

Having established the complexity of determining what an Indian tribe is from a legal-political perspective, we now turn to a brief but necessary examination of the equally if not more cumbersome question of "Who is an Indian?" This is important, as McClain and Stewart note, because "the question of who is an Indian is central to any discussion of American Indian politics."[40] The political relationship that exists between tribes and the federal government, bloated with issues of disparate power, cultural biases, and race and ethnicity, makes this so. Of course, like the concept of "Indian tribe," before Columbus arrived in 1492 there were no peoples in the Americas known as "Indians" or "Native Americans." Each indigenous community had its own name relating to the character of its people and the lands they inhabited.

Table 1.2
State Recognized Tribes

Alabama
Echota Cherokee
Northeast Alabama Cherokee
MaChis Lower Creek
Southeast Alabama Cherokee
Star Muscogee Creek
Mowa Band of Choctaw
Piqua Shawnee

Connecticut
Golden Hill Paugussett
Paucatuck Eastern Pequot
Schagticoke

Louisiana
Choctaw-Apache of Ebarb
Caddo Tribe
Clifton Choctaw
Four Winds Cherokee
United Houma Nation
Louisiana Cherokee Confederacy
Pointe-Au-Chien Indian Tribe

New York
Poospatuk
Unkechaug Nation

Montana
Little Shell Tribe of Chippewa

Oklahoma
Delaware Tribe of East Oklahoma
Loyal Shawnee Tribe
Yuchi Tribe

Washington
Chinook Indian Tribe
Duwamish Tribe
Kikiallus Indian Nation
Marietta Band of Nooksack Indians
Steilacoom Indian Tribe
Snohomish Tribe of Indians

California
Acjachemen Nation

Georgia
Georgia Eastern Cherokee
Cherokee of Georgia
Lower Muskogee Creek
Tama Tribal Town

New Jersey
Nanticoke Lenni-Lenape
Powhatan Renape
Ramapough Mountain

Michigan
Burt Lake Band of Ottawa & Chippewa Indians
Gun Lake Band of Grand River Ottawa Indians
Grand River Band of Ottawa Indians
Swan Creek Black River Confederated Tribes

North Carolina
Coharie Intra-Tribal Council
Haliwa-Saponi Tribe
Lumbee
Meherrin Tribe
Person County Indians
Waccamaw-Siouan Tribe

Virginia
Chickahominy Indian Tribe
Eastern Chickahominy Indian Tribe
Mattaponi Indian Tribe
Monacan Indian Tribe
Nansemond Indian Tribe
Pamunkey Indian Tribe
United Rappahannock Tribe
Upper Mattaponi Indian Tribe

West Virginia
Appalachian American Indians of West VA

Source: National Congress of American Indians, www.nca.org

With the political status of Indian nations defined, the question of deciding just "who is an Indian" would not appear to be a difficult one to answer. The decision rests with the tribal nations who retain, as one of their inherent sovereign powers, the power to decide who belongs to their nation. Unless this right has been expressly ceded in a treaty, it remains probably the most essential component of self-government. If tribes were to lose the right to decide who their citizens and members were, then it would logically follow that any government could dictate or influence what the tribe's membership should entail.

Since the identification of individuals as Indians depends upon or coincides with their association in a unique body politic and distinctive cultural and linguistic systems, historically, at least, "allegiance rather than ancestry per se [was] the deciding factor" in determining who was an Indian.[41] In other words, historically, to be considered an Indian one had to meet certain basic tribally defined criteria, including the social, cultural, linguistic, territorial, sociopsychological, and ceremonial. These criteria, of course, varied from tribal nation to tribal nation. However, as the federal government's power waxed by the late nineteenth century, with the corresponding waning of tribal power, indigenous cultural-social-territorial–based definitions of tribal identity were sometimes ignored and replaced by purely legal and frequently race-based definitions often arbitrarily articulated in congressional laws, administrative regulations, or court cases.

Congress, in particular, began to employ and still uses ethnological data, including varying fractions of blood quantum. See table 1.3, which is an official chart developed by the BIA describing the fractionalization of Indian identity. In fact, blood quantum remains one of the most important criteria used by the federal government and tribal governments to determine Indian status, despite the fact that its continued use "poses enormous conceptual and practical problems" since blood is not the carrier of genetic material and cultural traits as was thought in the nineteenth century.[42]

When blood quantum was first used in the Indian context in the early part of the twentieth century as a mechanism to reduce federal expenditures for Indian education, it

> was meant to measure the amount of Indian blood possessed by an individual. Because racial blood types could not be observed directly, Indian blood quantum was inferred from the racial backgrounds of parents. If both parents were reputed to have "unadulterated" Indian blood, then the blood quantum of their children was fixed at 100 percent. For children of racially mixed parents, their Indian blood quantum might be some fractional amount such as ¾, ½, or ⅛.[43]

Because, like the concept of *tribe*, there is no single constitutional or universally accepted definition of *Indian*, the federal government's principal function in formulating definitions of *Indian* is to "establish a test whereby it may be determined whether a given individual is to be excluded from the scope of legislation dealing with Indians."[44] The most widely accepted "legal" definition of "Indian" is from Felix Cohen, who wrote in 1943 that:

> The term "Indian" may be used in an ethnological or in a legal sense. Ethnologically, the Indian race may be distinguished from the Caucasian, Negro, Mongolian, and

Table 1.3

Chart to Establish Degree of Indian Blood

	NI*	1/16	1/8	3/16	1/4	5/16	3/8	7/16	1/2	9/16	5/8	11/16	3/4	13/16	7/8	15/16	4/4
1/16	1/32	1/16	3/32	1/8	5/32	3/16	7/32	1/4	9/32	5/16	11/32	3/8	13/32	7/16	15/32	1/2	17/32
1/8	1/16	3/32	1/8	5/32	3/16	7/32	1/4	9/32	5/16	11/32	3/8	13/32	7/16	15/32	1/2	17/32	9/16
3/16	3/32	1/8	5/32	3/16	7/32	1/4	9/32	5/16	11/32	3/8	13/32	7/16	15/32	1/2	17/32	9/16	19/32
1/4	1/8	5/32	3/16	7/32	1/4	9/32	5/16	11/32	3/8	13/32	7/16	15/32	1/2	17/32	9/16	19/32	5/8
5/16	5/32	3/16	7/32	1/4	9/32	5/16	11/32	3/8	13/32	7/16	15/32	1/2	17/32	9/16	19/32	5/8	21/32
3/8	3/16	7/32	1/4	9/32	5/16	11/32	3/8	13/32	7/16	15/32	1/2	17/32	9/16	19/32	5/8	21/32	11/16
7/16	7/32	1/4	9/32	5/16	11/32	3/8	13/32	7/16	15/32	1/2	17/32	9/16	19/32	5/8	21/32	11/16	23/32
1/2	1/4	9/32	5/16	11/32	3/8	13/32	7/16	15/32	1/2	17/32	9/16	19/32	5/8	21/32	11/16	23/32	3/4
9/16	9/32	5/16	11/32	3/8	13/32	7/16	15/32	1/2	17/32	9/16	19/32	5/8	21/32	11/16	23/32	3/4	25/32
5/8	5/16	11/32	3/8	13/32	7/16	15/32	1/2	17/32	9/16	19/32	5/8	21/32	11/16	23/32	3/4	25/32	13/16
11/16	11/32	3/8	13/32	7/16	15/32	1/2	17/32	9/16	19/32	5/8	21/32	11/16	23/32	3/4	25/32	13/16	27/32
3/4	3/8	13/32	7/16	15/32	1/2	17/32	9/16	19/32	5/8	21/32	11/16	23/32	3/4	25/32	13/16	27/32	7/8
13/16	13/32	7/16	15/32	1/2	17/32	9/16	19/32	5/8	21/32	11/16	23/32	3/4	25/32	13/16	27/32	7/8	29/32
7/8	7/16	15/32	1/2	17/32	9/16	19/32	5/8	21/32	11/16	23/32	3/4	25/32	13/16	27/32	7/8	29/32	15/16
15/16	15/32	1/2	17/32	9/16	19/32	5/8	21/32	11/16	23/32	3/4	25/32	13/16	27/32	7/8	29/32	15/16	31/32
4/4	1/2	17/32	9/16	19/32	5/8	21/32	11/16	23/32	3/4	25/32	13/16	27/32	7/8	29/32	15/16	31/32	4/4
1/32	1/64	3/64	5/64	7/64	9/64	11/64	13/64	15/64	17/64	19/64	21/64	23/64	25/64	27/64	29/64	31/64	33/64
3/32	3/64	5/64	7/64	9/64	11/64	13/64	15/64	17/64	19/64	21/64	23/64	25/64	27/64	29/64	31/64	33/64	35/64
5/32	5/64	7/64	9/64	11/64	13/64	15/64	17/64	19/64	21/64	23/64	25/64	27/64	29/64	31/64	33/64	35/64	37/64
7/32	7/64	9/64	11/64	13/64	15/64	17/64	19/64	21/64	23/64	25/64	27/64	29/64	31/64	33/64	35/64	37/64	39/64
9/32	9/64	11/64	13/64	15/64	17/64	19/64	21/64	23/64	25/64	27/64	29/64	31/64	33/64	35/64	37/64	39/64	41/64
11/32	11/64	13/64	15/64	17/64	19/64	21/64	23/64	25/64	27/64	29/64	31/64	33/64	35/64	37/64	39/64	41/64	43/64
13/32	13/64	15/64	17/64	19/64	21/64	23/64	25/64	27/64	29/64	31/64	33/64	35/64	37/64	39/64	41/64	43/64	45/64
15/32	15/64	17/64	19/64	21/64	23/64	25/64	27/64	29/64	31/64	33/64	35/64	37/64	39/64	41/64	43/64	45/64	47/64
17/32	17/64	19/64	21/64	23/64	25/64	27/64	29/64	31/64	33/64	35/64	37/64	39/64	41/64	43/64	45/64	47/64	49/64
19/32	19/64	21/64	23/64	25/64	27/64	29/64	31/64	33/64	35/64	37/64	39/64	41/64	43/64	45/64	47/64	49/64	51/64
21/32	21/64	23/64	25/64	27/64	29/64	31/64	33/64	35/64	37/64	39/64	41/64	43/64	45/64	47/64	49/64	51/64	53/64
23/32	23/64	25/64	27/64	29/64	31/64	33/64	35/64	37/64	39/64	41/64	43/64	45/64	47/64	49/64	51/64	53/64	55/64
25/32	25/64	27/64	29/64	31/64	33/64	35/64	37/64	39/64	41/64	43/64	45/64	47/64	49/64	51/64	53/64	55/64	57/64
27/32	27/64	29/64	31/64	33/64	35/64	37/64	39/64	41/64	43/64	45/64	47/64	49/64	51/64	53/64	55/64	57/64	59/64
29/32	29/64	31/64	33/64	35/64	37/64	39/64	41/64	43/64	45/64	47/64	49/64	51/64	53/64	55/64	57/64	59/64	61/64
31/32	31/64	33/64	35/64	37/64	39/64	41/64	43/64	45/64	47/64	49/64	51/64	53/64	55/64	57/64	59/64	61/64	63/64

Source: Department of Interior, Bureau of Indian Affairs, Phoenix area office. *Tribal Enrollment* (Washington: Government Printing Office, 1980).

Note: To determine the degree of blood of children, find degree of one parent in left column and the other parent in the top row; read across and down. For example, if a child has parents with 11/16 and 5/8 degrees of blood, then that child would be 21/32 degree Indian.

*Non-Indian.

other races. If a person is three-fourths Caucasian and one-fourth Indian, it is absurd, from the ethnological standpoint, to assign him to the Indian race. Yet legally such a person may be an Indian. From a legal standpoint, then, the biological question of race is generally pertinent, but not conclusive. Legal status depends not only upon biological, but also upon social factors, such as the relation of the individual concerned to a white or Indian community. . . . Recognizing the possible diversity of definitions of "Indianhood," we may nevertheless find some practical value in a definition of "Indian" as a person meeting two qualifications: (a) That some of his ancestors lived in America before its discovery by the white race, and (b) That the individual is considered an "Indian" by the community in which he lives.[45]

Because of the Constitution's silence on the issue of who is an Indian, Congress, the BIA, and the federal courts have had great latitude in developing specific meanings for specific situations that only sometimes reflect the definitions of particular tribes. But because of the plenary power doctrine and the trust doctrine, these federal actors, but especially the Congress, have vested themselves with the right to define "who an Indian is" for purposes relating to legislation and have sometimes established base rolls that actually identify who a tribe's members are. This was done in the case of the so-called Five Civilized Tribes of present-day Oklahoma. Congress, in 1893, enacted a law that all but secured to the federal government the right to determine the membership of these tribes.[46]

Over thirty "legal" definitions have been promulgated by various agencies, departments, and congressional committees and subcommittees that explain who is and is not an Indian eligible for federal services.[47] These definitions can be grouped into six categories. First, and most common, are those definitions that require a specific blood quantum, with one-fourth being the most widely accepted fraction. Second, there is a set of definitions clustered under the requirement that the individual be a member of a federally recognized indigenous community.

A third category includes definitions that mandate residence "on or near" a federal Indian reservation. A fourth class includes definitions grouped under descendancy. These entail definitions that extend eligibility not only to tribal members but also to their descendants up to a specified degree. For example, the definition of *Indian* found in a 1998 bill, Indian Trust-Estate Planning and Land Title Management Improvement Act, declares that "the term 'Indian' means any individual who is a member, or a descendant of a member, of a North American tribe, band, pueblo, or other organized group of natives who are indigenous to the continental U.S., or who otherwise has a special relationship with the U.S. through a treaty, agreement, or other form of recognition." The bill's sponsors described an "Alaska Native" as "an individual who is an Alaskan Indian, Eskimo, Aleut, or any combination thereof, who are indigenous to Alaska."

Under the fifth grouping are several definitions that rely on self-identification. The U.S. Census Bureau, for example, allows individuals to simply declare that they are Indian. Finally, the sixth class is a miscellaneous category that includes definitions that do not easily fit in the other categories.[48]

Defining "Indian" and "tribe" are not simple tasks in part because of the political and economic resources involved and because of the number and power of the respective actors: tribal governments, individual Indians, Congress, the president, the Department of the Interior, the BIA, federal courts, and, increasingly, state governments and the various agencies and individuals who constitute those sovereigns. But who does the defining and how these emotionally laden terms are defined are crucial in expanding our understanding of the politics of individual tribes, intertribal relations, and intergovernmental relations.

For example, in terms of identity, high outmarriage rates, steadily decreasing federal dollars, and an intensified tribal-state relationship have prompted questions about "whether the rules defining Indianness and tribal membership should be relaxed or tightened—that is, made more inclusionary or more exclusionary."[49] For instance, some tribes are eliminating blood quantum and adopting descent criteria, while others are pursuing an "ethnic purification strategy" by adopting a stricter set of blood quantum rules concerning tribal enrollment. These decisions impact tribes and their political relationship with the federal government.[50] For example, questions of who is Cherokee have put that nation at the risk of losing nearly $300 million in federal funds. The Cherokee Nation in 1988 changed the criteria for citizenship, an action that threatened the Citizenship of the Freedmen—the emancipated former slaves of the Cherokee and their descendants. The Freedmen challenged this action in federal and tribal courts. In 2006 the Cherokee Nation's Supreme Court ruled that the descendants of the Cherokee Freedmen had rights as Cherokee citizens. Following this decision, in 2007 the Cherokee Nation voted to amend its constitution, declaring that citizenship depended on one's ability to trace ancestry to one having "Indian blood" listed on the 1906 base roll. As a result, 2,867 Freedmen descendants and nine intermarried white descendants were disenfranchised. The Cherokee have maintained that, as a sovereign nation, they have the right to determine their own membership.

Cherokee opponents, however, have cited the Treaty of 1866 between the Cherokee Nation and the United States as evidence that the Cherokee are violating the law. Article IX of the Treaty of 1866 states, "They [the Cherokee Nation] further agree that all freedmen who have been liberated by voluntary act of their former owners or by law, as well as free colored persons who were in the country at the commencement of the rebellion, are now residents therein, or who may return within six months, and their descendants shall have all the rights of native Cherokee." The Congressional Black Caucus relied on this article when they urged the federal government to suspend funding to the Cherokee Nation. A 2007 bill was introduced by Representative Diane Watson (D-CA) that stated,

> [T]he United States hereby severs all relations with the Cherokee Nation, including all financial obligations or otherwise, until such time as the Cherokee Nation is meeting all of its treaty obligations and other federal statutory obligations (including all obligations of the Treaty of 1866, the Principal Chiefs Act, holding elections for tribal leaders that are in compliance with the Act, and has restored the rights of all Cherokee Freedmen disenfranchised from the Cherokee Nation in the March 3, 2007, Cherokee Nation vote).[51]

The bill also sought to suspend Cherokee rights to conduct gaming.

While tribes retain the right to establish their own membership criteria, the BIA in August 2000 published proposed regulations on the documentation requirements and standards necessary for Indians to receive a "certificate of degree of Indian blood," which is the federal government's way of determining whether individuals possess sufficient Indian blood to be eligible for certain federal programs and services provided exclusively to American Indians or Alaska Natives.[52]

But a number of Indian leaders, like W. Ron Allen, chairman of the Jamestown S'Klallam Tribe of Washington, charged that the federal government should not be in the business of determining who is Indian. The proposed regulations, he argued, by requiring applicants to show a relationship to an enrolled member of a federally recognized tribe, would potentially exclude members or descendants of terminated tribes, state-recognized tribes, and nonrecognized tribes.

Since the BIA's standard blood quantum is one-fourth, and with the high rates of outmarriage, Russell Thornton, an anthropologist, suggests that sometime in this century the proportion of the Indian population with less than one-fourth blood quantum will rise to 60 percent. If this trend is correct, from the federal government's standpoint "decreasing blood quanta of the total Native American population may be perceived as meaning that the numbers of Native Americans to whom it is obligated have declined."[53] This will not mean the extinction of Indian tribes, but it will mean a new form of federal termination of Indians who are eligible for federal aid and services.

Questions around whether a tribe is federally recognized, state-recognized, nonrecognized, or terminated have direct bearing on the internal and external political dynamics of tribes, and directly affect intergovernmental relations, since only recognized tribes may engage in gaming operations that are not directly subject to state law, may exercise criminal jurisdiction over their members and a measure of civil jurisdiction over nonmembers, and are exempt from a variety of state and federal taxes.

What Are Native Lands?

The first and most obvious difference between Indian peoples and all other groups in the United States is that Indians were here before anyone else. All the land in the continental United States, Alaska, and Hawaii was inhabited and revered by the over six hundred distinctive indigenous peoples who dwelt here. Gradually, however, from 1492 forward, various foreign nations—Russia, Holland, Spain, Great Britain, France, Sweden, and later the United States—competed for an economic foothold in North America. For the three most dominant European states, France, Spain, and Great Britain (and later the United States, as Britain's successor), this usually included efforts to secure title to indigenous lands through formal treaties, which were sometimes coercive and occasionally fraudulent, while some were fairly negotiated.[54]

When the United States declared independence in 1776, it wisely opted to continue the policy of negotiating treaties with tribes, which it continued to do until 1871, when Congress unilaterally declared that "hereafter no Indian nation or tribe within the territory of the United States shall be acknowledged or recognized as an independent nation, tribe, or power with whom the United States may contract by

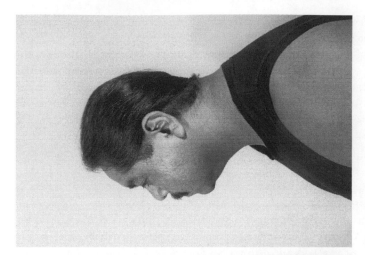

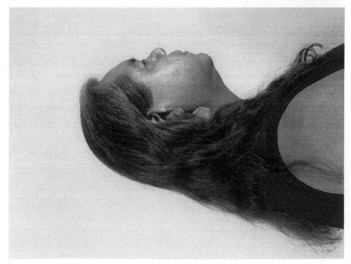

Photo 1.2
"Half Indian/
Half Mexican," 1992
by James Luna.
Courtesy of
James A. Luna.

Photo 1.3
"Half Indian/
Half Mexican," 1992
by James Luna.
Courtesy of
James A. Luna.

Photo 1.4
"Half Indian/
Half Mexican," 1992
by James Luna.
Courtesy of
James A. Luna.

treaty."[55] However, this stance proved unworkable and within a short period the United States was again negotiating agreements with tribal nations that were often referred to and accorded the legal status of treaties. The negotiation of agreements continued until 1912.

Many of these documents were primarily viewed as land cession arrangements by the federal government, in which the United States purchased varying amounts of tribal lands in exchange for monies, goods, and services. In addition, tribes "reserved" their remaining lands, or agreed to relocate to new lands, which were usually designated as reservations. These reserved lands were to be held "in trust" by the United States on behalf of the tribes, who were deemed the beneficiaries. As the tribes' "trustee," the federal government theoretically exercised the responsibility to assist the tribes in the protection of their lands, resources, and cultural heritage and pledged that it would hold itself to the highest standards of good faith and honesty in all its dealings with the tribes.

For example, article 1 of a treaty the Kickapoo signed on October 24, 1832, contained a cession of land:

> The Kickapoo tribe of Indians, in consideration of the stipulations hereinafter made, do hereby cede to the United States, the lands assigned to them by the treaty of Edwardsville, and concluded at St. Louis . . . and all other claims to lands within the State of Missouri.[56]

The second article, however, described the lands the tribe secured for their land cessions:

> The United States will provide for the Kickapoo tribe, a country to reside in, southwest of the Missouri river, as their permanent place of residence as long as they remain a tribe . . . [and] it is hereby agreed that the country within the following boundaries shall be assigned, conveyed, and forever secured . . . to the said Kickapoo tribe.[57]

In this case the Kickapoo agreed to relocate to a little over seven hundred thousand acres of new lands in Kansas that were to serve as their permanent "reservation."

In short, a *reservation* is an area of land—whether aboriginal or new—that has been reserved for an Indian tribe, band, village, or nation. Generally, the United States holds, in trust for the tribe, legal title to the reserved territory. The tribe in these instances holds a beneficial title to the lands, or, in other words, an exclusive right of occupancy. While tribes are able to petition to place newly acquired lands into "trust," the U.S. Supreme Court, in *Carcieri v. Salazar* (2009) created a bizarre distinction between tribes that had been recognized prior to the 1934 Indian Reorganization Act (IRA), which lays out the procedures for placing lands into trust on behalf of Indian nations, and tribes that had only recently received federal acknowledgment. The High Court ruled that the Narragansett Tribe, which had received formal recognition in 1983, was not eligible to have its land placed in trust because it was not under federal jurisdiction in 1934 when the IRA was enacted. This destabilizing decision effectively created two categories of native nations: those with lands under trust as of 1934, and those with lands not eligible for trust who became recognized after 1934. A vigorous campaign has been launched called the *Carcieri fix* that would remedy this bifurcation of native lands by putting all federally recognized nations on equal footing.

It is important to note that not all reservations were created by treaty. Congress has established a number of reservations by statute. The president, through the use of executive order power, established many other reservations. For instance, the state of Arizona has twenty-one reservations—twenty of which were created by presidents. The core foundation of the Navajo Reservation (the largest in the country), was treaty-established in 1868, though the many additions to it were mostly by executive orders. In 1919, Congress forbade the president from establishing any more reservations via executive order. Finally, the secretary of the interior is empowered under the 1934 IRA to establish, expand, or restore reservations.

As of 2010 there were 314 reservations and other restricted and trust lands in the United States (see map 1.1). These reserved lands are located in thirty-one states, mostly in the western United States. There are also twelve state-established reservations in Connecticut, Massachusetts, Michigan, New York, New Jersey, South Carolina, Georgia, and Virginia. Despite the large number of federally recognized Alaska Native groups, there is only one reservation, the Annette Island Indian Reserve.[58]

At present, the indigenous land base in the United States, including Alaska, is approximately one hundred million acres—fifty-six million in the continental United States and forty-four million in Alaska. This represents approximately 4 percent of all lands in the United States. Map 1.4 graphically shows the rapid and enormous loss of aboriginal territory to the United States from the birth of the American republic to the present day.

The roughly one hundred million acres constitutes territory over which tribal governments and Alaska Native villages and corporations exercise varying amounts of governmental jurisdiction, and where state laws are generally inapplicable, with exceptions. Of this acreage, Interior manages over one hundred thousand leases for individual Indians who own more than ten million acres.

Indigenous Hawaiian land claims remain as contested as their aforementioned political status. The United States recognized the independence of the Kingdom of Hawaii from 1826 until 1892. In 1893, however, a group of sugar planters and American businessmen conspired, with the support of American troops, to overthrow Queen Lili'uokalani and the lawful government of Hawaii. This provisional government, in 1894, declared itself to be the Republic of Hawaii and through a U.S. Congressional resolution in 1898 ceded 1,800,000 acres of crown, government, and public lands to the United States. In 1900 Hawaii was established as a territory and admitted into the Union in 1959.[59] Under the Admission Act, "the United States grant[ed] to the State of Hawaii, effective upon its admission into the Union, the United States' title to all the public lands and other public property within the boundaries of the State of Hawaii, title to which is held by the United States immediately prior to its admission into the Union."[60]

In 1993, on the centennial of the overthrow, President Clinton signed Public Law 103-150, known as the *Apology Resolution.* This apology to indigenous Hawaiians on behalf of the United States contained a poignant thirty-seven clause review of the history of Hawaii and recognized that "indigenous Hawaiian people never directly relinquished their claims to their inherent sovereignty as a people or over their national lands to the United States." Furthermore, the Resolution noted that:

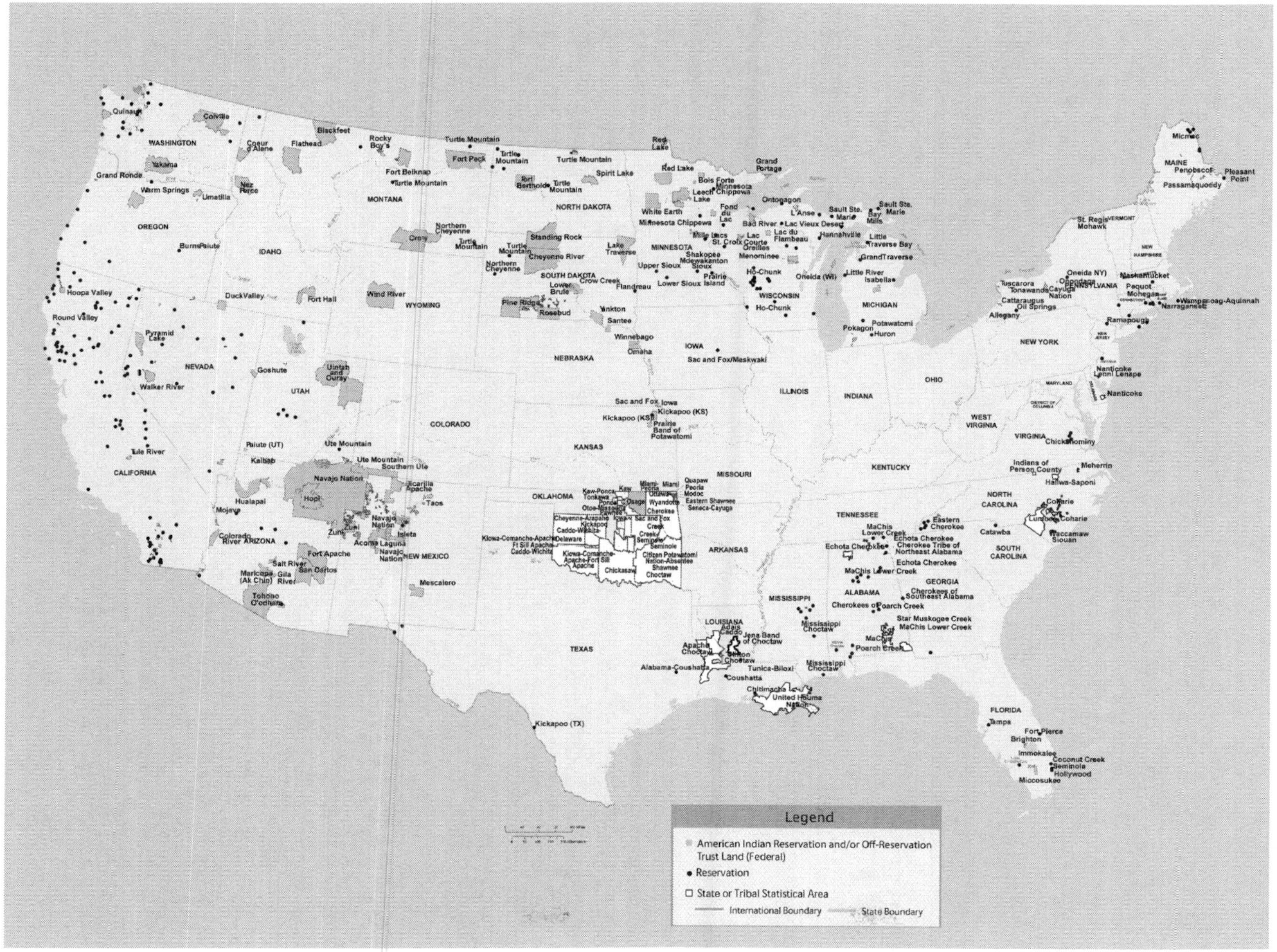

Map 1.1
Federal and State Indian Reservation Lands, 2000
Source: U.S. Census Bureau

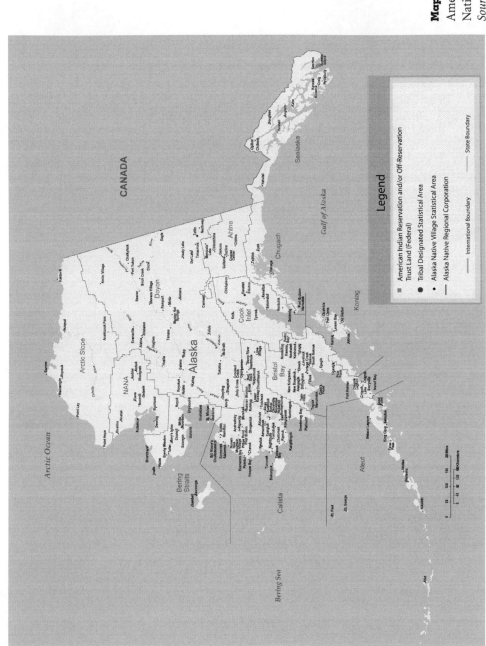

Map 1.2

American Indian and Alaska
Natives, 2000

Source: U.S. Census Bureau

the Congress . . . on the occasion of the 100th anniversary of the illegal overthrow of the Kingdom of Hawaii on January 17, 1893, acknowledges the historical signifi-cance of this event which resulted in the suppression of the inherent sovereignty of the Native Hawaiian people; . . .

apologizes to Native Hawaiians on behalf of the people of the United States for the overthrow of their Kingdom of Hawaii on January 17, 1893, with the par-ticipation of agents and citizens of the United States, and the deprivation of the rights of Native Hawaiians to self-determination; . . .

[and] urges the President of the United States to also acknowledge the ramifi-cations of the overthrow of the Kingdom of Hawaii and to support reconciliation efforts between the United States and the Native Hawaiian people.[61]

While the Apology Resolution seemed like a significant step toward reconciliation between the United States and indigenous Hawaiians, it has not restored any inherent rights or lands to Native Hawaiians. Indigenous Hawaiian claims to 1.2 million acres of land formerly held by the Hawaiian monarchy remain unsettled. The contested land base, held in public land trust, constitutes 29 percent of the total lands that make up the State of Hawaii. The State Supreme Court of Hawaii ordered an injunction that would prevent the Housing Finance and Development Corporation from removing the land from public trust and selling or transferring the lands to a third party until the claims of indigenous Hawaiians to the ceded land had been resolved, but the U.S. Supreme Court, in 2009, overturned this decision. The High Court argued that the Apology Res-olution, while having some legal effect, "did not change the legal landscape" and could not strip Hawaii of its sovereign authority to sell, transfer, or exchange these lands. Though Congress seemingly had the power to acquire indigenous Hawaiian lands via a resolution in 1898, the Court argued that "the Apology Resolution would raise grave constitutional concern if it purported to 'cloud' Hawaii's title to its sovereign lands."[62]

What Is Indian Country?

For an indigenous government to be able to exercise criminal or civil jurisdiction over their territory, their own citizens, and, in some limited cases, non-Indians, the land in question must be designated as *Indian Country.* In the colonial era, Indian Country encompassed all the lands beyond the frontier, lands "populated by tribes and bands of Indians who rejected contact with 'civilized' populations."[63] Today, however, the concept "has been elevated by federal law above other ideas because it transcends mere geo-graphical limitations and represents that sphere of influence in which Indian traditions and federal laws passed specifically to deal with the political relationship of the United States to American Indians have primacy."[64]

Indian Country: Beyond the Reservation

Broadly, the term *Indian Country* means land within which Indian laws and customs and federal laws relating to Indians are generally applicable. But it is also defined as all the land under the supervision and protection of the federal government that has been set aside primarily for the use of Indians. Federal law defines it, first, as all land within the boundaries of an Indian reservation, whether owned by Indians or non-Indians. Second, it includes all "dependent Indian communities" in the United States. These are lands—pueblos of New Mexico, Oklahoma Indian tribal lands, and California *rancherias*—previously recognized by other European nations and now by the successor government, the United States, as belonging to the tribes or as set aside by the federal government for the use and benefit of the Indians (see map 1.3).

Pueblo lands, because they were previously recognized as belonging to the pueblos under Spanish, Mexican, and later U.S. law, are not, strictly speaking, reservations, but are considered Indian lands and are held in trust by the federal government because they are held in communal ownership with fee-simple title residing in each pueblo. Some Pueblo Indian lands are held in equitable ownership by various pueblos, with the United States holding legal title. These lands include reservations created by congressional statute and executive order reservations established by the president.

Oklahoma's numerous Indian tribes also have a distinctive history, though their lands also constitute Indian Country. It is important to note that the nations in the eastern part of the state, what was called *Indian Territory,* home of the Five Civilized Tribes, have a somewhat different history from those in the western part of the state, or what was called *Oklahoma Territory,* home of the Cheyenne, Arapaho, Kiowa, Comanche, and so on. Until March 2010 there was a single reservation in Oklahoma, the Osage Reservation. But the Tenth Circuit Court ruled in *Osage Nation v. Irby*[65] that the Osage Allotment Act of 1906 had impliedly disestablished the reservation, unbeknownst to contemporary Osage citizens.

Some California tribes, because of heavy Spanish influence dating from 1769, live on *rancherias,* a Spanish term meaning "small reservation" and originally applied to Indians who had not been settled in Christian mission communities. The history of death and dispossession visited upon California's indigenous population may well be the worst of any aboriginal peoples in the United States. From a population of well over three hundred thousand at the time of contact, California Indians experienced a staggering rate of decline from diseases, outright genocide, and displacement.[66] That they have retained any lands at all is a remarkable testimony to their fortitude.

Finally, the Indian Country designation includes all individual Indian allotments (we discuss the allotment policy shortly) that are still held in trust or restricted status by the federal government—whether inside or outside an Indian reservation.[67]

For political and legal purposes, the designation of Indian Country is crucial because the reach of a tribal nation's jurisdiction is generally restricted to lands so designated. And it is Indian Country where most jurisdictional disputes arise between tribes and their members; tribes and non-Indians; and tribes and the local, county, state, or federal governments.

For example, this was the central question in the 1998 U.S. Supreme Court case involving indigenous people, *Alaska v. Native Village of Venetie Tribal Government.* In this case, the court had to decide whether the village of Venetie constituted Indian Country. If so, then the tribal government had the right to impose a tax on a construction company; if not, then it lacked such taxing power. In a harmful ruling for Alaska Native sovereignty, the Supreme Court held that the village's fee-simple lands did not constitute Indian Country, thus depriving Alaska villages and corporations of the power to exercise a number of governmental powers that tribal nations in the lower forty-eight states exercise routinely. The Supreme Court, however, need not have relied so exclusively on

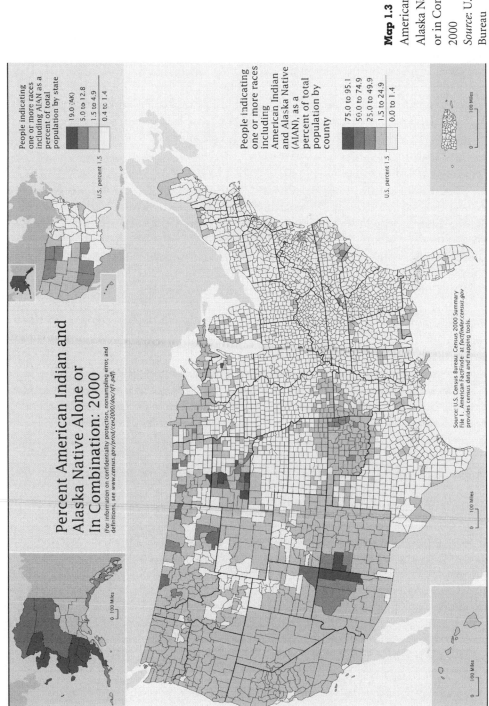

Map 1.3
American Indian and
Alaska Native Alone
or in Combination,
2000
Source: U.S. Census
Bureau

the question of whether or not Venetie constituted "Indian Country" since the statutes articulating this concept clearly did not encompass Alaska at the time they were enacted.

Demography and Indian Country

Estimates of the indigenous population prior to 1492 have been studied by a small group of scholars during the twentieth century and sparked sharp controversy. While population estimates and the measures used to determine these numbers vary, there is a general agreement that indigenous population ranged from three million to twelve million people, with many scholars settling at approximately seven million. While there is dissent regarding the demographic range of indigenous populations at contact, there is consensus that Native peoples experienced a profound population decline, which resulted in an indigenous population that barely numbered 250,000 in 1890. However, as Matthew Snipp notes, "From barely a quarter million at the beginning of the century, the American Indian population numbered nearly two million by the century's end."[68]

The 1980 Census publications were the first to include American Indians and Alaska Natives throughout its data. American Indians and Alaska Natives numbered 1,432,043 or a little more then one half of 1 percent of the total U.S. population. In the twenty-first century, the aboriginal population is larger and more heterogeneous than it has been in the past several centuries. Data from the 2000 U.S. census, which shows a total population of 281,421,906, indicate the continuing transformation of race and ethnicity in America. While the categories of white (211,460,626), Hispanic or Latino (35,305,818), black or African American (34,658,190), American Indian or Alaska Native (2,475,956), Asian (10,242,998), and Native Hawaiian or other Pacific Islander (398,835) were familiar, for the first time in history individuals could choose to self-identify as having more than one race. Some 6,826,228 people, 2.4 percent of the total population, claimed affiliation with two or more races.[69]

While this projected growth has potentially staggering political and economic implications, the fact is that the total indigenous population, despite the large number of indigenous nations—565 and counting—is comparatively quite small (see Figures 1.1–1.4). In 2000, there were a reported 2,475,956 self-identified Indians and Alaska Natives, a 26-percent increase since 1990. This is a drastic decline from pre-European figures of over seven million, but it is far more than the nadir of perhaps only 250,000 around 1900.[70] The 2000 figure represents only 0.9 percent of the total U.S. population of 281,421,906.

Although the overall population of self-identified American Indians and Alaska Natives is still quite small, because of the new category allowing individuals to identify as belonging to more than one race (sixty-three racial options were possible), the 2000 census data are not directly comparable with data from the 1990 census or previous censuses. Thus, while approximately 2.5 million individuals identified themselves as American Indian and Alaska Native alone, an additional 1.6 million people reported themselves as being indigenous and belonging to "at least one other race." Within this group, the most common combinations were "American Indian and Alaska Native and White" (66 percent of the population reported this), "American Indian and Alaska Native and Black or African American" (11 percent of the population), and "American Indian and Alaska Native and White and Black or African American" (7 percent). In sum, approximately 4.1 million people reported themselves as being American Indian and Alaska Native "alone or in combination with one or more other races."[71] By 2006,

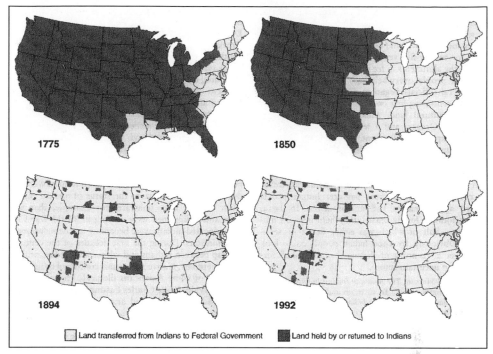

1775

1850

1894

1992

☐ Land transferred from Indians to Federal Government ■ Land held by or returned to Indians

Map 1.4
American Indian Land Losses
Source: Map from ENCYCLOPEDIA OF NORTH AMERICAN INDIANS, edited by Frederick E.
Hoxie. © 1996 by Houghton Mifflin Company. Reprinted by permission of Houghton Mifflin Har-
court Publishing Company. All rights reserved.

this number had grown to 4.5 million people. By 2008 American Indians composed
1.6 percent of the total population, totaling approximately 4.9 million people. Between
July 1, 2007, and July 1, 2008, alone, the American Indian population had increased by
83,250 people, a 1.7-percent growth.[72]

Suffice it to say, the amount of racial mixing acknowledged in the American Indian
context is extreme when compared with that of other racial and ethnic groups. As Russell Thornton, a Cherokee anthropologist, noted in his analysis of the 2000 census data,
American Indians have a racial mixture of 37 percent, which "far exceeds percentages
for other groups." Thornton noted that only about 5 percent of African Americans
reported mixed ancestry.[73]

In Alaska, there is only one small reservation, Annette Island Reserve, though for
census purposes lands are designated as "Alaska Native Village Statistical areas" that are
inhabited and recognized as indigenous areas. Approximately 47,244 Alaska Natives live
on these lands. In sum, more than 60 percent, over one million, of all Indian people do
not live on Indian reservations.[74] A majority of indigenous peoples, in fact some 56.2
percent, live in metropolitan or suburban areas. And roughly half of all urban Indians
can be found in as few as sixteen cities, largely as a result of the 1950s and 1960s termination, relocation, and educational programs of the federal government.

In the early days of relocation, the BIA generally helped send Indians to Chicago,
Los Angeles, Denver, or Salt Lake City. By 2000, Indians had migrated to a number of

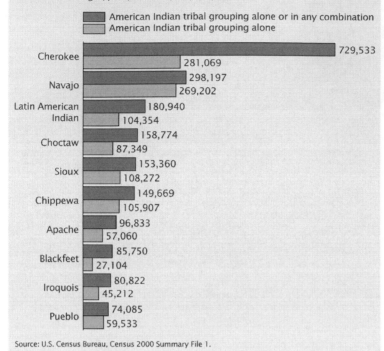

Figure 1.1
Ten Largest American Indian Tribal Groupings, 2000
Source: U.S. Census Bureau, Census 2000 Summary File 1.

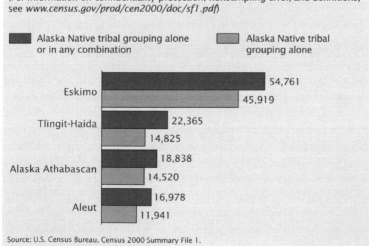

Figure 1.2
Largest Alaska Native Tribal Groupings, 2000
Source: U.S. Census Bureau, Census 2000 Summary File 1.

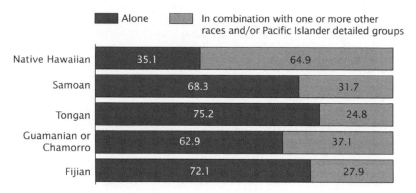

Figure 1.3

Percent Distribution of Selected Detailed Native Hawaiian and Other, 2000
Source: U.S. Census Bureau, Census 2000 Summary File 1.

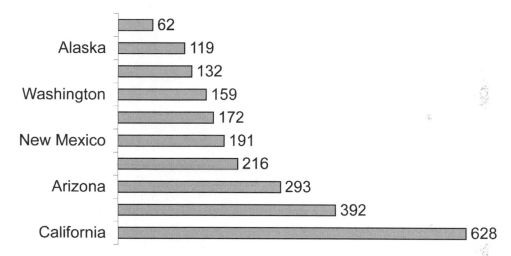

Figure 1.4

States with the Ten Largest American Indian Populations, 2000
Source: U.S. Census Bureau, Census 2000 Summary File 1.

other metropolitan areas. Cities with the largest self-identified Indian populations in 2000 were New York (87,241), Los Angeles (53,092), Phoenix (35,093), Tulsa (30,227), Oklahoma City (29,001), and Anchorage (26,995) (see table 1.4). These figures reflect those who identify as native "alone" or "in combination" with another ethnic group. Forty-eight percent of Indians still live in the western half of the United States, while nearly 30 percent live in the South.

The states with the ten largest indigenous populations in 2000 are shown in Figure 1.4. The District of Columbia had the fewest Indians, 1,466. As of 2008, California continued to have the largest indigenous population, totaling 738,978 people, while American Indians and Alaska Natives in Alaska made up the largest percentage of indigenous peoples in a single state, accounting for 18 percent of the total state population. Native Hawaiians and other Pacific Islanders compose 30 percent of the total state population for Hawaii.[75]

There is also great variation in the population of individual tribes (see Figure 1.1). The largest tribe, according to the 2000 census, is the Cherokee, with 281,069 self-identified members. By 2006 the Cherokee population had increased to 301,800. The Navajo Nation in this same year had a population of 296,100. The smallest tribes have fewer than one hundred members. The indigenous population is also a young population, with more than 35 percent younger than age seventeen. In fact, the median age for reservation Indians is more than ten years younger than that of the general U.S. population. The American Indian population is also growing at a faster rate than the U.S. population overall. There was a 26-percent increase among all native individuals—alone and in combination—between the 1990 and 2000 censuses. The U.S. population during this same period increased 13 percent. Although the 2010 census was unavailable for this edition, it is probable that the indigenous population will continue to grow. According to U.S. Census findings, the American Indian population, including those of more than one race, is predicted to total 8.6 million people by 2050, composing 2 percent of the total U.S. population. The indigenous population, like that of the Jews and the Japanese Americans in Hawaii, is also one that experiences an extremely high level of intergroup marriage (marriage between persons of different races). Although intergroup married couples accounted for only 4 percent of all married couples in the United States in 1990, American Indians had a 53-percent intergroup marriage rate. Potentially, this figure could have severe cultural and political implications for indigenous nations.[76]

As Snipp mused:

> The extraordinarily high level of racial intermarriage for American Indians provides a good reason to expect that growing numbers of American Indians and their descendants will choose non-Indians for spouses and to a greater or lesser degree become absorbed into the dominant culture. Some of these Indians will abandon their cultural heritage altogether, while others may make only minor accommodations as a result of having a non-Indian spouse. This raises a question that is extremely controversial within many quarters of the American Indian community: Are American Indians assimilating so quickly through racial intermarriage that they will eventually, in the not too distant future, marry themselves out of existence?[77]

Predicting the future is an impossible task and we will not hazard a guess as to whether this intermarriage rate will continue. Suffice it to say, this is viewed as a serious predicament by some tribes and raises some important questions. For instance, will Indians, like many intermarried Jews, be able to show a propensity for combining extensive intermarriage with a surge in ethnic and religious pride? For while the rate of Jewish intermarriage is higher today than at any earlier point, American Jewish culture and community life appear to be flourishing, including a resurgent interest in Yiddish.[78]

Other questions confront tribes as well. Will they continue to use blood quantum as their primary definitional criterion? Will the federal government claim that its legal and moral obligations to Indians dissipate if a tribal nation's blood quantum falls below a certain percentage? Will tribes be able to exercise jurisdiction over a multiracial citizenry? These are questions some tribes are beginning to address as data for the 2010 Census is being collected. Aware of the significant impact that numbers can have, the National Congress of American Indians (NCAI) has launched its "Indian Country Counts" 2010 Census campaign. Estimating that the actual population was undercounted by more then

Table 1.4.

Ten Largest Places in Total Population and in American Indian and Alaska Native Population: 2000

Place	Total Population		American Indian and Alaska Native Alone		American Indian and Alaska Native Alone or in Combination		Percent of Total Population	
	Rank	Number	Rank	Number	Rank	Number	American Indian and Alaska Native Alone	American Indian and Alaska Native Alone or in Combination
New York, NY	1	8,008,278	1	41,289	1	87,241	0.5	1.1
Los Angeles, CA	2	3,694,820	2	29,412	2	53,092	0.8	1.4
Chicago, IL	3	2,896,016	9	10,290	8	20,898	0.4	0.7
Houston, TX	4	1,953,631	11	8,568	10	15,743	0.4	0.8
Philadelphia, PA	5	1,517,550	24	4,073	21	10,835	0.3	0.7
Phoenix, AZ	6	1,321,045	3	26,696	3	35,093	2.0	2.7
San Diego, CA	7	1,223,400	13	7,543	9	16,178	0.6	1.3
Dallas, TX	8	1,188,580	18	6,472	18	11,334	0.5	1.0
San Antonio, TX	9	1,144,646	10	9,584	12	15,224	0.8	1.3
Detroit, MI	10	951,270	40	3,140	25	8,907	0.3	0.9
Oklahoma City, OK	29	506,132	6	17,743	5	29,001	3.5	5.7
Tucson, AZ	30	486,699	8	11,038	11	15,358	2.3	3.2
Albuquerque, NM	35	448,607	7	17,444	7	22,047	3.9	4.9
Tulsa, OK	43	393,049	5	18,551	4	30,227	4.7	7.7
Anchorage, AK	65	260,283	4	18,941	6	26,995	7.3	10.4

Source: U.S. Census Bureau, Census 2000 Summary File 1.

Note: For information on confidentiality protection, nonsampling error, and definitions, see www.census.gov/prod/cen2000/doc/sf1.pdf.

12 percent, NCAI President Joe A. Garcia said, "A true Indian count is just one of the steps that tribes must take on the path to regaining our economic, social, and governmental strength as Native people. This data directs billions of dollars in federal funding that flows into Indian Country. Often the most vulnerable are the hardest to count and consequently end up missing out on the resources they need."[79]

Conclusion

The power to define—what is a tribe, who is an Indian, what constitutes Indian Country, which group gets recognized—along with the power to decide whether or not to act in a colonial capacity in relation to indigenous nations are important means by which the federal government has gained and retains a dominant position vis-à-vis tribal groups. While on one hand supporting the right of indigenous polities to exercise self-determination, the United States on the other still insists that it has the power and the right to trump important tribal governmental decisions regarding identity and has shown throughout its history that it will so act if it deems it necessary to further its own economic, political, and cultural interests.

The demographic data presented glaringly show that diversity and uncertainty are hallmarks of Indian Country, with more than half the indigenous population living off reservations and Indians outmarrying at increasing rates. What the impact of such movement and marriage rates will be on tribal national identity, federal Indian policy, and the government-to-government relationship is, however, impossible to predict.

CHAPTER 2

Indigenous Peoples Are Nations, Not Minorities

We claim that the "constitution, and the laws of the United States which shall be made in pursuance thereof . . . shall be the supreme law of the land." But we also claim to recognize the sovereignty of Native American nations, the original occupants of this land. These claims—one to jurisdictional monopoly, the other to jurisdictional multiplicity—are irreconcilable. Two hundred years have produced no resolution of the contradiction except at the expense of the tribes and the loss to non-Indians of the Indians' gift of their difference.

—Milner Ball, 1987[1]

A QUICK PERUSAL OF recent national newspaper headlines searched under the category "Indian politics" uncovered a number of articles with fascinating headlines such as "Blazing New Trails in Native American Lands,"[2] "New York Wins Round in Fight Against Indian Tobacco Venders,"[3] "Quest to Save Tribal Languages,"[4] "Paterson Endorses Shinnecock Tribe's Bid for Recognition,"[5] and "U.S. Will Settle Indian Lawsuit for $3.4 Billion."[6] This small sampling of headlines is evidence of the significant breadth and depth of indigenous politics and identifies some of the topics that distinguish tribal nations and their citizens from other groups in the United States.

The situation of the 565 indigenous polities in North America is and has always been distinctive in comparison with the status and place of African Americans, Asian Americans, Latino Americans, women, and other racial or ethnic groups in the country. This is so for a number of important reasons, some obvious, some little known. First, tribal peoples are the original—the indigenous—inhabitants of North America and they are nations in the most fundamental sense of the word. That is, they are separate peoples inhabiting specific territories that they wield some governmental control or jurisdiction over. While speculation abounds in scientific circles about how long Native peoples have inhabited the Americas and whether they originated here or arrived from distant lands,[7] it is safe to say that they remain the original inhabitants of the Americas.

Photo 2.1
Mille Lacs tribal member Eric Gahbow in front of the U.S. Supreme Court after completing
Waabanong run for Ojibwe treaty rights.
Courtesy of Great Lakes Indian Fish & Wildlife Commission

Second, the preexistence of over six hundred independent tribal nations, bands, pueblos, and so on, well in advance of the formation of the United States, each having a number of integral attributes, including a bounded land base, an appropriate economic system, a governmental system, and sociocultural distinctiveness,[8] necessitated the practice of aboriginal sovereigns negotiating political compacts, treaties, and alliances with European nations and later the United States. The fact of treaty making, which no other resident American group (states are also precluded from negotiating treaties) participated in, and the products of that process—the actual treaties, agreements, and negotiated settlements—confirmed a nation-to-nation relationship between the negotiating tribal and nontribal parties. See Figure 2.1 for a graphical depiction of the structural relationship between American Indian nations and the United States, individual states, and local governments. A large number, over five hundred, of these important contractual arrangements form the baseline parameters of the political relationship between tribes and the United States and are still legally valid, though their enforceability has always been problematic.[9] A majority of these treaties involved land cessions by tribes and reservations of lands not ceded or sold to the federal government.

As tribes are treaty-recognized sovereigns, tribal rights are not based on or subject to U.S. constitutional law and are therefore not protected by the Constitution. This is because preexisting sovereign tribes do not derive their inherent governmental powers from the federal or state government. Thus, native nations have an extraconstitutional relationship to the United States that no other group has. However, according to Article 6 of the U.S. Constitution, "all treaties made, or which shall be made, under the authority of the United States, shall be the supreme law of the land; and the judges in

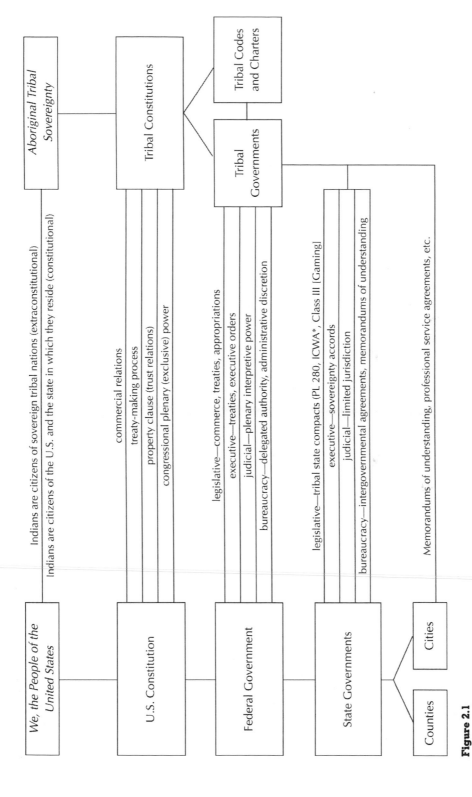

Figure 2.1
Indigenous Nations and the American Political System

every State shall be bound thereby, any thing in the Constitution or laws of any State to the contrary notwithstanding." Hence, while tribal sovereignty is not beholden to or rooted in American constitutional law, a tribe's treaty rights are, at least in constitutional theory, the supreme law of the land and should be subject to full protection under the Constitution's rubric.

A third feature differentiating indigenous peoples from other racial and ethnic groups is the trust doctrine. While the federal government and tribes have rarely been in agreement on what the trust principle entails,[10] President Obama, in a memorandum on tribal consultation deriving from the 2009 Tribal Nations Conference, recognized "The United States has a unique legal and political relationship with Indian tribal governments, established through and confirmed by the Constitution of the United States, treaties, statutes, executive orders, and judicial decisions."[11] In this statement the president sought to assure indigenous peoples that the United States recognizes that native nations have a sovereign status that the federal government, as a separate though connected sovereign, is bound to respect under its own law. The hundreds of treaties and agreements that were negotiated in which the native nations were guaranteed all the rights and resources (e.g., rights to water and lands; to hunt, fish, and gather; to exercise criminal and civil jurisdiction; to tax) they had not ceded to the federal government when they sold or exchanged the majority of their lands—most of North America— were contractual rights that were also protected by the trust doctrine, which is the federal government's legal and moral pledge to respect those reserved Indian rights.

More important was the president's use of the phrase "unique legal and political relationship." This is a declaration that the federal government has an obligation to support indigenous peoples legally, culturally, economically, and politically. It is best characterized by the phrase trustee (United States)-beneficiary (Tribes) relationship. As Vine Deloria Jr. (Standing Rock Sioux), the leading scholar of Indian law and politics, has stated:

> The trust responsibility of the federal government toward the Indian tribes is mandated by the fact that Indians are extra constitutional. No constitutional protections exist for Indians in either a tribal or an individual sense, and hence the need for special rules and regulations, special administrative discretionary authority, and special exemptions. This special body of law replaces the constitutional protections granted to other members of American society.[12]

Native nations tend to think of "trust" as entailing four interrelated components: that the federal government—or its agents—is pledged to protect tribal property and sovereignty and would not move for or against tribes without first securing tribal consent; that the United States would act with the utmost integrity in its legal and political commitments to Indian peoples as outlined in treaties or governmental policies (e.g., provide health care, educational support, housing assistance); that the United States would act in a moral manner regarding tribal rights, as the Judeo-Christian nation it historically professed to be in its dealing with tribes; and that the United States would continue to support any additional duties and responsibilities in its self-assumed role as the Indians' "protectors."

A fourth concept, *congressional plenary power,* is yet another distinctive feature of the tribal-federal relationship that separates tribal nations from all other racial and ethnic groups in the United States.[13] Basically put, *plenary* means complete in all aspects or meanings in federal Indian policy and law. First, it means exclusive. The federal Constitution, in the commerce clause (Article 1, Section 8, Clause 3), vests in Congress the sole authority to "regulate Commerce with foreign Nations, and among the several States, and with the Indian tribes." In other words, the founders of the American republic believed that the power to engage in treaty making with tribes should rest with the legislative branch of the federal government, not with the states, which, under the Articles of Confederation, had retained the right to deal with tribes in their proximity.

Second, and related to the first definition, *plenary* also means preemptive. That is, Congress may enact legislation that effectively precludes—preempts—state governments from acting in Indian-related matters. Finally, and most controversially, since this definition lacks a constitutional basis, *plenary* means unlimited or *absolute*. This judicially constructed definition (*United States v. Kagama*, 1886) means that the Congress has vested in itself, without a constitutional mooring, virtually boundless governmental authority and jurisdiction over tribal nations, their lands, and their resources. As recently as 2004, the Supreme Court, in *United States v. Lara*,[14] held that "Congress, with this Court's approval, has interpreted the Constitution's 'plenary' grants of power as authorizing it to enact legislation that both restricts and, in turn, relaxes those restrictions on tribal sovereign authority."[15]

Federal plenary power, when defined as unlimited and absolute, should give one reason to pause from a democratic theory perspective. The idea that a democracy has exercised and continues to assert that it has the power to wield absolute authority over native people—and without tribal consent—whose members are today citizens of the United States, is deeply disturbing, yet that reality persists for indigenous peoples and their citizens, notwithstanding their treaty and trust rights as citizens of sovereign governments and, since 1924, with citizenship status in the states and federal government as well.

Plenary power, like the trust doctrine, has proven to be a mixed blessing for Indian peoples. On the positive side, Congress, under its plenary exclusive and preemptive power, has been able to pass legislation that accords Indians unique treatment that other groups and individuals are ineligible for—medical care, Indian preference hiring practices in the Bureau of Indian Affairs (BIA), educational benefits, housing aid, tax exemptions, and so on. Such legislative and policy action is possible, again, because of the extraconstitutional status of tribes, which places them outside the protections of the Constitution. Tribal citizens are entitled to these distinctive considerations, and Congress is empowered to exercise a great deal of authority in Indian affairs because it must be "immune from ordinary challenges which might otherwise hamper the wise administration of Indian affairs."[16]

On the negative side, plenary power has been interpreted by the Supreme Court to allow the federal government to pass laws and enact regulations that prohibit Indians in some situations from selling their own land to whomever they wish.[17] Congress may also confiscate Indian lands held under aboriginal title and is not required to pay just compensation under the Fifth Amendment to the Constitution.[18] Congress may punish Indians under federal law for certain crimes, even if this means the individuals will be punished more severely than non-Indians who commit the same crime under state law.[19] And Congress may literally terminate the legal existence of tribal nations.[20]

How are Congress and the Supreme Court able to justify such discriminatory action if the Constitution prohibits discrimination on the basis of race? It is because while tribal nations certainly constitute separate racial groups, more important is the fact that they constitute separate political groups, recognized in the treaty relationship, the trust doctrine, and the placement of tribes in the commerce clause. In other words, European nations and the United States did not enter into treaties with tribes because of their racial differences, but because they were separate sovereigns—oftentimes with impressive military and economic clout—with whom the United States wanted and needed to establish diplomatic ties. Hence, the relationship the United States has with native nations is based on their political status as governments, and is at its heart a political, not racial, alliance. Congressional action, therefore, that is based on plenary power does not violate the equal protection and due process clauses of the Constitution that prohibit discrimination on the basis of race.[21]

What all the preceding concepts confirm is that native peoples, unlike any other groups in the United States, are sovereign nations, not minority groups. A sovereign nation is a distinct political entity that exercises a measure of jurisdictional power over a specific territory. It is not an absolute or fully independent power in a pure sense because no nation or state in the world today, regardless of its geographic girth, population base, or gross national product, is completely or fully sovereign. "Our industrial world of mass communication, soaring population and global transportation makes isolation of sovereign nations virtually impossible. Economic and political factors also encourage and necessitate governmental interdependency."[22]

In addition to the practical limitations of sovereignty, a nation's sovereignty is also restricted by self-limitation, according to Sam Deloria, "as when the United States Constitution puts limits on the expression of this country's sovereignty. In the case of the Indian tribes, the United States agrees to recognize our [Indian tribes'] political, cultural, and land rights. In recognizing these rights [in treaties and agreements] the United States has voluntarily limited its sovereignty."[23]

This statement, in part, addresses the fundamental issue raised in the quote that opened this chapter: that of jurisdictional monopoly versus jurisdictional multiplicity. In other words, the United States is certainly a distinctive sovereign entity and the U.S. Constitution is recognized as the "supreme law of the land." But the historical record and the Constitution itself also evidence the reality that the United States and the constituent states have always recognized, if not always supported, the preexisting sovereigns—the tribal nations—who have lived in North America for millennia. Thus, one of the tasks of this book is to discuss the reality that indigenous nations constitute the third set of sovereigns—along with the federal and state governments—whose politics deserve focused attention.

The sovereignty of tribes, it is important to note, was not delegated to them by the federal or state governments—it is original and inherent power. Tribal sovereignty has to do, on one hand, with a tribe's right to retain a measure of independence from outside entities and the power of regulating one's internal affairs, including the ability to make and execute laws, to impose and collect taxes, and to make alliances with other governments. On the other hand, tribal sovereignty has a unique cultural and spiritual dimension that differentiates it from the sovereign power of a state or the federal government. We define it this way: *Tribal sovereignty is the intangible and dynamic cultural force inherent in a given indigenous community, empowering that body toward the sustenance and enhancement of political, economic, and cultural integrity. It undergirds*

the way tribal governments relate to their own citizens, to non-Indian residents, to local
governments, to the state government, to the federal government, to the corporate world,
and to the global community.

Because of the doctrines discussed previously, the sovereign interactions of the tribes, the states, and the United States entail an ongoing and awkward minuet whose choreography has too often been unilaterally prepared by the federal government, with little regard for the inherent rights of the tribes, the original minuet partners. The distinctive cultural, political, geographical, and legal status of indigenous nations still does not fit within the U.S. Constitution's matrix, and is completely let alone by state constitutional documents, especially of western states, which were required by Congress to include clauses in their enabling acts and then in their constitutions forever disclaiming any jurisdiction over Indian tribes or their lands and promising never to tax Indian lands held in trust by the federal government.[24] These clauses continue in effect, even though tribal citizens have been citizens of the United States since 1924.

Consequently, native nations find that their collective rights, lands, and even inherent sovereignty lack substantive protection from the very government, the federal government, which is charged by treaties, by the trust doctrine, and by constitutional acknowledgment in the commerce clause with protecting Indian tribes. The internal political affairs of native nations and the relationship between native nations and the United States is, thus, full of perplexity.

Natives as Citizens and Subjects of the United States

One of the fundamental differences between indigenous peoples in their relationship with the federal government and that of other racial and ethnic minorities and the United States is that from the beginning the relationship was a political one, steeped in diplomacy and treaties. It was, in fact, a nation-to-nation relationship. The United States viewed Indian nations as small, largely "uncivilized" polities that it would have to deal with as separate entities.

This is evident in several provisions of some of the key documents of early U.S. political history:

The Declaration of Independence, July 4, 1776. Drafted mainly by Thomas Jefferson, this document proclaimed the right of the colonies to separate from Great Britain and outlined the rights of man and the rights to rebellion and self-government:

> He has excited domestic Insurrections amongst us, and has endeavoured to bring on the Inhabitants of our Frontiers, the merciless Indian Savages, whose Known Rule of Warfare, is an undistinguished Destruction, of all Ages, Sexes and Conditions.

Treaty with the Delaware Tribe, September 17, 1778 (7 Stat. 13). This is considered the first Indian treaty written in formal diplomatic and legal language:

> Article 6: . . . And it is further agreed on between the contracting parties [the United States and the Delaware Nation] should it for the future be found

conducive for the mutual interest of both parties to invite any other tribes who have been friends to the interest of the United States, to join the present confederation, and to form a state whereof the Delaware Nation shall be the head, and have a representation in Congress.

Articles of Confederation, March 1, 1781. The compact among the thirteen original states that established the first government of the United States:

> The United States in Congress assembled shall also have the sole and exclusive right and power of . . . regulating the trade and managing all affairs with the Indians, not members of any of the States, provided that the legislative right of any State within its own limits be not infringed or violated.

The Federalist Papers, No. 24, Alexander Hamilton, 1787–1788. Part of a series of eighty-five essays written by Alexander Hamilton, James Madison, and John Jay—all under the name Publius—published in New York newspapers to persuade New Yorkers to support the newly proposed Constitution:

> The Savage tribes on our Western frontier ought to be regarded as our natural enemies, their [Great Britain's] natural allies, because they have most to fear from us and most to hope from them.

The Northwest Ordinance, July 13, 1787 (*Journals of the Continental Congress* 321: 340–41). A congressional enactment under the Articles of Confederation for the government of the territory north of the Ohio River and west of New York to the Mississippi River. It is the most significant measure passed by the Confederated Congress, since it established the policy that territories were not to be kept in subjugation but were to be developed for admission to statehood on an equal footing with other states:

> Religion, morality, and knowledge, being necessary to good government and the happiness of mankind, schools and the means of education shall forever be encouraged. The utmost good faith shall always be observed toward the Indians; their lands and property shall never be taken from them without their consent; and, in their property, rights, and liberty, they never shall be invaded or disturbed, unless in just and lawful wars authorized by Congress; but laws founded in justice and humanity shall, from time to time, be made, for preventing wrongs being done them, and for preserving peace and friendship with them.

U.S. Constitution, 1789. The fundamental document that established the framework of government, assigned powers and duties of governmental agencies, and established the relationship of the people to the government:

> Article 1, Section 2, Clause 3: Representatives and direct Taxes shall be apportioned among the several States . . . according to their respective numbers, which shall be determined by adding to the whole Number of free Persons, including those bound to Service for a Term of years, and excluding Indians not taxed, three fifths of all other persons.

Article 1, Section 8, Clause 3: The Congress shall have Power to regulate Commerce with foreign Nations, and among the several States, and with the Indian tribes.

Trade and Intercourse Act, July 22, 1790 (1 Stat. 137). This act required white traders to secure license before trading with Indians and generally restricted transactions between settlers and Indians:

That no person shall be permitted to carry on trade or intercourse with the Indian tribes, without a license for that purpose under the hand and seal of the superintendent of the department.

Cherokee Nation v. Georgia **(1831) (30 U.S. [5 Pet.] 1).** The Cherokee had filed an original action in the U.S. Supreme Court challenging Georgia's extension of authority within Cherokee territory on the grounds that they were a "foreign nation" within the meaning of the Constitution. The Court denied it had jurisdiction to hear the case and went on to describe what it perceived the Cherokee status to be:

They [tribes] may, more correctly, perhaps, be denominated domestic dependent nations.

Worcester v. Georgia **(1832) (31 U.S. [6 Pet.] 515).** The Court, in holding that Georgia did not have the right to arrest white missionaries for having failed to obtain a state license, declared that federal law was supreme in relation to state law:

The Indian nations had always been considered as distinct, independent political communities, retaining their original natural rights as the undisputed possessors of the soil from time immemorial.

Each of these documents acknowledges that native peoples belonged to their own nations and were not citizens of the United States. The phrase "excluding Indians not taxed" was included in the Constitution as recognition that some individual Indians in the thirteen original states had merged with the general population. Nonetheless, the Indian commerce clause, the practice of treaty making, and the geographic and cultural separateness of native nations from the United States evidenced the reality that Indian tribes were seen as necessary political and economic allies and not as peoples whose citizens were likely to abandon their tribal nation in order to become American citizens.

Even as the nation-to-nation relationship was being reconfirmed via steady treaty negotiations, the U.S. Congress was already acting in ways that indicated its eventual goal was to extend American citizenship to certain individuals and groups of Indians. In such cases, Indians who requested U.S. citizenship were usually required to abandon their tribal citizenship and relinquish tribal property. For example, in 1817, in one of the earliest Indian removal treaties signed with the Cherokee Nation, a provision was included in Article 8 whereby individual Cherokee heads of family who opted to remain in the east rather than relocate to the new lands in the west were given the opportunity to become citizens of the United States and receive 640-acre tracts of land.[25]

Other native nations, like the Stockbridge and Munsee, the Ottawa, the Potowatomie, and the Wyandotte, also had opportunities for their members to become American citizens, but nearly always on the condition that the individual abandon or sever all tribal ties, adopt the habits and customs of Euro-Americans, become self-supporting, and learn to read and speak English. In some cases, however, special statutes naturalized particular tribes or individuals. In others, general statutes, like the Dawes General Allotment Act of 1887, conferred citizenship on Indians who accepted land allotments. And finally, there were some statutes that naturalized special classes of Indians: in 1888 Indian women who married white men[26] and in 1919 Indian men who fought in World War I and were honorably discharged.[27]

Along with these sporadic attempts to naturalize particular native nations or individual Indians, and notwithstanding Congress's enactment of a "Civilization Fund," an annual sum of $10,000 established in 1819 aimed at introducing Indians to the "habits and arts of civilization,"[28] the question of whether or not Indians were American citizens remained deeply problematic throughout the nineteenth and well into the twentieth century. In fact, the preponderance of evidence shows that, despite the several treaties and laws enfranchising some tribes and classes of individual Indians, the relationship between tribes and the United States remained one best described as a nation-to-nation association.

For example, in the devastating Supreme Court case *Dred Scott v. Sandford* (1857), which held that African Americans could not be citizens and lacked certain rights that whites had to respect, Chief Justice Roger Taney wrote that Indian tribes by contrast "were yet a free and independent people, associated together in nations or tribes, and governed by their own laws." "These Indian governments," said Taney, "were regarded and treated as foreign governments, as much so as if an ocean had separated the red man from the white."[29] Taney did indicate that individual Indians could be naturalized by Congress, but only if they left their tribal nation and adopted the habits and values of whites.

The next opportunity to examine Indian citizenship arose in the wake of interpreting the Fourteenth Amendment, ratified by the states in 1868. This amendment provided in the first clause that "all persons born or naturalized in the United States, and subject to the jurisdiction thereof, are citizens of the United States and of the State wherein they reside." A cursory reading of this amendment would lead one to believe that Indians, virtually all of whom were born in the United States, were now citizens of the United States.

However, the Senate Judiciary Committee, which had been asked to determine whether the Fourteenth Amendment had, in fact, enfranchised Indians, reported in 1870 that Indians who remained bound to their tribal nations were not and could not be subject to the Constitution's Fourteenth Amendment, including its citizenship clause:

> To maintain that the United States intended, by a change of its fundamental law, which was not ratified by these tribes, and to which they were neither requested nor permitted to assert, to annul treaties then existing between the United States as one party, and the Indian tribes as the other parties respectively, would be to charge upon the United States repudiation of national obligations, repudiation doubly infamous from the fact that the parties whose claims were thus annulled are too weak to enforce their rights, and were enjoying the voluntarily assumed guardianship and protection of this government.[30]

The committee did state that individual Indians who had "merged in the mass of our people" became subject to federal jurisdiction, but stopped short of declaring even detribalized Indians American citizens.

A year later three important developments occurred that addressed ongoing federal ambivalence about the political status of tribes. First, Congress, by way of a legislative rider attached to an Indian appropriation bill, declared that henceforth it would negotiate no more treaties with tribal nations, although it would remain legally bound by all preexisting ratified treaties. Second, and conversely, a federal district court in *McKay v. Campbell* (1871) ruled that a Chinook Indian was "born a member of an independent political community" and therefore "not born subject to the jurisdiction of the United States—not born in its allegiance." Finally, the Supreme Court in *Cherokee Tobacco* (1871) held that Indian treaty rights could be implicitly overridden by subsequent federal laws, a particularly egregious ruling because of the recent enactment of the treaty-termination law, which froze tribes in political limbo and left them completely vulnerable to the Congress. As a result of the *Cherokee Tobacco* precedent, any federal law enacted after March 3, 1871, could be interpreted as having overridden any prior treaty.

The status of tribes as separate yet domestic sovereigns, subject to increasing federal legislative power, yet lacking any constitutional protection and with increasingly little treaty protection, was summarized in 1872 in Commissioner of Indian Affairs Francis A. Walker's annual report to the secretary of the interior:

> In a word, in the two-hundred and seventy-five thousand Indians west of the Mississippi, the United States have all the elements of a large gypsy population, which will inevitably become a sore, a well-nigh intolerable, affliction to all that region, unless the Government shall provide for their instruction in the arts of life, which can only be done effectually under a pressure not to be resisted or evaded. The right of the Government to do this cannot be seriously questioned. *Expressly excluded by the Constitution from citizenship, the Government is only bound in its treatment of them by considerations of present policy and justice.* Even were the constitutional incapacity of these people not what it is, and were there nothing in the history of the dealings of the United States with them to form a precedent for their being placed under arbitrary control, still, the manifest necessity of self-protection would amply justify the Government in any and all measures required to prevent the miserable conclusion I have indicated.[31] [emphasis added]

This was the status of tribal nations and their citizens. But the status of detribalized Indian persons who had voluntarily left their nation was not addressed until the 1884 Supreme Court case *Elk v. Wilkins.* John Elk, an Indian whose tribal affiliation was never stated, left his nation and moved to Omaha, Nebraska. Elk registered to vote but his application was rejected by Wilkins, the city registrar, on the grounds that Elk was an Indian and therefore not an American citizen. The Supreme Court agreed with Wilkins's decision and denied Elk the right to vote. The Court held that Indians, like "the children of subjects of any foreign government," were not subject to the Fourteenth Amendment's provisions since they belonged to "alien nations, distinct political communities, with whom the United States might and habitually did deal as they thought fit, either through treaties . . . [or] legislation."[32]

In other words, Indians were not "subject to the jurisdiction of the United States," so could not be citizens by birth. In addition, the Court said that even if individual Indians met the same basic citizenship requirements expected of other noncitizens, they still could not be enfranchised unless Congress made an affirmative declaration—naturalization—authorizing by an act such a change in their standing.

However, federal policymakers, increasingly intent on the forced assimilation of Indians, continued their efforts to extend the franchise to Indians. In 1875 Congress extended the benefits of the Homestead Act of 1862 to those adult Indians who had or were willing to abandon their "tribal relations" and take up life as a homesteader on the public domain. These individuals were entitled to their per-capita share of tribal funds, lands, and other property, although their 160-acre homestead was to be held in trust by the government, not subject to sale or voluntary conveyance except by court decree for a six-year period.

As the Board of Indian Commissioners, a quasipolitical body that helped set federal Indian policy, declared in its seventh annual report, in 1876: "This legislation was a step in the right direction, since it aims to recognize the Indian's property rights as an individual man, instead of his tribal rights as simply a ward of the Government."[33] Nothing in this law, however, suggested that Indian homesteaders were to become American citizens. A similar measure was enacted in 1884, also known as the Indian Homestead Act. The next major Indian land law, the General Allotment Act, did finally address the issue of citizenship.

Congress enacted the General Allotment Act in 1887. In this act, Indians who received land allotments and those who voluntarily took up residence apart from their tribes were to be granted citizenship. But although the law seemed clear on this subject, it was complicated somewhat because the allotments of land were held in trust by the federal government for twenty-five years on the Indians' behalf. Some courts maintained that Indians gained American citizenship at the end of the twenty-five-year trust period; others held that citizenship was gained as soon as an allotment was received. Trust or not, for many in Congress there was a sense that "allotment of land in severalty, and citizenship [were] the indispensable conditions of Indian progress."[34] Nonallotted Indians remained citizens of their respective tribal nations.

Second, in 1890, Congress enacted the Indian Territory Naturalization Act, which provided that any member of the tribes in Indian Territory (present-day Oklahoma and Kansas) were entitled to American citizenship upon application to a federal court.[35] Unlike the Allotment Act's provisions, however, Indian applicants did not lose their tribal citizenship or the right to share in tribal assets. This law, "perhaps more than any other piece of legislation passed by Congress, seemed to imply that Indians held dual citizenship or could do so by performing the naturalization ritual in a federal court."[36]

In 1905 the question of the citizenship status of Indian allottees was firmly before the Supreme Court. In *Matter of Heff,* the Court held that upon receiving an allotment, an Indian immediately became an American citizen, and therefore federal laws prohibiting liquor sales to Indians were declared unconstitutional. Although the Court's ruling in Heff appeared to fit the thrust of what federal policymakers had been pushing for some time, namely, the unbridled assimilation of Indians, the outcry from a number of congressmen, the BIA, and Christian reform groups was immediate and vehement. These groups and individuals feared that Indians would be overrun by liquor-hawking whites, intent on defrauding the Indians of their remaining lands and funds.

Congress reacted in paternalistic fashion by enacting the Burke Act in 1906, which withheld federal citizenship from allotted Indians until the end of the twenty-five-year trust period or until the allottees had received a fee patent to their lands from the secretary of the interior. The government was concerned that if the Indian allottees were completely free of federal guardianship they would be subsumed by the "usual cycle of dissipation, drunkenness, disease, disaster, and death."[37]

Finally, in 1916, in *United States v. Nice,*[38] the Supreme Court expressly overturned the Heff ruling and enshrined in law the ambivalent status that Indians still have: they are citizens of their own nation and subject-citizens of the United States. Justice Van Devanter, problematically mixing the status of tribes as sovereigns with the status of individual Indians, held that "citizenship is not incompatible with tribal existence or continued guardianship, and so may be conferred without completely emancipating the Indians or placing them beyond the reach of congressional regulations adapted for their protection."[39]

Nice was decided three years before American Indian World War I veterans were given the opportunity of becoming citizens[40] and eight years before Congress enacted the general Indian citizenship law that enacted a mandatory extension of federal citizenship to all Indians who were not yet enfranchised.[41] The 1924 General Citizenship Act unilaterally declared all other noncitizen Indians as federal citizens, but the act retained a section that confirmed that such citizenship would not diminish the Indians' right to tribal or other property.

Equally important, a number of indigenous nations, including the Iroquois nations and members of the Five Civilized Tribes (Cherokee, Choctaw, Chickasaw, Seminole, and Creek—so named because of the remarkable social, educational, economic, and political progress made by the tribes before and after their forced removal from the Southeast to lands west of the Mississippi during the Indian removal era), refused to accept federal citizenship, arguing that their preexisting tribal nation status was sufficient for them. And since they had not requested American citizenship, they questioned how the United States could unilaterally extend its citizenship to their people, who constituted separate governmental bodies previously recognized in treaties. Evidence of this is seen in actions by a number of tribal nations who continue to seek recognition before the United Nations as distinctive peoples.[42] Some of these indigenous groups— Hopi and Iroquois—travel abroad on passports issued by their own governments.

This is one of the unique realities, that tribal members are citizens of three polities— their nation, the United States, and the state—that make the study of indigenous peoples such a dynamic pursuit. For if a native person's tribal citizenship is an active one and he or she resides on or near Indian Country, he or she has rights as an Indian that may be adversely affected by federal plenary power. At the same time, such Indians enjoy certain protections, services, and benefits because of their treaty or trust relationship with the federal government that are unavailable to other individuals or racial or ethnic groups in the nation.

The Politics of Ambivalence: Native Quandaries

There is nothing in the whole compass of our laws so anomalous, so hard to bring within any precise definition, or any logical and scientific arrangement of principles, as the relation in which the Indians stand toward this [the U.S.] government and those of the states.[43]

> In the opinion of your committee, the Constitution and the treaties, acts of Congress, and judicial decisions above referred to, all speak the same language upon this subject, and all point to the conclusion that the Indians, in tribal condition, have never been subject to the jurisdiction of the United States in the sense in which the term jurisdiction is employed in the fourteenth amendment to the Constitution. . . . Whenever we have dealt with them, it has been in their collective capacity as a state, and not with their individual members, except when such members were separated from the tribe to which they belonged; and then we have asserted such jurisdiction as every nation exercises over the subjects of another independent sovereign nation entering its territory and violating its laws.[44]

As these two quotes poignantly show, federal officials have struggled in their efforts to arrive at a consistent understanding of what the status of tribes is vis-à-vis the United States and what to do about Indian nations. Tribal nations and their individual members, as a result, have often suffered because of conflicting federal policies, which have vacillated between respecting the internal sovereignty of tribes and seeking to destroy tribal sovereignty in order to assimilate individual Indians into the American body politic. As such, the subject matter we are addressing encompasses at least four complicated quandaries about which we hope to provide some clarity.

First, tribal nations, as governments, face the conflicting tasks of "providing social services for people whose educational, health, and economic level is far below that of the general population in the United States, and running profitable and competitive businesses."[45] Gaming revenue, of course, has significantly improved the socioeconomic status of a number of tribes, as is discussed in chapter 6. In their efforts to balance these two very different forces, native nations encounter complications from within and without that states and the federal government do not confront. The difficulties that have arisen for some tribes who have been successful in the gaming market that came in the wake of the Indian Gaming Regulatory Act of 1988 entail intratribal, intertribal, intergovernmental, and tribal-corporate conflicts that are examples of what can transpire when a government is also the chief employer.

Second, native nations have a real desire to exercise political, economic, and cultural self-determination—to maintain a degree of exclusion from the American polity—but the federal government defines its trust responsibility in a paternalistic manner not only to protect but also to make decisions for tribes that fundamentally conflict with any genuine definition of tribal self-determination. This second quandary is complicated by the fact that most tribes insist that one of the primary obligations of the federal government under the trust doctrine is to protect and strengthen tribal sovereignty and the assorted rights and powers that accompany that doctrine.

Third, indigenous peoples are citizens of their own tribal nations, which are recognized as extraconstitutional governments. In other words, the federal Constitution does not apply to Indian tribes.[46] But by the middle of the twentieth century individual Indians had gradually been given the status of citizens of the United States, and of the states they resided in. Notwithstanding this treble citizenship, as described earlier, indigenous peoples have learned time and again that the U.S. Constitution provides only partial protection of their basic tribal and American citizenship rights. For example, the First Amendment has been interpreted by the Supreme Court as not protecting the religious freedom rights of tribal citizens.[47] The Fifth and the Fourteenth Amendments' due process and equal protection clauses are not extended to tribal citizens who continue to reside within a reservation's boundaries.[48] This is so, in part, because the Supreme Court determined in a major case in 1916, *United States v. Nice,* that U.S. "citizenship is not incompatible with tribal existence or continued guardianship, and so may be conferred without completely emancipating the Indians or placing them beyond the reach of congressional regulations adopted for their protection." In other words, Indians are indeed American citizens, but this status does not restrict the plenary (virtually absolute) powers of Congress with respect to Indians.

Fourth, indigenous tribal governments are nations inhabiting territorial units—reservations, pueblos, or dependent communities—in which the U.S. Constitution is largely inapplicable. The political status of tribes, because of their preexisting sovereignty and treaty-making power, has been held to be "higher than that of states."

However, over the last century, and due to the passage of a number of laws like the General Allotment Act of 1887, a large number of non-Indians moved within the boundaries of Indian reservations. What is the relationship between these non-Indians and the tribal governments whose lands they inhabit? What powers may tribal governments exercise over non-Indians who are not politically represented in tribal politics? How is the jurisdictional minuet between the tribal governments; the federal government; and the state, county, and local government to be administered since, constitutionally speaking, states and their political subdivisions have little or no jurisdiction in Indian Country because of Congress's exclusive authority under the commerce and treaty clauses?

These internal and intergovernmental quandaries are complicated by the indeterminate manner in which the federal government has dealt with indigenous nations, sometimes respecting, sometimes disrespecting their sovereignty. A brief, though not exhaustive, discussion of several of these federal indeterminacies, each rooted in legal precedent and political principles, makes clear why tribal nations enjoy little stability in their internal or external affairs.

First, tribes are sometimes treated as "distinct, independent communities" capable of exercising a significant measure of sovereign power, as when negotiating treaties or administering justice,[49] but they are also described as domestic dependent nations limited to exercising a reduced degree of internal sovereignty subject to federal dominance.[50] Second, tribal sovereignty has been defined as an inherent and reserved power,[51] but tribes have also been informed that they may exercise only those governmental powers that have been specifically delegated to them by express congressional action.[52]

Third, the tribal-federal relationship has sometimes been described as that of a "trustee" (federal government) to a "beneficiary" (indigenous group),[53] but on the other hand, the same relationship has been characterized as that of a guardian to a ward.[54] These are very different legal relationships. A "trusteeship" is a relationship that limits the property rights of the trustee, who is the beneficiary's servant; a guardianship relationship is one that limits the personal rights of the ward.

Fourth, a number of court cases have held that general acts of Congress are inapplicable to native nations unless they are specifically mentioned in the legislation, because of the extraconstitutional status of the tribes;[55] however, other cases have insisted that tribes are normally subject to congressional laws unless they are specifically exempted from the legislation, which would indicate that tribes are viewed as constitutional entities.[56]

Fifth, the federal government has sometimes acknowledged that its political power in relation to native nations is limited and must be based on specifically enumerated constitutional clauses (e.g., commerce, property);[57] on the other hand, federal law elsewhere asserts that the federal government has virtually unlimited political power over tribes and their property, and that this power is merely implied by constitutional clauses.[58]

Finally, there is much evidence that state laws have no force within Indian Country because of tribal sovereignty and federal supremacy under the commerce clause, unless the contrary is shown by an express act of Congress or some special circumstance;[59] but there is contrary evidence that state laws increasingly are valid in Indian territory unless they are expressly or implicitly prohibited by Congress.[60] There are other key inconsistencies in the way the federal government perceives its relationship to tribes that hinder stability in political affairs.[61]

These examples, with their radically different orientations, vividly point out that a tremendous ambivalence on the part of the federal government remains as to the actual political standing of tribal nations vis-à-vis their own peoples, the states, and the federal government. So long as this ambivalence persists, there can be no permanent resolution to many of the problems indigenous nations confront internally and externally.

A major reason for this ambivalence is that the status of native nations and individual Indians has three very different sources in law, policy, and popular attitudes.[62] One source is the cultural distinctiveness of native peoples. It was this cultural sovereignty that the federal government for the better part of its history sought to obliterate in its powerful push toward ethnocide—through Christian missionaries, boarding-school education, individualization of Indian lands, and so on. Now, the federal government sporadically seeks to protect cultural distinctiveness through bilingual education programs, protection of sacred sites, and allowances for Indians to practice traditional religions, but still finds ways to allow commodification and commercialization of American Indian culture—for example, the perpetuation of degrading sports mascots and Indian caricatures like the Atlanta Braves and their "tomahawk chop"; the Cleveland Indians' disfigured logo of an Indian; the derogatory football team name Washington "Redskins"; and countless products that exploit stereotypical images of Indians, including the Indian maiden on Land-O'-Lakes butter and margarine, the "rugged" Jeep Cherokee, and the noble savage images perpetuated in movies like *Dances with Wolves* and *Last of the Mohicans*.

A second source of Indian status is the property rights of tribes and individual Indians as landowners and possessors of other important rights, like hunting and fishing rights identified in treaties. Of course, the subject of the transfer of Indian land title to the federal government through treaties and other agreements is the single most important fact animating Indian-white relations. Native nations went from being the landlords of the entire continent to owning less than 4 percent of their original lands by the 1930s. Laws like the 1887 General Allotment Act and its amendments, and the allotting agreement that ensued, exacerbated the land loss and contributed to the state of poverty most native peoples found themselves in during the harshest days of Indian land dispossession.

As Vine Deloria notes, "Indian poverty was deliberately planned and [was] as predictable as the seasons," because of the allotment process and the way it was administered by the BIA.[63]

Hunting and fishing rights, water rights, and Indian tax exemptions from state law are the other major property rights of Indians reserved in treaties and federal laws. The manner in which these rights are exercised by the tribes, challenged by the local, state, or federal entities, or jointly administered by the tribal government, the states, and the federal government has important implications for Indian status.

A number of federal programs and agencies have historically been justified because a majority of Indians still suffered grinding poverty, high unemployment, and a host of other adverse socioeconomic circumstances compared with the U.S. population as a whole. Indians continue to suffer these conditions because of the manner in which their property rights, because of Indians' lack of a constitutionally recognized status, have been occasionally protected (when the right has been individually established, like an individual allotment of land) and more often exploited, when the rights are held in common by the native nation.

Some tribes have set up profitable gaming operations, other businesses, and resource-based enterprises in the form of cattle ranches, oil and gas operations, participation in timber industry, coal mines, recreational resorts, and electronic assembly plants.[64] Tribal economic development is discussed in chapter 6. But these tribal business successes remain greatly outnumbered by tribes whose governments and members struggle with intense poverty, largely artificial economies, and a virtual colonial relationship with the federal government.[65]

The third source, the rights of native nations as distinct political entities exercising inherent sovereignty, affirmed in international law, treaty law, the U.S. Constitution, and a wealth of congressional measures, Supreme Court cases, and presidential policy pronouncements, is the one source that is "constitutionally necessary to enable the society to make a legal distinction between Indian tribes and other cultural groups or other groups of poor people."[66] It is this political status of native nations and their treaty- and trust-based relationship to the United States that is the "foundation for the entire structure of policies, programs, and laws. Yet it is the one source of Indian status that, as a practical matter, probably cannot stand alone."[67]

Conclusion

These three sources—cultural distinctiveness, property rights, and political sovereignty—are braided together in the public and federal and state governments' perceptions of Indians. The inability or unwillingness of the public and the governments to distinguish between the three perpetuates the legal and political confusion of tribal status described earlier. In other words, tribal cultural distinctiveness and property ownership generally find some support in "the simultaneous humanitarian impulse and sense of cultural superiority that are the peculiar heritage of Anglo-American society."[68]

But as tribes have learned, their legal and political status as sovereigns will be and has been terminated or seriously diminished when they have been perceived to have "lost" their cultural uniqueness in the eyes of Euro-America, or, as is happening now, when tribes are deemed to be too well-off financially—the false perception that all Indians are wealthy because of gaming revenues—and are therefore perceived to no longer need federal protection or support. Phillip S. Deloria (Standing Rock Sioux) sums up the status dilemmas by noting that:

Indian governments are thus subjected to a different status than other governments. There are not constant reviews of the demographic status of all the little countries in Europe that are frequently compared in size and population with Indian tribes. No one asks whether Monaco and Liechtenstein are sufficiently culturally distinct from neighboring countries to justify their continued existence. Unlike that of Indian tribes, their political status is taken for granted.[69]

Clearly, this is complicated academic terrain. But by unbraiding and closely examining the four quandaries discussed, as well as the issue of treble citizenship for indigenous peoples, the national or sovereign status of indigenous polities, and the federal government's inconsistent understanding of its relationship to tribes, we hope to bring needed clarity to the status and internal and external powers of native nations as the First Nations in the Americas, nations who have entered into distinctive economic and political relations with other tribes, interest groups, the states, and the federal government.

CHAPTER 3

Indigenous Governments
Past, Present, and Future

> The aborigines of America are a very peculiar and strange people with very
> peculiar customs and ways very different from ours in Europe. Why, the people
> actually elect their own leaders and if the leaders do not abide by the will of the
> people, they are removed from office. This is a serious and dangerous thing.
> It is contagious. Our American colonies are now demanding a voice in their
> government.
>
> —A visiting Englishman, 1765[1]

PREVIOUSLY, WE HAVE emphasized that the core relationship between
native nations and the United States can best be characterized as nation to
nation. As one group of authors put it, "most important, any discussion of
American government must be based on the fact that native peoples inhabited this
hemisphere before the European invasion. Originally, North Americans dealt with
indigenous peoples as sovereign nations by signing formal treaties with them."[2]

These two important facts—the preexistence of First Nations and the succeeding
political recognition of tribal sovereignty in the form of hundreds of treaties, agreements, and compacts—necessitate that we take some time to describe the form and
essence of indigenous governments in three broad categories: (1) original, (2) transitional constitutional, and (3) contemporary constitutional.[3] Regardless of which of the
three types of indigenous governments we are describing, it is important to note that
the leadership of every tribal nation across time has sought to provide for the community's defense and safety, has allocated resources according to tradition and custom,
has overseen domestic and foreign relations, and has, in general, provided for the basic
needs and desires of their people.

First, a caveat. On one hand, many indigenous governments metamorphosed from
original to transitional to contemporary institutional structures. On the other hand,
there are other indigenous governments that still exhibit original or traditional structures of governance that link directly to ancient times, though there has, of course, been

some adaptation along the way. One study accurately concluded that "each tribe has retained, in varying degrees, traditional, cultural, and religious societal practices which influence the manner and form in which the tribal government is operated."[4] Moreover, a number of contemporary constitutional governments are opting to revitalize traditional governing components, while others appear to be taking on the form and functions of state and federal governments.

After describing these three categories of indigenous governments and the periods they are associated with, we briefly describe the separate though related status of Alaska Native governments. We conclude the chapter with some comments on the current status of tribes and the major issues they confront as they begin the new millennium.

Original Indigenous Governments

Indigenous origin accounts, as one might expect, vary widely, though a majority of them generally assert that their origins were on the North American continent or some other place besides Asia. For example, the Navajo origin account states that they arrived from within the earth. The Hopi and Colville describe transoceanic migrations in boats. Some nations even describe migrations from other worlds.[5] Rarely do indigenous origin accounts coincide with the theories proffered by Europeans or Euro-Americans that attempt to account for human presence in the Americas.

Historically, there have been exotic propositions that Indians were actually ancient Egyptians, or from the lost island of Atlantis, or were descendants from a lost tribe of Israel. But the theory that has come to be most accepted by Western scientists, though not by the majority of natives, is that indigenous peoples are the descendants of small bands of nomadic hunters who pursued game across a land bridge between Asia and Alaska during the last Ice Ages, from twelve thousand to one hundred thousand years ago.[6] Although this is the most widely accepted theory, the evidence for the land bridge, as Vine Deloria Jr. has shown in *Red Earth, White Lies,* is not very impressive and is, in fact, packed with major gaps and ambiguities.[7]

Regardless of the position one adopts on the Bering Strait, as Columbus's arrival loomed, indigenous societies were as varied as those found in Europe. An estimated five to ten million indigenous people, representing some six hundred independent nations, bands, and groups, inhabited every part of North America. Their societies ranged from simple bands to complicated confederated governments, and they had economies reflecting local conditions—from subsistence hunting, fishing, and gathering, to intensive horticulture and trading. Another gauge of the human diversity present is provided by language. In contrast to Europe, where most languages can be traced to a single Indo-European source, in North America there were perhaps "twelve quite distinct and apparently unrelated linguistic groups, in some cases more dissimilar than English and Chinese."[8]

Europeans were generally conflicted about the indigenous peoples they encountered and very quickly categorized Indians in terms of three essentially conflicting European traditions: the missionary, the Machiavellian, and the classical. "As a benighted heathen the Indian was to be saved; as a religious and racial inferior he was to be used or destroyed without compunction to suit the purposes of the civilized Christian; as a sweet-natured child, living in a Golden Age of primal innocence, he was to be envied and admired."[9]

While Spain, Holland, Great Britain, and France, the major European players during most of this period, each developed their own very distinctive and often ambivalent policies toward indigenous peoples, one common political reality emerged—many of the Indian nations the European states encountered were powerful economically and militarily and had to be dealt with accordingly. As a result of their formidable status, the treaty emerged as an important device with which to deal with tribes. Formal agreements between the European powers and tribal nations dealt with the subjects of peace, trade, territorial boundaries, and free passage, and "international norms compelled the Europeans to approach the indigenous political communities as international equals."[10]

And during much of the colonial period, even extending into the early U.S. period, the diplomacy that emerged frequently followed indigenous forms. "The protocols and ceremonies of this indigenous native North American language of diplomacy were rarely European because it was a language grounded in indigenous North American visions of law and peace between different peoples. The hierarchical, feudal symbols of seventeenth and eighteenth century European diplomacy simply did not translate well on the North American colonial frontier."[11] In other words, it was Indian traditions, symbols, values, and norms, and not Spanish, English, or French traditions, that formed the core and essential political-diplomatic parameters in many of the hundreds of treaty negotiations that occurred between tribal nations and European and early Euro-American states.

Countless books and monographs have been written by historians and anthropologists describing aboriginal nations. The focus in this chapter is more narrow. We briefly examine some of the governing systems that existed among these nations, since it would be an impossible task to chronicle the political systems of every indigenous community during this pre-European contact period.

As Deloria and Lytle point out, "it is difficult to generalize about traditional forms of tribal government because there was such a great variety of Indian social groupings."[12] Nevertheless, it is possible and it is certainly helpful to group certain tribal nations together because they share certain institutional structures or economic modes of living. An extensive quote encapsulates some of these tribal groupings:

> Many tribes were loose confederations of hunting groups who spoke the same language and ranged over a broad expanse of territory. Such groups as the Shoshone and the Paiutes, for example, were spread thinly in small groups over what is now the Great Basin area of the western United States. The Sioux, as the French called them, or the Dakota, as the Indians called themselves, once ranged from the area near Wisconsin Dells, Wisconsin, to the Big Horn Mountains of Wyoming, a distance of nearly 1,300 miles in width. By contrast, small fishing villages in the Pacific Northwest were scattered independently along the many rivers of that region and had commercial and trading contacts but little political organization above the village or longhouse level. Some tribes, such as the Creek, were occasionally aggressive and incorporated smaller groups into themselves as a result of marriages or wars and eventually had to evolve a national organization to maintain themselves within their expanding territorial domain. There were, of course, theocracies, such as the Pueblos of New Mexico and the Hopi of Arizona, who traced their form of government back to ancient times and organized their political and social life around a religious ceremonial year following basically religious rather than secular laws.[13]

■ The Iroquois Confederacy: A Case Study

As wide in scope as this quote is, it still does not encompass what was surely the most sophisticated and one of the most powerful indigenous governments—the Haudeno-saunee (Iroquois League)—which formed sometime between AD 1000 and 1500 in present-day upstate New York and part of Canada, from an alliance of five nations: the Mohawk, Oneida, Onondaga, Cayuga, and Seneca (later six, when the Tuscarora Nation joined).[14] The Iroquois are important for a number of reasons, most notably that they developed what Felix S. Cohen, a noted commentator on Indian law and government, called "the first Federal Constitution on the American Continent," the Gayaneshagowa, or Great Binding Law.*

The Iroquois Constitution, embodied in the symbolized writing of wampum belts made from sea shells, established the democratic ideals and principles of initiative, recall, referendum, equal suffrage, checks and balances, and specific delegations of war and peace responsibilities.[15] Furthermore, one also finds in this constitution the ideal of the responsibility of government officials to the electorate, and the "obligation of the present generation to future generations which we call the principle of conservation."[16]

The central governing unit of the confederacy was the Council, which had fifty seats filled by chiefs. The Council was presided over by an Onondaga, the Atotarho. It was organized into three bodies: the Mohawk (nine seats) and Seneca (eight seats) were identified as the Older Brothers; the Oneida (nine seats) and Cayuga (ten seats) were designated the Younger Brothers. The Onondaga, the Council's moderators, were the Keepers of the Fire (fourteen seats). The Council of fifty was convened at least once a year by the Onondaga to discuss issues of importance for the collective membership of the nations.[17] However, the internal sovereignty of each nation was respected.

Historically, the debate of the policies of the Confederacy began with the Mohawk. After being debated by the Mohawk and the Seneca, a question was then addressed by the Oneida and Cayuga leaders. Once consensus was attained among the Oneida and Cayuga, the issue was then sent back to the Seneca and Mohawk. If the Older and Younger Brothers disagreed on the issue, the Onondaga would seek a compromise and generate new discussion. The Onondaga would, upon their complete review, return the issue to the Older and Younger Brothers for additional discussion. If there was no disagreement between the two brotherhoods, the Onondaga "had a power simi-lar to judicial review in that they could raise objections to the proposed measure if it was believed inconsistent with the Great Law of Peace. Essentially, the legislature could rewrite the proposed law on the spot so that it would be in accord with the Constitu-tion of the Iroquois."[18]

The strength of this democratic process was that the Onondaga, after having heard the subject analyzed from multiple perspectives, were able to discern the general sense of the discussion and give their final consent to a decision that by the end of delib-erations reflected the collective voice of the assembled leaders.[19] This sophisticated yet clearly demarcated process reflects the strong emphasis the Iroquois placed on checks and balances, public debate, and consensus, the idea being to foster unity.

This process is similar to and established an important model for "the mechanisms of the Albany Plan of Union, the Articles of Confederation, and the U.S. Constitu-tion."[20] Evidence of this influence on American democratic thought is found in a state-ment made by Benjamin Franklin to the colonists in 1751. There he was urging the colonials toward some type of political union, a proposal that culminated in the Albany Plan of 1754:

> It would be a strange thing . . . if Six Nations of Ignorant savages should be capable of forming such a union and be able to execute it in such a manner that it has subsisted for ages and appears indissoluble, and yet that a like union should be impractical for ten or a dozen English colonies, to whom it is more necessary and must be more advantageous, and who cannot be supposed to want an equal understanding of their interest.[21]

In fact, there is a substantial body of evidence—both inferential and direct[22]—that supports the thesis that American democracy as it emerged in the late eighteenth century is a synthesis of indigenous and European political theories. As Vine Deloria Jr. put it: "Where else were ideas of distributing national sovereignty [between nation and state] articulated and practiced when the constitutional fathers were debating the organic documents of state? They certainly could not have looked to Europe for guidance, and there was no nation on earth at that time except the Six Nations that had grappled with this problem."[23]

It is important to note that the Gayaneshagowa is still a vital philosophical and structural force and remains the binding law for many traditional members of the Haudenosaunee confederacy, although it now competes with other forms of government that were introduced after the arrival of Europeans.

* Felix S. Cohen, Handbook of Federal Indian Law (Albuquerque, NM: University of New Mexico Press, reprint ed. 1972): 128.

Historic Values and Traits

We can discern a number of particular aboriginal values and structural traits that appear to have undergirded many of these systems of governance. First, the idea of the kinship group or household often formed the basic social building block for larger social, economic, and political structures. Indigenous societies were bound together in a complex interweaving of social relationships based on a variety of ties such as language, clan, ceremonial practices, and land boundaries.

Second, and interwoven with the first trait, was the idea that individual or personal autonomy was essential and to be protected and respected.[24] But unlike the rugged individualism of Euro-America, in virtually all tribal societies "the space and security provided by the sense of community allowed the concept of the individual . . . to flourish."[25]

Third, there was an emotional-spiritual-physical connection to one's homeland. The indigenous people, animals, plants, and virtually every other part of the landscape played integral roles in the balance of creation, of which humans were but a part. Technologically, indigenous peoples in North America required less sophisticated systems of agriculture and metallurgy—though some groups were quite advanced in both—because their mental, intellectual, creative, cognitive, and spiritual capacities were so great.[26]

As a result, most indigenous peoples' bonds with their environment are deeply personal. As one commentator stated: "People, animals and plants could change the form in which they appeared, a transformation recorded in myths and stories and represented today by the use of animal masks in dances and rituals. In many indigenous cultures, human beings were simply mediators of complex relationships between plants, animals and themselves, touching and consuming the spirits of those they hunted and cultivated."[27]

Fourth, traditional aboriginal cultures rarely separated the political world from the spiritual world. Political actions generally were carried out with "spiritual guidance and oriented toward spiritual as well as political fulfillment."[28] Fifth, sovereignty, the intangible bond that binds a people together with their environment, was vested in the community—the People—and not in the leaders. Native leaders were the servants of the people and an individual was not placed in a leadership position unless that person had "demonstrated over and over again that he or she has the spiritual and physical well-being of the rest of the tribe at heart."[29]

Sixth, Indian males tended to hold most of the elected or appointed political leadership positions. Historically, Indian women held significant influence in the family network, which is the center of aboriginal social life and political organization, and thus few were elected or chosen to serve formally as political leaders. This fact, of course, varied across tribes. Women were sometimes warriors or hunters, and the idea of gender itself is a subject with significant cultural variation among indigenous peoples.[30] Among some indigenous nations, like the Cherokee, the women of each of the seven clans elected their own leaders, who convened as a Women's Council. The chiefs, however, were men, although their decisions were sometimes overridden by the women if they believed it was in the best interest of the people.[31] In recent years, Indian women have made great strides in the number of elected leadership positions they hold in their nations.[32] A 2001 survey indicates that 36 percent of all tribal council members of federally recognized tribes are women, a much higher figure than that for any other level of government in the United States.[33] Wilma Mankiller became the first female chief of the Cherokee Nation of Oklahoma in 1985, when Ross Swimmer, her predecessor, was selected to become the assistant secretary of Indian affairs. Mankiller was reelected twice, in 1987 and 1991. In the 1991 election she received over 80 percent of the vote.

Seventh, the primary thrust of aboriginal government was more judicial than legislative. Adjudicating and mediating figured more prominently in coping with the unpredictability of human interactions, particularly for resolution of conflict, than did prosecuting or legislating. This adjudicatory nature of original indigenous governments was in distinct contrast to the predominantly legislative approach that Europeans introduced into Indian Country.[34]

Transitional Constitutional Governments

Most commentators writing about Indian affairs, if they discuss indigenous governments at all, tend to skip from a description of traditional governing structures to the Indian Reorganization Act governments of the 1930s, what we are calling the *contemporary constitutional governments.* They assume that the intervening years were so cataclysmic for tribes that little was left in the way of traditional tribal government structures or Indian self-determination. A typical passage of such oversimplified commentary is the following:

> The dwindling number of traditional Native governments which survived into the 1800s were almost totally disrupted by the end of the century. The principal causes were (1) contact with European culture, (2) removal and placement of tribes

within confining reservations, and (3) establishment of the powerful Indian agent system by the federal government. Only a few groups, most notably the Pueblos, escaped this political fate and have been able to continue their traditional governments largely intact to the present.[35]

While there are several bits of truth in this statement—there was tremendous disruption of tribes, forced removal, and the beginnings of an intense and comprehensive system of internal colonialism—it is not completely accurate to posit that the Pueblos "escaped this fate," since they were surely disrupted and suffered under dominant Indian agents and land-squatting Euro-Americans. More distressing is that this passage does a disservice to the many other tribal nations who, while certainly affected in fundamental ways by Euro-American interaction, continued to exercise a strong measure of self-determination. Of course, there is little doubt that they felt compelled to modify, in various degrees, the formal structures of their traditional institutions because of the increasing complexity of diplomatic and intergovernmental relationships that followed from their close encounters with Euro-Americans. But indigenous identities and their governing structures have proven to be "complex, resilient, and adaptable; despite substantial changes in the outward manifestations of culture, much survived, including distinctive self-concepts and world views."[36]

We may describe these types of synthesizing or adaptive tribal governments as *transitional constitutional,* since the tribal nations were clearly in a transitional mode and many of them, though not all, developed written constitutions as one response to changing circumstances. Importantly, these nations' governing systems changed in part as the result of forced colonial influence, but also as a deliberate result of efforts of the tribes' members to modify the method of government organization to reflect the community's evolution.[37]

Take, for example, the Pueblo peoples of the American Southwest. When the Spanish explorers and conquistadors arrived in what is now New Mexico, a majority of the indigenous peoples they met lived a sedentary existence in permanent settlements that consisted of compact, flat-roofed homes built around plazas or squares. The Spanish were reminded of their own homeland and called these settlements "pueblos," and the "village dwellers" were called "Pueblo Indians," in contrast to the nomadic or semi-nomadic peoples (i.e., Apaches, Navajos, and Utes) the Spaniards had encountered or would encounter in the region.[38] The various Pueblo communities, of course, retained their own names for themselves. The Santa Ana Pueblo members call themselves Tamayame; the Jemez Indians refer to themselves as He-mish.

At the point of first contact, there were between seventy and one hundred pueblos. But depopulation as a result of diseases and Spanish attempts to dominate had soon reduced the number to about twenty. Zuni, Acoma, and Laguna were located east of the Rio Grande and along the Pecos River. The remaining pueblos, Taos, Picuris, San Juan, San Ildefonso, Nambe, Pojoaque, Tesuque, Cochiti, Santa Clara, Santo Domingo, San Felipe, Zia, Santa Ana, Jemez, Sandia, and Isleta, were nestled along the upper reaches of the Rio Grande in central and northern New Mexico. The Hopi, who live in Arizona, are also considered to be part of the Pueblo family. Each pueblo was independent, with its own social organization, governing body, and distinctive language.

The Pueblos and other aboriginal peoples in the Southwest have been impacted, and have faced varying degrees of incorporation, by four state societies: (1) Meso-American state societies (prehistoric cultures inhabiting the region from Mexico to El

Salvador), which had the least influence; (2) Spain, which operated from the sixteenth to the nineteenth century; (3) Mexico, which had a brief period of rule in 1821–1846; and (4) the United States, which has been the dominant power since 1846.[39]

Some evidence suggests that the effects of states and their policies, people, and cultures on sedentary groups like the Pueblos have been different from their effects on nomadic groups like the Navajo. This is because Pueblos had centralized political structures, because they engaged in a significant trade relationship with the incorporating powers, and because their sociopolitical organization was that of a chiefdom, while groups like the Navajo have a scattered band structure and no central authorities.[40]

One of the most important adaptations in Pueblo political life that arose because of state intrusion, specifically Spanish influence, dates back to 1620. In that year, the king of Spain decreed that each pueblo (except at Hopi) would have a government modeled after Spanish custom. The imposed government, what Fisher called the "Spanish set" of governing officials, since traditional Pueblo officers remained in place, typically consisted of a governor *(adelantado)*, lieutenant governor, and other subordinate officers. For instance, at Santo Domingo, there was a governor (known as *dapop*), a lieutenant governor (called *dapop teniente*), and six helpers known as *capitani*. The capitani were messengers and errand runners for the governor and had a law enforcement role as well; they were to maintain the sanctity of discrete ceremonies and meetings.[41]

The Spanish set of Pueblo governors received metal-tipped canes from the Spanish, inscribed with the Spanish cross. These became the symbols of authority for these secular officers. Mexican officials, and President Abraham Lincoln in 1863, continued the tradition of bestowing canes to Pueblo governors, extending their authority and commission.

This set of officers, historically and today, plays an important role in Pueblo life. Rather than supplanting the preexisting traditional Pueblo religious-political institutions (e.g., various moieties, kiva groups, societies, orders, fraternities, and clans), they actually formed an effective screen—a parallel political world—concealing the existence of the extant Pueblo authorities, thus allowing Pueblo traditional ceremonial life to continue in relative obscurity from foreign eyes.

However, Spanish colonization of Pueblos, particularly because of Catholic priests and their efforts to eradicate traditional Pueblo ceremonies and beliefs, was very oppressive. Spain dominated the Pueblos from the early seventeenth century until the Pueblos revolted in 1680, driving the Spanish out of their territory. The Spanish eventually resettled among the Pueblos but did not regain the level of dominance they had exercised before the revolt.

Mexican independence in 1821 and the Americans' acquisition of the Southwest from Mexico under the 1848 Treaty of Guadalupe Hidalgo meant additional changes for the Pueblo peoples, but the "dual system of government, one religious and one secular, continues today to some degree in all the pueblos and reflects, to varying degrees, the acceptance of some distinction between the religious and secular worlds."[42]

Hence, while the Pueblos proved most adept at accepting and incorporating the Spanish secular offices into their communities, this transition has not been too disruptive of the ongoing Pueblo political-religious structures, which reach into the primordial past. As Reginald Fisher notes, "in a single generalization, it might be said that each individual pueblo has been [and still is] a miniature, theocratic, community-state."[43]

Photo 3.1
Shoshone Chief Washakie,
shown in this undated
photo, was considered one
of the greatest warriors,
military strategeists, and
orators in the American
West. He was also a complex
figure, criticized by some
for his willingness to coop-
erate with whites.
Source: AP/WIDE WORLD
PHOTOS

From the Pueblo example, along with the adoption of the Iroquois Constitution, to the IRA constitutions of the 1930s, there is "a fascinating history of political develop-ment that has never been pieced together."[44] Cohen made this statement nearly seventy years ago and called for a detailed analysis of tribal political development up to 1934, which is still needed. Let us say something more about these transitional constitutional governments than is usually laid out.

Prior to 1934, over sixty indigenous nations, including peoples as diverse as the Absentee Shawnee, the Cheyenne and Arapaho, the Hopi, the Kickapoo, and the Red Lake Ojibwe, operated under constitutions or constitution-type documents that were on file with the Department of the Interior.[45] By far the most sophisticated of these transitional constitutional governments were the governments of the so-called Five Civilized Tribes—the Cherokee, Choctaw, Chickasaw, Creek, and Seminole.[46] A number of texts have been written about these remarkable nations,[47] but for our purposes it is sufficient to provide a brief case study of one of them, the Cherokee. We will describe their precontact societal structure and then highlight some of the impressive adaptations they made in order to better cope with drastic changes resulting from sustained contact with Euro-Americans.

■ The Cherokee: A Case Study

At the moment of European contact, the Cherokee controlled an estimated forty thousand square miles of land in the southeastern United States. By the eighteenth century, they lived in as many as sixty-four mountain towns and villages and spoke three different dialects. Each settlement was home to some 350 to 600 people. Because they lived scattered over such a diverse geographical territory, there was no need for a centralized government, although they were a distinct ethnic group in a specific territory recognized by other nations.[48] Thus, joined as they were by blood ties, the Cherokee "regulated their lives in accordance with common cultural traditions. The names and values of this culture stressed mutual defense, discouraged conflict within the extensive community, and bound the Cherokee together through a tradition of unwritten clan law."[49]

The Cherokee's sixty-four towns were grouped in several regions: the Lower Towns, in the valleys and foothills of western South Carolina; the Middle Towns, along the Tuckasegee River and at the headwaters of the Little Tennessee; the Valley Towns, west of the Middle communities and along the Hiwassee River; and the Overhill (Upper) Towns, below the Cumberland Mountains. Hence, despite their shared ethnic heritage, there was no overarching national government and the people were governed largely through clan law and town councils. Three factors militated against a central government in this period—factional conflicts, linguistic troubles, and historical tradition.[50]

As whites moved into Cherokee territory, so too did enormous change: diseases, trade goods, missionaries, competition among European states and later between the U.S. and state governments for political and economic friendship with the Cherokee, and liquor all played significant roles in transforming the Cherokee people and their institutions. A succession of treaties between 1721 and 1819 with various foreign powers and the United States led to a massive reduction of Cherokee aboriginal territory. Given the weight of all these economic, cultural, and political-legal forces, the Cherokee survived remarkably well, by responding proactively rather than succumbing to the transformation. As one scholar put it,

> Through the selective incorporation and adaptation of non-Christian ideas and institutions, the Cherokee fashioned a course that allowed them to sustain many of their traditions and beliefs. In stages, in the first three decades of the nineteenth century, the Cherokee reorganized their economy and political structure. Farming and animal husbandry replaced fur trading as the most important economic activities. A mixed-blood elite emerged that profited from owning slaves and developed commercial ventures such as mills, trading stores, taverns, ferry services, and turnpikes. Political authority was centralized under the direction of certain traditional leaders in combination with the newly powerful mixed-blood leadership. By 1827 the Cherokee had adopted a republican style of government with a bicameral legislature, a court system, and a legal code responsive to the growing market and contract economy.[51]

Despite all these modifications, the Cherokee—some seventeen thousand strong—like the majority of the other "civilized" tribes, were forced to leave their homelands under Indian removal and march to present-day Oklahoma on the infamous "Trail of

Tears" in 1838 and 1839. During this grueling eight-hundred-mile march, an estimated 8,100 Cherokee died from illness, starvation, freezing temperatures, and trauma.[52]

However, showing their resiliency yet again, the Cherokee, despite intense internal conflicts exacerbated by the removal, devised a new constitutional government with a bicameral legislature and judicial system based on the democratic ideals they had already developed. The leadership emphasized public education and soon had a complex of 144 elementary schools and two higher education institutions. Their literacy rate before the Civil War was higher than that of the white populace.[53]

The Civil War brought this era of relative prosperity to an abrupt end. Although the Cherokee sought to remain neutral, they were eventually pulled into the conflict and some segments of the nation actually signed a treaty with the Confederacy. As a result, once the war ended the federal government forced the Cherokee leadership, in the Treaty of 1866, to cede additional lands and to allow right of way through their territory to the railroads.[54] Again, the Cherokee regrouped and struggled to retain their political and territorial autonomy. But by the 1880s, federal policy once more shifted and Indians faced the most concerted attack on their remaining lands, under the general allotment policy inaugurated in 1887.

Although the Five Civilized Tribes were initially exempted from this act because they held their lands in fee-simple title, the increasing number of white squatters indicated that a new round of political, economic, and cultural trauma awaited the nation. Thus, in 1897 and 1898, in direct violation of their preexisting treaties, the Cherokee and the other tribes in the Indian Territory were forced to sign new agreements that allotted their lands. By 1906 their tribal governments had been stripped of all their inherent powers except the power to supervise the disposal of tribal property.[55] These largely emasculated tribal governments were continued by congressional resolution.[56] But Cherokee political officers were actually appointed not by the tribal membership, but by the president of the United States until 1970, when that power was finally returned to the tribe.

Although the Cherokee political structure was weakened some years before the 1930s, a number of tribes, including large nations like the Iroquois and nations in the West, retained a significant—if modified—degree of their traditional form of governance, even after years of direct and extended contact with whites. The federal government's allotment and assimilation program from the 1860s forward empowered Indian agents to use whatever means were deemed necessary to dismantle and individualize the communalistic nature, structures, and lands of indigenous groups.

Other Tribes in Transition

The experience of many western tribes, including the Navajo Nation, can best be characterized "as a government-sponsored transformation of traditional forms into a more workable version of an informal council, which could be called upon by the agent whenever it became impossible for him to work without some form of approval from the people concerned."[57] This council generally reflected the tribe's preexisting political subdivisions but it also incorporated the principles of American democracy—like formal elections of leaders—the Indian agents were intent on bestowing to the tribes.

For example, the superintendent of one of the agencies on the Navajo Reservation, John G. Hunter, is credited with the development of local governments on the reservation called *chapters,* which were mostly gatherings of Navajos to discuss local issues like irrigation, livestock improvement, and agriculture. Chapter governments consisted of an elected president, vice president, and secretary-treasurer. Meetings were required to follow Robert's Rules of Order.[58] However, as chapters spread quickly throughout the reservation, they fit "easily into the traditional socio-political organization patterns. Like the natural communities that lay at the core of the traditional social system, the chapters were local organizations, composed of, and directed by, people with common interests."[59]

In the northern plains, tribal governing bodies varied from a general council type, with an unwritten constitution to a "small business committee made legitimate by a written document."[60] For example, the Blackfeet of Montana, from 1875 to 1935, faced concerted pressure from their Indian agents to adopt a Western-style government. But even in this the Blackfeet found a way to continue their reliance on their natural leaders by electing those individuals most likely to best represent their interests to the government. "Until 1911, the general council elected an eighteen member administrative body. These were 'reliable' men with 'good judgment' who exerted beneficial influence upon the rest of the community by maintaining discipline."[61] The Blackfeet were also prodded into adopting a legal code and a tribal tribunal, composed of the agent and three Blackfeet. This Court of Indian Offenses was like many established in the 1860s throughout Indian Country and overtly designed by the United States to eradicate traditional religious practices, and so on, but nonetheless enabled a measure of traditional leadership to continue.

Hence, while no native nation was left unscathed by the forces of American expansion and colonialism, it is clear that many integrated or selectively adopted, and then often modified, the governmental suggestions and demands offered by their Indian agents. Nevertheless, the ravages of allotment, diseases, forced assimilation, and reservation confinement had wreaked havoc on all indigenous nations, and by the 1930s tribal complaints were joined by the complaints of white reform groups and others interested in Indian, nay, human rights.

Contemporary Constitutional Governments

This groundswell of support fueled a number of congressional investigations into the living conditions of Indians. These investigations, coupled with the labor of a number of prominent individuals and organizations challenging the direction of federal Indian policy and with the direction provided by BIA head John Collier, culminated in a number of pieces of legislation in the 1930s aimed at reconstructing tribal governments, rehabilitating tribal economic life, reconstituting tribal land bases, and protecting tribal resources and Indian civil, cultural, and educational rights.

Examples of key legislation include the Leavitt Act of July 1, 1932, which dealt with Indian irrigation projects[62]; the act of March 4, 1933, which involved Indian timber[63]; the Johnson-O'Malley Act of April 16, 1934, which authorized the secretary of the interior to enter into contracts with states or territories to improve Indian education, medical care, and social welfare[64]; the act of April 30, 1934, which dealt with Indian heirship lands[65]; and the act of May 21, 1934, which repealed twelve sections of the U.S. Code that had restricted Indian civil liberties.[66] As important as each of these measures was, the Indian Reorganization Act (IRA) of June 30, 1934,[67] was the most comprehensive

Photo 3.2
The Wheeler-Howard Bill Becomes Law on the Flathead Reservation, 1935
Source: AP/WIDE WORLD PHOTOS

measure of the decade and one of the most important federal laws ever enacted insofar as Indians are concerned.

The IRA: A Revival of the Tribal?

According to Senator Burton Wheeler, one of the cosponsors of the act, the IRA had many purposes, including stopping the allotment of reservations, providing for the acquisition of lands for landless Indians, permitting tribes to organize themselves into business corporations, establishing a system of financial credit, supplying Indians with collegiate education and technical training, providing for Indian preference in employment in the BIA, and stabilizing tribal governments by "vesting such tribal organizations with real, though limited, authority, and by prescribing conditions which must be met by such tribal organizations."[68]

Section 16 of the act, which established the basis for the adoption of tribal constitutions, is most crucial. That section reads, "Any Indian tribe or tribes, residing on the same reservation, shall have the right to organize for its common welfare, and may adopt an appropriate constitution and by-laws." The adopted constitution became effective upon a majority vote of the adult members of the tribe and upon approval by the secretary of the interior.

The IRA gave tribes one year to vote on whether to accept or reject the act's provisions. In June 1935, Congress gave tribes an additional year in which to vote. But tribes could only vote once and could not revisit their decision. Within the two-year period, 258 elections were held: 181 tribes (129,750 Indians) accepted the act's provisions, while 77 tribes (86,365 Indians, including the 45,000-member Navajo Nation) rejected the act.[69]

Three controversies arose around these elections. First, "the IRA was to be considered adopted unless a majority of the adult Indians voted against its application, the vote being structured so that the majority of Indians had to vote against its application, placing the burden of action on those Indian factions that opposed the law's application."[70] This voting slant was made more controversial when the solicitor general issued an opinion that stated that all eligible Indian voters who opted not to vote would be counted as being in favor of adopting the act. For seventeen tribes, this opinion reversed an otherwise negative vote. Thus, for example, on the Santa Ysabel Reservation in California, where forty-three Indians voted against the IRA and only nine voted for it, the tribe came under the act's provisions "because the sixty-two eligible tribal members who did not vote were counted as being in favor of adoption."[71]

Second, the act allowed for a one-time vote for entire reservations, although in a number of instances more than one ethnic tribal nation inhabited a single reservation, thus leading to the consolidated or confederated status of a number of tribes. Some of the reservations and tribes affected were the Confederated Salish and Kootenai Tribes of the Flathead Reservation of Montana, the Confederated Tribes of the Colville Reservation of Washington, the Three Affiliated Tribes of the Fort Berthold Reservation (Mandan, Gros Ventre, and Arikara), and the Colorado River Indian Tribes of the Colorado River Indian Reservation (Mohave, Chemeheuvi, Hopi, and Navajo), to name but a few. In these cases, preexisting governing structures—sometimes still extant—were collapsed into a single constitutional-type government, regardless of the historical relationship between the various tribes.

Third, there was a question about the sequence in which the IRA elections were to be held. Under the IRA, the interior secretary was authorized to transfer federal surplus and submarginal lands to landless Indians. Upon the transference, an election could then be held by those now territorial-based Indians to adopt the IRA and establish a constitution.[72] But the question then arose whether a tribe had to have land before it could adopt a constitution or whether a constitution could be approved with the land transferred later. This issue has proven a major barrier for many contemporary nonrecognized tribes, who are often informed that they cannot be recognized by the United States because they have not held onto a communal land base.

Initially, the Indians of Oklahoma and Alaska Natives were excluded from most of the benefits of the IRA. But in 1936, through two separate measures, the Alaska Act and the Oklahoma Indian Welfare Act, the indigenous groups of those two regions had an opportunity to partake of the benefits of the IRA and regain a measure of self-government.

Because of the degree of indigenous governmental disorganization during the previous decades and the Western constitutional approach John Collier and the BIA were calling for, the newly revived tribes were not always in a position to set the parameters for their own new governments. In fact, while there is evidence that some BIA personnel would have preferred to dominate the tribal constitutional process, there is also evidence that tribal leaders and their allies fought hard to make sure their voices, customs, and knowledge were heard in the constitutions of these organic charters. In a 2000 study, *A Fateful Time,* Elmer Rusco noted that "there is still no thorough study of how the BIA organized itself to carry out the act and few studies of the actual writing of constitutions and related actions in specific Native American communities."[73] Rusco's statement is still generally correct, but a few recent studies are beginning to address this constitutional silence.[74]

Many tribal constitutions (see appendix C for a sample constitution) contained provisions describing the tribal territory and jurisdiction, specifying eligibility for membership, establishing the governing bodies and their powers, detailing elections, specifying civil rights, and setting the criteria for amending the document. Any amendments, of course, were also subject to approval of the secretary of the interior. In fact, the domineering presence of the BIA within the operations of constitutional tribal governments continued. Besides power over approval of constitutions and amendments, the secretary retained power over a tribe's bylaws, had to approve the selection of legal counsel, and could veto tribal resolutions on land use and civil and criminal codes. In addition, the secretary had to approve or review tribal council actions on such matters as levying assessments on nonmembers trading or residing on reservations, regulating the inheritance of real or personal property other than allotments, providing for the appointment of guardians for minors, and excluding from Indian lands individuals without a legal right to reside upon them.[75]

Native nations struggled in the late 1930s and 1940s to adjust to their new measure of self-government; for many this meant a shift away from historic traditions and unwritten customs and values that had served the communities well during and before the transitional period. Increasingly, tribes "were adopting the whites' legalistic perspective on government."[76]

However, this self-assumed tribal shift in political orientation toward a more Western approach did not forestall the termination period of the 1950s, in which federal lawmakers sought to eliminate reservations and expedite the assimilative process of Indians, which these lawmakers felt had been temporarily and wrongly derailed during the IRA period. Although a number of tribes, bands, and California *rancherias* were "terminated," the termination era, although powerfully destructive to those who experienced it, was short-lived. By the mid-1960s the policy had largely been scuttled, although the specter of termination continued to haunt tribes throughout the 1960s.

Besides the genuine fear of termination, most native nations during this period experienced the reality of intense levels of poverty, poor education, abysmal health conditions, inadequate and dilapidated housing conditions, transportation infrastructures that were virtually nonexistent, and a lack of communication facilities. Mamie Mizen, a professional staff member of the Senate Appropriations Committee, starting in 1953 and continuing through 1967 annually published reports on reservation conditions and the facilities and programs provided by the federal government for Indians.

Mizen's reports focused on BIA schools, health facilities, tribal business operations, welfare activities, law enforcement issues, housing, and irrigation installations; she also assessed the cities where Indians had been relocated in order to determine how the Indians were doing. Her annual reports showed how difficult life was on reservations in virtually all socioeconomic aspects. In 1967 she reported on the generally depressed conditions of most Indians. She noted in her introduction that,

the area of lack most visible to even a casual visitor to Indian reservations is housing . . . [and that] another plague that besets the Indian groups is unemployment.
For too many Indians are dependent on public welfare . . . [and] education . . . has
its problems. It must be said again and again that we forget too often that this is
a people who have all their education planned for them in a second language. [77]

On the Cheyenne River Sioux Reservation, in Eagle Butte, South Dakota, it was
reported in 1963 that 97 percent of the occupied housing structures were deficient,
dilapidated, or unsafe. It was also reported that unemployment exceeded 75 percent
due to limited opportunities. There was, at that time, practically no industry, and tourism and recreation were minimal operations. The Mescalero Apaches of southern New
Mexico, who had recently received a $120,600 Office of Economic Opportunity grant
for their community action program, appeared to be in a slightly better economic situation. They were using federal dollars to provide some employment service, home
improvement, child development (under Head Start), community development (under
Vista), manpower development training, and economic development in the form of
resort development and a ski lodge. Still, the other local Apache communities were
described as "dying communities" because of the lack of employment, the shortage
of community facilities, including hospitals, and the lack of roads. Regarding education, although virtually all children attended elementary school and most high-school-
age youth were enrolled, only 20 percent regularly attended high school and very few
entered college.[78]

These conditions, typical of reservations at the time, in Mizen's words left a "deep
impression of lack—lack of information on the part of all of us about our citizens; lack
of understanding of their problems and of their whole philosophy of living, of their
cultural heritage—all too often ignored—of their potentialities."[79]

Native Nations as Corporate and Poverty-Stricken Bodies

The Area Redevelopment Act (1961), Economic Opportunity Act (1964), and Great
Society social welfare programs, all pillars of the federal government's War on Poverty,
along with the national civil rights movement and the Red Power activism that emerged
in the late 1950s and 1960s, led to tribes' involvement as direct sponsors of a number
of federally funded programs.[80] For the first time, tribal governments "had money and
were not beholden for it to the BIA. This created an enormous change in the balance of
power on reservations and in Washington. Tribes could, to some degree, set their own
priorities. They could hire, supervise, and fire people on their own."[81]

But there was another dimension to tribal eligibility for non-BIA federal dollars.
Tribes became eligible to sponsor a multitude of new programs not directly as a result
of their political status as separate nations but because they acted in a corporate capacity or were perceived simply as poverty-stricken ethnic groups. In fact, the tribal councils had to become the sponsoring agencies if they were to be eligible to receive these
federal dollars.

In the language of the Area Redevelopment Act of May 1, 1961, which was designed
to alleviate conditions of substantial and persistent unemployment and underdevelopment in chronically depressed areas, federal assistance would "be extended only to

applicants, both private and public (including Indian tribes), which had been approved for such assistance by an agency or instrumentality of the state or political subdivision thereof in which the project to be financed is located."[82]

In a constrained sense, a *corporation* is something chartered by a government. In this sense, one could rightfully say that the Pueblos of New Mexico, incorporated by territorial legislation in the mid-1870s, and tribes incorporated under Section 17 of the IRA are corporations. And one federal court has held that IRA tribal courts are at least in part "arms of the federal government" since they were organized pursuant to federal law.[83]

But there is a broader sense of the term *corporation* that applies when there is no charter of incorporation. The United States is a body corporate, as are the non-IRA tribes. Thus, tribes have corporate status regarding the right to sue, the capacity of being sued, the power to execute contracts that bind the tribe, and the separation of tribal liability from the liability of tribal members. As a result, when the Area Redevelopment program was renewed and expanded in 1964 as the Economic Opportunity Act, all tribes were made eligible for the wide array of programs administered by this agency. Here again, tribes in their corporate and socioeconomic (poverty) status were being accorded economic and programmatic opportunities that had previously eluded them.

Of course, to be eligible for these specific federal programs, the tribes, as governing bodies, had to assure the federal agencies that they would administer the funds impartially and without regard to race, ethnicity, gender, and so on. In other words, tribal agencies were now required to provide assistance to any reservation resident (African Americans, Asian Americans, whites) who otherwise met the eligibility criteria for these programs. Tribes, as tribes, but also in their role as "corporate" bodies and as eligible recipients because of their low socioeconomic status, became quite skilled at maneuvering between these statuses and at lobbying various federal agencies and Congress. As a result, tribal nations became eligible for virtually every new program authorized during the rush of social, educational, and economic legislation during this period.

While tribes as corporations were now eligible for many new programs, tribes as governments came under increasing congressional scrutiny. In 1968 Congress enacted the Indian Civil Rights Act (ICRA), which imposed certain basic constitutional norms on the actions of tribal governments toward reservation residents; rights guaranteed by the Bill of Rights and the Fourteenth Amendment were inapplicable to tribes because of their preexisting sovereign status. Two of the primary purposes of the ICRA were to impose upon tribal governments restrictions applicable to federal and state governments and to protect individual rights of all persons on the reservations. This act, from an indigenous perspective, was a serious infringement on the internal sovereignty of native nations.[84]

The act was judicially tested the following year in a federal district case involving the Navajo Nation and Theodore R. Mitchell, the program director of Dinébeiina Nahiilna Be Agaditahe (D.N.A.), a nonprofit legal services corporation organized under the laws of the state of Arizona. D.N.A. was created to act as a delegate agency to receive funds made available under the Office of Economic Opportunity, administered by the Office of Navajo Economic Opportunity. Mitchell and D.N.A.'s board of directors had been embroiled in a battle with the Navajo Nation's Advisory Committee over a local school issue and over how much autonomy from the tribal council D.N.A.'s attorneys were entitled to.[85]

As the debate ensued, Mitchell was permanently excluded from the reservation for having offended Dr. Annie Wauneka, a tribal council delegate. The council asserted that the power to exclude was within the scope of its authority under article 2 of the Treaty of 1868, which reserved to the nation the power to ban non-Navajos from the reservation with a few specific exceptions. The district court agreed that the tribe retained the exclusion power but declared that in this case the tribe's actions violated Mitchell's rights to freedom of speech and due process of law, and constituted a bill of attainder, all of which were prohibited by Title II of the ICRA. In the court's words, non-Indians "are entitled to the assurance that they are not subject to be summarily ejected from their homes and separated from their employment because of the disfavor of the ruling segment of the Navajo Tribe."[86] As a result of tribal eligibility for programs under the various civil rights and social welfare measures, tribal governments and their business partners also learned that they could not disregard the rights of nonmember Indians.

In *Dawavendewa v. Salt River Project* (1998), a Hopi Indian filed suit against the Salt River Project Agricultural and Power District, an Arizona corporation operating a generating station on Navajo land. Salt River had entered a lease agreement with the Navajo Tribe in 1969, allowing Salt River to operate the power plant, which utilizes coal from Navajo lands to produce electricity for the Southwest. One of the conditions of the lease was that the corporation would extend preferential treatment to Navajos in its hiring practices. Harold Dawavendewa had applied for a position but was rejected. He filed a complaint alleging that Salt River was engaging in national origin discrimination in violation of Title VII of the 1964 Civil Rights Act. The court of appeals ruled in his favor, holding that discrimination in employment on the basis of membership in a particular tribe did, in fact, constitute national discrimination.

During the halcyon days of the 1960s and early 1970s, native nations were veering away "from a BIA-focused governmental structure into one adopted, perhaps awkwardly, to enable them to be treated consistently as governments."[87] The next major law, the Indian Self-Determination and Education Assistance Act of 1975, created a formal statutory environment for a more sustained period of tribal self-government by establishing that tribal governments could contract to perform services then being provided by the Departments of Interior and Health and Human Services.

The theory underlying the concept of tribal self-determination was that tribal governments knew best what their own problems were and would carefully allocate their resources to address these problems. However, "this ideology assumed a sophistication that did not exist and generated tremendous expectations in Congress that the tribes would suddenly respond to new opportunities with the expertise of a modern corporation."[88] The Indian self-determination era has produced mixed results—reduced unemployment, but continuing excessive federal regulations—which is one reason the self-governance policy was called for by a number of tribes in the late 1980s. Tribal nations continue to seek greater autonomy over their remaining resources, even as they remain locked in an inequitable power relationship with the federal government.

Despite these shifts, the original structures of most IRA tribal governments remain. Although there is increasing diversity in tribal governing structures under the related federal policies of Indian self-determination and self-governance, we can still make some generalized comments about contemporary constitutional native governments, although specific tribal constitutions should be read to clarify particular problems.[89]

Structures and Functions of
Contemporary Constitutional Governments

It is important to note that the IRA had virtually no effect on the substantive powers already vested in the native nations, but added some powers and recognition of powers tribes could exercise without first securing secretarial approval: veto power over the dispensation of tribal funds or assets; the right to negotiate with federal, state, and local governments; and the right to be advised of all appropriation estimates affecting the tribe before these are submitted to the Congress.[90]

Finally, tribal governments were recognized as having the right to exercise all inherent "existing powers." Of course, Congress was unclear as to what those "existing" powers were, and it was left to Nathan Margold, the solicitor of the interior, and John Collier, the commissioner of Indian affairs, to identify what those powers of self-rule were. On October 24, 1934, Margold issued an opinion, titled "Powers of Indian Tribes," some thirty-two pages long, that followed the premise that "those powers which are lawfully vested in an Indian tribe are not, in general, delegated powers granted by express acts of Congress, but rather inherent powers of a limited sovereignty which has never been extinguished."[91]

Inherent powers included recognition of a tribe's right to choose its own form of government, the right to define the conditions for tribal citizenship, and the power to regulate and dispose of tribal property. In other words, tribes had been completely sovereign in the past, but in establishing their political relationship with the United States in various treaties surrendered some of their sovereignty, while retaining all other powers of sovereignty.

We can now turn to a generalized assessment of the structure, functions, and powers of contemporary constitutional governments. A discussion follows about Alaska Native governments, which have structures that are quite different from indigenous communities in the lower forty-eight states. Finally, we close with some comments on the difficulties tribal governments continue to experience inside and outside the federal structure.

■ The Ft. Peck Reservation's General Council: A Case Study

If one adopts a broad perspective on the types of legislative bodies represented in Indian Country, the diversity is abundant: tribal councils (e.g., Ft. Peck Reservation Council), general councils (e.g., Sherwood Valley General Council), business committees (e.g., Cheyenne-Arapaho Business Committee), legislatures (e.g., Menominee Tribal Legislature), boards of directors (e.g., Tulalip Board of Directors), boards of trustees (e.g., Umatilla Board of Trustees), executive committees (e.g., Nez Percé Tribal Executive Committee), councils (e.g., Mashantucket Pequot Council), and tribal committees (e.g., Viejas Tribal Committee).[92] The following case illustrates one of these types.

The Fort Peck Reservation, established by an act of Congress in 1888, is located in the northeastern corner of Montana. It is home to two distinct tribal nations, the Assiniboine and the Yanktonai Sioux, who historically fought bitter wars with one another. Their forced confederation on a single reservation has led to many years of factionalism. Nevertheless, in 1927 the tribes adopted a constitution and formed a general council legislative body that allowed the entire electorate to debate and, hence, legislate for the two tribes. The tribes rejected the Indian Reorganization Act in 1934, opting to retain their earlier constitution. In 1960 the membership of the tribes formed a new constitution that established a seventeen-member Tribal Executive Board. As Lopach et al. state, "the Constitution retains the 'General Council,' but it no longer is the ordinary governing body. Instead it is designed to operate as an institutionalized initiative and referendum."[93] The Executive Board is still subject to the power of the General Council. In effect, the tribal chairman and the Executive Board act as partners in overseeing reservation government, since the heads of tribal agencies must report to both.

■ The Navajo Nation's President: A Case Study

Looking at the executive function in Indian Country, there is also great variety: president (e.g., Navajo Nation), governor (e.g., Isleta Pueblo), chairman (e.g., Yankton Sioux Tribe), spokesman (e.g., Enterprise Rancheria), chief (e.g., Miami Tribe), and principal chief (e.g., Cherokee Nation). Until 1989, the Navajo Nation's chief executive officer was called the *tribal chairman*. However, in that year, in the wake of political turmoil, the Navajo Nation's council drafted amendments to their Tribal Code (their organic governing documents) in an effort to separate executive and legislative powers and to curb the extraordinary power that had built up in the office of the chairman. These amendments created the positions of president and speaker of the council (the legislative branch's leader). The president is the chief executive officer of the executive branch and has full authority to conduct, supervise, and coordinate personnel and programs of the nation. Among the president's powers are the power to represent the nation in its relations with all other governments; the power to faithfully execute and enforce the nation's laws; the power to negotiate and execute contracts, subject to appropriate legislative approval; and the power to appoint supervisory executive personnel.[94]

■ The Crow Tribal Court: A Case Study

The judicial function is also present under a variety of names: supreme court (e.g., Rosebud Sioux Supreme Court), peacemaker court (e.g., Iroquois Confederacy Peacemaker Courts and Navajo Nation Peacemaker Courts), councils of elders (e.g., Mohegan Nation Council of Elders), tribal courts (e.g., Crow Tribal Court), courts of appeal (e.g., Cheyenne River Sioux Court of Appeals), and criminal tribal court (e.g., Mississippi Choctaw Tribal Courts), to name but a few.

The Crow Tribal Court is a creation of the tribe's legislative body, the General Council, and lacks clear independence. It is a three-member court. The judges are elected by the General Council's membership (all adult males and females). Judges serve four-year terms. The court is expected to serve as an appellate body should the need arise. Although the court is vulnerable to political influence, there are signs that it is acting with a greater measure of independence: its increasing use of contempt powers, decisions enforcing payment plans in contract disputes, and its use of the power of judicial review to nullify an executive committee election. In the Crow situation, however, the court is the weakest branch of the nation's political system.[95]

Tribal Councils (Legislative Functions)

Let us now turn to a necessarily brief description of the three broad functions most indigenous nations exercise: tribal councils (legislative function), tribal chairs (executive function), and tribal courts (judicial function).[96] It is important to note that while virtually every tribe has an executive and legislative branch, some lack a separate judiciary.

A majority of native nations, particularly those organized under the IRA, vest legislative authority in a tribal council, although it is sometimes called something else. Tribal councils or business committees are usually fairly small, ranging from as few as five members up to eighteen. However, the Navajo Nation, the largest reservation-based tribe, had until 2010 an eighty-eight member council. Tribal councils tend to be organized by districts, which in some cases date back to when reservations were divided into land management districts by agricultural and soil conservation agents in the New Deal era of the 1930s.

For example, the Navajo Reservation was divided into nineteen land management districts in the spring of 1936, with the districts ranging in size from 396,160 acres to 1,759,360 acres. Each district employed an administrator, whose duties included overseeing the work of other employees and developing range-management plans to conserve the depleted soil of the Navajo Nation. In addition, the Navajo Council members (seventy-four in 1936) were elected from these districts, in accordance with the population of each district.

Interestingly, in the post-IRA years of tribal government operations, the commissioner of Indian affairs still wielded a tremendous amount of power over tribal operations. In the case of the Navajos, who rejected the IRA but were still subject to the rule-making authority of the federal government, the commissioner no longer had the right to appoint tribal delegates, but council meetings still required the presence of a federal official, the superintendent, who occupied a position beside the chairman during the council meetings.

There is also a question of whether native nations are subject to the legislative reapportionment process (the assignment to a state of a new number of congressional seats) after the decimal census has been completed, and if population fluctuations warrant a change. In recent years, for instance, there has been tremendous population growth in the Sunbelt states stretching from Florida to California. That area and other states have gained congressional representatives as a result of their increased population base. Conversely, some states in the Northeast and Midwest have lost congressional representatives because of population decline. Tribes, it has been held, if they have adopted Anglo-Saxon democratic processes for selection of tribal political leaders, have been required to follow equal protection concepts like the "one person–one vote" principle.[97]

By contrast, the Crow Tribe of Montana operate under a non-IRA constitution and with a General Council government. Its membership consists of all enrolled tribal members who are eighteen or over.

Council members of most tribal nations, like U.S. or state legislators, generally serve for a specified period, usually two to four years. Satisfying the constitutional prerequisites for service in elected councils is not difficult. Generally, "they pertain only to minimum age, eighteen or twenty-one years; tribal membership; and being free of felonious convictions or indebtedness to the tribe. Otherwise it is left to the voters to decide whether the individual candidate is qualified for office. There are no other formal qualifications of an educational, occupational, or experiential sort."[98]

Tribal councils, first of all, exercise those powers either stated or implied in the tribal constitution or other organic political documents. Typical of these broad powers or goals of governance are enacting ordinances and resolutions (the equivalent of congressional statutes), establishing justice, ensuring tranquility and enjoyment of the blessings of freedom and liberty, conserving tribal property, managing tribal business enterprises, establishing or modifying judicial systems, delegating powers to committees of its choice, and providing for the tribes' welfare.

There are also a number of specific enumerated powers that may be exercised by the councils. Many of these derive from the list established in a 1934 solicitor's opinion written by Nathan Margold at John Collier's request. For example, the Rosebud Sioux Tribal Council may, among others, exercise the following powers:

1. to employ legal counsel for the protection and advancement of the rights of the tribe;
2. to purchase and to otherwise acquire land or other property for or on behalf of the tribe and prevent the sale of existing tribal land;
3. to regulate all economic affairs of the tribe;
4. to levy taxes upon members of the tribe and upon nonmembers doing business on the reservation;
5. to enact resolutions . . . governing the adoption and abandonment of membership;
6. to make and enforce ordinances governing the conduct of the members of the tribe and providing for the maintenance of law and order and the administration of justice by establishing a reservation court and defining its duties and powers;
7. to regulate the inheritance of property; and
8. to regulate the domestic relations of the tribe and to provide for the appointment of guardians for minors and mental incompetents.[99]

There is, however, one major qualification on tribal powers. Nearly all major tribal ordinances or resolutions that have a substantial effect on tribal powers or resources are subject to review by the secretary of the interior. "Some constitutions provide that the ordinances and resolutions are not effective until the Secretary approves; others provide that the Secretary may rescind ordinances of which he disapproves. Either way, the requirement represents a very substantial limitation upon the self-government of the tribes."[100] Such secretarial veto power, even though it is not used very often today, is proof that federal plenary power (read: absolute power) is a continuing reality tribal nations must cope with, although it is unclear what the basis for this power is.

It is important to recall, however, that tribal councils, acting for the tribal nation, derive their power to act from two other critical sources as well—inherent sovereignty and treaty rights. In fact, tribal constitutions themselves are, in some sense, a manifestation of tribal sovereignty, with treaties also being directly related since only sovereigns have the power to negotiate binding legal compacts.

Tribal Chairs (Executive Function)

Virtually all tribal constitutions provide for a tribal chairperson, who in some cases is called *president* or *governor*. The chair performs the executive function of government, which involves the daily operations of administration, continual decision making, and setting up and overseeing systems that give tribal government laws force and meaning. There are two basic components of the executive branch: the chief executive and the administration. Most tribal constitutions provide for at least four officers: the chair, the vice-chair, the tribal secretary, and the tribal treasurer. We discuss only the chair.

The chair is head of the government. His or her powers are prescribed in the tribal constitution and bylaws. The chair also draws power from customs, tradition, personal charisma, and the prestige of the position.[101] Powers and duties of a chair include seeing that the laws are being faithfully implemented; issuing directives and setting up administrative guidelines; handling negotiations with the BIA, Congress, local governments, and other tribes; presiding over all council meetings; and being responsible for the administration of the tribal bureaucracy.

In some native nations, the chair is elected by council vote. In other cases, he or she is directly chosen by the tribal electorate. For example, the Muskogee Creek Nation of Oklahoma have a principal chief and second chief who are chosen by tribal voters over the age of eighteen. These officers serve four-year terms. "The principal chief's responsibilities include organizing the executive department, overseeing tribal programs, preparing the annual budget, and informing the national council about the state of the nation's affairs."[102] The principal chief, with the tribal council's concurrence, also selects the election board's members and a citizenship board, and he or she chooses the justice for the nation's supreme court.

Tribal Courts (Judicial Function)

> Tribal courts, in both their present form and their "traditional" predecessors, however, have been centrally concerned with the overall concept of justice and have oftentimes managed to be free of the obsession with technicalities that has so often plagued non-tribal court systems.[103]

This quote serves as a reminder that the primary role of tribal government, at least historically and well into the contemporary era, was more judicial than legislative in nature. In other words, as our earlier discussion of traditional governments showed, tribal leaders and governing structures functioned primarily as adjudicatory bodies seeking to maintain harmony and balance and looking to amicably settle disputes when they arose.[104] Notwithstanding this primordial and inherently judicial orientation, the inaccurate perception of most Europeans and Euro-Americans toward tribal nations was that they were largely lawless, anarchical societies lacking even rudimentary systems of law and order.

An important pair of law review articles written in 1891 by a prominent Harvard Euro-American legal scholar, James Bradley Thayer, summed up this mischaracterization of tribes in the article titles: "A People without Law." Thayer was explicitly decrying the fact that tribes lacked legal systems resembling those he was familiar with, and thus in his view were essentially lawless communities in need of Western-style law and order systems that would speed their assimilation.[105]

The reality, however, is that tribes have had their own very effective systems of law and order since long before European contact. Obviously, with so many indigenous communities, no two systems looked alike and certainly none bore much resemblance to those brought to North America by Europeans. While the passage of time, the force of Euro-American colonialism, tribal adaptations to that force, the litigious nature of Americans, and the enactment of laws like the IRA and the ICRA have led to the development of similarities in tribal judicial systems, it is still "in the operation of the judicial branch that one finds the most variety amongst tribal governments."[106] This variety is intensified and complicated by the sheer volume of "law" that tribal courts must be aware of, respond to, and produce. As Deloria and Lytle note:

> If limited only to the written documents that could be used as a basis for finding "the" law, one would have to cover nearly 400 ratified treaties and agreements, 5,000 federal statutes, 2,000 federal court opinions, and over 250 tribal constitutions and charters. . . . Add to this massive accumulation the traditions and customs of 500 or more individual tribes and the task becomes formidable indeed. But these are simply basic documents. American Indian law also includes state opinions and state statutes (some of which originated before the Constitution of the United States), congressional hearings of legislation, reports of a series of investigative commissions, and field surveys of Indian conditions, many of which are themselves a massive compilation of data. Finally, American Indian law includes solicitor's opinions and memorandum opinions of the Department of the Interior and, more recently, other federal departments that have come to serve Indians in a variety of ways.[107]

Complicating matters even further are questions surrounding which entity or entities have jurisdiction over a specific dispute—tribal court, federal court, or state court. Figure 3.1 depicts the general linkage between the three sovereigns. It is important to know that cases involving Indians, tribes, and interpretations of aspects of Indian law, whether involving Indians or not, can begin in any of these courts.

At present there are three legal institutions that together compose the Indian judicial system—traditional courts, courts of Indian offenses (also known as *code of federal regulations [CFR] courts*), and tribal (IRA) courts.

Traditional Courts

There are only approximately twenty remaining traditional courts, including the religious courts of the Pueblos of New Mexico, the Peacemaker Courts of the Navajo Nation and the Iroquois, and the courts of some small fishing tribes in the Northwest, that administer unwritten customary law and follow little formal procedure.[108] In some cases, a council of elders, a tribal chief, religious leaders, or the warrior society leaders serve as mediators or dispute resolvers. These courts handle misbehavior through public scorn, the loss or restriction of certain privileges, or the payment of restitution to an injured party. In extreme cases, such as witchcraft or homicide, banishment from the nation might be called for.[109] In traditional courts the values of the community dictated that compensation to victims and their families and resolution of problems "in such a manner that all could forgive and forget and continue to live within the tribal society in harmony with one another was of great importance."[110]

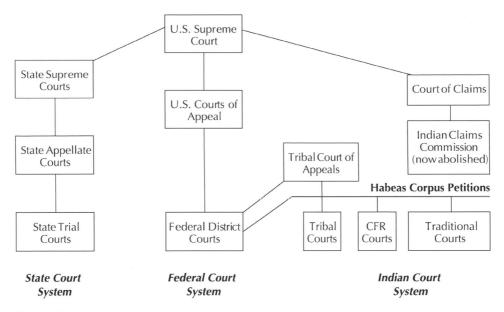

Figure 3.1
The American Judicial System and Indian Law
Source: From AMERICAN INDIANS, AMERICAN JUSTICE by Vine Deloria, Jr. and Clifford M.
Lytle, Copyright © 1983.

Courts of Indian Offenses

These courts, established by the secretary of the interior in the early 1880s, are also
known as *CFR courts* because they operate under guidelines laid out under the Code
of Federal Regulations (currently in Title 25). They were the product of the then-
dominant federal ideology of forced assimilation of Indians.[111] Their primary purpose
was to promote acculturation of Indians by educating them in Euro-American legal
and cultural values and norms.

Commissioner of Indian Affairs Hiram Price, of his own accord and without congressional authorization, originated the idea for the CFR courts. He compiled the first
set of guidelines for court organization and procedure and a short civil and criminal
code in 1883. The courts were staffed by local Indians, handpicked by the Indian agent.
They served at the pleasure of the agent. The primary task of the courts, as described
in *United States v. Clapox* in 1888,[112] was to serve as "mere educational and disciplinary instrumentalities by which the Government of the United States is endeavoring to
improve and elevate the condition of these dependent tribes to whom it sustains the
relation of guardian."

As tools of colonialism, the CFR courts were focused on imposing Western law and
order on Indian communities. At their apex around 1900, CFR courts were operating
on nearly two-thirds of all reservations. However, a number of tribal nations—the Five
Civilized Tribes, tribes in New York State, the Osage of Oklahoma, the Pueblos of New
Mexico, and the eastern band of Cherokee in North Carolina—did not have to endure
a CFR court system because they had preexisting tribal court systems the United States

chose not to supplant.[113] The tasks of the courts, already complicated enough, became even more complicated as a result of the allotment policy, which led to the individualization of Indian property and rights and a dramatic increase in the number of whites in Indian Country. This, of course, led to squabbles over jurisdictional authority, interracial tension, and, in turn, an increase in the workload of the courts.

As a progressive mood emerged in the early twentieth century, out of which flowed developments that would culminate in the IRA and the modern tribal constitutions and tribal courts authorized under that act, the CFR courts began to be replaced. Many of them were phased out altogether, while others were folded into the constitutionally based tribal courts. However, some CFR courts continued because tribes lacked sufficient resources to establish modern courts. Thus, today there are twenty CFR courts still operating in Indian Country.

Modern Tribal Courts

The tribal constitutions organized under the IRA and the court systems that followed were a vast improvement over the CFR courts, because tribal judges under the IRA constitutions were directly responsible to their tribe and not to the BIA. On the other hand, many tribal constitutions contained language, ideas, and structures that only sometimes comported with the tribes' historical methods of self-governance. The role of the BIA in the development of tribal constitutions also cannot be overlooked, although the agency acted differently with different tribes, and far more research is needed before any definitive conclusions can be drawn about the relationship between the bureau and tribal nations. More importantly, those constitutions "did not provide for any separation of powers and did not specifically create any court system."[114]

Nevertheless, despite the difficulties tribes had recovering from the previous decades of intense colonialism and the inherent flaws in the IRA system of Indian self-rule, tribal courts have grown and diversified tremendously over the last six decades. Although most tribal courts resemble their state or federal counterparts in structure and function, their jurisdiction has broadened from primarily criminal to include civil suits of increasing complexity.[115] In fact,

> Traditional non-judicial dispute resolution mechanisms continue to function in some tribes along with Peacemaker courts, courts of specialized jurisdiction, such as administrative commissions, gaming, small claims courts, and courts of general jurisdiction. These differences are a sign of creativity as tribal councils and courts balance variances among the tribes' traditions and present needs against the traditions and requirements of the dominant society's law.[116]

Of course, the Indian Civil Rights Act of 1968, which statutorily imposed qualified portions of the U.S. Bill of Rights on tribal court proceedings for the first time, pushed tribal judges more in a direction resembling non-Indian courts and provided a mechanism—the writ of habeas corpus—by which litigants could challenge tribal court decisions in federal courts. Several important U.S. constitutional provisions, however, were not incorporated in the act. For instance, the establishment of religion clause, indictment by a grand jury, and the restriction against quartering troops in homes are absent. Tribes may also discriminate in voting on account of race. Nor are tribes required to convene a jury in civil trials or, in criminal cases, to issue grand jury indictments or appoint counsel for poor defendants. Nevertheless, a significant portion of U.S. constitutional law was made applicable to tribal court affairs by the ICRA. This is one of the few federal laws that directly limits the power of tribes to govern their internal affairs.

Despite the fact that many tribal courts have assumed many of the forms and functions of Western-style governments, in part because of the anticipation of federal intrusion into tribal authority if they fail to do so, important differences remain between tribal courts and non-Indian courts. First, tribal judges are not usually attorneys. Although they receive legal training from the National American Indian Court Judges Association (NAICJA) or other bodies, this is not the equivalent of a J.D. degree. Second, tribal courts are not generally courts of record, and many opinions are not recorded. Finally, because modern tribal courts have a colonial origin, they "must continually build legitimacy within the tribe, both among tribal members and with the Tribal Councils."[117]

In some tribes, tribal judges are popularly elected, while in most they are appointed by the tribal council or chairperson. Tribal judges usually are tribal members, though in some cases they are non-Indians or members of other tribal nations.[118] Because of the doctrine of tribal sovereignty each tribe establishes its own qualifications for its judges, which may or may not include a requirement that they be state-licensed attorneys. However, nearly all tribal judges receive some measure of training in federal Indian law, sponsored by organizations like the NAICJA or the National Indian Justice Center. Judges typically serve a fixed term, usually two or four years, although one tribal nation, the Navajo, grants life tenure to its justices after they successfully navigate a probationary period.

Finally, many tribes have recently established appellate courts (usually consisting of three judges), though tribes are not required to have such a court. Some of the more developed tribal court systems, like that of the Navajo Nation, have appellate courts that sit permanently to hear appeals. Other tribes have established intertribal courts that hear appeals from a regional association of tribal councils.[119] Still others have panels of judges who are assembled ad hoc for each appeal.

On some reservations the tribal council serves as the appellate court. In December 1993, Congress enacted the Indian Tribal Justice Act, which authorized federal government assistance for the development of tribal justice systems, including not only individual tribal courts, but regional judicial systems as well.

Approximately 150 native communities have functional modern tribal courts and, as we have seen, there is tremendous diversity among them. Of the three branches of government discussed here, the tribal courts have been required to make the most adjustments, in their relations not only with their own governments but especially with their federal and state counterparts and with the non-Indians who live on or travel through the courts' jurisdictions.

Tribal courts have made great strides in recent years in performing their complicated and increasingly difficult tasks, especially considering that while crime rates appear to be receding in most of the country they are increasing exponentially in Indian Country. In a study completed by the Justice Department in 2004,[120] it was found that American Indians experienced a per capita rate of violence twice that of non-Indians in the United States. Moreover, for Indians aged 25–34, the rate of violent crime victimization was more than two and one-half times the rate for all other persons in the same age bracket. More distressingly, the study found that approximately 60 percent of those who committed violent crimes against Indians between 1992–2001 were white. Besides the interracial nature of most of this crime, the other alarming finding was that "the criminal victimizer is more likely to have consumed alcohol preceding the offense." This report's findings confirm that crime, alcohol, and interracial tensions remain major stumbling blocks to tribal prosperity and that the tribal courts will have their hands full for the foreseeable future.

Increasing crime is but one of the difficulties tribal courts face. Others include their susceptibility to political influence by tribal politicians, inadequate tribal laws, lack of qualified personnel, and a lack of planning.[121] Still, tribal courts are becoming more effective in their assorted and diversifying tasks and are slowly gaining legitimacy in the eyes of federal and state courts. For example, on July 28, 2005, tribal court judges from five Wisconsin tribal nations ceremonially signed into law the "Teague Protocol," with judges from the Ninth Judicial District. The purpose of this tribal-state court protocol was to "effectively and efficiently allocate judicial resources by providing a legal mechanism which clearly outlines the path a legal dispute will follow when both a tribal court and a circuit court have each determined it has jurisdiction over a matter." While not altering or expanding the jurisdiction of either party, this cooperative measure establishes an institutional judicial framework that is helping to ease tensions between the tribes involved and the Ninth Circuit Court judges. Equally important, they are finally gaining federal financial assistance and support from organizations like the Law Enforcement Assistance Administration.

In addition, they, better than the other two branches, seem to be more willing and are structurally and normatively capable of synthesizing traditional norms and culture with Western traditions. In fact, "the ability of the tribal court to interpret law to the Indian people and to interpret Indian culture to other legal institutions may be the most important of all assets flowing from the tribal court system."[122]

Alaska Native Governmental Organizations

Alaska Natives, which include American Indians (e.g., Tlingits and Haidas), Inuit (formerly called Eskimo), and Aleut, had very little contact with non-Indians before or even after Russia "ceded" Alaska to the United States in 1867, a cession Alaska Natives protested. In fact, from 1741 to 1867, the Natives retained their political independence, never signed any treaty with the Russians, and sold them no land.[123] The aboriginal people of the territory lived in over two hundred scattered villages, located primarily along the southern and far northwestern coasts. Hunting and fishing were their primary means of subsistence.

Generally, from 1923 to the passage of the Alaska Native Claims Settlement Act (ANCSA) in 1971, the legal position of the Alaska Native was similar to that of American Indians. In fact, the Indian Naturalization Act of 1924 expressly included the Eskimo, Aleut, and Indians of the Alaska Territory. The IRA of 1934 partially included Alaska Natives among its beneficiaries when it declared that "the provisions of this Act shall not apply to any of the Territories, colonies, or insular possessions of the United States, except that sections 9, 10, 11, 12, and 16, shall apply to the Territory of Alaska." It was also declared that "for the purposes of this Act, Eskimos and other aboriginal peoples of Alaska shall be considered Indians."[124] A separate act in 1936,[125] an amendment to the IRA, extended the rest of the IRA's original provisions to Alaska Natives. Some seventy Alaskan groups organized under these two acts. Native property and affairs were also under the trust protection of the federal government.[126] Moreover, federal and state policy encouraging the incorporation of Alaska Native communities under state law began in 1963. Approximately 127 Native communities have organized under Alaska's state municipal incorporation statutes. These state-chartered entities coexist alongside the federal IRA-chartered entities.

Despite this seeming comparability, "the distinctions between Alaska natives as governments and as landowners, however, have remained clouded." This is evidenced in a 1955 Supreme Court ruling, *Tee-Hit-Ton v. United States,* in which the court held that Alaska Natives lacked recognized title to their aboriginal territory and that the federal government could take "unrecognized" Native lands without having to pay just compensation under the Fifth Amendment to the Constitution.

On top of this ruling came the Alaska Statehood Act of 1958, which authorized the state to select 108 million acres of public land, including prime Native hunting and fishing territory, as its proprietary land based on Alaska's admission as a state. These two events prompted the formation of the Alaska Federation of Natives, an interest group whose primary goal was the eventual settlement of their aboriginal claims.[127] Oil discoveries on the North Slope of Alaska in 1968 only intensified indigenous determination to secure control of their remaining territory. Energy corporations, the state, and other interests were also excited about the possibility of a final settlement of the Natives' land claims.

In 1971 Congress responded with passage of ANCSA,[128] a comprehensive law regarding the land rights of Alaska's eighty thousand indigenous inhabitants. This law significantly modified the nature of the federal government's relationship with Alaska Natives. Unlike most Indian reservations, which are held "in trust" by the United States on behalf of the tribes, Native land in Alaska under the act was granted in fee-simple title. The act required the establishment of both regional and village business corporations to receive and manage the money and land conveyed by the act. In addition, forty-four million acres were conveyed to these corporations, along with $962.5 million in compensation for the extinguishment of all Native claims to the rest of Alaska. ANCSA also extinguished aboriginal hunting and fishing rights to "public lands." However, a subsequent amendment restored protection of subsistence hunting and fishing for rural natives.

Between 1972 and 1974, twelve regional corporations (later a thirteenth was formed for Alaska Native nonresidents) and nearly two hundred village corporations were formed as "profit-making business corporations under the laws of the State of Alaska."[129] All Alaska Natives were enrolled as individual shareholders of the ANCSA corporations. The corporations were required to distribute 10 percent of the funds to all stockholders and 45 percent (after five years it increased to 50 percent) to village corporations and to stockholders who did not live in a village. All persons living on December 18, 1971, and possessing at least one-fourth or more Native blood were issued one hundred shares of corporate stock in their regional corporation. There were some 74,300 initial shareholders.[130] The act required each regional corporation to use its land and resources for the profit of its shareholders.

Congressional intent in this legislation was clear: "Congress intended to promote economic development and the economic assimilation of Alaska Natives to the American mold. The results of this decision have been mixed. Some corporations became financially successful, while others remained inactive and a few faced bankruptcy."[131] But Donald C. Mitchell also points out that "more than a quarter century after its enactment, ANCSA remains the most generous aboriginal claims settlement in United States history."[132] And while conceding that economic assimilation was a principal ANCSA objective, it is important also to note that the idea of using state of Alaska–chartered business corporations to implement the settlement was first recommended by the Alaska Federation of Natives and was not a congressional imposition.[133]

As originally enacted, ANCSA prevented shareholders from selling their shares for twenty years, or until 1991. Thereafter, these shares could be sold to any person. And corporate-owned lands were to be exempt from state and local taxation for this same period. Alaska Natives became concerned about the potential long-term impact of these measures, and they successfully lobbied Congress in 1988 to amend the act and extend the restrictions on sale of stock and on state taxation "indefinitely." But Congress also allowed each corporation to issue and sell stock to non-Natives, and rejected the Natives' request to allow these corporations to transfer their land to tribal governments in order to give this acreage additional protection.[134]

By the late 1990s, Alaska Natives and their villages and corporations fought to make their organizations profitable and gain greater political autonomy, while preventing non-Natives and the state from gaining any additional power over them. But in 1998, their efforts received a significant blow from the Supreme Court. In *Alaska v. Native Village of Venetie Tribal Government,* the court held that Venetie's 1.8 million acres of fee-simple land did not qualify as "Indian Country" and thus the tribal government lacked authority to impose a 5-percent business tax on a non-Native contractor building a school in the village.

Notwithstanding this judicial loss, many Alaska Natives are continuing their push for clearer recognition of their status as "tribal governments," sensing that neither ANCSA nor other laws are sufficient to protect their traditions and rights.[135] Encouragingly, the Department of the Interior in 1993 acknowledged that the over two hundred Alaska Native entities were federally recognized governmental bodies.[136] But what governing powers these bodies have in the wake of the Venetie ruling is unclear. Additionally, and more problematically, Senator Ted Stevens (R-AK), in 2003 in a video-taped speech to the Alaska Federation of Natives, said that "tribal sovereignty is not the answer to the problems Alaska Natives face. It merely brings authority to some, power to others, and legal fees to advocates that bring incessant litigation."[137] He then sponsored legislation that was aimed at terminating federal funds for Alaska Native village courts and law enforcement. The language in the bill would divert the money to the state. Still, it is fairly certain that a number of Alaskan communities will continue to act as sovereign as they can. In a number of cases they "have therefore acted independently to establish tribal courts, to dissolve city governments, to restrict outside interference, to claim jurisdiction over their lands and resources, to pursue relief in international forums, and to form regional and intervillage compacts."[138]

Issues Confronting Native Governments

As this chapter has shown, native governments, like those of other sovereigns, have never been static. But because of federal dominance, tribal governments have often faced unrelenting pressure to modify their institutions or face the prospect of legal termination. Unbridled federal power is less often used today over tribes and their resources, but these small nations are always aware that the courts, the Congress, the president, the BIA, and increasingly, state governments may at any time require something new from them.

Still, most indigenous governments exercise a plethora of governmental powers. These include, but are not limited to, a variable mixture of civil and criminal jurisdiction over their own members and nonmember Indians, and to a lesser extent over non-Natives; the power to define their membership criteria; the power to administer justice via their own court systems; the power to regulate domestic and family relations (e.g., marriage, divorce, child welfare); the power to regulate, zone, exchange, purchase, and sell property; the power to exclude nonmembers from tribal lands; the power of extradition; the power to regulate hunting, fishing, and gathering rights; the power to regulate all economic activity; the power to tax; the power to negotiate with other governments; and the power to provide social, health, housing, and educational services for tribal and nontribal citizens.[139]

But the exercise of these and other inherent and delegated powers is complicated and is frequently contested from within and without tribal communities. As Lopach et al. learned in their study of tribal governments on Montana's Indian reservations, "two essential characteristics of reservation politics are used as shorthand for the values of Indian political culture. The two composite features are a politics of scarcity and a politics of interference."[140] This holds true in varying degrees for other reservations as well.

A politics of scarcity derives from the fact that Indian tribes remain among the most disadvantaged and impoverished groups in American society. The extreme social problems and economic poverty, "coupled with pronounced loyalty on reservations to the social group, influences the political behavior of tribal leaders." Tribal leaders, in their quest to alleviate poverty, have historically been led to seek outside support and funding. Of course, reliance on outside help of necessity leads to "compliance with outside regulations and acceptance of other forms of interference."[141]

A politics of interference, to be discussed in more detail in chapters 6 and 7, can be summarized briefly. There are two types of political interference within Indian Country. The first is socioculturally based and derives from within the tribal membership; the second is governmentally or corporate-based and is from the outside. The former centers on the reality that for many Indians their primary allegiance is to the family, clan, village, or social group with whom they share values, lands, religious views, and language. And depending on the tribe, sometimes this loyalty does not extend to the reservation-wide tribal government that theoretically represents all groups and sometimes even different tribes.

For example, among the Hopi, a number of the twelve villages maintain the traditional leadership provided by the Kikmongwi[142] and clan leaders. As Wayne Taylor, chairman of the IRA-recognized Hopi Tribal Council put it: "We're called an IRA tribe. We had an election to form a constitution back in 1934. We've had a kind of rocky history with the tribal government. Not all the communities, not all the Hopis, wanted to have the government. So we have some villages that don't quite accept this government, even today."[143]

Outside interests that may interfere include Congress; the Department of the Interior and its key agency, the BIA; other federal agencies; state and local governments; and corporate interests, which have directly or indirectly interfered in tribal government decision making throughout the last century and a half. External interference has serious implications for tribal powers of governance and challenges the idea that the federal government is truly supportive of tribal self-determination and self-governance. It also affects the views of tribal members about the representational legitimacy of their own government.

Specific issues, both internal and external, variably confront many tribal governments. From an internal perspective, there are problems centered on the poor administrative capabilities of some tribes. "Tribal government officials are routinely criticized as being incompetent, ineffective, weak, wasteful and inefficient. In some cases, they may even be corrupt and criminal."[144] Second, there is an issue of the legitimacy, representation, and stability of tribal institutions of self-governance, since "for many American Indian tribes, there is a very good possibility of a mismatch between their formal governments and the standards of political legitimacy found in their cultures."[145] This, of course, refers generally to the IRA constitutional governments that in some cases were forcibly imposed on various tribes. Even when these bodies are seen as legitimate, the issue of whether the councils fully represent their constituencies may remain.[146]

Third, there is the concern that the adoption of non-Indian judicial procedures is supplanting the remaining vestiges of traditional dispute-resolution mechanisms.[147]

From an external perspective, tribal governments face an equally daunting set of conditions. The major factor is the ongoing existence of congressional plenary power, which the federal government may use at any time as a justification to reduce or eliminate Indian rights. Alongside this is the inordinate amount of power the BIA still wields over many tribal leaders and their decision-making capabilities. Among the difficulties caused by the BIA's power is the conflict-of-interest problem. The BIA is lodged within the Department of the Interior, which is also home to agencies like the Bureau of Land Management, the Fish and Wildlife Service, and the Bureau of Reclamation, which sometimes have policy goals that clash directly with those of the tribes. This structural dilemma has existed since the middle of the nineteenth century.

Third, and related to the previous issues, is tribal economic dependency on non-Indian governments, agencies, and other interests. Despite gaming revenues, most tribes still receive a majority of their operating budgets from the federal government. As such, tribes are beholden to those funding sources and can be restricted in how they can utilize those monies.[148] More important, those funding agencies may decide to reduce or in some cases eliminate their expenditures to tribes, which has happened with some regularity since the late 1970s.

Conclusion

Indigenous governments are distinct sovereigns in that they retain and exercise a significant measure of sovereignty; yet because of federal colonialism, their sovereign powers may be ignored, reduced, or in some cases completely terminated. Nevertheless, tribal governing institutions will continue to evolve and make the necessary adaptations required to address the increasingly diverse needs of their citizens and in their diverse and unpredictable relations to the other polities they are linked to by treaty, trust, and citizenship.

CHAPTER 4

Actors in Native Politics

We were here since time immemorial. People will come to understand that we're still here and we're getting stronger. There are three different sovereigns within the United States: the federal government, the state governments, and the tribal governments. We can take our place among the family of nations, the family of governments, and participate.

—John Echohawk, 1997[1]

FEDERALISM—A SYSTEM of governance in which a national, overarching government shares power with subnational or state governments—is experiencing another growth spurt. It is a political, legal, and economic spurt spearheaded by the states and sanctioned by the Supreme Court and to a lesser, though still impressive, extent, the Congress and the president. This is not unusual given the nature of federalism, which Woodrow Wilson said in 1911 cannot be settled "by the opinion of any one generation." Wilson observed that changes in the social and economic condition of society, in the public's perception of issues needing to be addressed by government, and in the dominant political values require each successive generation to deal with federal-state relationships as a "new question" subject to comprehensive and searching analysis.

While such an analysis is indeed called for in issues such as welfare policy, religious matters, or economic regulation, the subject matter of the United States' dealings with Indian nations is distinctive because of the preexisting and sovereign nature of tribes and is not constitutionally open to such a balancing test. This is because the Congress was given exclusive jurisdiction in the commerce clause and by practical application in the treaty and property clauses. Exclusive federal jurisdiction over Indian Country affairs was most powerfully brought out in the landmark case *Worcester v. Georgia* (1832), in which the Supreme Court ruled that tribes were distinct, independent political bodies in which the laws of the states can have no force "but with the assent of the Cherokees themselves, or in conformity with treaties, and with the acts of Congress. The whole intercourse between the United States and this nation is by our Constitution and laws vested in the Government of the United States."[2]

Native nations stand, then, as preconstitutional and extraconstitutional polities situated alongside, but not constitutionally subject to, the federal government. Connected by treaties, agreements, the trust doctrine, and the commerce clause to the national government, tribes are nevertheless playing a direct role in the latest rearticulation of the doctrine of federalism. For example, in 1996 the Supreme Court, in *Seminole Tribe v. Florida*,[3] struck down important provisions of the 1988 Indian Gaming Regulatory Act that had authorized federal courts to resolve disputes between tribes and the states in certain instances. And in 2005, in an even starker case for tribal nations in their relations with local governments, the High Court in *City of Sherrill, New York v. Oneida Nation of New York* ruled 8–1 that the city of Sherrill had the right to impose property taxes on lands the Oneida Nation had repurchased within the tribe's historical land base.

In this chapter, we examine in a general way the relations between tribes and the Congress, tribes and the BIA, tribes and the courts, and tribes and the states.

Native Nations and the U.S. Congress

Over the last two hundred years, the various tribal nations and the federal government have assumed an untold number of reciprocal political, legal, social, and cultural obligations toward one other. From 1775 to 1914 these obligations, especially the political-legal variety, were most clearly espoused in the hundreds of treaties and dozens of agreements negotiated between a majority of tribes and the federal government. These documents, many of which from a Western perspective are binding legal contracts, were drawn and executed by the American president via the treaty-making authority vested in the executive branch by Article 2, Section 2 of the Constitution, and then ratified by the Senate. They were then implemented by congressional laws necessary to fulfill the U.S. treaty obligations. Congress receives the authorization to deal with tribes under Article 1, Section 8, Clause 3 of the Constitution, where it is stated that the legislative branch is empowered to "regulate commerce . . . with the Indian tribes."

The indigenous perspective on treaty making is much more complex, of course, because of the tremendous degree of tribal differentiation reflected in the hundreds of tribal groups the United States treated with[4] and, more importantly, because treaties were not viewed as merely legal instruments by the tribes but as sacred covenants.[5] While the various Iroquois nations, for example, had clearly recognized individuals responsible for the negotiation and signing of such covenants and a well-defined process by which the intercultural relations were codified and ratified, other less politically centralized groups like the Navajo, Apache, and Lakota often had individuals empowered to deal with alien nations, but these persons and the tribal nation itself lacked institutions that could effectively wed nonparticipatory bands or clans to the agreed upon instrument.

The U.S. Constitution's treaty and commerce clauses have been of important, if inconsistent, benefit to tribes and individual Indians. They provide a certain structural level of protection to Indians that is virtually nonexistent for most other indigenous groups worldwide (indigenous peoples in Canada and New Zealand are important exceptions). Unfortunately, there is nothing in either of these clauses or in any other provision of the U.S. Constitution that emphatically declares that the federal government has a constitutional obligation to protect tribes or even individual Indians from the federal government. In fact, "the Constitution itself is the greatest barrier Indians have faced in attempting to deal with the United States"[6] because of the division of sovereignty inherent in the federal system of government, which is further complicated by the checks and balances and separation of powers theories. In other words, no individual branch of either the state or federal government actually represents the "whole functioning of that political entity unless the two remaining branches refuse to become involved in the issue under consideration."[7]

Thus, when Madison proposed in *The Federalist*, No. 42, that the clause regarding the regulation of commerce with Indian tribes outlined in the Articles of Confederation was "obscure and contradictory," he set the stage for the federalization and congressionalization of Indian affairs. Madison argued that the clause needed correction because, while it authorized federal control of Indian affairs, it did so only so long as that control did not interfere with each individual state's freedom to legislate in its own affairs with tribes. The U.S. administration of its affairs with tribes now was to be the exclusive province of the Congress. Initially, Congress's principal responsibility was in the carrying out of the obligations and the execution of the powers outlined in the presidentially executed treaties. Many of these obligations were articulated in statutes "relating to or supplementing treaties"[8] and included the obligations "to secure them in the title and possession of their lands, [and] in the exercise of self-government, and to defend them from domestic strife and foreign enemies."[9]

The second principle of congressional power is in the regulation of commerce with Indian tribes. This, we have already noted, is the only explicit grant of power to the government mentioned in the Constitution. The questions of what constitutes "commerce," and what are the jurisdictional boundaries of such trade, if any exist, have been hotly debated over time. A quick review of the legislation enacted and policies pronounced by Congress from 1789 to 1834 reveals, as Francis Paul Prucha has shown, that the federal government needed to control and police its own citizens in their intercourse with Indian tribes. These policies dealt primarily with establishing trading houses or factories, with issuing licenses for the Indian trade, and with fulfilling specific treaty provisions that spoke to the question of commerce.[10]

There was, in fact, no federal effort to regulate Indians or tribes per se. Gradually, however, Congress, reflecting the general sentiment of many high-level policymakers and Christian missionaries, began to unilaterally introduce laws designed to assimilate individual Indians into the American polity[11] and introduce Western criminal law proceedings against interracial crimes involving Indians.[12] These early laws were ad hoc precursors to much more systematic and sophisticated eras of federal Indian policy: first, from 1871, when treaty making was unilaterally ended, to the period just before the Indian Reorganization Act of 1934; and second, from the end of World War II through the termination/relocation period of the 1950s and 1960s, when Congress enacted a litany of laws and policies aimed at the ultimate destruction of tribalism.

Conversely, the Indian Reorganization period (1934 to the early 1940s) and the Indian self-determination and self-governance era (1970 to present) entailed a measured congressional effort to show respect for the sovereignty of tribal nations by occasionally restoring some tribal lands, sometimes enforcing vested tribal treaty rights, providing more protection of Indian religious rights, and periodically reaffirming tribal governing authority.

Congress has certainly not operated alone[13] in administering the federal government's affairs with tribes; nevertheless, it remains the focal point of much scrutiny because of constitutional requirements and because tribes are keenly aware that it is to the political branches of the federal government that they must look for proper enforcement of their vested extraconstitutional, treaty-based (tribal) or constitutionally defined, citizenship-based (individual Indian) rights.

Congressional Committees and Indian Affairs: 1820–1977

Congressional committees are at the heart of federal-level governance. Committees, the subdivisions of legislatures, prepare legislation for action by the respective houses and also may conduct investigations. Most standing (full) committees are divided into subcommittees, which study legislation, hold hearings, and report their recommendations to the full committees. However, only the full committee can report legislation for action by the entire legislature.[14] First, a review of the historical process is in order.

During the first several decades of federal administration of Indian affairs—Indian-related matters involving war, trade, treaties, and boundaries, and general Indian-white intercourse—were handled either by the entire Senate or House, by select committees, or by other committees. It was not until 1820 that the Senate first established a Standing Committee on Indian Affairs.[15] This was followed the next year by similar action in the House of Representatives.

Throughout the remainder of the nineteenth century and through the twentieth century there were numerous other standing committees in the Senate, and various select and joint committees in both Houses, that exercised jurisdiction over Indian issues. Table 4.1 charts all the committees that have had a direct role in Indian affairs. Although Indian affairs are the purported exclusive domain of Congress because of the constitutional allocation of authority to this body, in reality the executive branch (via

Table 4.1.

U.S. Congressional Committees Having Jurisdiction over Indian Affairs, 1820–2010

Year(s)	Senate	House
1820	Standing Committee on Indian Affairs.	
1821		Standing Committee on Indian Affairs.
1838		Select Committee on Indian Fighters.
1878	Joint Committee on Transfer of the Indian Bureau.	
1879-1880	Select committee to Examine into Removal of Northern Cheyennes.	
1881	Select Committee to Examine into Circumstances Connected with Removal of Northern Cheyennes from the Sioux Reservation to the Indian Territory.	
1836-1892	Select Committee on Indian Traders.	Select Committee on Expenditures for the Indians and Yellowstone Park.
1888-1892	Select Committee on Indian Traders. Select Committee on the Five Civilized Tribes.	Select Committee on Indian Depredation Claims (1888-1891).

Year(s)	Senate	House
1893–1908	Select Committee to Investigate Trespassers on Indian [Cherokee] Lands. Select Committee on the Five Civilized Tribes. Standing Committee on Indian Depredations.	
1909–1920	Standing Committee on Indian Depredations. Standing Committee on the Five Civilized Tribes. Standing Committee to Investigate Trespassers on Indian Lands.	
1921	Committee on Indian Affairs (all existing Standing Senate Committees were Consolidated in this Committeee).	
1947	Public Lands Committee (subsumes Committee on Indian Affairs and Four Others).	Public Lands Committee (subsumes Committee on Indian Affairs).
1948	Interior and Insular Affairs (subsumes Public Lands Committee and Indian Affairs).	
1951		Committee on Interior and Insular Affairs (subsumes Public Lands Committee).
1951	Joint Committee on Navajo-Hopi Administration (64 St. 44). This committee abolished by the Navajo-Hopi Settlement Act of 1974 (88 St. 1712).	
1975		Committee on Education and Labor (give jurisdiction over Indian Education).
1977	Select Committee on Indian Affairs (temporary Two-year Status). Committee on Interior and Insular Affairs Abolished.	Subcommittee on Indian Affairs and Public Lands (within the Committee on Interior and Insular Affairs).
1978	Select Committee on Indian Affairs (granted Two-Year Extension).	
1979		Subcommittee on Indian Affairs Established (jurisdiction vested in entire committee). [Note: This was the first time since 1920 that a body of Congress Had Neither a Committee nor a Subcommittee on Indian Affairs.]
1980	Select Committee on Indian Affairs (granted Three-year Extension).	
1984	Select Committee on Indian Affairs (becomes Permanent Committee).	
1993	Select Committee Redesignated as Committee on Indian Affairs.	Subcommittee on Native American Affairs (within the newly formed Committee on Resources).
Present	Committee on Indian Affairs, 15 members	Subcommittee on Native American Affairs ended on 105th Congress. Committee on Resources as a whole exercises jurisdiction over Indian affairs, land, and claims.

Source: Updated from Richard S. Jones, "America Indian Policy: Background, Nature, History, Current Issues, Future Trends." *Congressional Research Service Report 87-227* GOV (Washington, D.C.: Government Printing Office, 1987): 80.

the treaty-making authority) and the judicial branch (via the Supreme Court's development of numerous legal doctrines) were the coordinate powers during the first three quarters of the nineteenth century that articulated tribal political status, tribal property rights vis-à-vis the federal government, and the federal and state positions in relation to tribes. Notwithstanding the fact that both houses of Congress had full standing committees by the early 1820s, the legislature "paid little attention to its role as the architect of Indian fortunes apart from providing legislative confirmation of presidential policies such as forced removal."[16]

This legislative acquiescence, however, began to change slowly by the mid-nineteenth century, when Congress began to authorize federal commissions to treat with the western tribes. Over the next two decades, congressional power to define Indian policy waxed, while the president's role as chief treaty negotiator was reduced from that of a "negotiator of treaties to an administrator of domestic disputes."[17]

The zenith of legislative power over Indian affairs was reached in 1871 when, after several years of internal conflict over which house would control Indian policy, the House Committee on Indian Affairs attached an amendment to the Department of the Interior's appropriations bill that declared that the United States would no longer recognize tribes as sovereigns capable of making treaties with the United States.[18] The ramifications of this rider and its effect on tribal political status and the tribal-federal relationship have been widely debated by federal policymakers and scholars. Preexisting ratified treaties remained in force, and Congress continued until 1914 to negotiate "agreements" with tribes that Cohen says "differed from formal treaties only in that they were ratified by both houses of Congress instead of by the Senate alone."[19] Still, the relationship between native nations and the federal government had been fundamentally affected. "Indians as a subject of congressional debate were moved from the national agenda to an item on a committee agenda, and they were never again seen as having an important claim on the national government."[20]

In subsequent years, federal Indian affairs and indigenous political status have been dominated by the confluence of actions by the Supreme Court (which has been extremely deferential to congressional enactments, never having invalidated a single Indian-related law as being beyond Congress's authority), congressional committees, the states, and the BIA (which has been delegated much of its authority by Congress, but which has also, by a process of "jurisdictional aggrandizement," empowered itself to act sometimes in ways destructive of tribal interests but usually as a paternalizing influence that refuses to allow tribes to act on their own behalf). Tribes are not an inherent part of this system. They interact with and lobby each of these government players but lack significant power to force compromises.[21]

The confluence is far from smooth or consistent, and sometimes the converging influences crosscut one another in vicious and unpredictable ways. For instance, at various times state interests have had a dominating influence, at other times the federal bureaucracy has stifled tribal efforts at self-government, and at still others, like the present, the Supreme Court has functioned in a way that directly clashes with congressional policy that is more favorable to tribal self-determination and self-governance.

The roles of Congress and the various committees and subcommittees addressing Indian affairs have been equally as sporadic, haphazard, and conflicting—vacillating between policies designed to assimilate Indian tribes, policies created to perpetuate tribal dependency and wardship, and policies centered on enhancing tribal autonomy.

Both because of their parallel sovereignty (Indians tend to serve in their own legislatures) and because of their lack of numbers (and therefore lack of political clout), very few American Indians have been elected to the U.S. Congress. Table 4.2 lists those who have and are continuing to serve. However, Congress alone has ultimate responsibility for federal Indian policy, and under the Constitution it has plenary (read "exclusive" and "preemptive") power to act.

As a result of the Legislative Reorganization Act of 1946,[22] the Indian Affairs Committees in both houses were reduced in status to minor subcommittees. This was the state of things from 1947 until 1977. On the Senate side, a subcommittee existed under the auspices of the Committee on Interior and Insular Affairs. On the House side, Indian issues were subsumed by a subcommittee under the Public Lands Committee, which in 1951 became the Committee on Interior and Insular Affairs.[23] During this thirty-year period, this subcommittee arrangement "failed to provide a truly adequate forum for legislating appropriate solutions to problems affecting Indian people. Indian legislation could no longer be reported to the floor of the Senate directly from a full Indian Affairs Committee, and legislative jurisdiction over Indian affairs was fragmented in a number of committees."[24]

Table 4.2
American Indians Who Have Served in the U.S. Senate and House of Representatives

	Tribe	State	Service Years
SENATE			
Matthew Stanley Quay	Abenaki or Delaware	Pennsylvania	1887-1899, 1901-1904
Charles Curtis*	Kaw-Osage	Kansas	1907-1913, 1915-1929
Robert I. Owen	Cherokee	Oklahoma	1907-1925
Ben Nighthorse Campbell	Northern Cheyenne	Colorado	1992-2004
HOUSE OF REPRESENTATIVES			
Charles Curtis	Kaw-Osage	Kansas	1893-1907
Charles D. Carter	Choctaw	Oklahoma	1907-1927
W.W. Hastings	Cherokee	Oklahoma	1915-1921, 1923-1935
William G. Stigler	Choctaw	Oklahoma	1944-1952
Benjamin Reifel	Rosebud Sioux	South Dakota	1961-1971
Ben Nighthorse Campbell	Northern Cheyenne	Colorado	1987-1992
Brad Cannon	Cherokee	Oklahoma	2000-2004
Tom Cole	Chickasaw	Oklahoma	2002-

*Curtis served as Herbert Hoover's vice president from 1929-1933 and president of the Senate during that time.
Source: From Paula D. McClain and Joseph Stewart Jr., *"Can We All Get Along?" Racial and Ethnic Minorities in American Politics*, 5th ed. (Boulder, Colorado: Westview Press, 2010). Reprinted by permission of Westview Press, a member of the Perseus Book Group. Drawn from a table developed by Gerald Wilkinson, National Indian Youth Council, and provided to McClain and Stewart by the office of Senator Ben Nighthorse Campbell, and data from the Congressional Research Service. The Congressional Research Service indicates that the American Indian background of Quay has not been verified.

The activism and political and social disquiet of the 1960s and 1970s—fueled by the civil rights movement; the Vietnam War; Watergate; and a number of disturbing events in Indian Country centered around the aftermath of termination policy, BIA incompetence and mismanagement of tribal and individual trust property, and tribal reassertion of once-dormant cultural and political attributes—convinced the Johnson and Nixon administrations of the need for a new policy: a policy of Indian self-determination.

This change in executive policy was followed closely by Congress's establishment of a bipartisan committee charged with the responsibility "to conduct a comprehensive review of the historical and legal developments underlying the Indians' relationship with the Federal Government and to determine the nature and scope of necessary revisions in the formulation of policy and programs for the benefit of Indians."[25] This two-year congressional investigation, led by Senator James Abourezk (D-SD), culminated in 206 policy recommendations in areas as diverse as trust responsibility, tribal government, federal administration of Indian policy, economic development, community services, off-reservation Indians, and terminated and nonreservation Indians.

With regard to government actors in Indian affairs, recommendation 77 under the category "Federal Administration of Indian Affairs" was the most important. It reads: "Congress [should] establish permanent standing or special select committees for Indian affairs in each House or place all jurisdiction, oversight, and legislative authority in a joint select committee."[26] In providing a detailed rationale for why the establishment of permanent committees on Indian affairs in both houses was essential, the American Indian Policy Review Commission gave several reasons. First, congressional plenary (read "exclusive") authority in the administration of the federal government's legal obligations to tribes was constitutionally well established.

Second, the distinguished status of native nations as the only groups specifically identified in the Constitution as separate polities with whom Congress was charged to regulate trade clearly evidenced their separate political status. Congress was the most essential actor on the federal side of the tribal-federal relationship because it ratified the legally binding treaties and agreements and had enacted subsequent policies and laws regarding native nations and indigenous citizens. Congress had a clear responsibility for maintaining the treaties, policies, and laws it had participated in or created. While the United States acknowledged that Indians and tribal-related issues no longer warranted the nation's full-fledged attention that they occupied during the first century and a quarter of its existence, the nation's political and legal obligations—both reciprocal and unilateral—to the tribes and their members remained intact.

Third, the commission noted that when the standing Indian committees were terminated in the 1946 congressional reorganization, the subsequent merger of the subcommittees into the Interior Committees caused tremendous conflicts of interest, with tribes and individual Indians often in direct competition with powerful governmental and nongovernmental organizations and monied interests like the Army Corps of Engineers, mining companies, and recreation and fish and wildlife interests.[27]

Finally, the bipartisan committee acknowledged that the complexity of federal Indian law and the unique issues confronting Indian people necessitated a permanent standing committee on Indian affairs.[28] Some of the complexities mentioned included the resolution of eastern Indian land claims cases against the state and federal governments; a review, consolidation, and codification of Title 25 of the U.S. Code; and most important, the tedious and ongoing oversight responsibilities the Congress possessed in relation to the tribes.

The Senate, under S.J. Resolution 4 earlier in the 95th Congress (February 4, 1977), had created a temporary Select Committee on Indian Affairs (select committees are created for specific purposes and are to be disbanded once those purposes have been fulfilled) with full jurisdiction over all proposed legislation and other matters relating to Indian affairs. This committee was to be abolished at the start of the 96th Congress, with jurisdiction over Indian matters going to the Human Resources Committee.

It became increasingly evident that if Congress was to keep pace with its constitutional, legal, moral, and historical responsibilities to tribes and Indian people, an ongoing permanent or standing committee with sufficient expertise and resources needed to be established. Hence, the Senate Select Committee was reauthorized several times, until it was made a permanent, though still "select," committee in 1984.[29]

The life, therefore, of the Senate Select Committee on Indian Affairs extended a full sixteen years: February 4, 1977, to February 24, 1993. And despite the sound reasons given by the American Indian Policy Review Commission for establishing permanent standing committees for Indian affairs, the committee remained "select" for this entire time. Moreover, on the House side, Indian affairs in 1977 were vested in a newly created Subcommittee on Indian Affairs and Public Lands within the Committee on Interior and Insular Affairs. But in 1979, the subcommittee was abolished and jurisdiction was vested in the full committee. This represented the first time since the early nineteenth century that neither the House nor the Senate had any committees or subcommittees devoted to Indian Affairs.[30]

This changed, however, in January 1993, when a Subcommittee on Native American and Insular Affairs, chaired by Rep. Bill Richardson (D-NM) was formed under the newly created Committee on Natural Resources.[31] However, by 1999, the Committee on Resources, as it was now called, had dropped the subcommittee on Native American affairs. The committee as a whole now exercises jurisdiction over federal relations with Indian nations although the Office of Native American and Insular Affairs continues to function. During the 105th Congress, Representatives J. D. Hayworth (R-AZ) and Dale Kildee (D-MI) established, and served as co-chairs of, the Congressional Native American Caucus, a thirty-nine-member nonpartisan organization. The Caucus was created to educate congressional members about the unique sovereign and treaty rights of tribes in the wake of the budget cuts affecting tribes and passed during the 104th Congress.[32] It now has over one hundred active members.

Senate Select Committee: The Legislative Record—1977 to 1992

The February 4, 1977, Senate Resolution 4, which contained the committee-system reorganization amendments, charged the select committee as follows:

> It shall be the duty of the Select Committee to conduct a study of any and all matters pertaining to problems and opportunities of Indians, including but not limited to, Indian land management and trust responsibilities, Indian education, health, special services, and loan programs, and Indian claims against the United States.[33]

The existence of the "select" committee spanned eight congresses—the 95th Congress (1977–1979) to the 102nd Congress (1991–1993), after which it was redesignated as the Committee on Indian Affairs CIA.

Although the focus of this section of the chapter is on the historical evolution of Congress's Indian committees, in particular the Senate select committee's legislative activity, and not the motives or goals of individual senators, it is appropriate to note in passing that the membership has been predominantly from western states. This is understandable considering that the majority of reservations and Indians in general live in states west of the Mississippi. More research is necessary to determine the motives of western, and the handful of eastern, senators who joined the committee. Using Vogler's approach we would try to ascertain whether the senators see the select committee as a power committee, a policy committee, or a constituency committee,[34] or whether because of the unique nature of tribes and their members, senators served on the committee for reasons that do not fit the standard goals posited by the literature.

In terms of the states, North Dakota, South Dakota, Montana, Arizona, Washington, Oregon, Alaska, Nevada, Hawaii, New Mexico, and Colorado have each had representation. The only nonwestern states with representation were Ohio (Howard Metzenbaum in the 95th Congress), Maine (William S. Cohen in the 96th and 97th Congresses), Mississippi (Thad Cochran in the 101st and 102nd Congresses), Minnesota (Paul Wellstone in the 102nd Congress), and Illinois (Paul Simon in the 102nd Congress). It appears that partisanship has historically had little significance in the way senators vote on Indian bills.[35] Votes on controversial bills tend to follow regional rather than party lines.

Not surprisingly, each of the chairs of the committee was from a western state, with the single exception of William S. Cohen. Cohen, it is important to note, assumed the chairmanship of the committee during the height of eastern Indian land claims, when a number of tribes, beginning with the two in Cohen's own state—the Penobscot and the Passamaquoddy—successfully argued that huge chunks of their aboriginal lands had been taken away from them illegally by states without federal approval.

The Maine case was the leading and potentially most disruptive of these land claims. Confronted with a series of federal suits against individuals and companies with large land holdings, Maine reluctantly agreed to an out-of-court negotiated settlement, with the federal government picking up the bulk of the bill. The Maine Indian Claims Settlement Act of October 10, 1980,[36] saw the Penobscot and Passamaquoddy tribes secure a $27 million federal trust fund and three hundred thousand acres of forest land purchased with federal dollars. By the time this conflict was legislatively resolved, fourteen other tribes had filed suits against the states and federal government.[37] Considering the importance of the Maine claims, Cohen's tenure as chair is less puzzling.

The Committee on Indian Affairs is the authorizing committee for programs of the BIA in the Department of the Interior, the Indian Health Service and the Administration for Native Americans in the Department of Health and Human Services, and the Office of Indian Education in the Department of Education. Furthermore, the committee has oversight responsibility for programs affecting Indians in all other federal agencies, including the Indian Housing program of the Department of Housing and Urban Development.

These responsibilities dovetail with those specified in Senate Resolution 4, which include matters relating to tribal and individual lands; the federal government's trust responsibilities; and Indian education, health, Indian land claims, and natural resources. In effect, this committee (like the subcommittee in the House) is charged with an enormous task: the oversight of Congress's continuing historical, constitutional, and legislative responsibilities to 565 distinctive indigenous entities. The committee's responsibilities are therefore extremely broad, "literally spanning the breadth of federal, state, and local government responsibilities, but with the additional responsibility for the protection and management of Indian trust resources for which the U.S. has a trust responsibility."[38]

It should come as no surprise, therefore, to learn that the committee has had an exceptionally active agenda. Senator Daniel Inouye (D-HI) has stated that this committee turns out more bills, and has more bills approved, than any other Senate committee. The select committee examined a plethora of issues, including land-related topics, health concerns, housing, education, economic development, water claims, land claims, trust funds, gaming, recognition, natural resource and environmental concerns, religious freedom, the committee administrative tasks, Alaska Natives, Indian child welfare, and tribal-state relations. Some of the hearings and reports combined more than one issue (e.g., tribal courts and civil rights).

Also unsurprising is that the top tier of broad issue categories listed here encompasses the major themes distinguishing the tribal-federal relationship: the perpetuation of tribal sovereignty and the unique rights generated from this doctrine, treaty-derived rights, and the trust relationship as defined by the federal government. The issues producing the most documentation were land claims, health, education, and environment and natural resources. The grouping "committee," given previously, represents production of documents pertaining to the select committee's own activities: legislative summaries of the activities during the previous Congress, reports on the committee's budget, and transcripts of hearings on the nomination and confirmation of various administrative personnel (the assistant secretary of the interior, National Gaming Commission members, and members of various special committees).

The importance of two other categories, recognition, acknowledgment, and restoration (RAR) and water rights, is self-evident. RAR is a fairly contemporary category. It has generated much legislative activity, largely because of two developments: (1) efforts to restore tribes, bands, and *rancherias* that had been terminated by the federal government in the 1950s and 1960s and (2) the BIA's establishment in 1978 of regulations and criteria to establish or deny "that an American Indian group exists as an Indian tribe."

Water rights, by contrast, is a complex issue that has been on the congressional Indian affairs agenda for well over a century. Beginning in 1867,[39] the federal government enacted laws for the construction of canals for irrigating Indian land as part of the larger plan to "civilize" Indians by forcing them into agricultural pursuits. The *Winters v. United States* decision of 1908 held that, where land in territorial status was reserved by treaty to an Indian tribe, there was an implied reservation of water to the tribe. This reserved water right was to be protected by the federal government and, legally, neither the states nor the federal government could act to reduce the amount of water inside a reservation below the amount necessary for irrigating the Indian lands.

The subsequent history of Indian water rights, however, indicates that the tribes' well-established legal (paper) right to water has often not translated to an appropriation or protection of the actual (wet) water that they are legally entitled to. As Lloyd Burton notes, "It is nevertheless possible to characterize the last two centuries as a period during which State governments and some federal elected officials generally did what they could to divest indigenous people of their natural resource heritage, while (until quite recently) federal judges generally did what they could to preserve that heritage for the tribes' use and enjoyment."[40]

Burton's parenthetical statement, "until quite recently," is important because, as he shows later in his study, since 1970 the Supreme Court has become an inhospitable arena for tribes seeking to have their water rights protected. In that time, tribes have lost over 90 percent of the water-related cases that have gone before the Supreme Court—generally on jurisdictional grounds.[41] These judicial losses have compelled a number of tribes to seek, as Daniel McCool has shown, negotiated legislative solutions with states to solve their water rights problems.[42] For example, the Zuni Indian Tribe Water Rights Settlement Agreement and the Shivwits Band of Paiute Indians Water Rights Settlement Act were both enacted by Congress in 2003.

At the low end of the committee's activity scale, we saw that a number of important topics generated little legislative attention. Categories with three or fewer hearings, reports, or publications included mental health, allotment, aging, civil rights and Constitution, reburial and repatriation, the National Indian Policy Research Institute, self-determination and self-governance, impact aid, Indian veterans, eastern Indians, emergency assistance, and California Indians.

Mental health, for example, is a major issue, since Indians suffer from a higher rate of mental illness than most other racial and ethnic groups. However, contrary to popular opinion, there is virtually no evidence to support a genetic predisposition to such illness. Instead, most forms of mental illness among Indians, evidenced by the high suicide, alcoholism, and violence rates, appear to correlate with the effects of the colonial legacy and poverty that burden most Indians. The stress associated with these realities often results in hopelessness, depression, and family dissolution.[43]

Reburial and repatriation of Indian remains, grave items, and cultural artifacts has been one of the thorniest issues confronting tribes in their efforts to regain control over their identity. While most Americans can rest assured that disinterment of their dead is strongly disfavored, Indian peoples historically, and to some extent today, have little such assurance. As Jack F. Trope and Walter Echo-Hawk point out, "national estimates are that between 100,000 and 2 million deceased native people have been dug up from their graves for storage or display by government agencies, museums, universities and tourist attractions."[44]

Indian anger and lobbying eventually culminated in Congress's passage of Public Law 101-601, the Native American Graves Protection and Repatriation Act (NAGPRA) of 1990, which finally recognized the rights of Indians to their ancestors' remains and to cultural items by providing for the return of such remains, funerary objects, sacred objects, and cultural patrimony to the living descendants. Despite indigenous objections, archaeologists and anthropologists continue to claim they have the right to examine these human remains and cultural items. Their response is indicative of the significant tensions that remain over this issue.

Committee on Indian Affairs and Indians: 1993 to Present

When Republicans, led by Newt Gingrich of Georgia, took control of the House of Representatives in 1995, it was the first time they controlled both houses of Congress since

Photo 4.1
Nine-year-old Inyan Barta holds a sign calling for the reburial of his ancestors' remains outside the capital in Lincoln, Nebraska, on August 31, 1998. Protestors marched from the state capitol to the University of Nebraska campus to demand the proper treatment and the return of American Indian remains discovered there. Some estimates show that up to two million deceased native people have been disinterred without tribal consent for storage, display, and research.
Source: AP/WIDE WORLD PHOTOS

1953–1955. Basking in their "political revolution," Republicans believed they were in a position to force action on a number of issues considered staples of the conservative agenda: economic deregulation, reduced taxes, return of prayer in public schools, and limits on abortion.

Native nations, of course, pondered where they fit in the Republican "Contract with America." They were wary, because they remembered that it was during the last Congress in which the Republicans held legislative power, 1953–1955, that tribes endured the beginning of the termination policy. In that two-year period, the government, anxious to assimilate Indians in the cost-cutting and culturally homogenizing postwar years, and equally anxious to free up Indian lands and resources for economic exploitation, used their political power under the Eisenhower administration to begin the implementation of the political and legal termination of tribes, to initiate the relocation program that sent Indians from reservations to urban areas, and to create Public Law 280, which extended state criminal and some civil jurisdiction over Indians, without tribal consent, in five states and gave all other states the option of gaining such jurisdictional power. It is important to note, however, that both termination and Public Law 280 were first discussed while the Democrats still controlled both houses and the presidency.

The GOP's "100-day" legislative surge of activity in 1995 centered on the G.I. Bill for America's Workers; measures regarding welfare reform; and bills promising to repeal or at least pare down the Food Stamp Act, the Commodity Food Distribution program, the School Lunch program, and regulatory reform, to name but a few. While none of these measures focused directly on Indians, they were still viewed with trepidation because items like the Food Stamp bill would have affected at least 50 percent of the Indian population. Indians, as American citizens, are disproportionately poor and dependent on a number of the federal government's antipoverty programs that were slated for termination, downsizing, or block grants to states.[45]

Tribal governments, as sovereigns, were more nervous about the Congress's plans that would adversely affect their sovereignty by reducing their inherent powers or by cutting federal expenditures, goods, and services they receive based on treaties or agreements, and on the trust doctrine, or as service providers for citizens who dwell in impoverished communities. Bills to terminate tribal sovereign immunity; to tax Indian gaming proceeds; to cut or drastically reduce badly needed public housing funding, monies for youth summer jobs, and funding for adult education and job-training programs; and to reduce tribal court funding and Indian business development grants were quickly drafted and began to wind their way through the legislative process.

Senator Slade Gorton (R-WA) was a leader in the anti-Indian forces, until he was defeated in his bid for reelection in December 2000, in part because of the organized and well-funded campaign of a number of Indians and tribal organizations.[46] From his early years as Washington State's attorney general (1965–1980), when the state brought a number of lawsuits against the tribes challenging their treaty right to fish, Gorton has fought Indians on a number of fronts. When he was reelected to the Senate in 1994, Gorton gained membership on several key committees from which he continued to challenge Indian rights—Appropriations, Budget, Energy and Natural Resources, and most importantly, Indian Affairs. During the 104th Congress, he also became chairman of the Interior appropriations subcommittee, which controls matters as diverse as parks and funding for the National Endowment for the Arts. This chairmanship provided Senator Gorton with significant power to make deals, thus making it difficult to defeat his proposals.[47]

It was from this position that Gorton began his most persistent and powerful assault on tribal rights. In 1995 he attempted through an amendment attached as a legislative rider (a dubious way to make public policy, since there is little or no debate and since the rider provision often bears little relation to the subject of the bill it is "riding" on) to the Department of the Interior's appropriations bill, H.R. 1977, to take away self-governance funds for the tribes and to punish tribes for filing lawsuits with which non-Indian reservation residents might disagree.

A year later, Gorton focused his attack on tribal sovereign immunity. As sovereign entities, tribal governments, like the states and the federal government, are immune from lawsuits unless they expressly consent to be sued. This is one of the inherent powers of any sovereign. Tribal sovereign immunity defenses, however, are not a shield against suit by the United States, and it was this vulnerability that encouraged Gorton to focus his attack on tribes. Once again he used the approach of attaching a rider to the Interior's appropriations bill, for fiscal year 1997, as his mechanism. Section 329 of his proposal reads as follows:

> In cases in which the actions or proposed actions of an Indian tribe or its agents impact, or threaten to impact, the ownership or use of the private property of another person or entity, including access to such property that might arise from such impacts or which impact the receipt of water, electricity, or other utility to such property, an Indian tribe receiving funds under this Act or tribal official of such tribe, acting in an official capacity, shall—No. 1 not be subject to the jurisdiction, orders, and decrees of the appropriate State court of general jurisdiction or Federal district courts for requests of injunctive relief, damages or other appropriate remedies; and No. 2, shall be deemed to have waived any sovereign immunity as a defense to such court's jurisdiction, orders and decrees.[48]

Another provision Gorton introduced, known as *means-testing*, was equally problematic for tribes. It would have denied federal money to tribes if their incomes were above a certain level and would have forced tribes to report their income in order to receive government benefits. When the bill was brought before the full Senate Appropriations Committee, Gorton agreed to an amendment to delete the two provisions from the bill so that the CIA could conduct a hearing on the issue.

The CIA held a hearing on tribal sovereign immunity in September 1996 in Washington, D.C. But this did not mollify Gorton, and in July 1997 he renewed his efforts via appropriations riders to strip away tribes' legal immunity from suit and to force tribal nations to report their income.[49] However, under intense lobbying from tribes, and because of the efforts of lawmakers like Senators John McCain (R-AZ), Daniel Inouye (D-HI), and Ben Nighthorse Campbell (R-CO), Gorton again agreed to drop his effort in exchange for the Senate's promise to hold additional hearings on the immunity question and to schedule a vote by the early summer of 1998. The hearings were held as planned, but Gorton did not relent in his attack on Indian rights, continuing to introduce legislation that would negatively impact tribal sovereignty, until he was voted out of office in 2000 in the closest Senate race of the year.

Fortunately for the tribes, most of the potentially disastrous funding cuts were either defeated or scaled back considerably due to the power and influence of two prominent and influential senators who also happened to be the chair and vice-chair of the CIA—John McCain and Daniel Inouye at the time—and the work of the then lone Indian congressman, Senator Ben Nighthorse Campbell, who also served on the CIA, first as a member and then as the chairman until he left office in 2004. These three senators throughout their careers have maintained that the federal government is legally and morally obligated to protect tribal sovereignty, natural resources, and funding entitlements. As Inouye noted in January 1999, the beginning of his twenty-first year as a CIA member,

> [T]oo few Americans know that the Indian nations ceded millions of acres of lands to the United States or that while the terms of the treaties naturally varied, the promises and commitments made by the United States were typically made in perpetuity. History has recorded, however, that our great nation did not keep its word to the Indian nations, and our preeminent challenge today as lawmakers is

to assure the integrity of our treaty commitments and to bring an end to the era of broken promises.[50]

In recent years, the Senate Indian Affairs Committee has remained committed to tribal trust reform and has paid needed attention to youth suicides, violence against American Indian women, economic development, Indian health care reform, tribal public safety and justice, the federal acknowledgment process, and the Native Hawaiian Government Reorganization bill. The Senate Committee on Indian Affairs, currently led by Chairman Byron Dorgan (D-ND) and Vice-Chair John Barrasso (R-WY), held a 2009 Senate Tribal Leaders Summit in which 224 tribal leaders took part to discuss some of these areas of concern. Summarizing many of the key issues addressed by tribal leaders in their recommendations for American Indian program funding, Dorgan and Barrasso noted "the economic conditions that our nation has been recently experiencing are both long-standing and magnified when it comes to our Native American communities." Finding that many native peoples continue to face inadequate access to health care, law enforcement services, economic opportunity, education, and housing, they made several recommendations.

First, the committee called for the strengthening of Indian health care. An issue of concern throughout the 110th and the 111th Congress, the Committee on Indian Affairs held hearings on the state of health care in Indian Country, finding that American Indians "have a 670% higher death rate from alcoholism, a 318% higher death rate from diabetes, and a 650% higher death rate from tuberculosis than the general population."[51] To address and eliminate deficiencies in the health status and resources of Indian tribes, President Obama first provided provisions in the American Recovery and Reinvestment Act of 2009 (ARRA) to maintain current facilities, build new facilities, and increase provision of medical equipment and health information technology. With strong support from several members of Congress, such as House Speaker Nancy Pelosi and Senator Dorgan, Obama made permanent the Indian Health Care Improvement Act (IHCIA), the legislative authority for the provision of health care to American Indians and Alaska Natives, in late March 2010.[52] Originally enacted in 1976, the IHCIA authorization for appropriations had expired in 2000. This legislation outlines many improvements for Indian Health Services (IHS), which provides services to 1.9 million of the estimated 3.3 million American Indian and Alaska Natives in the United States.

The second recommendation issued by the CIA was for the improvement of public safety on Indian lands. The United States has a distinct legal obligation, outlined in treaties and congressional legislation, to provide public safety in Indian Country. During the 110th Congress, the CIA held eight hearings to examine violent crime in Indian Country, which revealed that the primary cause of these severe and long-standing problems stemmed from "(1) a divided system of justice that limits local tribal control to combat reservation crime, and forces dependence on federal officials to investigate and prosecute crime in federal court rooms that are often hundreds of miles from the reservations; and (2) an across the board historical lack of funding for federal and tribal justice systems responsible for Indian Country crimes." They further noted that:

> As a result of the lack of funding, rates for violent crime, domestic abuse, and sexual assault on Indian reservations remain significantly higher than the national average. A February 8, 2008 report, released by the Centers for Disease Control

(CDC), found that American Indian and Alaska Native women experience the highest rates of domestic violence in the United States. The survey found that two in five Native women (39%) will suffer intimate partner violence in their lifetime, compared with one in four (25%) women overall. . . . [M]ore than one in three Native women will be raped or sexually assaulted in their lifetimes.[53]

Congress included provisions in the Violence Against Women Reauthorization Act of 2005 to address the epidemic of violence that native women face. The CIA made recommendations to increase funding in this area as well as providing for the construction of jails, tribal law enforcement, tribal court assistance, and youth programs aimed at reducing gang activity and controlling crimes relating to the distribution and use of controlled substances. Yet, many of these conditions stem from a legacy of colonialism, discrimination, and poverty that often result in disproportionate rates of violence and crime. Programmatic funding is, of course, only the first step in restoring American Indian families.

The committee's third recommendation focused on strengthening tribal economies. Their findings revealed that despite recent improvements on some reservations and various policies to increase economic development, unemployment in Indian Country was still 49%, with some reservations exceeding 80%, indicating that many parts of Indian Country continue to be extremely impoverished. The CIA focused their recommendations on increasing energy development on Indian lands, increasing loan opportunities for tribal businesses, and Indian land consolidation. It concluded with recommendations to improve Indian education and housing. Native peoples continue to have the lowest levels of educational attainment in comparison with all other racial and ethnic groups in the United States. "The national graduation rate for American Indian high school students was 49.3% in the 2003–2004 school year, compared with 76.2% for white students. Further, only 13.3% of Native Americans have an undergraduate college degree, compared to the national average of 24.4%."[54] Housing statistics remain equally troubling. Facing some of the worst housing and living conditions in the United States, approximately 40% of reservation housing is characterized as inadequate, lacking heating and electrical equipment, compared with 5.9% of national households. As seen with health care, the ARRA included provisions to fund Indian housing, education, public safety and justice, BIA programs, and energy and water projects. However, the committee's members noted that these provisions alone will not sufficiently address and alleviate these major concerns across Indian country.

Besides the issues raised here, the committee also held hearings on both the Native Hawaiian Government Reorganization Act (the Akaka bill) as well as the effect of the U.S. Supreme Court ruling in *Carcieri v. Salazar*, which ruled that the secretary of the interior was not authorized to acquire lands in trust status for Indian tribes acknowledged by the federal government after 1934, and what actions might be required by Congress. As the committee seeks to carry out its enormous task of the oversight of Congress's continuing treaty and trust responsibilities to native nations, the coming years will prove equally active.

Congressional Recognition of Tribal Self-Determination

Under the U.S. Constitution, the Congress is charged under the commerce clause with regulating the nation's affairs with Indian tribes. Although the president had the authority to negotiate treaties, it fell to the Congress to appropriate the funds to fulfill the government's treaty obligations and to develop an appropriate legislative agenda to maintain amicable relations with tribes. It also is incumbent upon the Congress to fulfill the federal government's self-assumed trust obligations to tribes.

Since 1975 the Congress's Indian policy has been tribal self-determination, articulated in the Indian Self-Determination and Education Assistance Act of that year. Self-determination has evolved for some tribes into the congressionally enacted policy of Indian self-governance, institutionalized in 1994. Under the Self-Governance Act, tribes are able to negotiate directly with Congress as a compacting party. The compact of self-governance defines the government-to-government relationship between a given tribe and the federal government, and the roles and responsibilities of each government are outlined in the compact.

Although the federal government is still in the stronger position from a political standpoint, self-governance is an important step that recognizes the national capacity of tribes to negotiate and bargain on their own terms. The compacting process in a real sense is the modern-day equivalent of the historic treaty-making period, which technically ended in 1871.[55]

The Executive Branch and Tribal Nations

The President

Although the president has no express constitutional responsibility for Indian tribes, he does have the primary role in conducting the nation's foreign affairs. And because Indian nations were considered "foreign" in a political sense to the United States during much of the first century of the country's existence, the president's role in treaty making with Indian affairs was very important (see appendix A, "1778 Delaware-U.S. Treaty"). The president, either by himself or with instructions from the Congress, "nominates treaty commissioners, supervises the preparation of treaty provisions, and submits the treaty for senatorial advice and consent prior to ratifying the treaty."[56] However, when Congress unilaterally decided on March 3, 1871, that the United States would negotiate no more treaties with tribes, an act the president did not challenge, this signaled a dramatic reduction of the president's role in federal Indian policy. Besides being of questionable constitutional validity, since it was a direct assault on the separation of powers doctrine, the action represented a weakening in the perceived sovereignty of tribes even though treaties, thereafter named *agreements,* would continue to be negotiated with tribes until 1911.[57]

Along with this implied treaty power, Congress has, of necessity, also delegated much power in Indian affairs to administrative officials, including the president, the secretary of the interior, and the assistant secretary for Indian affairs (formerly the commissioner of Indian affairs). Administrative powers of the president include the consolidation of Indian agencies, the use of executive order to create reservations and enact other measures, the releasing of unnecessary or inattentive Indian agents, and the transference of agents from one reservation to another. Of these powers, the use of executive orders for, among other things, creating reservations is arguably the most important and has had the greatest impact on Indian nations.

Franklin Pierce, in May 1855, became the first president to establish an Indian reservation by executive order, when he set aside lands for the Ottawa and Chippewa of

Michigan. This practice continued until it was terminated by Congress in 1919 at the behest of white settlers and western state officials. Although the legal title of executive order reservations was debated for some years, it was one of the most important means many Indian tribes had of gaining some measure of recognized title. All of the twenty-one reservations in Arizona were created by executive order, except for the core part of the Navajo Reservation, which was established by treaty in 1868.

President Clinton, during his two terms, issued several executive orders affecting Indians on topics such as tribal colleges and universities, Indian sacred land sites, and distribution of eagle feathers for Indian religious purposes. President Bush, at the height of his campaign for reelection in September 2004, issued a memorandum in which he declared his administration's views on trust and tribal sovereignty in an attempt to downplay previous statements on the subject that had alarmed many indigenous leaders and organizations. And in November 2009 President Obama signed a presidential memorandum seeking to renew and enhance the spirit of tribal consultation and collaboration previously outlined by Clinton (see appendix D).

The executive branch, then, frequently provides the content of Indian programs and treaty rights, and the office of the president provides the symbolic and moral focus of Indian policy. This is evident in an excerpt of a speech delivered by several Seneca Indian leaders, Corn Planter, Half-Town, and others, to President George Washington in Philadelphia on December 1, 1790, in which the Indian leaders expressed their respect for Washington and their concerns over the federal government's lack of treaty enforcement:

> Father: The voice of the Seneca nation speaks to you, the great councillor, in whose heart the wise men of all the Thirteen Fires [the original colonies] have placed their wisdom. It may be very small in your ears, and we therefore entreat you to hearken with attention: for we are about to speak of things which are to us very great. When your army entered the country of the Six Nations, we called you the town destroyer; and to this day, when that name is heard, our women look behind them and turn pale, and our children cling close to the necks of their mothers. Our councillors and warriors are men, and cannot be afraid; but their hearts are grieved with the fears of our women and children, and desire it may be buried so deep as to be heard no more. . . .
>
> When you gave us peace, we called you father, because you promised to secure us in the possession of our lands. Do this, and, so long as the lands shall remain, that beloved name will live in the heart of every Seneca.[58]

Some presidents, like Andrew Jackson in the 1820s and 1830s, presided over major tribal land and sovereign rights losses because of the Indian removal he firmly supported. Other presidents, like Franklin D. Roosevelt and Richard Nixon, acted to protect and even enhance the rights of tribes by restoring lands, ending disastrous policies like allotment and termination, supporting policies like the Indian Reorganization Act of 1934, and, in Nixon's case, establishing the Indian self-determination policy in 1970.

The Reagan and Bush administrations represented a period of neofederalism (states reasserting rights with administrative and judicial acquiescence), a severe downsizing of the federal budget for social service programs aimed at assisting Indian tribes (and minority and poor people in general), and a federal Indian policy enunciated on

January 24, 1983 (reaffirmed by Bush on June 14, 1991), devoted to reducing tribal reliance on federal financial support and increasing tribal dependence on the private sector and individual entrepreneurship. Despite tribes' massive losses of federal revenue, tribal political status was somewhat emboldened, whether inadvertently or not, by Reagan and Bush's description of the "government-to-government" tribal-federal relationship and by the Congress's and the tribes' mutual call for a return to negotiated agreements.

President Bill Clinton, by contrast, used his executive order authority and the symbolic power of his office to establish relatively close ties with many tribal leaders. On April 29, 1994, Clinton met with 322 indigenous leaders on the White House lawn, after having extended an open invitation to the leaders of every recognized American Indian and Alaska Native group in the nation. This was deemed a historic meeting since it was the first time a president had requested a meeting with all indigenous leaders. Clinton, ever the diplomat, issued a directive saying his administration would treat the native leaders with the utmost respect:

> In every relationship between our people, our first principle must be to respect your right to remain who you are and to live the way you wish to live. And I believe the best way to do that is to acknowledge the unique government-to-government relationship we have enjoyed over time. Today I reaffirm our commitment to self-determination for tribal governments. I pledge to fulfill the trust obligations of the Federal Government. I vow to honor and respect tribal sovereignty based upon our unique historic relationship. And I pledge to continue my efforts to protect your right to fully exercise your faith as you wish.[59]

The moral power exercised here, which President Obama now subscribes to in relation to native peoples, along with the president's veto power and appointment authority—especially of Supreme Court justices, other federal judges, and cabinet officers—provides the president with a potent array of powers that can work both good and ill toward the sovereign rights of tribes. George W. Bush's deeply contested election in December 2000 had many tribes worried, since he stated during his campaign that he believed that states' rights were senior to tribal rights. While he later downplayed that remark and his staff distributed a statement that said that Bush "recognizes and reaffirms the unique government-to-government relationship between Native American tribes and the federal government," tribes remained concerned because of Bush's record of dealing with Texas's tribes, and because of various policy choices he made during both terms as governor. According to the U.S. Commission on Civil Rights, while Bush acknowledged the great debt the United States owes to indigenous peoples, his actions never reflected that admiration. In a report produced in 2004, the commission noted that "the President has not effectively used the stature of his office to speak out on ending discrimination against Native Americans. Nor has he engaged in a consistent effort to alleviate their problems. He has not applied resources to improving conditions or adequately funded programs that serve Native people."[60]

The commission staff gave the following specific examples of Bush's failures:

- Bush has not requested sufficient funding for tribal colleges and universities, has proposed terminating $1.5 billion in funding for education programs that benefit

Indian peoples, and has not provided adequate resources to meet No Child Left
Behind goals that apply to Indian Country.

· For 2004, the administration requested $3.6 billion for the Indian Health Service,
the primary provider for Indian people. This amount is far short of the $19.4 bil-
lion in unmet health needs in Native communities.

· The president's budget requests for housing programs have not approached the $1
billion that is required to meet the large demand. As a result, American Indians still
need an additional 210,000 housing units.

· In 2003, Bush ended funding for vital law enforcement programs, including the
Tribal Drug Court Program. Many experts agree that criminal justice problems in
Indian Country are of a profound nature and need much more attention.

More distressing to First Nations was Bush's response in August 2004 to a question
from journalist Mark Trahant (Shoshone/Bannock) at the Unity conference organized
by four journalists of color organizations, including the Native American Journalists Association. Trahant asked Bush what he thought tribal sovereignty meant in the
twenty-first century and how conflicts might be resolved between tribes, the federal
government, and states. Bush responded awkwardly, saying that "tribal sovereignty
means that, it's sovereign. You're a . . . you're a . . . you've been given sovereignty and
you're viewed as a sovereign entity."[61] Later in the interview he noted with more clarity
that "the relationship between the federal government and tribes is one between sovereign entities," but his prior comment about sovereignty having been "given" to tribal
nations caused a great stir in Indian Country.

In the fall of 2005, Bush's nomination and later renomination of John G. Roberts
Jr., first to be an associate justice when Justice Sandra Day O'Connor retired, and then
to be chief justice, replacing the deceased William Rehnquist, had tribal nations concerned, since several of his legal briefs written as a private lawyer strongly hint that
Judge Roberts favors state power over tribal sovereignty.[62] With Robert's confirmation
as chief justice, and Associate Justice Samuel Alito's later appointment, Bush effectively
placed a conservative ideological stamp to the Supreme Court.

President Barack Obama stopped the conservative slide when he nominated a Latina,
Sonia Sotomayor, in May 2009. Associate Justice John Paul Stevens's retirement in 2010 has
provided Obama with another opportunity to change the ideological complexion of the
court. In addition, Obama has sought to provide a stronger voice for American Indians
in his administration, appointing Larry EchoHawk (Pawnee) as the head of the Bureau of
Indian Affairs, Kimberly Teehee (Cherokee) as senior advisor for Indian issues, Wizipan
Garriot (Rosebud Sioux) to the newly-created position of First Americans Public Liaison,
Jodi Gillette (Standing Rock Sioux) as the deputy associate director for White House intergovernmental affairs, Mary Smith (Cherokee) as assistant attorney general for the Depart-
ment of Justice, Hilary Tompkins (Navajo Nation) as solicitor of the Department of the
Interior, and Yvette Robideaux (Rosebud Sioux) as the director of Indian Health Services.

The executive branch also influenced Indian tribal status in 1953, when it supported amendments to two laws that were known as the "federally impacted area" legislation (Public Law 874 and Public Law 815). The amendments brought Indians under
the law's provision by enabling the federal government to provide funds to school districts where there was a need for additional facilities due to Indian enrollment.[63] Indian
eligibility for such broad social programs rapidly expanded in the 1960s during the War

on Poverty and Great Society programs. But Indian eligibility to receive federal funding for such programs arrived not because of their sovereign political status as nations, but "because of their public nature and semi-corporate status established by the adoption of constitutions and by-laws under the Indian Reorganization Act."[64]

Even as tribes were being accorded a new status, as minority groups eligible for federal funding because of their poverty, in 1975 the Indian Self-Determination Act was passed, providing tribes, as governments, an opportunity through self-determination contracts to administer programs that had previously been run by the BIA. Tribes, in effect, were made a part of the executive branch insofar as these programs were conceived. The 1994 Tribal Self-Governance Act expanded this process while providing tribes with greater leeway in how they could use their funds.

The scope of federal executive power vis-à-vis tribes and individual Indians remains very broad; it generates problems in regard to tribal and individual Indian lands, tribal funds, and questions of tribal membership as well. In part this is because the BIA, an executive agency and still the primary representative of the federal government to Indian tribes, entails a synthesis of both the legislative and executive functions of the government.[65] As an administrative agency it exercises new powers, while historically the actions and decisions of administrative officers have been given great weight by federal courts, so that tribal challenges of such authority are often turned aside, leaving Indians little recourse.

The Secretary of the Interior and the Bureau of Indian Affairs

The Interior Department, created in 1849, was originally responsible for overseeing the westward migration of the American people and the distribution of public lands and resources. For much of its history it was a center of controversy over corruption and opportunism as well as the sometimes brutal control of indigenous peoples and the frequent mismanagement of their lands and natural resources.[66] But the secretary of the interior, who has been described as the "guardian of all Indian interests," acts on behalf of the president in administering federal Indian policy. In fact, the Supreme Court has held that the secretary's acts are "presumed" to be the acts of the president.[67]

Interior is home to a number of diverse and frequently competitive agencies: the Bureau of Land Management, the Fish and Wildlife Service, Minerals Management, the Bureau of Reclamation, the National Park Service, the Bureau of Mines, the U.S. Geological Survey, and, of course, the BIA. Theoretically, Interior is also the nation's principal conservation agency, and it has responsibility for most of the nationally owned public lands and natural resources, including over five hundred million acres of federal land and trust responsibilities for approximately fifty-six million acres of aboriginal lands.

From 1786 to 1849, Indian affairs were handled by the War Department. In 1824, the secretary of war, John C. Calhoun, created the BIA in the War Department and gave its employees such duties as administering appropriations for treaty annuities, approving expense vouchers, and managing funds designed to "civilize" Indians. Eight years later, in 1832, Congress authorized creation of a commissioner of Indian affairs to head the BIA. In 1834, Congress finally acted to officially acknowledge a Department of Indian Affairs, also housed within the War Department. But the Office was transferred to the Department of the Interior in 1849 in an effort to reduce the amount of armed conflict between tribes and the U.S. military.

The BIA has been engaged in a variety of sometimes devastating tasks toward indigenous peoples over its long history: from Indian removal in the 1830s, to enforced confinement on reservations in the 1850s–1890s, to land allotment and forced assimilation in the 1880s–1930s, to termination in the 1940s–1960s. Today, however, its primary tasks are centered on fulfilling the federal government's trust responsibilities (at a minimum, protecting tribal lands, natural resources, and moneys) and implementing the related policies of Indian self-determination and Indian self-governance.

The bureau is the largest agency in the Interior Department and employs approximately 10,200 employees, nearly 90 percent of whom are Indian. The bureau, despite having as its principal purpose that of serving the needs of Indian tribes and their members, historically did not employ many Indians. Indians were supposed to receive preference in employment as early as the 1830s, and again under a provision of the Indian Reorganization Act of 1934 it was stated,

> [T]he Secretary of the Interior is directed to establish standards of health, age, character, experience, knowledge, and ability for Indians who may be appointed, without regard to civil-service laws, to the various positions maintained, now or hereafter, by the Indian Office, in the administration of functions or services affecting any Indian tribes. Such qualified Indians shall hereafter have the preference to appointment to vacancies in any such positions.[68]

However, the percentage of Indians in the BIA rose from 34 percent in 1934 to only 57 percent in 1973. The majority of the positions held by Indians were in the lower ranks, and few Indians held supervisory positions.[69] As of 2010, six of the forty-five Commissioners of Indian Affairs to head the BIA have been American Indian or Alaska Native. Louis Bruce (Mohawk-Sioux), the third Indian to head the BIA (Ely S. Parker, a Seneca, was the first in 1869; Robert Bennett, an Oneida, was Bruce's predecessor in 1966–1969), was appointed in 1969, and in 1972 forcefully pushed to institute Indian preference in hiring. This decision prompted a legal challenge by several non–Indian Bureau employees who contended that Indian preference violated the Equal Employment Opportunity Act of 1972.

The Supreme Court in *Morton v. Mancari*[70] disagreed and held that the BIA's preferential policy did not constitute racial discrimination but was rather a means to further the congressional goal of greater Indian self-government, was meant to further the government's trust obligations to Indians, and was designed to minimize the negative effects of having non-Indians administering Indian matters. In short, this opinion reconfirmed that the relationship between Indians and the United States was based in the political realm and not the racial realm.

Since this decision, Congress has included Indian preference provisions in the enabling legislation of other federal agencies that also administer to the needs of Indians, including the Indian Health Service in the Department of Health and Human Services and the Office of Indian Education in the Department of Education. The Indian preference policy, like affirmative action programs for minority groups, has not gone unchallenged.

On October 19, 2000, Representative Curtis Weldon (R-PA), introduced a bill, H.R. 5523, that would have repealed the Indian preference policy. It was euphemistically titled the "Native Americans for Equal Rights Act," and, had it been enacted, would have repealed all the preference policies applicable to indigenous peoples dating back to the 1934 Indian Reorganization Act. Weldon's bill did not generate much support because the Supreme Court in the *Cayetano* decision earlier that year had strongly reaffirmed the federal government's trust relationship to federally recognized tribes, though not for Hawaiian natives, and expressed its support for the *Mancari* precedent, upholding the political nature of tribes in their relations with the United States. Thus, the Indian preference policy has survived the efforts of those who have assailed and sought to dismantle affirmative action programs.[71]

Currently, the BIA has a number of specific organizational policies:

1. To act as the principal agent of the United States in fulfilling the nation-to-nation relationship with recognized indigenous communities
2. To carry out the responsibilities of the United States as trustee for property and moneys it holds in trust for recognized tribes and individual Indians
3. To encourage and assist Indian and Alaska Native people to manage their own affairs under the trust relationship to the federal government
4. To facilitate with maximum involvement of all indigenous people the full development of their human and natural resource potential
5. To mobilize all public and private aids to the advancement of recognized indigenous people for use by them
6. To promote self-determination by utilizing the skill and capabilities of indigenous people in the direction and management of programs for their benefit

One strength of the BIA's organizational structure that makes it capable of handling matters in a manner that benefits tribal nations is that "tribes are recognized as legal entities or equivalent rank by the office regardless of what level the office is on. Thus a tribe is able to exercise its fundamental sovereignty at all levels of government."[72] Tribes, in other words, always can draw upon their basic legal rights as governing bodies, which sometimes gives them a competitive edge over other applicants for federal funding.

The BIA has provided services directly to tribes, through self-determination contracts initiated in 1975, or for some tribes since 1988, through self-governance compacts. These compacts are contractual arrangements between the United States and compacting tribes designed to "ensure the continuation of the trust responsibility of the United States to Indian tribes and Indian individuals, . . . [and] to permit an orderly transition from Federal domination of programs and services to provide Indian tribes with meaningful authority to plan, conduct, redesign, and administer programs . . . that meet the needs of the individual tribal communities."[73]

The BIA provides services directly or through contracts or compacts to 565 recognized native polities, with a population of over 1.9 million American Indians and Alaska Natives in over thirty states. The range of BIA programs is extensive and covers virtually the entire range of services provided by state and local governments for non-Indians: elementary, secondary, and postsecondary education; social services; law enforcement; judicial courts; business loans; land and heirship records; tribal government support; forestry; agriculture and rangelands development; water resources; fish, wildlife, and parks; road construction and maintenance; housing; adult and juvenile detention facilities; and irrigation and power systems.

More important, as a result of the tribal self-determination and self-governance policies, over 90 percent of all appropriations are expended at the local level, with tribes and tribal organizations under contracts or self-governance compacts utilizing some 70 percent of that amount. Of course, although tribes today have greater control over the federal dollars they receive, they are receiving in real terms less money than they were in 1977.

In a 2003 report, "A Quiet Crisis: Federal Funding and Unmet Needs in Indian Country," the Commission on Civil Rights reported that "despite a marked increase in government-wide funding beginning in 1993, a decline in spending power has been evident for decades."[74] As Figure 4.1 graphically shows, per capita spending by the federal government has increased far more for the U.S. population overall than it has for indigenous peoples.

Specifically, from 1998 through 2004 the percentage of the total Department of Interior budget for the Bureau of Indian Affairs has fluctuated, declining from 2000 to 2002. During this period, the BIA's "funding of tribal priority allocations (grants to Native American governments for such basic services as child welfare), for example, also declined from 42 percent of BIA's budget in 1998 to 35 percent in 2002, and may only be 33.3 percent of the budget in 2004."[75]

The assistant secretary of Indian affairs, a position established in 1977, assumes the authority and responsibility of the secretary of the interior for activities related to Indian affairs. The assistant secretary is responsible for (1) providing the secretary with advice on Indian matters, (2) identifying and acting on issues affecting Indian policy programs, (3) establishing policy on Indian affairs, (4) acting as liaison between the

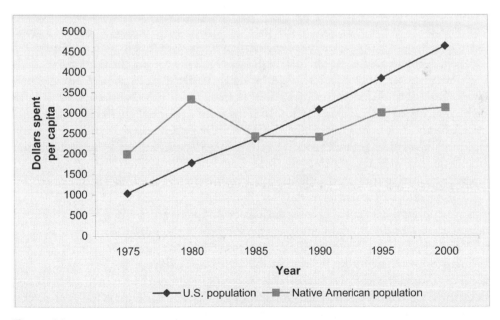

Figure 4.1

Per Capita Government Expenditures, U.S. Population vs. Native American Population, 1975-2000. *Source*: Roger Walke, specialist in American Indian policy, Domestic Social Policy Division, Congressional Research Service, memorandum to the Senate Committee on Indian Affairs, March 1, 2000, re: Indian-related federal spending trends, 1975-2001, appendix, table 1.

Department of the Interior and other federal agencies that provide services to Indians, (5) representing the department in congressional transactions, and (6) exercising secretarial direction and supervision over the BIA. Larry EchoHawk (Pawnee) was nominated to this position by President Obama and was confirmed May 20, 2009. EchoHawk, a former U.S. Marine, was the first American Indian to be elected as a state attorney general (for Idaho) in 1990. He has held a number of political positions, including service as a state legislator and appointee, by President Clinton, to the Coordinating Council on Juvenile Justice and Delinquency Prevention.

The BIA, as of 2010, has twelve regions, or "area" offices. The area offices, and the smaller "agency" and other offices within the areas (there are eighty-three agencies, three subagencies, six field offices, and two irrigation project offices), have the majority of the bureau's direct contact with the tribes.[76] Since the tribal self-governance project was established in 1988, providing tribal governments with greater flexibility in the decision making and administration of their contracted programs, the BIA has been under pressure from Congress to restructure itself and to downsize. This has come about because of the general sense that the federal government should be reduced in size, and because tribal governments have assumed greater control and responsibility for the administration of federal programs. However, in 1998 Congress enacted a moratorium on the negotiation of new tribal contracts and compacts, and failed to pass H.R. 1833, Title V, the permanent self-governance legislation for the Indian Health Service. Consequently, at a time when tribes were regaining a measure of genuine self-governing authority, Congress chose to stymie the process.

The BIA, despite some improvement in its handling of Indian affairs, still has a very uneven record when it comes to fulfilling its primary role as the principal trust agent of the federal government. This record was evidenced by the class-action lawsuit and subsequent Cobell pending settlement discussed in the introduction, in which the United States was sued for having grossly mismanaged individual and tribal trust accounts.

Besides mismanagement, incompetence, and failure to fulfill the trust responsibility to tribes and individual Indians, the BIA has also been charged with being extremely paternalistic toward Indian peoples and their resources.[77] This approach dates back to the late nineteenth century, when Indians were declared "legally incompetent" and treated as wards and the Indian agents literally assumed control of Indian lives. Although the express focus of federal Indian policy today is Indian self-determination and self-governance, the BIA and the Department of the Interior still act occasionally in ways that are contrary to the idea of tribal autonomy.

The secretary of the interior must still sign off on certain tribal decisions—for example, amendments to tribal constitutions or transactions involving trust resources. Herein is a conundrum. The principle, and sometimes the practice, of trusteeship is, in some respects, opposed to the idea of tribal self-determination. For example, if the Navajo Nation Council seeks to issue a lease with a coal company under terms the BIA considers unfair, the BIA may interpret its trust responsibility as requiring it to disapprove the lease. This is clearly frustrating to Navajo sovereignty, but is in keeping with the BIA's understanding of the trust doctrine.[78] Along with paternalism is the characterization of the BIA as a "fear-ridden" organization, an entity whose members too often fail to take action simply for fear that the action may be the wrong one.

Yet another criticism of the BIA also involves its mother agency and the Department of Justice, and centers on the issue of conflict of interest. The BIA is legally and morally responsible for protecting the Indians' trust assets from other interests. However, oftentimes threats to Indian resources come from one of the Department of the Interior's other agencies, such as the Bureau of Mines or the Bureau of Land Management. Although the BIA is the largest agency in the department, it lacks the political support other agencies have. Thus Indians often lose when compromises are made at the secretarial level between the adversarial bureaus. It is important to note that "although this type of political compromise goes on within every executive agency, it carries the danger that the tribes will be viewed merely as a weak political interest rather than as a group to whom a fiduciary duty is owed."[79]

This conflict extends to interdepartmental affairs as well. In the initial stage of such conflicts, the BIA is represented by the solicitor of the Department of the Interior. If the matter proceeds to court, the Department of Justice steps in. Lawyers for both departments, however, at times represent not only tribal and Indian interests, but those of other agencies or departments. As William Canby Jr. notes, "a private attorney could not ethically undertake the representation of such clearly competing clients, but the government attorneys regularly do."[80] Although President Clinton established the Office of American Indian Trust in 1996 to ensure that the secretary of the interior's legal and moral obligations under the trust responsibility are performed in accordance with the standards required by treaty, statutory, and case law, there is still no solution to the inherent structural conflict of interest.

In the fall of 2000, however, the BIA took two steps that have somewhat improved its relationship with indigenous nations. First, on September 8, Assistant Secretary Kevin Gover, in remarkably candid comments during a ceremony acknowledging the 175th anniversary of the BIA, officially apologized for all the harm his agency had done to America's aboriginal peoples. This admission, approved by the Clinton administration but not spoken on behalf of the United States, warrants an extended quote, since it represents the first time a leader of the BIA has apologized for its treatment of tribes:

> We have come together today to mark the first 175 years of the . . . BIA. . . . Before looking ahead, though, this institution must first look back and reflect on what it has wrought and, by doing so, come to know that this is no occasion for celebration; rather it is a time for reflection and contemplation, a time for sorrowful truths to be spoken, a time for contrition. . . . [T]he first mission of this institution was to execute the removal of the southeastern tribal nations. By threat, deceit, and force, these great tribal nations were made to march 1,000 miles to the West. . . . [A]s the nation looked to the West for more land, this agency participated in the ethnic cleansing that befell the western tribes. War necessarily begets tragedy, . . . yet in these more enlightened times, it must be acknowledged that the deliberate spread of disease, the decimation of the mighty buffalo herds, the use of poison alcohol to destroy mind and body, and the cowardly killing of women and children made for tragedy on a scale so ghastly that it cannot be dismissed as merely the inevitable consequences of the clash of competing ways of life. . . . And while the BIA employees of today did not commit these wrongs we acknowledge that the institution we serve did. We accept this inheritance, this legacy of racism and inhumanity. And by accepting this legacy, we accept also the moral responsibility of putting things right.[81]

It is ironic that such an apology and admission of guilt came during a time when the assistant secretary himself was an Indian (Gover was Pawnee) and 90 percent of the BIA's personnel were American Indian. In essence, American Indian peoples are apologizing for historical actions and events conducted against their own people by non-Indians who staffed the BIA until late in the twentieth century.

Former Assistant Secretary Gover's "apology" for the BIA's sordid historical treatment of Native peoples appears to have inspired a similar movement in Congress. On May 6, 2004, Senator Sam Brownback (R-KS) and two others introduced S.J. Resolution 15, "Native American Apology Resolution," that would formally "acknowledge a long history of official depredations and ill-conceived policies by the United States Government regarding Indian tribes and offer an apology to all Native People on behalf of the United States."

As Brownback noted in his remarks accompanying the resolution, this measure would not authorize or serve as a settlement of any claim against the United States, nor would it settle the many ongoing challenges Native peoples continue to face. "But," he said, "it does recognize the negative impact of numerous deleterious federal acts and policies on Native Americans and their cultures. Moreover, it begins the effort of reconciliation by recognizing past wrongs and repenting for them."[82]

This resolution was signed by President Obama in December 2009 as part of a defense appropriations spending bill. This version, watered down from the original resolution introduced in 2004, does not make a direct apology from the government but instead apologizes "on behalf of the people of the United States to all Native peoples for the many instances of violence, maltreatment, and neglect inflicted on Native peoples by citizens of the United States."[83] Perhaps more telling than the measure's significance was the sheer silence that followed. Neither President Obama nor any member of his administration has issued any statement as of March 2010 acknowledging this apology, begging the question by many native peoples of whether an apology has to be spoken aloud to hold any meaning. Brownback said in an interview that "political games shouldn't be played with something as important as a Native American apology, but he senses the White House may be facing pressure, and it does not want to appear weak or overly politically correct."[84]

The awkward relationship between native nations, the Interior Department, and the BIA will no doubt continue. But as Robert McCarthy noted in his extensive article on the BIA,

> [T]ribes undoubtedly will assume a greater role not only in administration of federal and tribal trust resources but also in resolving the vexing issues of trust reform and reorganization of the BIA. . . . The growing tension between greater tribal self-governance and the continuation of the federal trust responsibility raises important questions for the future of federal Indian policy. Their resolution may present an opportunity to remedy an equally difficult dilemma: the persistent conflict between aggressive enforcement of the federal trust responsibility and competing government interests.[85]

In their continued efforts to develop a more comprehensive, department-wide policy for meaningful consultation with indigenous nations, as directed by President Obama during the November 2009 Tribal Nations Summit and his subsequent memorandum (see appendix D), the Interior Department held a series of meetings focused on consultation between December 2009 and January 2010 with approximately 300 tribal representatives and over 250 officials from various federal agencies. As of March 2010, the department is in the process of constituting a tribal consultation team, which will consist of a tribal official and alternate from each of the twelve BIA regions, as well as a federal member and alternate from each Interior bureau or office. It is too early to know whether these efforts toward meaningful consultation will result in an application of the trust relationship consistent with indigenous understandings of this doctrine.

The U.S. Supreme Court and Indian Affairs

Section 1 of Article 3 of the Constitution creates "one Supreme Court." In the early years of the American republic, the federal judiciary was considered the weakest of the three branches because, according to Alexander Hamilton, it lacked the "strength of the sword or the purse" and had neither "force nor will, but only judgment." The individual most responsible for changing this perception was Chief Justice John Marshall. In the pivotal case *Marbury v. Madison* in 1803, the justices, in an opinion read by Marshall, held that the Constitution is "the fundamental and paramount law of the nation" and that "an act of the legislature repugnant to the constitution is void." This decision established the Supreme Court's power of judicial review. This is the power to declare congressional acts invalid if they violate the Constitution.

Throughout its history, the Supreme Court (and to a lesser extent the federal courts of appeal and the U.S. district courts) has played a seminal role in elaborating on the distinctive status of tribes and the tribal-federal-state relationship. In fact, besides establishing the power of judicial review, the Supreme Court has also established several important doctrines of law that still are available for use, including that the U.S. Constitution is not applicable to tribal nations who derive their sovereignty not from the American people but from their aboriginal status (see appendix B, which prints the text of *Talton v. Mayes* [1896], the case that established this doctrine), that Indian treaties are equal in stature to foreign treaties, that tribes reserve all those rights not expressly ceded in treaties or agreements, and that Indian land title is as "sacred as the fee-simple title of whites."

By contrast, the Court has also developed a number of legal doctrines that have been used at times to diminish or even quash the sovereign rights of tribes and individual Indians, including the doctrine of discovery (giving European nations and later the United States legal title to Indian-occupied lands), the doctrine of plenary power (that the United States has virtually "absolute and unlimited authority" over Indians), the idea of Indians as "wards" of the government with the Congress acting as "guardian" of Indian interests, the political question doctrine (which until 1980 often denied tribes a legal forum to test their complaints against the government, since the Court frequently ruled that disputes between tribes and the government were "political," not legal, issues), and the rule that the Supreme Court may implicitly abrogate Indian treaty rights.

The Supreme Court's role in elaborating the status of indigenous peoples has been chronicled by a variety of scholars. Some posit that the Court is the most helpful branch for tribes and is their best hope of securing justice.[86] Others stress that the Court is "the most dangerous branch" to Indians and acts as the tribes' chief antagonist.[87] Recent scholarship, on the other hand, points out that while the Court appears to be the most logical place for tribes to secure justice, the present trend in defining the political status of tribes and their relationship to the states and federal government threatens to wipe out or dramatically reduce the important legal strides tribal nations have made since the 1970s in such areas as hunting and fishing rights, tribal-state relations, criminal and civil jurisdiction, taxation, and sovereign immunity.[88]

President Bush's nomination of the conservative judge John Roberts Jr. in 2005 to replace the retired Sandra D. O'Connor and then his renomination of Roberts to fill the chief justice position after William Rehnquist's death from thyroid cancer was a profoundly important development for the court and the nation, and for the field of federal Indian law. O'Connor, while also a conservative jurist, in recent years had rendered several strong rulings supportive of tribal sovereignty and treaty rights (e.g., *Minnesota v. Mille Lacs Band of Chippewa Indians,* 1999), though her overall voting record on indigenous issues was usually less supportive of native rights. With Rehnquist's passing in the fall of 2005, President Bush was given the opportunity not only to change the chief justiceship, but also to nominate yet another conservative to the bench. After the debacle with Harriet Mier's nomination, Bush tapped Samuel Alito, a federal appeals judge with even more impressive conservative credentials. President Obama's nominee, Sonia Sotomayor, who replaced Supreme Court Justice David Souter in 2009 will likely prove less transformative. While Sotomayor is only the third racial minority and third woman on the Supreme Court, she heard few Indian cases during her tenure on the Second Circuit Court. Souter's votes had tended to favor Indian interests in treaty and trust cases, but he often voted against tribal interests in jurisdiction and taxation cases. Yet, as legal scholar Matthew Fletcher points out with a measure of skepticism, "a new Justice could force the remainder of the Justices to reconsider Indian law principles. Right now . . . the Court merely ignores inconvenient Indian affairs history, or Congressional intent, or its own precedents."[89]

One positive development that has emerged on the judicial scene in recent years, largely as a result of the many harsh rulings handed down by the Supreme Court in the last two decades, has been the collaborative effort of the Native American Rights Fund and the National Congress of American Indians (NCAI), which joined forces in 2002 to create the Tribal Supreme Court Project. This joint effort was called for "to coordinate and strengthen the advocacy of Indian issues before the Supreme Court, and ultimately to improve the win-loss record of tribes before that tribunal."[90] The Working Group presently has over two hundred lawyers and academics who specialize in Indian law. They share e-mail and regularly hold conference calls to discuss pending cases, to assess legal strategy, and to share ideas.

Tribal-State Relations

As we have seen, the political relationship between native nations and the federal government is outlined simply in the commerce clause of the Constitution. But the equally important relationship between Indian nations and the states is not outlined in the organic documents of the United States, state constitutions, or tribal constitutions or codes. It is generally accepted by all three sovereigns that the primary relationship for most native nations is at the federal level. In fact, one federal court declared in 1959 that tribes have "a status higher than that of states."[91] This is because of the nation-to-nation relationship tribes enjoy with the federal government, rooted in internationally recognized treaties and the trust doctrine.

States, for their part, cannot enter into treaties; only nations may do that. Moreover, eleven western states (North Dakota, South Dakota, Montana, Washington, Wyoming, Idaho, Utah, Oklahoma, New Mexico, Arizona, and Alaska) in their constitutions forever disclaimed jurisdiction over Indian property and persons and declared that the state would never attempt to tax lands held in trust for the Indians by the federal government. For example, the Arizona Constitution declares in Article 20, Section 4:

> The people inhabiting this State do agree and declare that they forever disclaim all right and title to the unappropriated and ungranted lands lying within the boundaries thereof and to all lands lying within said boundaries owned or held by any Indian or Indian tribes, the right or title to which shall have been acquired through or from the United States or any prior sovereignty.

Despite the clarity of such constitutional provisions, states have tended to disregard these important clauses. The history, therefore, of tribal-state relations has been contentious for a long time. Tribes and states today stand as mutual, if different, sovereigns. In the thirty-four states where federally recognized tribes live, the two sovereigns share contiguous lands, with every reservation or Indian community being surrounded by a state's borders. Equally important, the two polities share common citizens. That is, tribal citizens who live within reservations enjoy tribal, state, and federal citizenship, while non-Indian residents of reservations enjoy state and federal citizenship but are not tribal citizens.

Although sharing a level of citizenship and land masses, the two sovereigns have jealously guarded and been protective of their collective political, economic, and cultural resources. Tribes resent the states' constant attempts to tax and regulate their lands, wages, and industries, and are displeased that many states are still reluctant to concede the reality of tribal sovereignty and recognized tribal competence to handle increasing amounts of regulatory, judicial, and administrative duties. States, especially the western states, resent the fact that they lack basic jurisdiction over Indian lands and may not tax those territories without congressional and tribal consent.

The reasons for this tension date back to the colonial period and the debates about whether a central government or the individual colonies and states should manage Indian affairs. At the Philadelphia convention in 1787 it was determined that Congress would have exclusive control over trade relations with the sovereign tribes and that the national government would continue the treaty relationship with indigenous nations that other European sovereigns had practiced.

Later, as the United States expanded west, the enabling acts admitting most states to the Union were required to contain disclaimer clauses recognizing the federal government's exclusive jurisdiction over the nation's Indian affairs. These three factors—congressional plenary (exclusive) power, treaties, and state disclaimer clauses—along with tribal sovereignty effectively excluded states from any direct involvement in tribal affairs.

The Supreme Court in *Worcester v. Georgia* (1832) provided the first focused analysis of the tribal-state relationship. The court held that state laws could have no force within Indian Country unless Congress authorized such state action. Chief Justice John Marshall declared that "the treaties and laws of the United States contemplate the Indian territory as completely separated from that of the states; and provide that all intercourse with them shall be carried on exclusively by the government of the Union." Along with federal exclusivity, the doctrine of tribal sovereignty was also relied on by Marshall to bar state intrusion into internal tribal affairs.

The Marshall doctrine, which judicially firmed up the constitutional wall separating tribes from states, gradually grew porous, however, as non-Indians moved into Indian Country. For as whites moved in, so too did various elements of state jurisdiction. There have been five major state intrusions. Ironically, each of these was precipitated by federal action: (1) *United States v. McBratney* (1881), which held that states had criminal jurisdiction over non-Indians who commit crimes against other non-Indians within reservations; (2) the General Allotment Act (1887), which in individualizing Indian lands gave states jurisdiction over descent and partition and also authorized the state to tax any Indian allotment that left federal trust status; (3) Public Law 280 (1953), which initially gave five states complete criminal and some civil jurisdiction over Indian reservations located within their borders; (4) termination laws (1953–1960s), which legally ended the life of the "terminated" tribe, save for treaty rights; and (5) the Indian Gaming Regulatory Act (1988), which required tribes who wanted to operate lotteries, slot machines, blackjack, and other casino-type games to negotiate compacts with the states.

Notwithstanding these intrusive measures and the special political circumstances of the Indians in the states of New York and Oklahoma, which enjoy considerable jurisdiction over the tribes because of unique historical circumstances, until recently the general rule remained that state laws were of no force within the territory of an Indian tribe in matters affecting Indians. This was the case unless Congress had expressly delegated authority to the state, or unless a question involving Indians also involved non-Indians to a degree significant enough to give the state jurisdiction.

States for their part have frequently sought ever greater jurisdiction within Indian Country, despite the important constitutional and legal barriers that preclude this. By 1980, the Supreme Court had shifted away from a reliance on tribal sovereignty as a major check on state law. In its place the Court had erected a two-part test to determine which state laws could be applied in Indian Country without congressional consent: the federal preemption test (if a state law is inconsistent with federal law or interferes with overriding federal and tribal interests, it is voided) and the infringement test (if a state's action infringes on the rights of reservation Indians to be self-governing, it is nullified).

The importance of these tests, however, has been seriously eroded by a series of Supreme Court rulings in the 1980s, 1990s, and 2000s: *Montana v. United States* (1980), *Cotton Petroleum v. New Mexico* (1989), *Brendale v. Confederated Tribes and Bands of Yakima Indian Nation* (1989), *County of Yakima v. Yakima Nation* (1992), *South Dakota v. Bourland* (1993), *Seminole Tribe of Florida v. Florida* (1996), *South Dakota v. Yankton Sioux Tribe* (1998), *Alaska v. Native Village of Venetie Tribal Government* (1998), *Atkinson Trading Co. v. Shirley* (2001), *Nevada v. Hicks* (2001), *City of Sherrill, New York v. Oneida Indian Nation of New York* (2005), and *Wagnon v. Prairie Band Potawatomi Nation* (2005). These cases have turned the previous century and a half of federal Indian policy and judicial precedent on its head, and they threaten tribal sovereignty at a time when the doctrine of tribal self-determination is evolving into a permanent presence after a century of direct attacks.

The operating presumption of the John Roberts–led Supreme Court is that state law now is applicable in Indian Country unless the affected tribe can show that the state's action will have a significantly adverse impact on the tribe or its resources. As the Court put it in *Brendale,* "The impact must be demonstrably serious and must imperil the political integrity, the economic security, or the health and welfare of the tribe." "This standard," insisted Justice White, "will sufficiently protect Indian tribes while at the same time avoiding undue interference with state sovereignty and providing the certainty needed by property owners."

Tribes and States as Cooperative Sovereigns

Since before the Supreme Court began its direct assault on tribal rights, tribes and states have occasionally cooperated to avoid expensive litigation when their rights have conflicted or when both have seen it was in their interests to negotiate. They have done so at times with support of federal law or presidential directive and at times independently of federal involvement.

In 1978, for example, three national organizations—the National Conference of State Legislatures, the NCAI, and the National Tribal Chairman's Association—formed the Commission on State-Tribal Relations. This was the first nationally organized effort to better intergovernmental relations between tribes and states. The commission's broad goal was "to enable states and tribes to coordinate their responsibilities and activities without threatening or challenging the jurisdiction of either government."[92] The commission's leaders assumed that the federal government would continue to wield its extraordinary power in the field of Indian affairs but believed that it behooved states and tribes to seek solutions through agreements and compacts when possible.

This commission was active into the 1980s, but with the demise of the National Tribal Chairman's Association, a new cooperative entity was forged within the National Council of State Legislatures (NCSL) in 1990 at the behest of a number of concerned state lawmakers who realized a renewed need to find more amicable approaches to state-tribal relations. These lawmakers created a task force on state-tribal relations that sought to develop new institutional arrangements and because they worked to "publicize effective working relationships and agreements between Indian tribes and state governments."[93]

The task force arranged a dozen meetings around the country and provided a forum for tribal members, state legislators, federal officials, and others to speak on topics like gaming, government-to-government relations, tribal sovereignty, taxes, state-tribal agreements, and other topics. Acknowledging that "cooperative state-tribal government relationships are difficult to establish," the task force nevertheless proceeded to craft a short book, *States and Tribes: Building New Traditions* (1995), that outlined and discussed the numerous achievements in intergovernmental agreements that had already been put in place. The book discussed the opportunities available through agreements, but also included chapters that focused on cooperative arrangements that had been put into place in areas such as health, education and welfare, economic development, taxes, natural resources, and environmental regulation.

Soon, a new joint proposal between the NCSL and the NCAI was established in 1998 with funding from the W. W. Kellogg Foundation that set out to promote intergovernmental cooperation between states and tribes by researching, assessing, and disseminating vital information, particularly in the face of federal devolution of pro-grams.[94] Specifically, the broad goals of the project include the following:

- Promote an understanding of tribal sovereignty and governance by state legislators, and promote an understanding among tribal leaders regarding issues and processes of state governance in an attempt to alleviate some of the basic and historical mis-trust that tribes may feel toward states.
- Create and maintain neutral forums that are comfortable for and conducive to fostering improved state-tribal leader relationships.
- Understand how to form effective state-tribal agreements to meet mutual interests.
- Create and institutionalize resource networks.[95]

The staff of the NCSL/NCAI Project has produced several helpful reports in the *States and Tribes: Building New Traditions* series on critical topics under the guid-ance of the project's interracial and interinstitutional advisory council. Topics have included "Welfare Reform on Tribal Lands: Examples of State-Tribal Collaboration" (2004), "Tribal Trust Lands: From Litigation to Consultation" (2004), "Traffic Safety on Tribal Lands" (2004), "Indian Gaming in the States: Dispelling Myths and Highlighting Advantage" (2005), "Criminal Jurisdiction and Law Enforcement" (2006), and "Sustain-able Development: State and Tribal Initiatives" (2007).

■ Traffic Safety on Native Land: A Case Study

Traffic safety is an important subject for citizens and lawmakers alike. As Melissa Sav-age noted in a 2004 report, each year nearly 42,000 Americans are killed in vehicular crashes in the United States, with hundreds of thousands more being injured. In fact, vehicle crashes cause more deaths for people between the ages of one and thirty-four than any other social problem. Besides dealing with the trauma of death or injury, these accidents, in 2000, cost society about $230 billion. States have enacted many laws to confront this problem—forty-nine states have seat belt laws (except for New Hamp-shire) and all fifty states have child passenger protection laws. As a result, child pas-senger fatalities have decreased by nearly half in the last twenty-five years. Moreover, in August 2004 it was announced that safety belt use had reached 79 percent, saving an estimated one thousand lives and $3.2 billion.

However, statistics for minorities are much less flattering, with studies show-ing that Latinos, African Americans, and American Indians have more crashes, greater reluctance to wear seat belts, and more drinking and drug problems. In fact, "Native Americans have the highest risk of motor-vehicle related deaths of all ethnic groups. In some tribes fatality rates are two to three times higher than all other races."[96] See figures 4.2 and 4.3, which chart this depressing reality over the last twenty-five years.

A severe shortfall in police officers, an increasing lack of jurisdiction over non-Indian traffic violators, and a critical shortage of funding for roads are just some of the challenges facing tribal governments in their efforts to cope with traffic safety issues. Savage concludes her report by suggesting that tribal leaders, state lawmakers, public health professionals, and other interested parties partner with advocacy groups like Mothers Against Drunk Driving; develop public awareness and educational campaigns

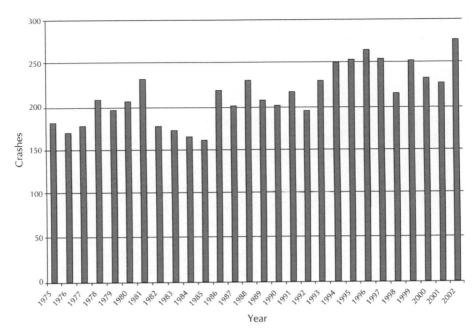

Figure 4.2
Fatal Motor Vehicle Crashes on Indian Reservations
Source: NCSA, NHTSA, FARS 1975-2002. Melissa Savage, "Traffic Safety on Tribal Lands" (Denver, Colo.: NCSL, October 2004): 2.

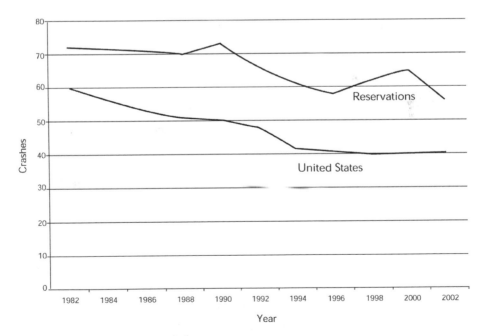

Figure 4.3
Percent of Alcohol-Related Crash Fatalities
Source: NCSA, NHTSA, FARS 1982-2002. Melissa Savage, "Traffic Safety on Tribal Lands" (Denver, Colo.: NCSL, October 2004): 3.

that address the distinctive cultural issues in Indian Country; and that tribal governments enact more stringent laws regarding passenger protection, drunk driving, and child passenger safety.[97]

■ Northwest Tribes and the State of Washington: A Case Study

Historically, the twenty federally recognized treaty tribes in what is now Washington State, including the Yakima, Nisqually, Puyallup, Snohomish, Squamish, and others, lived on the major river systems. Their cultures, ceremonial life, and economies evolved around fishing, hunting, and gathering of natural resources. As whites moved into the territory, the federal government negotiated treaties with the tribes in 1854 and 1855 in which the Indians sold a majority of their lands but retained some as their exclusive homeland, and secured treaty guarantees of specific rights like fishing for salmon both on and off the reservation. A common provision in most of these treaties dealt with the all important right to hunt and fish. One treaty read, "The right of taking fish, at all usual and accustomed grounds and stations, is further secured to said Indians in common with all citizens of the Territory, and of erecting temporary houses for the purpose of curing, together with the privilege of hunting, gathering roots and berries, and pasturing their horses on open and unclaimed lands."[98]

These treaty provisions were subsequently ignored by local whites, state officials, and federal officials. By the 1960s, Indians had begun legal efforts to reclaim their ignored and abused treaty right to fish. As Indians sought to exercise these rights, they faced intense resentment and outright violence from non-Indian fishermen (both commercial and sport) and were often arrested by state wildlife officials who had come to view salmon fishing as their exclusive domain. The federal government, as the tribe's treaty partner and trust agent, filed suit on behalf of the twenty tribes in 1971. The three-year case was heard by federal district court judge George Boldt. Judge Boldt rendered his decision in 1974 in *United States v. Washington,* which reaffirmed the treaty fishing rights of the Indians, recognizing that they were entitled to 50 percent of the harvestable salmon and steelhead trout, but also established that there should be co-management of the fish by the tribes and the state.

The state continued to challenge the Indians and their hard-won fishing rights victory until 1983, even though the U.S. Supreme Court upheld the lower court's ruling in 1979. In the subsequent three decades, despite many fits and starts, a number of cooperative measures have unfolded between the tribes, the state, and the federal government aimed at achieving the common goal of protecting, restoring, and enhancing the productivity and diversity of salmon and their habitat. Several specific features have made this possible:

- In 1974 the treaty tribes formed the Northwest Indian Fisheries Commission (NWIFC) to assist them in carrying out orderly and biologically sound fisheries policies and to provide member tribes with a unified voice on fisheries management and conservation issues.
- In 1984–1985 a tribal-state plan (called the Puget Sound Management Plan) for cooperative management of fisheries in the Puget Sound was jointly developed by the tribes and the state and approved by the federal court that had been overseeing management of the fishery because of the conflict ongoing since 1974.

- In 1985 the Pacific Salmon Treaty was negotiated between Canada and the United States, with tribes, the state, federal fisheries officials, and sport and commercial fishing groups playing an important role in its development.
- In 1986 the treaty tribes and Washington State's Department of Fisheries developed a number of watershed management plans throughout Puget Sound.
- In 1987 a final version of the Timber-Fish-Wildlife agreement was approved. This agreement between tribal delegates, the timber industry, environmental organizations, and state officials provides for a joint decision-making process in which these various entities cooperatively manage all these vital resources.
- In July 1989 a memorandum of understanding was negotiated between the tribes and the state. This memorandum focused on the environmental protection of the fisheries and wildlife resources, and all parties agreed that it was imperative that a plan be developed to protect, restore, and enhance habitat for these resources. It was also agreed that successful restoration and enhancement efforts would require educational outreach efforts involving constituencies of each of the parties. Priorities were to be developed within the government-to-government relationship envisioned in the memorandum.
- In August 1989 Governor Booth Gardner and the leadership of the state's twenty-six federally recognized tribes signed a "Centennial Accord." This measure established a framework for a government-to-government relationship and instituted procedures to ensure execution of that relationship. Importantly, each party to the accord expressed respect for the sovereignty of the other party.[99]
- Between 1999 and 2002 treaty tribes implemented the Hatchery Reform process, which is a systematic and science-driven effort to address how salmon hatcheries can help recover and conserve naturally spawning salmon populations.
- In 2004 the Skokomish Tribe purchased 175 acres of floodplain and wetlands along the lower Skokomish River in an attempt to preserve that important salmon spawning habitat.
- In February 2005 the treaty tribes named Michael Grayum as executive director of the NWIFC. Grayum replaced James Anderson, who was executive director for over two decades. NWIFC employs seventy-five full- and part-time employees who provide services and support to the twenty member tribes.
- Billy Frank Jr., Chairman of NWIFC, was awarded the Seventh Generation Legacy Award in 2006 to acknowledge "the great importance of team spirit between tribal and non-tribal communities, particularly in the pursuit of environmental protection and natural resource management."
- In 2006 Treaty Indian tribes in western Washington released 3.1 million hatchery salmon. Some of the salmon released by the tribes were produced in cooperation with the Washington Department of Fish and Wildlife, U.S. Fish and Wildlife Service, State Regional Enhancement Groups, and other sport or communities groups. The combined tribal, state, and federal hatchery system in Washington State is the largest in the world.
- The Stillaquamish Tribe, in 2009, restored forty acres of flood plain with the aid of the Washington State Department of Transportation and a work-release crew of minimum-security inmates.[100]

But deep fault lines remain between the two sovereigns, and progress is slowed by cultural misunderstandings, skepticism, and the finiteness of resources. Litigation, therefore, remains the most common technique to settle differences, though there is little evidence that it helps to promote a deeper mutual understanding of problems and needs.

The intergovernmental relationship between native nations and states is a dynamic one. It is complicated by the overarching presence of the federal government, which on one hand has treaty and trust obligations to tribal nations, but on the other hand is constitutionally wedded to the states. Relations will improve, from an indigenous perspective, only if states recognize the fact that tribes are sovereign entities entitled to govern the lands and peoples within their borders. Tribes, states contend, must be willing to consider the interests of the state if they are embarking on economic development or environmental decisions that may have implications beyond the reservation's borders (e.g., whether a tribe should be a "host" to low-level nuclear radioactive wastes despite state objections).

And while jurisdictional uncertainties and economic competition will persist, there is growing hope that the two sovereigns will come to recognize the rights of the other to protect the health, safety, and welfare of its own citizens; to engage in economic development that is appropriate for their communities; and to regulate their natural resource endowments and environmental quality, and that this may lead to more cordial relations.

Conclusion

The study of an intergovernmental relations matrix that includes tribes will remain a complex and tedious field. Complicating factors are legion. They include the sheer diversity of tribes (565 indigenous polities) in Indian Country; the political and economic powerlessness of a majority of these tribal groups, who must turn to Congress for assistance; the frequent contentiousness of the western states; the inherent conflicting goals of the BIA[101] and larger conflicts of interest within the Department of the Interior; the fact of the tribes' persistent extraconstitutional status, based on preexisting treaties and agreements and inherent sovereignty; and the generally anti-Indian stance of the Rehnquist Court on various substantive issues—for example, criminal jurisdiction, religious freedom, state taxation, and zoning of Indian lands.

How the committees and subcommittees on Indian affairs, the Supreme Court, the president and his Indian affairs appointees, the BIA, the general public, and the tribes interact will largely determine the future of U.S. Indian policy. The Committee on Indian Affairs, under the leadership of Senators Byron L. Dorgan and John Barrasso, has developed fairly amicable political relations with many tribes. President Obama has also taken important initial steps in reorienting federal-Indian relations. Whether these efforts will be sustained in the face of the conservative ideology of the Supreme Court and ever-increasing state attacks on tribal sovereignty, or revert to some older pattern emphasizing assimilation versus the recognition of tribes as small nations whose members also happen to have American citizenship, is impossible to know.

CHAPTER 5

A History of Federal Indian Policy

The Indians must conform to "the white man's way," peaceably if they will, forceably if they must. They must adjust themselves to their environment, and conform their mode of living substantially to our civilization. This civilization may not be the best possible, but it is the best the Indians can get. They cannot escape it, and must either conform to it or be crushed by it.

—Commissioner Thomas J. Morgan, 1889[1]

History has shown that failure to include the voices of tribal officials in formulating policy affecting their communities has all too often led to undesirable and, at times, devastating and tragic results. By contrast, meaningful dialogue between federal officials and tribal officials has greatly improved federal policy toward Indian tribes.

—President Barack Obama, 2009[2]

A Federal Indian Policy Overview

The indigenous nations' struggle to retain and exercise a measure of their original political independence in the face of persistent and, at times, oppressive federal policies aimed at the forced Americanization and coercive assimilation of tribal citizens forms the bulk of the story in this book. But there is more to it. The federal government's policies, most of which were aimed at the absorption of Indians, have had a discernible if variable impact on tribal nations, variable in part because these policies themselves were ambivalent—created at different times, by different individuals and administrations, for different purposes, and for varied tribal nations. And as a result of the undulating and unpredictable nature of history, combined with the interaction between the force of federal policies and the responses of indigenous nations to those policies, Native America is, not surprisingly, vastly different today than it was in 1900, 1800, or 1700.

Table 5.1 provides a general overview of the major policies and laws, and indigenous responses to those directives, from the early American period to the present. Of course, such linear charts, as useful as they are, are inherently flawed in that policies do not simply terminate at particular dates. For example, Indian removal, the forced relocation of Indians from their homelands to lands west of the Mississippi, did not begin and certainly did not end in the so-called Indian removal period of the 1830s–1850s. Many tribes, in fact, had already been forced out of their homes prior to the 1830 Indian Removal Act, and many thousands of Indians were required to relocate or remove long after the official policy ceased in the 1840s. These later removals were the result of land conflicts (e.g., the Navajo-Hopi land dispute from the 1860s to the present) or the construction of dams that required Indians to abandon their homes (e.g., Seneca Indians being forced to relocate because of the construction of the Kinzua Dam in the Northeast).

As another example, reservations were still being established after the 1890s, and they may still be established today. The secretary of the interior is authorized under the Indian Reorganization Act (IRA) of 1934 to create new Indian reservations at his discretion. Nevertheless, table 5.1 provides an accurate, if overgeneralized, way to assess the historical unfolding of the indigenous-federal relationship.

Students and interested readers seeking details of these policies and tribes' reactions to them can find this information in a number of texts, including Francis Paul Prucha, *The Great Father: The United States Government and the American Indians,* 2 vols. (1984); Angie Debo, *A History of the Indians of the United States,* (1970); Wilcomb E. Washburn, ed., *The American Indian and the United States: A Documentary History,* 4 vols. (1973); Peter Nabokov, ed., *Native American Testimony: A Chronicle of Indian-White Relations from Prophecy to the Present, 1492–1992* (1992); Philip J. Deloria and Neal Salisbury, eds., *A Companion to American Indian History* (2002); and Colin G. Calloway, *First Peoples: A Documentary Survey of American Indian History,* 3rd ed. (2008).[3] While it is not possible to provide a detailed policy history here, a synopsis of the major eras provides some needed historical context.[4]

The Formative Years (1775–1820s)

Within the first decade of the federal government's existence the fledgling democracy's inexorable need to expand led to increased conflict between indigenous and nonindigenous peoples.[5] This expansion was overseen by a Congress and president intent on exerting their authority in Indian affairs by following certain policies: the promotion of civilization and education of Indians, the regulation of trade and commerce with tribes, the establishment of territorial boundaries between the two peoples, the use of treaties to maintain peace with tribes and to purchase Indian lands, and letting states know that they lacked any constitutional authority in the field of Indian policy.[6]

The U.S. Supreme Court during these crucial embryonic years signaled it was a part of the ruling alliance when it handed down an important decision, *Johnson v. McIntosh* (1823), that set a new tone in federal Indian policy. Chief Justice John Marshall declared that, based on the doctrine of "discovery," the European states, and the United States as their successor, secured a superior legal title to Indian lands. Indian land rights were not entirely disregarded, but were necessarily reduced even though native peoples were not direct parties in this lawsuit and were in fact separate nations.

Table 5.1

Historical Development of the Federal–Tribal Relationship

Dates	Policy	Major Laws	Relationship	Tribes' Status	Tribal Responses
1770s–1820s	International sovereign to international soverign	1787 Northwest Ordinance 1790 Trade & Intercourse Act Treaties	Protectorate	International sovereigns	Diplomacy; some armed resistance
1830s–1850s	Removal	1830 Indian Removal Act Treaties	Government-government and trust relationship	Domestic dependent nations	Armed resistance; negotiation under duress
1850s–1890s	Reservation	Reservation Treaties	Guardianship	Wards in need of protection	Waning resistance; accommodation
1870s–1930s	Assimilation	1871 End of treaty making 1885 Major Crimes Act 1887 Allotment Act (Dawes Act)	Guardianship	Wards in need of projection	Accommodation; foot dragging; religious movements
1930s–1950s	Indian self-rule	1934 Indian Reorganization Act (Wheeler-Howard Act)	Renewal of government-government and trust relationship	Quasi-sovereigns	Increased political participation; growing inter-tribal activity
1950s–1960s	Termination (assimilation)	1953 Resolution 108 1953 Public Law 280 Urban Relocation Program	Termination of trust relationship	Termination of quasi-sovereign status	Growth of inter-tribal politics; beginnings of modern resistance

(*Continued*)

Table 5.1

Historical Development of the Federal–Tribal Relationship (*Continued*)

1960s–1988	Self-determination	1968	Indian Civil Rights Act	Renewal of government-government and trust relationship	Domestic dependent nation/quasi-soverigns	Continued spread of political activity; radical activism until 1970s; interest group activity
		1975	Indian Self-Determination Act			
		1978	Indian Child Welfare Act			
		1978	Indian Religious Freedom Act			
1988–Present	Self-determination	1988	Indian Gaming Regulation Act	Government-government trust relationship	Domestic dependent nation/quasi-sovereigns	Interest group activity; increase of international activity
	Self-governance	1988	Tribal Self-Governance Act			
		1990	Native American Graves Protection and Repatriation Act			
		1994	Indian Self-Determination Act Amendments			
		1996	Native American Housing Assistance Act			
		2000	Indian Tribal Economic Development and Contract Encouragement Act			
		2004	American Indian Probate Reform Act			
		2006	Esther Martinez Native American Languages Preservation Act (PL 109-394)			
		2010	Tribal Law and Order Act			

Sources: Modified from Sharon O'Brien, *American Indian Tribal Governments* (Norman: University of Oklahoma Press, 1989): 258; and Stephen Cornell, *The Return of the Native* (New York: Oxford University Press, 1988): 14.

Indian Removals, Relocations, and Reservations (1830s–1880s)

Despite laws like the Trade and Intercourse Acts (1790, 1802, and 1834), which placed severe restrictions on whites who had aspirations of entering Indian lands to trade or settle, and the Civilization Fund Act of 1819, which established the U.S. goal to "civilize" the Indians as an act of humanity, friction continued to mount between the ever-increasing and land-hungry non-Indian population and the tribal nations. As a result, the eastern tribes, particularly those in Georgia, faced mounting pressure from state and local authorities to surrender their lands and political status. The proposed "solution" to the conflict was the removal of Indians to country west of the Mississippi River, where it was thought the tribes would be able to live in isolation, apart from the corrupting influence of whites.

The idea for Indian removal was first proposed by Thomas Jefferson and was also supported by Presidents Monroe and Adams. However, it was President Andrew Jackson who would see to it that a removal policy was implemented by Congress via a congressional law in 1830.[7] Tribes were compelled to sign a number of removal treaties in which they ceded virtually all their aboriginal territory in the east in exchange for new lands west of the Mississippi.[8]

The 1830s and 1840s witnessed the coerced migration of thousands of Indians from the southeast, to the Ohio and beyond the Mississippi valley, under a program "that was voluntary in name and coerced in fact."[9] The harshness of removal was most vividly seen in the brutal experiences of the Five Civilized Tribes. The Cherokee Nation, who termed their trip to Indian Territory the "Trail of Tears," lost four thousand of their citizens during the march from their homelands in the Southeast to present-day Oklahoma.

Federalism was another factor that complicated relations between Indian nations and whites during this period, since there was intense conflict between the federal and state governments over which sovereign was ultimately in charge of Indian policy. The tension peaked in the so-called Cherokee cases: *Cherokee Nation v. Georgia* (1831) and *Worcester v. Georgia* (1832). In *Cherokee Nation*, the Supreme Court declared that Indian peoples constituted "domestic dependent nations" whose citizens were nonetheless "in a state of pupilage and subject to the guardianship protection of the federal government."

In Worcester, however, Chief Justice Marshall stated that tribes were "distinct political communities, having territorial boundaries, within which their authority is exclusive." Tribal nations, said Marshall, retained enough sovereignty to exclude the states from exercising any power over Indian peoples or their territories. Why the seemingly different conclusions by the same court? In large part because Marshall and the Court had been asked to decide different questions. In *Cherokee Nation*, Marshall provided a definition of the relationship between tribes and the federal government. In *Worcester,* the chief justice and the Court were called on to articulate the tribal-state relationship. Hence, Deloria and Lytle assert that "The *Cherokee Nation* Cases should be considered as one fundamental statement having two basic thrusts on the status of Indian tribes."[10] Furthermore, two related aspects of tribal sovereignty emerge from these cases: "Tribes are under the protection of the federal government and in this condition lack sufficient sovereignty to claim political independence; tribes possess, however, sufficient powers of sovereignty to shield themselves from any intrusion by the States and it is the federal government's responsibility to ensure that this sovereignty is preserved."[11]

In the wake of Indian removal, the federal government implemented the reservation policy by the mid-1850s. The new policy was administered by the Bureau of Indian Affairs (BIA), which was moved from the War Department, where it had been since its inception in 1824, to the newly formed Department of the Interior. From the federal government's perspective, reservations had become necessary because of the discovery of gold in the 1830s, new land acquisitions by the United States (e.g., Texas in 1846 and much of the Southwest in 1848 under the Treaty of Guadalupe Hidalgo), and the construction of railroads that linked both coasts and expedited westward travel.

Gradually, however, expansionist forces largely out of the government's control precluded keeping the Indians and whites apart, and slowly reservations came to be viewed as social laboratories for "civilizing" the Indians.[12] As Commissioner of Indian Affairs Francis A. Walker explained in 1872:

> The reservation system affords the place for thus dealing with tribes and bands, without the access of influences inimical to peace and virtue. It is only necessary that Federal laws, judiciously framed to meet all the facts of the case, and enacted in season, before the Indians begin to scatter, shall place all the members of this race under strict reformatory control by the agents of the Government. Especially it is essential that the right of the Government to keep the Indians upon the reservations signed to them, and to arrest and return them whenever they wander away, should be placed beyond dispute.[13]

Indians on reservations, in other words, were not merely fodder for social experimentation but were also, in effect, prisoners on their own lands.

Indian agents, BIA administrative personnel who historically had served as diplomatic liaisons between tribal nations and the United States, eventually became the key figures in charge of acculturating and fostering the assimilation of Indians. They had virtually unlimited power over the Indians under their care on reservations and often abused that power. As Senator Henry Teller of Colorado, a staunch opponent of Indian allotment and agents' autocratic rule in the 1870s and 1880s, said in testimony before Congress of many Indian agents:

> They are a class of men that, as a general thing, are sent out [to reservations] because they cannot make a living in the East. They are picked up as broken-down politicians, or one-horse preachers that have been unable to supply themselves with a congregation. They go to an Indian agency at a salary that will not employ, in the West in most cases, an ordinary clerk, and hardly a porter. They take these positions; they desire to keep them, whether it is for the salary or whether it is for the perquisites I leave to others to say, but they desire to keep them, and it is their interest that they make these statements that little by little these [Indian] men are progressing; and yet when a new and honest agent goes he frankly says, "these people [Indian tribes] can have made no progress at all."[14]

Christian churches, by the late 1860s, were also assuming a dominant role in Indian lives, a clear indication that the separation of church and state outlined in the First Amendment was irrelevant insofar as tribal nations were concerned. In fact, when President Ulysses S. Grant initiated his peace policy in 1869 as a way to quell the interracial violence on the frontier, involving Christian missionaries directly in the administration of Indians on reservations, this was probably the first explicit example of the federal government crossing the boundaries of constitutional prohibition by seeking to establish a religion among Indian tribes.[15] As part of their authority, church leaders were given the right to nominate Indian agents and to direct Indian educational activities.

Another example of the domestication of indigenous peoples occurred in 1871, when Congress, by way of an appropriations rider, enacted a provision that no tribe thereafter was to be recognized as an independent nation with whom the United States could make treaties. As mentioned, however, previously ratified treaties were not abrogated, and the Congress continued to negotiate many agreements with tribes. While it is constitutionally problematic whether the Congress had the right to terminate the Indian treaty-making power of the president, the fact is that this action signaled a significant shift in indigenous-federal relations, as an emboldened Congress now frequently acted unilaterally to suspend or curtail Indian rights, including treaty rights, when it suited the government's purpose.

Allotment, Americanization, and Acculturation (1880s–1920s)

By the 1880s the federal government's efforts to assimilate Indians had become quite coercive. Beginning in this era, a U.S. assimilation policy, as Wilmer shows, developed in several stages. These included "replacing the traditional communal economic base with a system of private property; intensified education, primarily through boarding schools; the regulation of every aspect of Indian social life, including marriage, dispute settlement, and religious practice; the granting of citizenship; . . . and finally allowing the Indian tribes to become self-governing by adopting constitutions ultimately subject to the approval of the U.S. government."[16]

Each of these laws and policies played a critical role in undermining the confidence, hopes, and self-respect of indigenous communities. But most observers suggest that the single most devastating federal policy adopted during this period was the land allotment system, under the General Allotment Act of 1887[17] and its multiple amendments, and the individual allotting agreements negotiated between various tribal nations and the United States. Most white philanthropists agreed that the Indians' tribal social structure, generally founded on common stewardship of land, was the major obstacle to their "progress" toward civilization. These individuals, and the organizations they often formed, firmly believed in the need to break up the reservations, distribute small individual plots of land to individual Indians (heads of households received 160 acres, single persons over eighteen received 80 acres, those under eighteen received 40 acres), and then require the allotted Indian to adopt a Euro-American farming existence.

The allotments, however, were to be held in trust—they could not be sold without express permission of the secretary of the interior—for twenty-five years. This was deemed a sufficient period for the individual Indian to learn the art of being a civilized yeoman farmer. U.S. citizenship accompanied receipt of the allotment. Tribal land not allotted to members was declared "surplus," and this "extra" land was sold to non-Indians, whose settlement among the Indians, it was believed, would expedite their acquisition of white attitudes and behavior.[18]

Tribal land estates were diminished very quickly by these policies. For example, the Iowa Tribe's members after their allotment went into effect retained only 8,658 acres;

the federal government purchased over 200,000 acres of the tribe's "surplus" land, a loss of over 90 percent of tribal territory. In Oklahoma, the Cheyenne and Arapaho Indians kept 529,682 acres after allotment, but were required to sell over three million acres that had been declared "surplus," a loss of over 80 percent of their lands.[19]

The allotment policy was, in the words of President Theodore Roosevelt, "a mighty pulverizing engine to break up the tribal mass." By 1934, when it was finally stopped, 118 out of 213 reservations had been allotted, resulting in the loss of nearly ninety million acres of tribal lands.[20] The accompanying program that ensued included removal of allotments from trust-protected status by forced-fee patent, sale by both Indian landowners and the United States, probate proceedings under state inheritance laws, foreclosure, and surplus sale of tribal lands. This program had disastrous economic and cultural consequences that still adversely affect allotted tribes and individual Indians today.

The Oglala Sioux of the Pine Ridge Reservation in South Dakota, after their military struggles with the United States in the late nineteenth century, slowly began to rebuild their economic life on the basis of a tribal livestock operation. With the able assistance of a committed and honest Indian agent, they built a herd of some forty thousand by 1912. But, required to sign an allotment agreement with the United States, by 1916 their 2.5-million-acre reservation had been completely subdivided. In 1917 a new agent encouraged the Oglala to sell their herd and grow wheat as part of the war effort. Because the tribe had neither the capital nor the experience for arable farming, most of their lands were leased to whites. James Wilson writes,

> By 1930, about 26% of the allotted land had been sold by individual owners, 36% had passed into heirship status and been rented out on a virtually permanent basis to non-Indians, and the reservation had become so fragmented and checkerboarded that the kind of cooperative enterprise for which the tribe's land and traditions fitted them had become almost impossible.[21]

Reservations that were allotted have a number of problems that continue to bedevil the efforts of tribal governments at economic development. The major problem is the fractionation of allotted lands. The sale of surplus land and the loss of many of the fee allotments by Indians left large areas of formerly consolidated lands in a checkerboard pattern, with areas of Indian, non-Indian, state, and federal ownership existing side by side. Efforts to consolidate allotted lands are complicated because allotments, whether held in trust or not, are subject to state inheritance laws if an Indian allottee dies without a will. It is virtually impossible in these circumstances to put together economic grazing or farming units on allotted reservations, because generally there are not enough allotments or fragments of allotments adjacent to one another to form an economically viable block of land for leasing or other forms of economic development.[22] Their highly fractionated ownership has thus left the Indian allotted lands largely undeveloped.

By the 1920s, however, it was clear that coercive assimilation and allotment were not having the desired results, since Indian allottees had experienced fraud and many Indians had actually become landless as a result. This, along with a general mood of progressivism in American political and popular thought, convinced federal policymakers to rethink federal Indian policy.

The Revival of Limited Tribal Self-Rule (1920s–1940s)

In 1926, Secretary of the Interior Hubert Work authorized Lewis Meriam and the staff of the Institute of Government Research in Washington, D.C., to conduct an investigation of socioeconomic conditions among Indian people. Their two-year study resulted in a major publication, *The Problem of Indian Administration*, the first fairly comprehensive description and analysis of what had happened to indigenous peoples since the end of the last of the Indian wars. The report's authors detailed the plethora of disastrous conditions affecting Indians at that time: high infant death rates and high mortality rates in general, poverty, horrendous health conditions, inadequate education, poor housing, and the problem of migrated Indians (Indians forced to leave the reservation because of land loss). The policy of forced assimilation, Meriam stated, "has resulted in much loss of land and an enormous increase in the details of administration without a compensating advance in the economic ability of the Indians."[23]

Although most commentators suggest that the Meriam Report was the basis for the IRA and other reforms instituted during the New Deal era, "there is not much evidence to support this contention."[24] In fact, the underlying tone and direction of the report's many recommendations "continued to assume that Indians had to be led benignly, if not driven, to certain preconceived goals, which were assimilation or a mutually imposed isolation within small Indian enclaves."[25]

In actuality, there were a number of other equally important, if little known, federal studies and a major and long-term congressional investigation conducted during this period that also played key roles in setting the stage for Indian reform. These studies were the Preston-Engle Report on Indian irrigation, a report on "Law and Order on Indian Reservations of the Northwest," a study of Indian agricultural lands, "An Economic Survey of the Range Resources and Grazing Activities on Indian Reservations," and a multiyear investigation conducted by a subcommittee of the Senate Indian Committee, which gave senators personal experience with the depth of Indian poverty caused by their own government's policies and under the BIA's mismanagement.[26]

The combination of evidence from all these reports led to important changes in federal Indian policy, changes that favored restoration of some measure of tribal self-rule. Of course, the federal strategy was to employ tribal culture and institutions as transitional devices for the gradual assimilation of Indians into American society. The vehicle for this transition was the IRA of 1934, which represented a legitimate but inadequate effort on the part of Congress to protect, preserve, and support tribal art, culture, and public and social organization.[27]

For those nations who voted to adopt the measure, the IRA succeeded in ending the infamous allotment policy, provided measures whereby Indian land could be restored or new reservations created, established a $10 million revolving credit fund to promote economic development, permitted tribes to hire attorneys, and authorized tribal governing bodies to negotiate with non-Indian governments. Also included were provisions for the regulation of resources, for establishment of an affirmative action policy for Indians within the BIA, and, importantly, for writing charters of incorporation and chartering and reorganizing tribal governments.

This final provision, the establishment of tribal governing and economic institutions, specifically authorized tribes to organize and adopt constitutions, bylaws, and incorporation charters subject to ratification by vote of tribal members. But problematically, these constitutions and bylaws were also subject to the approval of the secretary of the interior, as were any proposed future amendments to these organic documents. This is ironic in a sense, because one of the goals of John Collier, as commissioner of Indian affairs and principal sponsor of this broad measure, was to "minimize the enormous discretion and power exercised by the Department of the Interior and the Office of Indian Affairs."[28]

The act produced a mixed bag of results whose legacy continues today. On one hand, the act was effective in stopping the rapid loss of indigenous land and provided the institutional groundwork for tribal governments, whose powers have increased considerably since this period. One of the strengths of this act was that while it did not provide tribes with new governing powers, it "did recognize these powers as inherent in their status and resurrected them in a form in which they could be used at the discretion of the tribe."[29]

On the other hand, the act's goal of reestablishing Indian self-rule was less successfully achieved. For example, the tribal constitutions adopted only rarely coincided with tribes' traditional understandings of how political authority should be exercised. Furthermore, for those tribes who had been able to retain some semblance of traditional government, the IRA sometimes supplanted those institutions, thus intensifying internal tribal conflicts.[30]

Tribal Termination and Relocation (1940s–1960s)

The ending of World War II and the cost-cutting measures that ensued in Washington, D.C., John Collier's resignation in 1945, the Indian Claims Commission Act of 1946 (which allowed Indians to sue for monetary compensation from the United States), a sense among conservatives in Congress and the BIA that the IRA period's policies were "retarding" the Indians' progress as American citizens, and a sense among liberals that Indians were still experiencing racial discrimination in the BIA's still overly colonial relationship with tribes all fueled a drive to abandon tribal reorganization goals and terminate federal benefits and support services for tribes.[31]

The Committee on Indian Affairs (CIA) developed criteria to identify those indigenous groups thought prepared for termination. Federal lawmakers and BIA personnel believed that some tribes—the Menominee of Wisconsin and the Klamath of Oregon—were already sufficiently acculturated and no longer needed the federal government to act as their trustee. These tribes faced immediate termination. Other tribes, those in the Southwest, for example, were to be given more time to acculturate before they too would be legally terminated.

The definitive statement of the termination policy was House Concurrent Resolution 108, adopted by Congress in 1953. This resolution declared that "at the earliest possible time" the Indians should "be freed from all Federal supervision and control and from all disabilities and limitations specially applicable to Indians."[32] Between 1945 and 1960 the government processed 109 cases of termination "affecting a minimum of 1,362,155 acres and 11,466 individuals."[33]

Along with the termination resolution, Congress, just a few days later, also enacted Public Law 280, which conferred upon five states (California, Minnesota, Nebraska, Oregon, and Wisconsin) full criminal and some civil jurisdiction over Indian reservations (with certain reservations being exempted) and consented to the assumption of such jurisdiction by any other state.

The final part of the termination policy trilogy was relocation, a federal policy aimed at the relocation of Indians from rural and reservation areas to designated urban "relocation centers." In 1956 alone, the federal government spent $1 million to relocate more than 12,500 Indians to cities. The relocation policy was a coercive attempt to destroy tribal communalism.

The two largest terminated tribes were the Menominee of Wisconsin and the Klamath of Oregon. Prior to termination, both nations were comparatively well off, with sizable reservations and more than sufficient natural resources. But after termination, several harsh consequences resulted: tribal lands were usually concentrated into private ownership and, in most cases, sold; the trust relationship was ended; federal taxes were imposed; the tribes and their members were subject to state law; programs and services designed for federally recognized tribes were stopped; and the tribes' legal sovereignty was effectively ended.[34]

Indigenous Self-Determination (1960s–1980s)

The period from the end of termination in the 1960s to the 1980s was a crucial time in indigenous-federal relations. It was, according to most knowledgeable commentators, an era when tribal nations and Indians in general—led by concerted indigenous activism—won a series of important political, legal, and cultural victories in their epic struggle to terminate the termination policy and regain a measure of real self-determination.

Many of these victories arose out of activities and events like the fishing rights struggles of the Pacific Northwest in the 1950s–1970s; the American Indian Chicago Conference in 1961; the birth of the American Indian Movement in 1968; the Alcatraz occupation in 1969; the Trail of Broken Treaties in 1973; the 1973 occupation of Wounded Knee in South Dakota; and untold marches, demonstrations, and boycotts.

The federal government responded to this activism by enacting several laws and initiating policies that recognized the distinctive group and individual rights of indigenous peoples. In some cases the laws supported tribal sovereignty; in other cases they acted to erase or diminish tribal sovereignty. For example, in 1968 Congress enacted the Indian Civil Rights Act (ICRA), the first piece of legislation to impose many of the provisions of the U.S. Bill of Rights on the actions of tribal governments vis-à-vis reservation residents.[35] Until this time, tribes, because of their extraconstitutional status, had not been subject to such constitutional restraints in their governmental actions. The ICRA was a major intrusion of U.S. constitutional law upon the independence of tribes, and it is important to remember that the Indian bill of rights also does not protect tribes or their members from federal plenary power aimed at reducing tribal sovereignty, treaty rights, or aboriginal lands.

Two years later, by contrast, President Nixon explicitly called on Congress to repudiate the termination policy and declared that tribal self-determination would be the goal of his administration.[36] Congress responded by enacting a series of laws designed to improve the lot of tribal nations and Indians generally in virtually every sphere: the return of Blue Lake to the Taos Pueblo people, the Indian Education Act of 1972, the restoration of the Menominee Nation to "recognized" status in 1973, the establishment of the American Indian Policy Review Commission in 1975, the Indian Self-Determination and Education Assistance Act of 1975, the Indian Child Welfare

Act of 1978, the American Indian Religious Freedom Act of 1978, and the Maine Land Claims Settlement Act of 1980.

However, by the late 1970s, these Indian political victories (and a number of judicial victories as well) had provoked a backlash among disaffected non-Indians. The backlash was spearheaded by a number of non-Indian organizations, western state officials, and congressional members from states where tribes had gained political and legal victories. Subsequently, bills were introduced that threatened to abrogate Indian treaties, there was renewed discussion of abolishing the BIA, and some lawmakers argued that Indians should be completely subject to state jurisdiction. While tribes and their supporters repelled most of these anti-Indian efforts, they could not prevent the Supreme Court from handing down a series of decisions, beginning in 1978, that dramatically limited the law enforcement powers of tribes over non-Indians (*Oliphant v. Suquamish*, 1978), weakened tribal jurisdiction over hunting and fishing by non-Indians on non-Indian land within reservations (*Montana v. United States*, 1981), and reduced the water rights of tribes (*Nevada v. United States*, 1983).

The Reagan administration (1981–1989) was a time of much less certainty for indigenous self-determination. Although Reagan acknowledged that there existed a "government-to-government" relationship between the United States and recognized tribal nations, his budget cuts devastated the federally dependent tribes. In part to offset these financial losses, Reagan's administration encouraged tribes to consider establishing gaming operations. Indian gaming would have a profound economic impact on a number of tribes and would affect their political relationship with the states and federal government as well.

Tribal Self-Governance in an Era of New Federalism (1980s–Present)

By the late 1980s, federal policy was a bizarre and inconsistent blend of actions that, on one hand, affirmed tribal sovereignty and, on the other, aimed at severely reducing tribal sovereign powers, especially in relation to state governments. For example, in 1988, Congress enacted the Indian Gaming Regulatory Act, which affirmed the tribes' right to engage in certain forms of gaming if states engaged in comparable gaming.

Also in 1988, and at the behest of several tribes, Congress adopted an experimental tribal self-governance project aimed at providing self-determined tribes a much greater degree of political and economic autonomy. As leaders of the tribes put it:

> Self-Governance is fundamentally designed to provide Tribal governments with control and decision-making authority over the Federal financial resources provided for the benefit of Indian people. More importantly, Self-Governance fosters the shaping of a "new partnership" between Indian Tribes and the United States in their government-to-government relationships. . . . Self-Governance returns decision-making authority and management responsibilities to Tribes. Self-Governance is about change through the transfer of Federal funding available for programs, services, functions, and activities to Tribal control. Tribes are accountable to their own people for resource management, service delivery, and development.[37]

This originally experimental policy, which has been fairly successful for those tribes who chose to enter into a compacting relationship with the federal government (thirty in 1995), was made permanent in 1994 with the passage of Public Law 103-413.

Conversely, the U.S. Supreme Court, also in 1988, handed down two important decisions involving Indian religious rights. In *Lyng v. Northwest Indian Cemetery Protective Association,* the Court ruled that the Constitution's free exercise clause did not prevent governmental destruction of the most sacred sites of three small tribes in northern California.[38] And in *Employment Division, Department of Human Resources v. Smith,* the Court granted certiorari and remanded back to the Oregon Supreme Court a case involving whether an Oregon statute criminalizing peyote provided an exception for Indian religious use.[39]

President Clinton issued several executive orders and memorandums during his two terms (1993–2001) that provided Indians a measure of recognition and protected certain Indian rights. "Together," said Clinton, "we can open the greatest era of cooperative understanding and respect among our people ever . . . and when we do, the judgment of history will be that the President of the United States and the leaders of the sovereign Indian nations met . . . and together lifted our great nations to a new and better place."[40] Clinton issued executive orders in the following areas: consultation and coordination with Indian tribal governments, Indian sacred sites, tribal colleges and universities, American Indian and Alaska Native education, and the distribution of eagle feathers for Native American religious purposes.

Although Clinton generally maintained cordial relations with the tribes, Congress, especially after the Republicans gained control of both houses in 1994, and the Supreme Court continued to act in ways that threatened to unravel the political and economic improvements tribal governments had made in the first part of the self-determination era. In particular, a majority of the Supreme Court's decisions involving conflicts between tribes and states have supported state sovereignty over tribal sovereignty, a dramatic departure from historical and constitutional precedent.[41] The issue of Indian gaming seems to be at the vortex of much of this conflict, which has led to a redefinition of federalism that threatens to destabilize tribal status just at a time when the doctrines of tribal self-determination and self-governance are evolving into a permanent presence after a century of direct federal assaults.

The Bush administration's two terms continued this troublesome period, with Bush paying scant policy attention to tribal nations, except in the area of education where his office issued two executive orders. One of the orders (EO 13,270) expressed support for tribal colleges and universities; the other (EO 13,336) sought to assist Indian students in meeting the academic standards of the No Child Left Behind Act. Congress enacted the Esther Martinez Native American Languages Preservation Act of 2006 (PL 109-394) to ensure the survival and continuing vitality of Native American languages through Native language immersion programs and other purposes supporting language preservation.

Indian Country responded enthusiastically to President Obama's campaign for change. The National Congress of American Indians identified a number of key issues where transformation was needed in the way that the federal government interacted with native nations, including trust reform and tribal natural resource management, treaty rights and consultation, funding of tribal government services, law enforcement, and taxation. The Obama administration has begun to address some of these critical concerns. The first decade of the twenty-first century was dominated by trust accounting litigation. On December 7, 2009, the government reached a tentative $3.4 billion settlement in *Cobell v. Salazar* (as outlined in the introduction). However, implementation of the settlement of one of the largest class-action lawsuits against the United States has not gone according to schedule. Needing congressional approval, lawmakers had until December 31, 2009, to complete the legislation. As of March 2010, that deadline has twice been extended and has yet to be finalized as this edition went to press.

Recent national legislation has also included key provisions for American Indians and Alaska Natives. The American Recovery and Reinvestment Act of 2009 contained provisions for Indian health care, BIA programs, public safety and justice, tribal roads and bridges, Indian housing, education, energy and water programs, and food distribution programs. And on March 23, 2010, President Obama signed into law the Patient Protection and Affordable Care Act, which included the permanent reauthorization of the Indian Health Care Improvement Act, aiding in efforts to improve Indian Health Services.

Conclusion

The policy ambivalence evident in the conflicting goals of sometimes recognizing tribal self-determination and sometimes seeking to terminate that governing status has lessened only slightly over time. Tribal nations and their citizens find that their efforts to exercise inherent sovereignty are rarely unchallenged, despite their treaty relationship with the United States and despite periodic pledges of support in various federal laws, policies, and court cases.

CHAPTER 6

Tribal Political Economy

Indian people have been bound by three iron chains: paternalism, exploitation, and dependency. These chains gained their crippling power through the decades as lawmakers vacillated about whether tribes should continue to exist as separate sovereigns or whether their separate rights should be terminated. Many of those who advocated "freeing the Indian" through each period of history were well-meaning but paternalistic. Others were merely greedy and wanted to exploit Indian resources. Whatever their motives, the effects of the vacillating policies were the same: The tribes and individual Indians lost more and more of the land and other resources they needed to make them self-sufficient again. This exploitation left them increasingly dependent upon the federal government yet, ironically, resistant to change, because so often in the past change had brought disaster.

—Marjane Ambler, 1990

An attack on the Seneca Nation is an attack on the economy of western New York.

—J. C. Seneca, 2010[1]

Largely as a result of Indian gaming operations, there is a heightened perception among many non-Indian Americans and federal and state policy makers that tribal nations are all now economically well off and no longer need federal financial aid, or at the very least can withstand severe reductions in the federal expenditures they receive. This perception is grievously flawed, however. The most reliable statistics we have paint a portrait of a Native America that remains largely mired in oppressive levels of poverty. See tables 6.1 and 6.2 for these grim socioeconomic statistics.

The U.S. Commission on Civil Rights, in their detailed analysis "A Quiet Crisis: Federal Funding and Unmet Needs in Indian Country" (2003), brought these statistics to life. They reported that, while federal efforts have long sought to improve the living conditions of Native peoples, Native peoples "still suffer higher rates of poverty, poor

Table 6.1

Selected Characteristics of the Non-Latino Black, Asian American, American Indian, and White Populations, Latest Estimates

	Black (2006)	Asian American (2006)	American Indian (2006)	Whites (2006)
Population (in thousands)	36,435	12,945	2,036	198,777
% of Total U.S. Pop.	12.2	4.3	0.7	66.2
Median Age (Yrs.)	31.5	35.3	31.6	40.6
% ≥ 18 Yrs. Old	70.6	77.9	71.7	78.7
% of H.S. Grad. (of Pop. > 25 Yrs.)	79.6	85.7	78.9	88.9
% Unemployed (of Pop. > 16 Yrs.)	7.9	3.3	7.2	3.3
Males	8.5	3.6	7.8	3.6
Females	7.4	3.0	6.6	3.0
Median Family Income (in 2006 inflation-adjusted dollars)	$38,424	$72,437	$39,122	$65,180
% Owning Home	46.5	60.4	57.4	74.0
% Living in Poverty	25.3	10.7	27.0	9.3

All figures reflect data from the 2006 U.S. Census Bureau, Americna Community Survey; http://factfinder.census.gov

Sources: From Paula D. McClain and Joseph Stewart Jr., *"Can We All Get Along?" Racial and Ethnic Minorities in American Politics*, 5th ed. (Boulder, Colo.: Westview Press, 2009). Population Data: "Total Population." Age Data: "Median Age (Years)" and "18 Years and Older." Education Data: "High School Graduate or Higher." Unemployment Data (found or computed: "Employment Status: Unemployed." Median Income Data: Income in the Past 12 Months: Median Family Income (Dollars). "Home Ownership Data: Housing Tenure." Poverty Data: "Poverty Rates: All People." (February 6, 2008).

educational achievement, substandard housing, and higher rates of disease and illness. Native Americans continue to rank at or near the bottom of nearly every social, health, and economic indicator."[2]

A 2010 National Health Statistics report further demonstrates the conditions affecting Indian country, noting that Indians and Alaska Natives continue to have a lower life expectancy than any other racial or ethnic group. And they have higher rates of diabetes, suicide, tuberculosis, and that constant bane, alcoholism.[3] In regard to housing, various studies have found that existing housing structures are substandard; approximately 40 percent of on-reservation housing is considered inadequate,[4] since it lacks adequate plumbing, kitchen facilities, and utility gas.[5]

Explanations for Indian Underdevelopment

Reservation-based tribal nations exist in a paradoxical world. They are recognized political sovereigns, with rights and resources and lands that can be systematically quashed or reduced. What is the basis for this seeming contradiction? Why is it that

Table 6.2

Changes on Reservations other than Navajo

	Non-Gaming	Gaming	U.S.
Real Per Capita Income	+21%	+36%	+11%
Median Household Income	+14%	+35%	+4%
Family Poverty	-6.9	-11.8	-0.8
Child Poverty	-8.1	-11.6	-1.7
Deep Poverty	-1.4	-3.4	-0.4
Public Assistance	+0.7	-1.6	+0.3
Unemployment	-1.8	-4.8	-0.5
Labor force participation	-1.6	+1.6	-1.3
Overcrowded homes	-1.3	-0.1	+1.1
Homes lacking complete plumbing	-4.6	-3.3	-0.1
Homes lacking complete kitchen	+1.3	-0.6	+0.2
College graduates	+1.7	+2.6	+4.2
High school or equivalency only	-0.3	+1.8	-1.4
Less than 9th grade education	-5.5	-6.3	-2.8

even those tribes with impressive gaming revenues, the forty-plus tribes with producing mineral leases (e.g., coal, gas, uranium, and oil) and other tribes with significant natural resources including land, water, and timber still lag far behind the rest of society in many socioeconomic categories?

Many Americans have some awareness of the historical exploitation Indian nations have experienced at the hands of the federal government, corporate America, and state officials, and in untold interactions with non-Indian individuals with an eye on native resources. This massive exploitation, best explained by the related theories of colonialism, internal colonialism, and dependency, describe a devastating story of "U.S. political and economic control and exploitation of Indian resources."[6] These theories are well suited to explain the pronounced levels of tribal poverty and economic underdevelopment, and the decay of tribal political, social, and cultural institutions, because they focus on tribes' historical relations with the United States, how underdevelopment occurred, and why it persists for most tribes.

The tribal economic situation is compounded by several factors. First, while billions of dollars have indeed been appropriated for tribal Indians, less than 30 percent of that money ever reached the reservation. Second, studies have shown that despite the fact that tribes suffer the worst socioeconomic conditions of any group in the country, over the last two decades they have experienced a decline in spending power focused on indigenous needs. This is compounded by the fact that the American Indian population has grown at a faster rate than the U.S. population as a whole. Third, an increasing number of state governments are encroaching on tribal economic sovereignty, primarily through their attempts to inhibit or supplant tribal jurisdiction, to tax tribal lands, and to extract additional gaming revenue. The misconception that native peoples pay no taxes (although native trust lands are not taxed, Indians pay federal income tax and numerous business and sales taxes) and therefore should not receive state programs is also a significant problem that tribes must cope with on a consistent basis. Fourth, revenues from tribes with significant natural resources, particularly oil, gas, and timber, have also declined in recent years. Finally, there has been a significant backlash among states and Nevada casino operators that has resulted in a growing movement to restrict, tax, or even abolish Indian gaming operations.

Issues of Significant Impact for Tribal Development

Socioeconomic conditions, however, are not dire uniformly across Indian Country. And during the last thirty years, as a result of vibrant tribal leadership, an inspired Indian population, and constructive federal laws like the Indian Education Act (1972), the Indian Self-Determination and Education Assistance Act (1975), the Tribal Self-Governance Act (1988, 1994), and the Indian Gaming Regulatory Act (IGRA; 1988), some tribes like the Mashantucket Pequot of Connecticut, the Confederated Salish and Kootenai of the Flathead Reservation in Montana, the White Mountain Apache of Arizona, the Mescalero Apache of New Mexico, the Cochiti Pueblo of New Mexico, the Mississippi Choctaw of Mississippi, and the Muckleshoot of Washington, to name but a few, have begun to enjoy a measure of economic success in areas such as gaming, energy and mining, water rights, agriculture, timber, fisheries and wildlife, livestock raising, tourism and hotels, arts and crafts, and manufacturing and assembly.[7] The remainder of this chapter explores the following major economic development issues in more detail: land consolidation, Indian gaming, agriculture, natural resources (energy and timber), and tourism. The chapter ends with some discussion of the relationship between tribes and states.

Land Consolidation

Land—who owns it, how can it be retained or regained, and the best uses of it—has been the major theme animating the Indian–non-Indian relationship. As late as 1887, tribes controlled nearly two billion acres of land. By 1924, because of laws like the General Allotment Act and its amendments, the sale of surplus lands, lease arrangements, and other policies, the total amount of Indian-owned land had been reduced to 150 million acres. By 1975, tribal lands in the lower forty-eight states totaled only a little more than 54 million acres. But it was the allotment of reservations—over 118 were allotted—that has generated the most intense and persistent problems for tribes who were allotted.

The General Allotment Act of 1887 was the first piece of comprehensive legislation dealing with tribal trust land. Allotted reservations were divided into individual parcels of varying sizes (160, 80, and 40 acres). In order to protect the allottee from having his or her rights abused, the allotment was to be held in trust by the federal government for a twenty-five-year period, during which time the land could not be sold, taxed, or mortgaged without explicit federal consent. The policy also provided that if the allottee died while the property was still in trust status, the estate would be divided among heirs according to state or territorial regulations. The allotment policy proved disastrous for Indians. The money generated by the sale of "surplus" lands was placed in the U.S. Treasury for the Indians' benefit, and many of the allottees became little more than petty landlords, with the BIA leasing their allotments to white ranchers or farmers.

One of the major failures became clearer as successive generations of Indian heirs came to hold the allotted lands. The original 160-, 80-, and 40-acre parcels became splintered into multiple individual interests in land, with some parcels having hundreds of owners. Since the land was in trust status, it only rarely was alienated or partitioned. Thus the fractionation problem multiplied enormously. Although the allotment policy was ended in 1934 with the enactment of the Indian Reorganization Act, this did not prevent the compounding of the existing heirship problems, since each property owner was likely to have more than one heir.

Studies conducted by both the House and Senate in 1960 showed that one half of the approximately twelve million acres of allotted trust lands were held in fractionated ownership, with over three million acres held by more than six heirs to a parcel. The Sisseton-Wahpeton Lake Traverse Reservation is a powerful example of how devastating fractionation has been for tribes and how this single issue practically precluded economic development. Forty-acre tracts on the reservation, which lease for about $1000 yearly, are typically subdivided into hundreds of undivided interests. Some of these interests generate only pennies a year in rent. The average tract of allotted land has 196 owners; and the average owner has undivided interests in at least fourteen tracts.

According to a report by Michael Lawson, the administrative problems associated with such fractionation are best seen by examining a particular parcel of land within the Sisseton-Wahpeton reservation, Tract 1305. Lawson dubbed this "one of the most fractionated parcels of land in the world."[8] An extended quote from Lawson's report reveals how complicated the heirship problem is on the Sisseton-Wahpeton reservation and why economic development is extremely difficult:

> The original allottee, a member of one of the most prominent and prolific Sisseton families, died in 1891. By 1937 there were 150 heirs to the allotment and probating the estate cost $2,400 and required more than 250 typewritten pages. At present there are 439 heirs and the lowest common denominator (LCD) used to determine fractional interests is 3,394,923,840,000. A portion of the allotment consisting of forty acres of farmland is currently leased at the rate of $1080 per year. When it comes time to distribute this money, it requires three full days for a realty clerk to calculate the heirship interest values. A breakdown of the current lease distribution reveals that more than two thirds of the heirs receive less than $1.00 per year from the estate, that approximately one-third receive less than 5 cents, and that the interest of 100 of the heirs entitled them to a fraction of 1 cent. The largest interest holder receives $82.85, but the value of the smallest heir is $.0000564. At the current lease rate, it would require 177 years for the smallest heir to earn 1 cent, and 88,652 years to accumulate $5.00, which is the minimum amount for which the Bureau of Indian Affairs will issue a check. If this portion of the allotment was sold at its appraised value of $8000, the share of the smallest heir would be $.000418, and if it were physically partitioned, the smallest heir would be given title to approximately 13 square inches.[9]

Stranger still, the administrative costs of handling just this one tract of land exceeded $17,000 annually, while the total revenue generated on Tract 1305 only amounted to a little over $1,000 annually, divided between the 439 owners.

The difficulty of consolidating Indian lands and the ongoing fractionated heirship issue together constitute one of the major economic problems for tribes. Until tribal governments or individual Indians own land in solid blocks, long-term economic planning will remain problematic. For example, to have a successful livestock operation requires 2500 to 3000 acres in the plains states, while allotments, and particularly fractionated allotments, provide on average much less than 160 acres of land. Thus, individual allottees tend to express a desire to sell their allotments, lease them, or simply let them lie idle.

Consolidation of lands has other consequences as well, however. As Deloria and Lytle have observed, tribal civil and criminal jurisdiction rests upon the existence of trust lands. And when an allotment is sold to non-Indians or is taken out of trust, the tribes generally lose jurisdiction over the area and must negotiate an agreement with the state and county officials in order to exercise jurisdiction over the area. In addition, zoning for economic development and housing, and enforcement of tribal hunting and fishing regulations, are extremely difficult over nontrust land.[10]

Tribes for years have attempted to develop land acquisition and consolidation programs to solve the problem by using meager tribal funds and, sometimes, federal loans. But until the advent of gaming dollars the funds were grossly inadequate. The Mille Lacs Band of Ojibwe in Minnesota, for example, a successful gaming tribe, is using some of its gaming proceeds to establish a Land Purchase Trust Fund in an effort to consolidate its tribal lands. But not all allotted tribes have successful gaming operations. As one congressional report stated in 1977, at least $1.5 billion would be needed to buy the 10.2 million acres of existing allotted lands.[11]

Congress, which created the problem, attempted to bring some relief in 1983 with passage of the Indian Land Consolidation Act. This act was designed to stop the further fractionation of Indian trust lands by regulating the terms under which heirs to such lands received property. Under this act, tribes could establish inheritance codes to regulate the disposition of real property. But several Indian heirs challenged the constitutionality of a core provision of the act that stated that when an owner of Indian trust land died, if his or her interests represented 2 percent or less of the total acreage or had earned its owner less than $100 in the preceding year, it would escheat (revert back) to the tribal government rather than to an heir.

The Supreme Court in a 1987 case, *Hodel v. Irving*,[12] held that Congress had indeed violated the Fifth Amendment property rights of the Indian heirs by taking their fractionated interests without paying just compensation. This is one of the few cases where the Court applied a constitutional amendment in support of the rights of Indians. In this case the rights were to property that had been individualized, thus clashing with the sovereign rights of the tribal nation.

Congress amended the act in 1994 in an effort to address the escheat issue. Despite the changes, the amended act was also challenged by several Indian heirs in *Youpee v. Babbitt*.[13] Relying on *Hodel*, an 8–1 majority once again struck down Congress's attempt to address fractionated heirship lands, holding that the law violated Youpee's individual property rights.[14]

There is still no simple solution to the problem of fractionated lands and the heirship situation, although Congress has enacted two recent laws, one in 2000 (Public Law 106-462) and the other in 2004 (Public Law 108-374) with subsequent technical amendments, in an effort to address the fractionated heirship lands problem.[15] It is too early to tell whether these acts' provisions are sufficient to the task or whether they will survive judicial scrutiny. As it stands, poorer tribes who lack the money to purchase lands for consolidation purposes will continue to have the greatest difficulty. However, tribes who have ample gaming revenues now have the means to make such purchases, and we are beginning to see efforts by these tribes to consolidate their lands. The Standing Rock Sioux Tribe, for example, has begun repurchasing lands, about half of which were owned by non-Indians through the sale of Indian allotment.

Indian Gaming

In 1976, when the Commission on the Review of the National Policy Toward Gambling issued its final report, legalized gambling was still relatively limited. Only thirteen states had lotteries, New York and Nevada were the only two states that had approved off-track wagering, and casinos did not exist outside Nevada. Much has changed since then. Legal gambling, euphemistically known as *gaming,* is now widespread and is an accepted part of the social landscape throughout the United States and in many other countries as well.[16]

In the United States, gaming has increased tenfold since 1975. In 2006 a person could make a legal wager in every state except Utah and Hawaii. Thirty-seven states have lotteries, twenty-one have casinos, and more than thirty have off-track betting. In a telling statistic, in 2003 nationwide consumer spending on legal gambling was $73 billion. State lotteries generated $19.9 billion, commercial gaming produced $28.7 billion, and pari-mutuel wagering and charitable gaming generated $7.4 billion.[17]

Similarly, gaming has increased exponentially in Indian Country since native governments were encouraged to enter the field during President Reagan's administration as a means to offset Reagan's devastating budget cuts (the president, with congressional support, cut $1 billion from the $3.5 billion budgeted for Indian affairs, terminated job-training programs, and cut funds for Indian housing).[18] In 2008, the National Indian Gaming Commission (NIGC) reported that Indian gaming revenues were approximately $25.9 billion for fiscal year 2008. Related hotels, resorts, restaurants, and entertainment businesses attached to tribal gaming generated an additional $3.2 billion in gross revenue. In 2008, data showed that 233 tribal nations are running 411 gaming operations in 28 states. Indian casinos supported 636,000 jobs and paid out approximately $20.7 billion in wages in 2008. Figure 6.1 depicts the growth of gaming from 1999 to 2008.

In terms of federal revenue, even though Indian casinos are exempt from state and local property taxes under federal law, Indian gaming still generated $6.4 billion in federal tax revenue from employees and affiliated businesses. According to Ernest L. Stevens Jr., chairman of the National Indian Gaming Association, "In 2008 the federal treasury revenues grew over $8.0 billion because of income taxes and other taxes related to the employees of tribal gaming. State governments obtained an additional $2.5 billion in revenue from income tax, payroll tax and sales tax paid from employees of tribal gaming."[19] In addition, states gained revenue from tribal payments outlined in tribal-state compacts. Local taxes, increased sales taxes, and other revenue sharing agreements generated $100,000 million for local governments (figures 6.2 and 6.3). In fact, it is Indian gaming and the sometimes impressive revenues gaming generates that have had the largest positive impact on the economic situation of a number of tribal nations.[20]

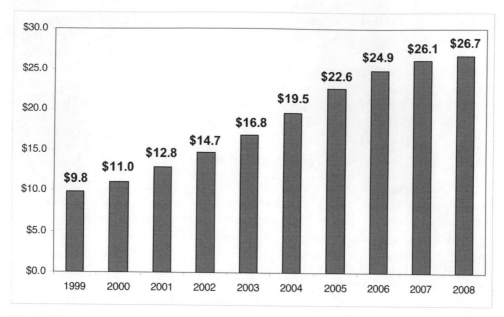

Figure 6.1
Growth in Gaming Revenues, 1999-2008
Source: National Indian Gaming Commission

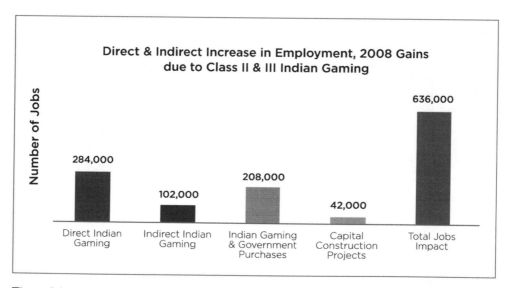

Figure 6.2
Direct and Indirect Increase in Employment, 2008. Gains due to Class II and III Indian Gaming
Source: National Indian Gaming Commission

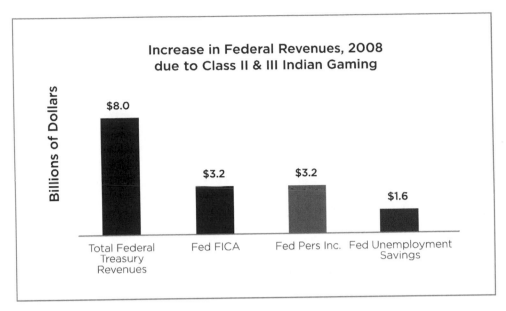

Figure 6.3
Increase in Federal Revenues, 2008, due to Class II and III Indian Gaming
Source: National Indian Gaming Commission

It was not until 1979 that a tribe, the Seminole Nation of Florida, opened the first high-stakes bingo parlor. Although tribes were simply engaging in activities comparable to those of states and private gaming operators in Las Vegas and New Jersey, state officials nevertheless sought to extend their regulatory authority over tribes. The tribes contested this and in *California v. Cabazon Band of Mission Indians* (1987), the Supreme Court supported the tribes by declaring that, once a state has legalized any form of gambling, Indian tribes within a state's borders are entitled to offer the same or similar games on trust land and cannot be interfered with or restricted by state actions.

The Court stressed that tribal self-sufficiency and economic development, and the federal government's role in supporting that, outweighed California's interest in regulating Indian gaming for the alleged purpose of controlling organized crime. The decision forced Congress to expedite enactment of legislation to address Indian gaming, since it was clear that tribes had legal authority to engage in gaming. The IGRA was enacted in 1988. IGRA had several goals: (1) establish a statutory basis for Indian gaming as a means of promoting tribal economic development and self-sufficiency and strengthening tribal governments, (2) provide a regulatory basis to protect Indian gaming operations from the criminal elements and to ensure that the tribe was the principal beneficiary of gaming revenues, and (3) establish an independent authority known as the National Indian Gaming Commission (NIGC) to meet congressional concerns and to protect gaming.[21]

The act also divided gaming into three classes:

Class 1: These are traditional social games played for prizes of nominal value, usually in connection with social events or ceremonies. The tribe has exclusive jurisdiction over these games.

Class 2: These consist of bingo, instant bingo, pull tabs, lotto, punch cards, and card games that are authorized by state law. Such games are subject to tribal jurisdiction with oversight by the NIGC.

Class 3: These consist of all other games, including casino-style gambling, keno, pari-mutuel racing (horse and dog), and jai alai. Such games, the most lucrative of all, require a tribal ordinance and approval by the NIGC. They also require a negotiated tribal-state compact, which might include provisions like division of regulatory authority between the two polities; establishment of terms of criminal jurisdiction and allocating of division of labor; payments to the state to cover enforcement or oversight costs; procedural remedies if there is a breach of the compact; and regulations for the operation of gaming, including licensing. States may not insist that the compact contain a tax, fee, charge, or other assessment. The compacting process is designed to balance the interests of the state (concerns over alleged crime, traffic congestion, social ills generated by gaming) with the economic (pursuit of self-sufficiency) and political (respect of tribal sovereignty) interests of the tribe.

Indian gaming is solely the province of the sovereign, the tribal government, as revenues for gaming may only be used to fund tribal government operations, provide for the general welfare of the tribal government and its members, promote tribal economic development, or help the operation and funding of local governments. Tribal governments may also use some of the money to make charitable donations. In 2008 gaming tribes contributions to charities totaled $150 million.

As a result of gaming revenues, some tribes, for the first time since the late nineteenth century, have been able to attain a measure of economic self-determination, improve their relationships with local and state governments, and increase their political clout. Conversely, Indian gaming has also unleashed a powerful backlash from Nevada and New Jersey gaming operations, created tension between some tribes and state governments resulting in litigation, and exacerbated tensions within and between tribes over concern about the cultural impact of gaming on tribal communities. Let us briefly examine some of the positive and negative consequences associated with gaming.

Positive Consequences of Indian Gaming

In January 2005 a broad study, "American Indians on Reservations: A Databook of Socioeconomic Change Between the 1990 and 2000 Censuses," of the demographic, economic, and social impact of Indian gaming was completed by Jonathan B. Taylor and Joseph P. Kalt. The authors comparatively studied the 1990 and 2000 Census data on American Indians living on reservations and in other statistical areas and compared Indian gaming and non-gaming areas and compared them with the United States overall. Fifteen measures were used, including housing, employment, and poverty. The data indicate that, while there are still fundamental socioeconomic disparities between Native peoples and non-Indians, "rapid economic development is taking place among gaming and non-gaming tribes." Here are a few of their findings:

- Having started the 1990s with incomes lagging far behind those for the general U.S. population, American Indians in Indian Country experienced substantial growth in income per capita. Even with this Indian population rising by more than 20 percent between 1990 and 2000, real (inflation-adjusted) per capita Indian income rose by about one-third. For both gaming and non-gaming tribes, the overall rate of income growth substantially outstripped the 11-percent increase in real per capita income for the United States as a whole.

- From 1990 to 2000, family poverty rates dropped by seven percentage points or more in non-gaming areas, and by about ten percentage points in gaming areas. U.S. family poverty dropped eight-tenths of a percentage point.
- Unemployment rates dropped by about two-and-a-half percentage points in non-gaming areas and by more than five percentage points in gaming areas. U.S. unemployment dropped by half a percentage point.
- Housing overcrowding decreased during the decade, particularly in Indian areas without gaming. The percentage of American Indians living in homes with plumbing increased markedly in both gaming and non-gaming areas.[22]

Besides these general findings, in a number of cases the relationship between various tribes and state governments has improved considerably, especially for those tribes who provide substantial revenue to state governments. In 2004 alone, states received approximately $900 million directly from tribes, up from $733 million in 2003.[23]

Incidentally, a number of tribes have voluntarily provided additional monies to support state, local, and county governments, and educational institutions as well. For example, the San Manuel Band of Mission Indians in Southern California has donated over $40 million to charities since 2001. The following is a sample of the gifts they have made in recent years:

- In January 2010 the tribe contributed $1.7 million to the American Red Cross and Doctors without Borders to assist ongoing relief and recovery efforts in Haiti after the country was ravaged by an earthquake.
- In March 2010 the tribe donated $3.7 million to the University of Redlands, $500,000 to the Dorothy Ramon Learning Center in Banning, California, and $600,000 to the Community Hospital of San Bernardino.
- In February 2010 the tribe donated $220,000 to assist the American Red Cross to provide aid to nine tribal communities affected by severe winter weather. In 2008 the tribe donated $1 million to aid in the economic recovery of the Havasupai Tribe impacted by flood waters and in 2007 and 2003 made contributions to California Tribes affected by wildfires.
- In January 2009 the tribe donated over $7 million to twenty-five non-profit organizations and community groups in recognition of the outstanding services each provide to their local communities.
- In 2009 the tribe gifted the Second Harvest Food Bank serving Riverside and San Bernardino counties with five new semi trucks.

The Shakopee Mdewakanton Sioux Community (SMSC) in Minnesota has also made significant contributions to local, state, federal, and tribal programs and communities. Between 1998 and 2009, the tribe donated more than $132 million, making contributions totaling over $40 million in 2008 alone. The following is a sample of how that $40 million was distributed:

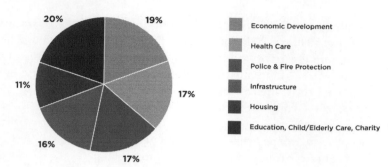

Figure 6.4
Tribal Spending of Gaming Revenue
Source: National Indian Gaming Commission

- The University of Minnesota received $10 million for the construction of the Minnesota Tribal Nations Plaza at TCF Bank Stadium, the largest private gift ever given to Golden Gopher Athletics. An additional $2.5 million was donated for a matching endowment fund for American Indian student scholarships.
- Over $16 million was donated to other tribal nations to fund community and economic development; elderly housing and services; day care facilities and youth centers; water-quality, fish and wildlife management; and to purchase school clothes and supplies.
- Over $2 million was given to native organizations to aid youth shelters, recovery programs, renewable energy programs, indigenous language preservation, and music and the arts. The tribe donated over $700,000 to charitable organizations.

The SMSC also makes voluntary annual payments to cover the costs of services provided by local jurisdictions totaling more that $14.4 million, with $2.4 million paid in 2008. The SMSC Business Council, reflecting on the year's giving, stated, "We are firm in our commitment not only to tribal sovereignty but also to helping the larger community. As Dakota people we have a long tradition of aiding others, and when our needs are met, we have the good fortune to assist others."[24]

Besides the tangible social, educational, and economic benefits gaming revenues support, these funds also enable those nations so inclined to get much more directly involved in local, state, and even national politics. This is discussed in greater detail in chapter 7, but for now it is sufficient to note that since 1990 some tribal governments have made significant financial contributions to the political campaigns of non-Indian politicians. Tribes have also been able to utilize gaming revenue to invest in diverse economic endeavors locally, nationally, and with the Seminole tribe's purchase of the Hard Rock business, internationally (figure 6.4). Seminole Tribal Vice-Chairman Max Osceola, referring to the sale of Manhattan Island by Indians to the Dutch for "trinkets," stated "We're going to buy Manhattan back one hamburger at a time."[25]

■ The Mashantucket Pequot: A Case Study

The tribe most often discussed when addressing the successful side of Indian gaming is the small Mashantucket Pequot Tribe of Ledyard, Connecticut, population 350. Until 1983 the Pequot were not even federally recognized, but in that year they gained not only a recognized sovereign status, but also $900 million in a land claims settlement that they used to start reconstructing a land base and an economy. In 1986 they opened a 2,100-seat bingo hall. However, in 1992, in the wake of the *Cabazon* ruling, the tribe opted for high-stakes casino gaming and opened Foxwoods High Stakes Bingo and Casino. They subsequently negotiated a compact with the governor of Connecticut, Lowell Weicker. The compact allowed a forty-six-thousand-square-foot gaming area with 120 table games: roulette, poker, craps, blackjack, and others. It was the only casino in the eastern United States to offer poker. Initially, Foxwoods employed 2,300 people, mostly from Connecticut and Rhode Island.

In 1993 an agreement was reached between the Mashantucket Pequot and the state that allowed Foxwoods to offer slot machines. The tribe agreed to pay the state 25 percent, or a minimum of $100 million, of its overall slot revenues each fiscal year. The agreement would be declared void if casinos were legalized elsewhere in the state.[26] The agreement provided the state with more than $30 million in 1992–1993 and $117 million in 1993–1994. This agreement was modified in April 1994, when the Pequot and the Mohegan Tribe negotiated a revised agreement that allowed the Mohegan to open a casino without breaching the Pequot's exclusive slot revenue arrangement with the state. Each tribe agreed to pay the state 25 percent of their slot revenue, or 30 percent if the payment for each tribe in one year fell below $80 million. The Pequot gaming operation annually generates about $1 billion, has directly created thirteen thousand jobs, and generated nearly forty-one thousand jobs in the state of Connecticut since 1992. Since 2007, the Pequot have actively pursued new market opportunities in gambling, competing with other large casino operators and beating out Trump Entertainment Resorts, Pinnacle Entertainment, and several others to lead the development of a $500-million slot parlor and hotel to open in Philadelphia. However, facing economic difficulties, the project has been delayed and will be financed by Wynn Resorts of Las Vegas. Tribal gaming has also felt the impact of the recession and declining national economy that began in 2007. Preliminary research shows that the Foxwoods casino is down almost $10 million in net dollars, while the Mohegan Sun is down more then $6 million when comparing July of fiscal year 2009–2010 to July of fiscal year 2008–2009. Thaddieus W. Conner and William A. Tagart note, "the Indian gaming industry is not as recession proof as was once thought. Conversations with various state gaming officials indicate it is difficult to determine what the landscape of Indian gaming will look like as the country emerges from the depths of the current economic recession. At this juncture, a return to the days of years past does not appear imminent."[27] Nonetheless, native governments have proven resilient, and will likely continue with gaming and pursue further economic diversification as well.

Negative Consequences of Indian Gaming

Gambling, no matter who controls it, can cause or exacerbate problems for individuals and communities. Tribes and their members are not immune from social and economic ills sometimes generated by legalized gambling, and some communities and tribal members have voiced concerns about some of these issues. From an internal perspective, one key issue has been concern about crime. There is fear, expressed by Indians, states, and federal officials, that (1) gaming may allow organized crime to infiltrate Indian gaming operations or that (2) the increased number of non-Indians coming onto Indian lands because of the presence of gaming operations may lead to an increase of interracial crime. For instance, in 1992 federal agents arrested two Chicago crime figures, John "No-Nose" Difronzo and Samuel Carlisi, and eight of their associates on charges of racketeering, extortion, and fraud in an effort to gain control of the Rincon Indian Reservation's gaming operations near San Diego, California.[28]

Nevertheless, most evidence suggests that the regulation and oversight apparatus put into place by the IGRA, and the compacting process, appear to be sufficient at keeping crime at a minimum. As one of the studies notes, "The highly regulated atmosphere in [Indian] casinos appears to be a crime-deterrent. Customers and employees are subject to constant video surveillance, which is highly coordinated with gaming floor security. In other words, a casino is not the place where criminals choose to operate."[29]

Another concern is gambling addiction, or compulsive gambling, which has been linked with psychiatric disorders (including alcohol and substance abuse and depression-related conditions), family problems (including physical violence, suicide attempts, and child abuse), and emotional problems among children of gamblers (including depression and substance abuse).[30] Addictive gambling is a real concern for tribes, the states, and the federal government, and some tribes are proactively developing programs and policies to address the issue. A number of casinos ban alcohol; some tribes provide financial assistance to organizations fighting addictive gambling, as in the case of the Standing Rock Sioux, who have contributed to the Mental Health Association of North Dakota for maintenance of a compulsive gamblers' crisis counseling hotline; and other tribes run programs aimed at promoting awareness of problem gambling.[31]

A third issue is that gaming in some tribes causes or heightens tensions among tribal members, with some segments expressing concern about the impact of gaming revenues on the political and cultural integrity of the nation. In some cases, physical violence has erupted between tribal members. In 1990 on the Mohawk's Akwesasne Reservation in upstate New York, tension between a progambling segment and those opposed to gaming erupted in gunfire, leaving two Mohawk men dead.[32] In other cases this intratribal tension has resulted in some tribal government officials "banishing," disenrolling, or expelling some tribal members who have raised questions about the tribal leadership's management of the gaming operations.[33]

In the case of the Lumbee of North Carolina, a state-recognized people in pursuit of complete federal recognition, the lure of potential gambling revenues—"potential" because they are currently ineligible to engage in gaming as an unrecognized tribe—has sparked a divisive split within the community. In December 2009 the tribal council, in a closed-door session, signed a multimillion dollar "recognition services contract" with Lewin International of Nevada that effectively jettisoned their previous lawyer, the noted Lumbee attorney Arlinda Locklear, who had skillfully represented the Lumbee for over two decades in their recognition efforts.

When word of the contract was received in the community, a group of Lumbees formed the Lumbee Sovereignty Coalition and raised a series of probing questions about the methods and reasons behind the Council's decision to contract with Lewin. First, it directly contradicts section four of the Lumbee Recognition bill (H.R. 31), which states that "the tribe may not conduct gaming activities as a matter of claimed inherent authority." Second, the tribe's constitution expressly states that an ordinance authorizing gaming has to first be submitted to the people via a referendum vote. As a result, in 2010 the contract was voided.

The Haudenosaunee Council of Chiefs, representing the traditional-minded peoples of the Iroquois Confederacy, formally issued a statement in 2005 through Sidney Hill, the Tadadaho (leading spokesman), expressing their collective opposition to gambling. According to the chiefs, "Casino culture destroys the social, cultural and spiritual fabric of our people, and will lead to more serious disruption of the overall health and welfare of our people."[34]

Fourth, the relative success of Indian gaming has generated a powerful political and economic reaction from certain states, some members of Congress, the Supreme Court, and the private gaming industry. States were required under the IGRA to make a "good faith" effort to negotiate a compact with those tribes who wanted to pursue Class 3 gaming ventures. The act authorized tribes to bring lawsuits in federal court against states that failed to negotiate. But in an important decision on the gaming act and federalism itself, *Seminole Tribe v. Florida* (1996), the U.S. Supreme Court held that Congress lacked the power under the Indian commerce clause to force states to waive their sovereign immunity and subject them to suits by tribes. The Court said that a state could assert an Eleventh Amendment immunity defense to avoid a tribal lawsuit alleging that the state did not negotiate in good faith.

Since this decision, tribes have been unable to request judicial mediation if the state asserts sovereign immunity. States, in effect, now have veto power over the IGRA dispute resolution system, a situation that has stalemated the compacting process for some tribes. The secretary of the interior must now step in when such a stalemate occurs to mediate and issue procedures for the conduct of Class 3 gaming.[35]

Although many states and tribes have voluntarily negotiated compacts, and although tribes have never attempted to stifle state gaming operations or sought to tax such operations, some states, like New Mexico, Arizona, Minnesota, California, and Florida, have furiously fought tribes over their right to game with a minimum of state regulation and have sought to impose state taxes on tribal proceeds from gaming.

In the fall of 2004, Governor Tim Pawlenty of Minnesota notified the eleven Ojibwe and Dakota tribes in the state that he expected them to pay the state $350 million a year to maintain their current gaming status. This demand arrived even though the present tribal-state gaming compact was still in place, and even though the state had already received a reasonable $150,000 for regulation and inspection purposes. Pawlenty's assault on the economic sovereignty of the tribes was eventually tabled.

At the same time, Governor Arnold Schwarzenegger of California, upon his election, began to insist that the gaming tribes pay what he called a "fair share" of their net earnings, or about 25 percent, to the state. While some tribes, as recently as 2008, have agreed to renegotiate their compacts with the state, giving the state a higher percentage of their revenues in exchange for larger gaming operations, Chairman Deron Marquez of San Manuel more accurately noted that "what people forget—especially in the governor's office—is that there is no right for the state to share revenue with a sovereign nation."[36]

Assaults on tribal gaming from politicians such as Pawlenty and Schwarzenegger fueled anti-Indian sentiments expressed in rhetoric that positioned tribes as special interest groups. This discourse, as Kevin Bruyneel points out, is amplified by the notion that "1) the tribe's claims are based upon archaic premises or promises, from another time, which are not applicable in modern American time; and 2) contemporary indigenous economic and political development has outpaced the historical boundaries of tribal sovereignty, and thus it is not an expression of sovereignty at all, but is rather a wild, reckless

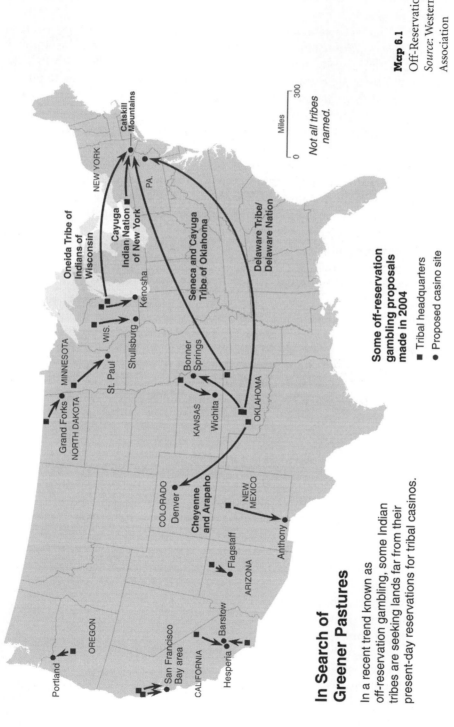

In Search of Greener Pastures

In a recent trend known as off-reservation gambling, some Indian tribes are seeking lands far from their present-day reservations for tribal casinos.

Some off-reservation gambling proposals made in 2004

■ Tribal headquarters

● Proposed casino site

Miles

0 — 300

Not all tribes named.

Map 6.1

Off-Reservation Gambling

Source: Western Governors Association

form of special interest activity."[37] Politicians have utilized this misconstruction of tribal sovereignty to not only gain election but, once in office, to push policies that seek to diminish or deny assertions of tribal sovereignty that allow indigenous nations to endure. "Indian gaming is not a special interest," noted an official for the National Indian Gaming Association. "It is but one outcome of tribal sovereignty, and tribe's rights to self-govern and try to prosper through various economic development means."[38]

Another major area of contention, both within and between tribes and between tribes and the states and federal government, has been the attempt by some tribes to establish gaming locations in areas the tribes no longer inhabit but that may now be located in or near major metropolitan areas. For example, the Cheyenne and Arapaho Indians once held land in Colorado, but they were forced out in the nineteenth century to Oklahoma. In 2005, the two tribes offered the state of Colorado $1 billion and a willingness to abandon their land claims against the state "all in exchange for a 500-acre piece of land near Denver on which they hope to build one of the world's largest casinos, complete with a five-star hotel, golf course, shopping mall, and a cultural center."[39]

Pressure from the states also led to action by Congress to target Indian gaming income for taxation, an unprecedented consideration since state lotteries are not subject to federal taxes. In 1997 Congressman Bill Archer of Texas went so far as to propose a 34-percent corporate income tax on tribal gaming revenue and other Indian businesses. Archer asserted that tribal gaming operations had unfair advantages over non-Indian casinos and businesses. Tribal leaders and congressional supporters of Indian gaming, like Senator John McCain of Arizona and then Senator Ben Nighthorse Campbell of Colorado, successfully fought to defeat this measure, arguing that one sovereign did not have the right to tax the income of another sovereign. It had not been the first such tax proposal, however. In 1994 the Clinton administration briefly considered a special tax on tribal casinos to finance welfare revisions. But the administration dropped the idea in the face of considerable tribal opposition.[40]

Bills have been introduced to amend IGRA every year since its enactment in 1988. In the 110th Congress (2007–2008) alone, six bills were introduced to modify the act (H.R. 1555, H.R. 1654, H.R. 2562, H.R. 3752, H.R. 2643, and S. 2676). Among other things, these bills, if enacted, would have imposed a moratorium on the approval of new state-tribal compacts, regulated casino development on newly acquired lands, limited casino expansion, and limited the application of IGRA to tribes that had been federally recognized for twenty-five continuous years.

Because of the inherent risks and potentialities associated with gaming, a number of tribes, like the Hopi Tribe, have chosen not to engage in high-stakes gaming as an economic-development venture. Opponents have expressed grave concerns about the perceived diminishment of their sovereignty, since they would be forced to negotiate gaming compacts with the states under the provisions of the IGRA if they wanted to engage in the more lucrative games of chance. They have also expressed concern about the moral consequences of gaming and its long-term impact on the social welfare of the tribe. In fact, only one third of the 565 recognized native nations operate casino-style gambling on their lands.[41]

Native nations accept the reality that Indian gaming will not last indefinitely, since legalized gaming is increasing throughout America as a means of producing income. They also are keenly aware that there is an anti-Indian dimension that hopes to curtail Indian gaming efforts.

As a result, many tribes are as rapidly as possible diversifying their economic portfolios so that if and when gaming proceeds dwindle or are stopped altogether, the tribal government will have alternative economic means in place to sustain their development. Indeed, as Figure 6.5 illustrates, Indian gaming is just one of many spending choices available to consumers. The Ho-Chunk Nation, for instance, has established a construction company and built an RV park and campground, motels, a gift shop, and a restaurant. The Mohegan Tribe of Connecticut is establishing an aquaculture business, is engaged in wholesale electricity and gas marketing, and has built an arts and crafts store. The Oneida of Wisconsin have tobacco shops, an industrial park, an electronics manufacturing facility, a cellular communications company, a printing enterprise, an Internet service business, and other projects.[42]

Agriculture and Natural Resources

Since land is the central issue structuring tribal sovereignty and animating indigenous–non-indigenous relations, it should come as no surprise that the natural resources appurtenant to Indian lands are critical for the perpetuation of tribal nations as political and cultural sovereigns and that these resources have major impacts on the political-economic relationships of tribes to states, the federal government, and the corporate world. It is no coincidence, therefore, that Indian affairs have been administered by the Department of the Interior since 1849. That department's primary charge is to encourage the management, preservation, and operation of the public lands and natural resources of the United States, and to work closely with tribes and their lands and resources to ensure that reservations and their members receive sufficient economic, educational, and social services through proper administration of the trust responsibility.

First Nations, as with all human societies, have utilized their natural resources to sustain themselves economically. Although by the early twentieth century most tribes had been required to surrender a majority of their lands to the United States through treaties, laws, and policies like Indian removal and the General Allotment Act, the lands and resources reserved and the rights and resources they retained on ceded lands provided them some basis on which to maintain their livelihood, although in a greatly diminished fashion.

Of course, the 1887 General Allotment Act, the central component of the government's policy of forced assimilation, set a chain of events in motion that vested virtually unlimited power in the Interior Department's commissioner of Indian affairs and his delegates (the local Indian agents) to sell, lease, or administer lands and natural resources of tribal communities. Yet as the Select Committee on Indian Affairs found in 1987 after a two-year investigation of the U.S. treatment of Indians, "despite the federal government's long standing obligation to protect Indian natural resources, they have been left unprotected, subject to, at best, benign neglect and, at worst, outright theft by unscrupulous private companies."[43]

In addition, it is evident that Congress, the ultimate trustee under the Constitution, bears the greatest responsibility for its handling of Indian natural resources, largely because it has failed to understand the larger dynamics of the economics of given time periods. The allotment policy, for example, was begun when the American family farm was becoming an anachronism and when agriculture demanded a sizable investment

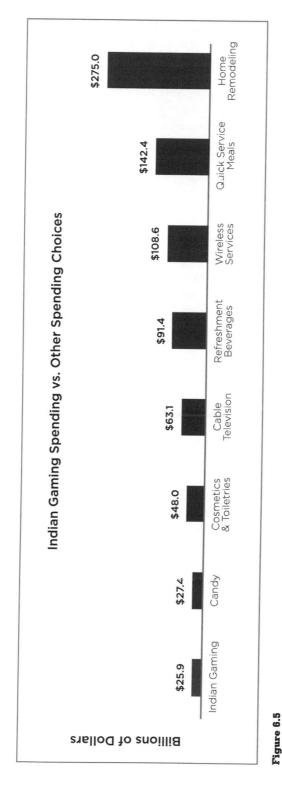

Figure 6.5
Indian Gaming Spending *vs.* Other Spending Choices
Source: National Indian Gaming Association

in machinery; tribal governments did not have the right to veto Interior Department leases of their lands until the 1920s, during the last years of the first great industrial spurt before the Great Depression of the 1930s; the termination period of the 1950s and 1960s occurred when private capitalism was thought to be the tribes' savior; and the rush to exploit the tribes' nonrenewable energy resources in the 1960s and 1970s came during an era when such practices were being called into question by other segments of society.[44]

Despite the numerous and oppressive constraints imposed on tribes and their resources by their federal trust agent, the Interior Department, Indian tribes have found the means to cope within these confines, although only a few tribes were able to generate or sustain much positive economic development before the advent of Indian gaming. Let us turn our attention, however briefly, to the areas that have provided tribes with a measure of economic support over the years.

Agriculture

Of the over fifty-four million acres owned by the tribes under trust status, some forty-four million are rangeland (5 percent of the nation's total) and about 2.5 million are cropland (about 1 percent of the U.S. total). Thus range and croplands are important resources that provide tribes and individual Indians with real income and job opportunities. However, because of Bureau of Indian Affairs (BIA) lease arrangements of Indian allotments with non-Indians, inadequate water and irrigation systems, the high cost of agricultural implements and machinery, lack of financial credit, the fractionated heirship nature of tribal lands, and the lack of general economic infrastructure (e.g., roads and communications systems), the potential yield from agricultural activity is not what it could be.[45]

In fact, according to the BIA, in 1975 the gross value of agricultural products grown on Indian range and croplands was $394 million. However, Indians received only $123 million, or less than one third of that amount, with the remaining $231 million going to non-Indians. More recently, in November 1999, 213 Indian farmers and ranchers (on behalf of nineteen thousand Indians) filed a $19 billion class-action lawsuit against the Department of Agriculture, alleging a twenty-year history of discrimination in the granting of federal loans.[46] As Tex Hall, one of the Indian plaintiffs, said, "as indigenous people we are the first farmers and ranchers of this land. All we wanted is a fair chance to become successful." This suit was similar to one African-American farmers had filed against the government that was settled in April 1999 for an estimated $2 billion.

The major types of agriculture practiced on Indian lands include livestock grazing, dry land farming, and irrigation. Indian farmers typically have concentrated their energy and resources on grazing, which tends to be the least profitable of these three types of farming.[47] Associated with grazing are the cattle industries started by a number of tribes of the northern plains and the Southwest in the late nineteenth century and continuing today. Indian cattle ranching provided an economically viable way of life for some tribes, even though it was discouraged by the BIA, which insisted that Indians become farmers.[48]

Some tribes have sought to break the lease cycle by developing their own tribally operated farm enterprises. Such operations provide a greater rate of return for the community from their lands and they also provide employment. For example, the Indians of the Ak-Chin Reservation in Arizona in 1962 established Ak-Chin Farms once the non-Indian lease expired. In less than a decade the enterprise was grossing over $1 million a year. The tribe had to reduce its operation in the mid-1970s because the underground water supply was being exhausted by non-Indian farmers who lived adjacent to the reservation. However, in 1984 the tribe, after a lengthy court battle against the federal government, gained a permanent water supply from the Colorado River for its agricultural needs.[49] The tribe, through Ak-Chin Farms Enterprise, grows cotton, barley, potatoes, alfalfa, and corn on the 16,000-acre farmland, generating $9.7 million of the total tribal income.[50]

Despite the relative success of the Ak-Chin, most other tribes and individual Indians had insufficient land or inadequate money to operate successful farms. Nevertheless, because of Indians' connection to the land, farming will more than likely remain one form of economic development that they will continue to pursue, however difficult the conditions.

Energy

Since well before the oil embargo of the Organization of the Petroleum Exporting Countries (OPEC) in 1973, and before the rise of high stakes gambling, energy-related mineral deposits—coal, gas, oil, uranium—on Indian lands dominated the economic spectrum for tribes whose resource endowments contained such deposits. In fact, the media and the public in this era had the mistaken impression that energy-rich tribes were the rule rather than the exception, a situation similar to that facing tribes today as a result of the incorrect perception that all gaming tribes are wealthy.

It is certainly true, as Marjane Ambler found, that some tribes own very large amounts of the nation's energy minerals: Indians own 30 percent of the strippable low-sulfur coals west of the Mississippi River, 50 to 60 percent of the uranium resources in the United States, and 5 percent of the country's oil and gas reserves.[51] In 1990, more than 15 million barrels of oil, 135 million cubic feet of natural gas, and 27 million tons of coal were extracted from Indian lands.

However, these resources are not evenly distributed among the tribes. Of the 326 Indian land areas in the lower forty-eight states, only about 40 contain these resources in sufficient amounts to be profitable. Moreover, natural resources, particularly minerals, have historically been subject to strong cyclical price fluctuations. So just as their dependency on federal dollars has left tribes subject to vacillating political tides, dependency on natural resource revenues makes them vulnerable to the changing trends in commodity prices.[52]

Since the allotment era, the development of these resources has been largely out of the control of the tribal governments or Indian allottees, as the secretary of the interior, exercising his tremendous discretionary power, leased out tribal lands to various oil, coal, and gas companies. The exploitation of these nonrenewable resources had a profound political-economic impact on tribes. The Navajo Nation's first tribal council was formed in 1922 as a direct result of pressure exerted by oil companies on the Interior Department. The oil companies were required by law to secure the Indians' consent before drilling. The Navajo agent and Commissioner of Indian Affairs, Charles Burke, convinced the Navajo to create a Business Council, the forerunner of the Navajo Nation Council, in 1922.[53]

Oil and gas were discovered in great quantities on Osage Indian land in Oklahoma even earlier, around 1896, and this discovery created the perception by 1906 that the Osage people, per capita, were "the richest people on earth."[54] Osage wealth, however, was viewed with great envy by many, and the Interior Department arranged a blanket lease that encompassed the entire reservation for exploitation of Osage resources. This leasing arrangement "caused problems that haunted Indian people for years to come—for example, lack of surface owner and environmental protection; lack of competition; speculation; and bribery of both Interior and tribal officials."[55]

In the 1950s and 1960s, coal and uranium began to be mined in great quantities on the Crow and Northern Cheyenne reservations in Montana and on Navajo and Hopi lands in Arizona and New Mexico, although the nature and extent of reservation mineral deposits had been known and actually mapped twenty to forty years before they were leased and developed. Economics and politics, rather than geological discourse, determined the rate and extent of Indian mining.[56]

Moreover, the vast majority of these leases were inequitable arrangements that ensured that Indian revenues generated from these nonrenewable resources were only a fraction of what they should have been. A major deficiency in the leases negotiated by the Department of the Interior "on behalf of the tribes" was that "royalty rates [were] usually too low and fixed in dollars per unit of production of the resources which, of course, ignores increases in value rather than percentage of value, which increases income as minerals increase in value."[57] As an example, in four of the five Navajo coal leases negotiated between 1957 and 1968, the tribe's royalties were fixed between $0.15 and $0.375 a ton. But the average value for a ton of coal rose from $4.67 in 1968 to $18.75 in 1975.

Low royalty rates were just a small part of the problem tribes faced regarding their mineral resources. By the late 1960s it was clear that the entire decision-making process employed by the BIA and the Department of the Interior regarding the authority and manner in which the leases occurred was flawed, that tribes had rarely been informed of the true value of their resources, that they lacked any control or self-determination over these resources, and that environmental degradation was becoming a major concern of all Indian people. Even as tribes were struggling to gain greater rights over these resources, the 1973 oil embargo imposed by OPEC, an international cartel of oil-producing states, led to an energy crisis and an escalation in prices in the United States, which brought the focus on tribes who owned large amounts of mineral resources. Because the federal government felt compelled to develop the country's own natural resources as a hedge against future embargos, it approached tribes about the need to exploit their reserves. While these natural resource discussions were taking place, twenty-six tribes of the northern plains formed the Native American Natural Resource Development Federation as a way to protect their mineral, water, and agricultural resources by collecting and sharing information regarding these materials.[58]

A year later, twenty-five energy-resource-rich tribes, with federal and public interest group financial support, organized the Council of Energy Resource Tribes (CERT). The tribes told federal officials that they had organized because they wanted:

> resource-related education; a clearinghouse for exchanging information; help arranging financing for development; expertise on alternative contractual arrangements; studies on using resources on the reservations rather than continuing the

tribes' role as colonies exporting energy; impartial environmental studies; and a means for advising the federal government about Indian energy development.[59]

But the fact that CERT received ample funding from the Department of Energy and the BIA undercut its claim to be "domestic OPEC"; also, some tribes questioned CERT's merits, since the BIA would sometimes refuse funding to tribes on the grounds that it had already sent money to CERT. Nevertheless, CERT continues to play an important role for its member tribes by, among other things, helping them monitor and negotiate energy contracts. There are now more than fifty member tribes in the organization. See table 6.3 for a list of these tribes and their resource endowments. One member tribe, the Southern Ute, after struggling for many years to gain control of its natural resources from large energy companies, now control roughly 1 percent of the nation's natural gas supply, worth approximately $40 billion.

The year 1982 was important for energy-owning tribes. Congress enacted the Indian Mineral Development Act, which authorized tribes to join with industry as mineral developers and to choose which development ventures to pursue. And the U.S. Supreme Court handed down *Merrion v. Jicarilla Apache Indian Tribe*,[60] which recognized the right of tribes to impose a severance tax on energy companies engaged in mining on tribal lands. The Merrion case was somewhat muted by a 1989 ruling, *Cotton Petroleum Corporation v. New Mexico*,[61] which held that the state of New Mexico could impose its own severance tax on oil and gas produced on tribal land by a company already paying a similar tribal tax. This "double-taxation" of business entities in Indian Country could cause severe problems, since it could cause companies to move off reservations to avoid paying double taxes.

An interesting yet problematic form of tribal economic development directly related to energy issues is the disposal of hazardous and radioactive waste on or near Indian lands. Reservation lands are nonpublic and are generally not subject to state

TABLE 6.3

CERT Member Tribes

Tribe	State	Known and Potential Resources
Acoma Pueblo	NM	Coal, Geothermal, Natural Gas
Blackfeet	MT	Coal, Oil, & Natural Gas
Cherokee	OK	Coal, Oil, & Natural Gas
Cheyenne & Arapaho	OK	Oil & Gas
Cheyenne River Sioux	SD	Oil, Gas, & Coal
Chippewa-Cree (Rocky Boys)	MT	Coal, Oil, Natural Gas, & Uranium
Confederated Colville	WA	N/A
Crow	MT	Coal, Oil, & Natural Gas
Eastern Shoshone Flathead (Salish & Kootenai)	MT	Hydroelectric & Natural Gas
Fort Belknap	MT	Coal, Oil, Natural Gas, & Geothermal
Fort Berthold	MT	Coal, Oil, Natural Gas, & Geothermal
Fort Hall	ID	Geothermal & Natural Gas

(Continued)

TABLE 6.3
CERT Member Tribes (*Continued*)

Tribe	State	Known and Potential Resources
Fort Mojave	CA	N/A
Fort Peck	MT	Coal, Oil, Natural Gas, & Geothermal
Hopi	AZ	Coal, Uranium, Oil, & Natural Gas
Hualapai	AZ	Uranium, Oil, Natural Gas, & Hydro
Iowa of Oklahoma	OK	N/A
Jemez Pueblo	NM	Uranium, Natural Gas, Geothermal, & Oil
Jicarilla Apache	NM	Oil, Natural Gas, Coal, & Geothermal
Kaibab Paiute	AZ	N/A
Kaw Nation	OK	N/A
Laguna Pueblo	NM	Coal, Uranium, Oil, & Natural Gas
Lummi Nation	WA	N/A
Morongo Band of Mission Indians	CA	N/A
Muckleshoot	WA	Coal, Natural Gas, Oil, & Hydroelectric
Navajo	AZ	Coal, Natural Gas, Oil, Uranium, & Geothermal
Nez Perce	ID	Hydroelectric
Northern Arapaho	WY	N/A
Northern Cheyenne	MT	Coal, Oil, & Natural Gas
Oglala Sioux	SD	Oil, Natural Gas, & Uranium
Ohkay Owingeh	NM	N/A
Osage	OK	N/A
Pauma Band of Mission Indians	CA	N/A
Pawnee	OK	Oil & Gas
Penobscot	WA	N/A
Picuris Pueblo	NM	N/A
Ponca	OK	Oil & Gas
Ramona Band of Cahuilla	CA	N/A
Rosebud Sioux	SD	Oil, Natural Gas, Oil Shale, & Geothermal
Round Valley	CA	N/A
Saginaw Chippewa	MI	Oil & Gas
Saint Regist Mohawk	NY	N/A
Santa Ana Pueblo	NM	Geothermal
Southern Ute	CO	Coal, Oil, & Natural Gas
Standing Rock Sioux	SD	N/A
Tule River	CA	Hydroelectric
Turtle Mountain (Chippewa)	ND	Oil, Natural Gas, & Coal
Uintah Ute & Ouray	UT	Oil, Natural Gas, Coal, Tar Sand, & Oil Shale
Umatilla	OR	Geothermal & Hydroelectric
Ute Mountain Ute	CO	Coal, Oil, Natural Gas, & Uranium
Walker River Paiute	NV	Uranium, Geothermal, & Hydroelectric
Yakima	WA	Oil, Natural Gas, & Hydroelectric
Zia Pueblo	NM	Uranium, Geothermal, Oil, & Natural Gas
Canadian Tribes		
Ermineskin Nation of Cree	AB	N/A
Louis Bul Band of Cree	AB	N/A
Montana Nation of Cree	AB	N/A
Samson Cree Nation	AB	N/A

Source: Amended from C. Matthew Snipp, "Public Policy Impacts on American Indian Economic Development," *Public Policy Impacts on American Indian Economic Development* (Albuquerque: University of New Mexico, 1988), 13; and www.certredearth.com.

regulations governing solid and hazardous waste materials. Moreover, federal laws governing such matters are not as strong as those already in place in many states. By the early 1990s, as many landfills were closed, neared capacity, or failed to meet stricter federal standards, the waste industry and the Department of Energy viewed Indian lands as possible landfill sites to store spent nuclear fuel.

Some tribes, like the Mescalero Apache of New Mexico, openly discussed becoming a host to such materials to offset unemployment and bring needed capital. These discussions have increased tensions among the tribe's members and the tribal government and between the tribal government and New Mexico, which is deeply resistant to allowing such materials in their midst; the discussions have also placed the Mescalero at odds with environmentalists and sparked animosity with other tribes.[62]

However, tribes like the Yakima of Washington State have forcefully rejected the entreaties of companies and the federal government to allow their homelands or former homelands to serve as storage places for such materials, since their members view the land as sacred and because they distrust the safety claims of the companies and the United States. As Russell Jim, a council delegate for the tribe, stated: "By placing hazardous radioactive wastes near our reservation, they may well undermine our treaty rights. . . . Our lands may be contaminated irretrievably by action on nearby non-Indian land or from faulty transportation of radioactive wastes."[63]

Other tribes fight against economic development plans that pose a risk to their sacred traditional homelands and cultural practices. The Quechan Indian tribe in Arizona is challenging the construction of a planned $4 billion oil refinery that could destroy sites located 40 miles off of the reservation but considered sacred to the tribe. Tribal leader Mike Jackson already found success in preventing two other planned projects—a low-level nuclear dump and a $50 million gold mine—both also a distance from the reservation. Tribes across the nation have sought with inconsistent success to protect sites of considerable religious significance from destruction or degradation as a result of economic development. The Navajo, Hopi, and eleven other tribes in Arizona sought without success to protect the San Francisco Peaks from further development for a ski resort; and the Northern Cheyenne have sought to block drilling for coal-bed methane near their Montana reservation that was affecting their sacred springs. In Alaska, the Inupiat fear the impact oil drilling will have on their long-standing whaling practices. These tensions persist.

Global awareness of climate change and its relationship to energy development is ripe within Indian Country. The Navajo Nation remains divided over the development of a coal-fired power plant that could generate $50 million a year in taxes, royalties, and other income by selling power while also emitting twelve million tons of carbon dioxide. The Nez Perce people in Idaho are working to bridge local needs for economic development and energy with global concerns for the environment. They are converting their reservation lands, cleared in the nineteenth century for farming, back to forest land because timber is a sustainable form of economic development. While tribal carbon sales have had mixed results since the 1990s, as Jim Robbins notes, "The market for carbon credits promises to be a boon for some land-rich but casino-poor tribes."[64]

Timber

Unlike fish and wildlife, which have generally been considered as belonging to the Indians as a property right, timber, since 1874, has been understood as a part of the trust lands belonging to the federal government and held for the benefit of the Indians. Thus, as the property of the United States, timber could not be cut without express federal authorization and timbering had to be done strictly for "the improvement of the land."[65]

Of the 56 million acres owned by tribes outside Alaska, about 5.3 million have commercially valuable timber reserves. This acreage translates to forty-two billion board feet, or 1.5 percent of the nation's supply of lumber. Forestry provides significant revenue to at least fifty-seven reservations, mostly in the Pacific Northwest, although fourteen of those reservations generate 96 percent of all timber revenues.[66] The reservations producing the most timber revenue in the 1980s were the Yakima ($19.7 million) and Colville ($17.7 million) reservations of Washington and the Warm Springs Reservation ($11.6 million) of Oregon.

A number of tribal mills, like the Menominee Mill in Wisconsin and the Navajo Forest Product Industry in Arizona, receive support from the BIA and the Economic Development Administration (EDA). Despite this support, a congressional investigation of government policies toward tribes involving timber management found in 1989 that the BIA's management of tribal timber resources was inadequate. "Although timber is potentially a major source of income for several dozen reservations," said the report, "especially in the Northwest, the BIA's own internal assessment indicates serious deficiencies in its Division of Forestry."[67] And while stating that a lack of funding was a major cause of the BIA's problems, the report noted that tribes had lost more than $300 million between 1979 and 1989 because of poor management of their forests and woodlands.

The other major issue for timber is that, like energy prices, timber prices declined sharply in the 1980s from the peaks reached in the late 1970s. Thus, by 1982 the total Indian revenues had fallen from the 1979 peak of $117.2 million to $39.7 million.[68]

Some tribes, under self-determination contracting procedures established by Congress in 1975, have attempted to take control over their own forestry programs, but even these groups have faced great difficulty stemming largely from the BIA's unwillingness to surrender power to the requesting tribe. The Quinault Nation of Washington State has one of the most advanced forestry management programs. But even their operations faced a shutdown because the BIA contract funds did not arrive consistently.[69]

Nevertheless, by the late 1970s tribes were becoming increasingly involved in decisions regarding their timber. For instance, in 1979 a number of tribes together established an Intertribal Timber Council to help in timber management decisions. Similar to CERT, this body encourages the development of tribal forest programs and products and encourages tribes to participate in studies aimed at forest management and conservation.[70] And research has shown that as tribal control increases vis-à-vis BIA control, the productivity of workers increases, costs go down, and income improves. In fact, even the price received for logs improves.[71]

At the regional level, tribes are also persisting in their efforts to exercise greater sovereignty of these and other valuable resources through the negotiation of agreements like the Timber, Fish and Wildlife Agreement negotiated in 1987 between a number of western Washington tribes, the timber industry, environmental organizations, and the state of Washington.[72] This agreement, following in the wake of a state-tribal fishery management plan, provides a process for resolving differences that are bound to arise when different parties are managing the same resources.

In addition, laws like the National Indian Forest Resources Management Act of 1990 increased tribal management and gave financial support for the forestry activities of tribes. As a result of this measure and the 1975 Indian Self-Determination Act, tribes are increasingly making their own determination on what is best for their forests.

Tourism

Because a segment of the American population has always had a genuine curiosity about Indian peoples, their lands (especially those in the desert Southwest), and their cultures, tourism has offered possibilities for tribal economic development. Cultural tourism, as Susan Guyette calls it, is in fact the marketing of cultural heritage.[73] Examples abound.

The Eastern Cherokee, who live in the Smoky Mountains of North Carolina, sell baskets and sculptures and put on an annual pageant play; the Pueblos of New Mexico sell distinctive pottery and silver work and exhibit unique architectural patterns that are pleasing to the non-Indian eye; the Navajo produce beautiful rugs and turquoise jewelry and inhabit lands like the Four Corners area and Monument Valley, Arizona, that provide outstanding vistas; and many tribes have museums and art galleries and hold annual powwows and other ceremonies that have attracted tourists for several generations. Most recently and most spectacularly, the Mashantucket Pequot have used some of their vast gaming wealth to build a world-class museum and cultural research center. The $130 million, 308,000-square-foot facility is the largest of its kind in the United States.

In 1967 the EDA, established by the Public Works and Economic Development Act of 1965 and a major agency in the federal government's War on Poverty, created an Indian desk and made a major commitment to promote economic development projects on Indian reservations. EDA funds were directed toward infrastructure investments, industrial parks, and tourism facilities, among other projects. From 1966 to 1976 EDA spent more than $272 million in an effort to advance Indian economic development.[74]

EDA administrators believed that tourism offered some of the best prospects for new businesses on reservations, and they made a major effort to fund tourism projects, citing Indian Country's attractive physical environments and the availability of desirable recreational opportunities as key factors justifying their optimism. But a 1972 study funded by the Ford Foundation, titled "The Gift That Hurt the Indians," said that most Indian tourism projects had been failures. The authors concluded that "the numbers of tourists being attracted were far short of the numbers needed for financially successful operations. The $67 million in federal funds spent for Indian tourism since 1967 had yielded projects running a total annual deficit in 1977 of $5.0 million—creating a continuing major drain on tribal as well as federal financial resources."[75]

Reasons for the failure included the geographic isolation of many reservations, inadequate transportation systems, harsh climates, lack of hotels, inadequate skill levels of the labor force, and attitudes among some tribal members that did not favor private entrepreneurship or the loss of privacy that accompanies many forms of tourism. Indian tourism, like other forms of economic development, also has a cyclical nature, depending in part on the overall condition of the U.S. economy and the relative attractiveness to tourists of the reservations in a given region.

Arizona, which is home to twenty-one tribes and some of the most beautiful scenery in the nation, is a major player in Indian tourism. A study concluded in 1994 by the Center for Applied Research for the Arizona Department of Commerce, designed to ascertain the economic and fiscal impact of Indian reservations on the state's economy, found that while the state government's expenditures for the Indian population in 1993 were an estimated $41 million, in that same year nearly two million tourists visited Arizona's reservations, spending $511.8 million. Table 6.4 vividly shows the tremendous impact tourism has on the overall economy of the state. Moreover, this table shows that the Indian reservation population alone accounted for $32.5 million in state revenue in 1993, $23 million of which came from transaction privilege tax sources and $9.5 million of which came from corporate income tax sources. In other words, and contrary to popular opinion, tribal members and the tourist dollars their lands and cultures generate produce far more income for the state, at least in Arizona, than the state expends for the tribes.

With the rise in indigenous tourism, in 1999 the American Indian Alaska Native Tourism Association (AIANTA) was founded "to help define, introduce, grow and sustain American Indian and Alaska tourism."[76] The AIANTA, composed of tribes, tribal businesses, and entrepreneurs, seeks to protect and promote the integrity of tribal culture and traditions.

Table 6.4

The Economic and Fiscal Impacts of Tourism: Impacts Attributed to Indian Reservations in Arizona

1993 Arizona tourists drawn by Indian reservations/culture	1,881,662
Average Arizona tourist party (people)	4
1993 Arizona tourist parties drawn by Indian reservations/culture	470,415
Average Arizona tourist party expenditures per day	$272
Average stay of Arizona tourist party (days)	4
Average Arizona tourist party expenditures per stay	$1,088
Total 1993 Arizona statewide tourist expenditures attributable to Indian reservations/culture	511,811,958
Total taxable expenditures	$460,630,762
Statewide Fiscal Impact	
Arizona transaction privilege tax	$23,031,538
Arizona corporate income tax	$9,519,702
Total fiscal impact	$32,551,241
Statewide Economic Impact	
Direct and induced income	$479,055,993
Direct and induced employment	20,278

Source: Center for Applied Research, *The Economic and Fiscal Impact of American Indian Reservations in Arizona* (Denver, Colo.: Center for Applied Research, 1994), 17.

Tribal-State Economic Partnerships

Although historically tribes and states have fought bitterly over many issues and continue to struggle to find common ground, tribes and states have increasingly entered into innovative partnerships in recent years to promote tribal economic development. Some of these partnerships, like those involving the fishing rights controversies in Washington State and the Great Lakes, and like Class 3 gaming compacts, have been driven by federal law and court mandates. But in other cases, tribal and state leaders have voluntarily worked out arrangements that provide benefits to both parties.

In 1973 the Minnesota legislature established an Indian business loan program to provide Indians with a chance to start new businesses or improve existing enterprises. Funds to support the loan program are derived from mineral rights taxes that are collected annually by counties. These funds are divided between the eleven tribal nations in the state. Although the program is administered by the state, each tribal government determines which of their tribes' businesses and projects will be funded.

In Oklahoma, the Small Business Division of the Oklahoma Department of Commerce has a Tribal Government Assistance program that provides support and technical assistance for Indians living on trust lands. The state office helps to draft and analyze business plans, identifies capital sources, coordinates meetings between businesses and tribal leaders, and generates investment procedures that comply with the distinctive trust status of Indian lands and resources. The program also developed an Indian advisory council, which meets quarterly.[77] And some tribes and states are working more closely to promote tourism. To facilitate this, Arizona, Montana, New Mexico, Oklahoma, and South Dakota have passed legislation to protect Indian arts and crafts from competition from imitations.

More recently, the North Dakota legislature directed its legislative council to analyze rural economic development efforts, including those located within or near Indian Country. And the Office of Rural Community Affairs in Texas was implemented to examine community leadership, economic diversification, and telecommunication in the state's rural areas, including Native communities.[78] Tribes and states have also found some success in developing cooperative agreements that involve multiple parties and interests. As recently as February 2010 Secretary of the Interior Ken Salazar joined the Oregon and California governors; chairmen of the Klamath, Yurok, and Karuk tribes; and the chief executive officer of PacifiCorp in announcing the final agreements for the Klamath Basin Restoration Agreement and the Klamath Hydroelectic Settlement Agreement. The largest river restoration project in U.S. history, these agreements, contingent on congressional approval and scientific assessment, outline a process for the removal of four dams by 2020. "The Klamath River, which for years was synonymous with controversy, is now a stunning example of how cooperation and partnership can resolve difficult conflicts," said Secretary Salazar. He noted, "The Agreements provide a path forward to meet the needs of local communities, tribes, farmers, fishermen, and other stakeholders while restoring a beautiful river and its historic salmon runs."[79]

Conclusion

The diversity that is the hallmark of Indian Country means that there is, by definition, a remarkable variety in the kinds of economic development tribes are undertaking as they struggle to cope with the legacy of their internal colonial relationship with the federal government. And while some tribes have made significant strides in their political-economic status because of gaming and other factors, poverty is still the norm and not the exception. This is so for a number of reasons.

First, the trust status of Indian lands and resources, originally designed to prevent the loss or exploitation of those resources, is sometimes viewed by the corporate and business sector as a hindrance to reservation economic development. Second, the ongoing fractionated nature of allotted reservations poses real problems. Third, thick layers of BIA regulations, and the bureau's insistence on approving certain business decisions, still clog the efforts of tribal governments and individual entrepreneurs to exercise self-determination. Fourth, many tribes with significant natural resource endowments are still locked into long-term leases that were negotiated by the BIA years ago. Fifth, many tribes lack the economic connections that are essential to build and sustain economic development. And since there are few reservation businesses, tribal members frequently have to drive long distances to purchase or sell necessary goods and services. Lacking a solid economic base, most locally generated income and revenue on reservations is passed on to non-Indian businesses, with little entering the reservation economy.[80]

Since tribes have a sense that the gaming boom cannot be sustained indefinitely because of the issue of saturation and the forces that have aligned to confront Indian gaming, and since poverty remains deeply entrenched for most tribal communities, there is a real desire by gaming tribes to secure as much capital as they can, to diversify their economies, and to prepare to make do with less in the days ahead. In the meantime, the tribes without gaming or with only marginal gaming operations will continue to struggle economically for the reasons discussed.

We have seen that some tribes, however, have attained a measure of economic stability, notwithstanding the difficult structural and perceptual conditions they confront. For those tribes it comes to this:

> The critical factor in achieving economic stability seems to be in encouraging tribal officials to develop programs that are perceived by the people as natural extensions of things they are already doing. A natural economy maximizes the use of the land in as constructive a manner as possible, almost becoming a modern version of hunting and gathering in the sense that people have the assurance that this kind of activity will always be available to them. . . . The Lummis and some of the other tribes have developed sophisticated aqua-cultures, and this kind of development relates directly to the tribal traditions, even though it is today expressed by and based on highly technical skills.[81]

Such decisions occur and are most often acted upon when the tribal people have a commitment to such enterprises, when the tribal governments have fundamental control over their economic resources, and when tribes have the political will and the political institutions necessary to develop the kinds of economic programs appropriate to their communities and environments.

CHAPTER 7

Indigenous Political Participation

Patriotism, Suffrage, and Partisanship

> You [the federal government] have passed a law [the 1924 General Indian Citizenship Act] that says that we are U.S. citizens. . . . We did not agree to be citizens and we did not agree that your governments could have jurisdiction over us. We do not accept these laws. We are not citizens of the U.S.
>
> —Chief Irving Powless Jr., 1994[1]

WHEN WE SET OUT to examine the various forms and patterns of native political participation in the three polities they are connected to—tribal, state, and federal—we are delving into a most complicated subject. It is complicated in large part because native individuals are citizens of separate extraconstitutional nations whose members have only gradually been incorporated in various ways by various federal policies and day-to-day interactions with non-Indians. Tribal nations, of course, have never been constitutionally incorporated and still retain their standing as separate political bodies not beholden to either federal or state constitutions for their existence.

These realities—tribes as continuing sovereign nations and individual Indians as citizens of not only their tribes but also of the United States and the states—exist simultaneously. If this were not complicated enough, since the late 1980s, and largely as a result of Indian gaming, some tribal governments are now acting, they assert, in a sovereign capacity, not only by proactively supporting state and federal office seekers through financial contributions, but also by weighing in on issues, like the national tobacco litigation, that seem unrelated to tribal affairs.

First Nations have been lobbying in Washington and in state capitals since the beginning of the republic to protect treaty and individual rights, but gambling wealth is providing some tribes with opportunities to employ skilled lobbyists and savvy public relations firms, and make large campaign contributions "to win influence, make friends and crush opponents" in a manner heretofore unknown.[2]

For example, Indian political influence at the state and national level was substantial in 2000 when Indian voters cast their support for the Democratic challenger, Maria Cantwell, who successfully defeated the powerful and entrenched Republican senator of Washington State, Slade Gorton, who had long opposed tribal sovereignty and Indian treaty rights.[3] In 2002, Indian voters in South Dakota exercised their electoral power and helped incumbent Senator Tim Johnson (D-SD) defeat his Republican challenger, U.S. Representative John Thune. Johnson won by a mere 524 votes, and he and many others credit the Indian vote with having made the difference, since 8.3 percent of the state's population is indigenous. In 2006, Montana Democratic challenger Jon Tester defeated Republican incumbent Conrad Burns, having gained strong support from native voters. Data revealed that 2,461 people voted in the precincts on the Blackfeet Reservation, with 83 percent supporting Tester. Montana Senator Carol Juneau, a Mandan and Hidatsa, noted that Indian support was critical in the close election, stating "It shows the power of the Indian vote in Montana and the power of things we can change nationally."[4]

Along with their increasing voting turnout, native contributions to political campaigns also increased tremendously from the mid-1990s through the first decade of the twenty-first century (Tables 7.1 and 7.2). Tribal nations are exempt from the overall individual donor limits of $95,000, and this once gave them a key advantage over individual and corporate donors. But this once distinct indigenous advantage has been at least partially muted by the Supreme Court's 2010 decision, *Citizens United v. Federal Election Commission,* which held that the federal government could not ban political spending by corporations in candidate elections. The court overturned two earlier precedents involving the First Amendment rights of corporations and declared that the government lacked the power to regulate the political free speech rights of corporations who now have the right to directly spend unlimited sums of money on political campaigns.

The Center for Responsive Politics, which tracks political contributions, found that tribal contributions climbed to just over $10 million in 2000 and reached a record high of $21.7 million in 2003.[5] Tribes, however, like others, are not allowed to make unlimited donations, otherwise known as "soft money," although they may challenge this restriction in the wake of the Citizens United ruling.[6] Of the more than $21 million, contributions largely came from tribes that operate gaming facilities. Two tribes gave the most: the Agua Caliente Band of Cahuilla Indians of California donated $2,060,000 and the Saginaw Chippewa in Michigan donated $2,200,000.[7]

Although native governments had some success in the candidates they supported, they were not as successful as they had hoped to be in the 2004 presidential, congressional, or gubernatorial elections, despite a significant "Get Out the Native Vote" campaign organized by the National Congress of American Indians (NCAI), National Voice, and other organizations and individual tribes. Even though John Kerry campaigned hard in Indian Country and received a majority of the votes cast by Indians, including the endorsement of the Navajo Nation, he was defeated by Bush. The Democratic senator, Tom Daschle of South Dakota, who also received overwhelming Native support, also was defeated. He lost to a conservative Republican, John Thune. And despite

Table 7.1

Indian Gaming: Long-Term Contribution Trends

Election Cycle	Total Contributions	Contributions from Individuals	Contributions from PACs	Soft Money Contributions	Donations to Democrats	Donations to Republicans	% to Dems	% to Repubs
2010*	$5,295,949	$5,240,149	$55,800	N/A	$3,741,400	$1,532,349	71%	29%
2008*	$10,428,400	$10,270,660	$157,740	N/A	$7,887,720	$2,537,730	76%	24%
2006*	$7,714,154	$7,534,560	$179,594	N/A	$4,791,927	$2,882,373	62%	37%
2004*	$7,412,615	$7,275,367	$137,248	N/A	$4,975,858	$2,436,757	67%	33%
2002	$6,792,396	$4,218,190	$115,575	$2,458,631	$4,503,515	$2,288,881	66%	34%
2000	$4,509,167	$2,173,654	$62,565	$2,272,948	$3,578,160	$913,358	79%	20%
1998	$1,627,024	$346,796	$91,128	$1,189,100	$978,544	$648,480	60%	40%
1996	$2,035,799	$375,496	$114,782	$1,545,521	$1,725,398	$310,151	85%	15%
1994	$704,500	$168,550	$28,950	$507,000	$573,550	$130,950	81%	19%
1992	$168,681	$54,510	$0	$114,171	$134,460	$34,221	80%	20%
1990	$11,350	$11,350	$0	N/A	$7,400	$3,950	65%	35%
Total	$46,700,035	$37,569,282	$943,382	$8,087,371	$32,897,932	$13,719,200	70%	29%

Source: Center for Responsive Politics

Notes: *These figures do not include donations of "Levin" funds to state and local party committees. Levin funds were created by the Bipartisan Campaign Reform Act of 2002. Methodology: The numbers on this page are based on contributions of $200 or more from PACs and individuals to federal candidates and from PAC, soft money, and individual donors to political parties, as reported to the Federal Election Commission. While election cycles are shown in charts as 1996, 1998, 2000 etc., they actually represent two-year periods. For example, the 2002 election cycle runs from January 1, 2001 to December 31, 2002.

Data for the current election cycle were released by the Federal Election Commission on Sunday, May 16, 2010.

Note: Soft money contributions to the national parties were not publicly disclosed until the 1991-92 election cycle, and were banned by the Bipartisan Campaign Finance Reform Act following the 2002 elections.

Table 7.2
Indian Gaming: Native Nations' Contributions (2009)

Client	Total
Gila River Indian Community	$1,310,000.00
Crow Tribe	$730,000.00
Seminole Tribe of Florida	$730,000.00
Miccosukee Tribe of Indians of Florida	$560,000.00
Jicarilla Apache Nation	$490,000.00

Source: Center for Responsive Politics, www.opensecrets.org

spending some $12 million to defeat Arnold Schwarzenegger in the California recall election, with tribes providing heavy financial support to Lieutenant Governor Cruz Bustamante, Schwarzenegger was elected.

As many American Indian nations have gained entrance to political and economic halls of power because of their gambling enterprises, some have felt compelled to try to navigate, as do many corporations, the even trickier world of Washington lobbyists and public relations specialists who, the tribes believe, can help them maintain and even expand their connections to long-denied political power.

Six tribal nations—the Coushatta Tribe of Louisiana; the Mississippi Band of Choctaw; the Saginaw Chippewa of Michigan; the Agua Caliente Band of Cahuilla Indians of California; the Tigua Indians of Ysleta del Sur Pueblo of El Paso, Texas; and the Pueblo Sandia Tribe of New Mexico; each of which presently operates or desires to operate casinos—beginning in 2001, engaged in a complicated set of financial relationships with two men, Jack Abramoff, a Republican lobbyist, and Michael S. Scanlon, a public relations specialist who formerly served as an aide to the House majority leader, Tom DeLay of Texas. The tribes paid the two men more than $66 million in less than four years to curry influence that they hoped would benefit them and their members, sometimes to the express detriment of other tribes.[8] Upon the advice of the two lobbyists, the tribes also donated millions to various GOP-connected conservative groups like Americans for Tax Reform, the Capital Athletic Foundation, and Ralph Reed's Atlanta-based political consulting firm.

But during a 2004 Senate hearing before the Committee on Indian Affairs, it became clear during review of a long list of subpoenaed documents that the two men had, in fact, been manipulating the tribes in order to secure contracts worth millions of dollars. The lobbyists went so far as to involve themselves in tribal elections so as to gain the favor of tribal leaders who would then, upon election, reward them with lucrative tribal contracts. Senator John McCain said during the 2004 hearing that "what sets this tale apart, what makes it truly extraordinary, is the extent and degree of the apparent exploitation and deceit."[9]

The Senate committee's investigation of the two lobbyist's activities was joined by the Justice Department, the Federal Bureau of Investigation, the Internal Revenue Service, and the Interior Department. These probes proved successful and Scanlon pleaded guilty in November 2005 to conspiring to defraud Indian tribes, while Abramoff pleaded guilty in January 2006 to conspiracy, fraud, and tax evasion for his even larger role in bilking several tribal nations of millions of dollars. Tribal contributions declined after this lobby scandal, as tribes and congresspersons alike were more cautious about how donations would be publicly perceived. Still, tribal donations totaled just over $17 million in 2008 and $15.7 million in 2009.[10]

As indigenous political influence has increased at the state and national level, there are two dimensions that warrant attention. First, Indian gaming has spawned a severe backlash among some state and federal policymakers. This is evident in the increasing tension between some state legislatures and their governors and tribal governments and their leaders. And it is evident in federal lawmakers like former Senator Slade Gorton of Washington State, who derisively labeled Indians "super-citizens." He and some of his colleagues in the Senate and the House sought to force tribes to surrender their sovereign immunity in federal courts for cases brought by non-Indians, tried to impose federal taxes on Indian gaming revenues, and would have liked to deny money to tribes if their income was above a certain level. These and other measures have arisen, tribes say, "because of a perception that Indian reservations are prospering with casino gambling, disregarding the fact that most of them remain among the poorest places in the nation."[11]

The increase in tribal contributions has only perpetuated this misconception and, coupled with the Abramoff lobbying scandal that garnered national attention, escalated state and federal attacks on tribal sovereignty. In 2004 alone, the Agua Caliente Band of Cahuilla Indians, one of Abramoff's top clients, spent $6 million to promote Indian gaming propositions that were ultimately rejected by California state voters. Though the tribe publicly listed their contributions on their website, they neglected to report their contributions from 1998 to 2002, totaling more then $8 million, to the state's Fair Political Practices Commission (FPPC). The FPPC sued the tribe for violation of the Political Reform Act of 1974, which regulates aspects of the election process on the state and local level and requires that political contributions be reported. The Agua Caliente Band claimed that, under the doctrine of tribal sovereign immunity, they were immune from suit. Pitting tribal sovereignty against state sovereignty, the trial court denied the tribe's motion and argued "that to apply tribal sovereign immunity from suit in this case would (1) intrude upon the state's exercise of its reserved power . . . to regulate its electoral and legislative processes and (2) would interfere with the republican form of government guaranteed to the state."[12] The Court of Appeals agreed with the trial court and asserted that the interest of the state to preserve its political process from corruption outweighed Aqua Claiente's claim to sovereign immunity. On December 21, 2006, the California Supreme Court, in a 4–3 ruling, affirmed the Court of Appeals' ruling.[13] While the Agua Caliente Band considered taking their case to the U.S. Supreme Court, they worried about the broader impacts this case could have for other tribal nations and in 2007 agreed to enter into a settlement with the FPPC in which they will report their campaign contributions.[14]

Second, and more disturbing from an internal tribal perspective, is what long-term impact gaming and the tribes' increasingly active participation in American politics might have on tribal sovereignty. If tribal members are so actively engaged in non-Indian electoral politics, as seen with the Agua Caliente Band of Cahuilla Indians, can they still legitimately claim to belong to separate if connected sovereign nations?[15] Or have they finally acquired the political status—"domestic-dependent nations"—that Chief Justice John Marshall first inaccurately used to describe tribes in 1831?

Some native citizens from some indigenous nations, like the Haudenosaunee Confederacy, consider the act of voting in an American election—at any level—to be a virtual act of treason, a betrayal of one's own indigenous nationality.[16] And yet many native nations in New Mexico, Arizona, California, and North Carolina appear to rest comfortably in the knowledge that their tribal sovereignty is not jeopardized by active participation in state and federal elections. Many of these native nations argue, in fact, that from their perspective, voting may be the best and possibly only realistic way to protect their remaining land rights, economic rights to conduct gaming operations, and cultural rights like bilingual education.

The diversity of the reality and indigenous conceptions of self-determination makes it clear that there is no single definition of sovereignty that uniformly covers all the native nations in Indian Country. But one wonders whether native citizens and their governments' full-throttle participation in the American political process might bring darker days in the future when the collective rights of sovereign tribes might be curtailed or even terminated.

The issue of indigenous political participation in non-Indian politics is of tremendous interest to those intent on invigorating tribal sovereignty, not solely because greater participation necessarily produces better policy decisions, but also because of the developmental value of participation in educating and socializing people, which enhances both the meaning of their lives and the value of their relationship to one another and their respective indigenous community.

In the remainder of this chapter, we examine the political attitudes of Indians and some of the actual ways Indians engage in politics. The emphasis is on indigenous participation in nontribal political affairs (e.g., voting, ideology, partisanship, electoral politics, and endorsements), in large part because there is such scant social science research available on native participation in indigenous political systems.

Litigation is another important method through which indigenous persons and polities seek to protect and enhance their distinctive political, legal, economic, and cultural rights. In fact, the U.S. Supreme Court "often decides more Indian cases than the number of Indians relative to the population as a whole would seem to justify."[17] This suggests three important points: (1) something more than just indigenous rights and resources is involved in such proceedings; (2) indigenous peoples and their rights and resources are subject to more litigation than any other racial, ethnic, or gender group; and (3) indigenous peoples still believe that the rule of law will one day be duly enforced and thus their rights will be safeguarded by a nation that maintains that the rule of law is an essential feature of democracy.[18] Direct-action politics in the form of protests, demonstrations, and so on, has also proven useful.

Native Nations and the Pursuit of Justice

We have already noted the astounding lack of research by political scientists about indigenous peoples as political entities situated in sovereign-to-sovereign relationships with the U.S. and state governments. This paucity is palpable considering the preexisting nature of indigenous governments and the wealth of political issues and questions that are an inherent part of the tribal situation singly and intergovernmentally—constitutional origins, political development and underdevelopment, the unique body of federal Indian law and policy, social movement organizations, legislative party dynamics, and the roles of Congress, the president, the courts, and the bureaucracy in formulating, implementing, or stymieing Indian policy, to name but a few.

Part of the reason for the reluctance or refusal of political scientists to examine indigenous political participation rests on the fact that tribal nations, generally, do not consider themselves to be part of the pluralistic mosaic that is predominant in political science literature. Many tribes perceive themselves not only as preconstitutional entities, but more importantly, as extraconstitutional polities. For example, comparing Indians to African Americans, one commentator puts it thus:

> The overriding goal of the black civil rights movement was to achieve individual equality and individual rights as promised within the philosophy of liberalism. Native American leaders, on the other hand, have historically demanded recognition of their tribal [national] rights as guaranteed by treaties, executive agreements, and congressional statutes.[19]

The noted native scholar and activist, Vine Deloria Jr., said it more pithily when he stated that the primary difference between blacks and Indians was that blacks were pursuing equality of acceptance and equal opportunity in American society while Indians pursued justice. By "justice," Deloria meant the Indians' right to maintain their sovereign integrity and to rest assured that their treaty and trust rights would be protected. These goals are evidenced in the tribes' focus on tribal sovereignty and maintaining and enhancing their separate land base—goals dissimilar from those of America's other racial and ethnic minority groups.

Indians as Patriots: But of Which Nation?

Because of the inherent tension between the doctrine of tribal sovereignty and the federal government's historical effort to assimilate native peoples, native peoples have developed a complicated set of attitudes and values about their relationships to their nations and to the United States that affects their involvement or lack of involvement in tribal, state, and federal elections. These assorted attitudes have been influenced by the high rates of American Indian military service. Native individuals have the highest record of service per capita when compared with any other American ethnic groups.[20] Participating in U.S. military actions for over two hundred years, American Indians served as allies for both the British and the Americans in the War of 1812 and also aided both sides in the Civil War. However, in 1866 indigenous military participation began to transform from an external position as military allies to the incorporation of individual Indians when the U.S. Army established its Indian Scouts, an act of Congress officially authorizing the recruitment of American Indians, which was active until 1947 with the retirement of their last soldier.

By 1900 indigenous peoples had been greatly impacted by disease, warfare, and colonization. Federal Indian policy, as discussed in chapter 5, aimed at the assimilation of American Indians into American society through a three-pronged approach: education of Indian children, the allotment of Indian lands, and the extension of U.S. citizenship to individual Indians. These federal aims would bear on indigenous expressions of patriotism, both to their own nations and to the United States. Even though many were not U.S. citizens, more than twelve thousand native peoples served in the U.S.

military in World War I (1914–1918). Motivations to serve were multifarious. Susan Applegate Krouse, an anthropologist, has attributed high rates of service in World War I to native people's desire to demonstrate their loyalty to their own nations and the United States, to carry out long-standing family and tribal traditions, and as a response to boarding school practices that emphasized patriotism. In addition, Krouse notes that military service provided economic opportunities, the prospects of travel, and the chance to demonstrate important aboriginal values such as leadership and bravery. Many indigenous peoples also desired to defend their homelands and some hoped that their service would bring about greater justice for their nations in their relations with the federal government.

These motivations and desires have persisted throughout the twentieth and into the twenty-first century. In World War II (1939–1945) indigenous participation per capita surpassed all other racial groups, with about twenty-five thousand American Indians serving in the military. Although they were by then citizens of the United States, American Indians still predominately served in the military on a voluntary basis, with a 60-percent volunteer rate. Much of the success on the battlefield in World War II at key moments has been attributed to native code talkers, who created codes using their native languages. Indigenous military service garnered national attention on February 19, 1945, when Ira Hayes, a Pima Indian, became one of five marines, along with a U.S. Navy Corpsman, captured in an iconic photograph raising the U.S. flag on Iwo Jima.

By the 1950s however, native Korean War veterans returned home to find their peoples vilified in "Cowboy and Indian" films that had captured the American imagination.[21] Yet indigenous military participation continued during the Vietnam War, with nearly 90 percent of the forty-two thousand American Indians who served volunteering at a time when the United States relied on the draft to get the required enlistment rates for this controversial war.[22] The American public was again reminded of indigenous military participation in 2003 when Private First Class Lori Ann Piestewa, a Hopi Indian and daughter of a Vietnam veteran and granddaughter of a World War II veteran, became the first woman in the U.S. armed forces to die in the 2003 Iraq War and possibly the first American Indian woman to die in combat while in service in the U.S. military.[23] (For representation of American Indians in the U.S. military see tables 7.3 and 7.4.) Thus military service has contributed significantly to indigenous patriotism and has considerably shaped American Indian response to and participation in American political systems.

Diane Duffy, a political scientist, in some preliminary research on the subject of Indian patriotism based on interview data, arrived at the following diverse categories of patriotism:

1. Indigenous (traditional) patriotism: Native Americans' sole allegiance is to the tribal nation. This allegiance is expressed in positive Indian, not antiwhite, language.
2. Measured-separatism patriotism: primary allegiance is to the tribe, but also there is some (measured) support for the United States and willingness to "serve" as "allies" with the United States in the armed services in battles with foreign nations.
3. Anti-American patriotism: against the United States (rather than for their tribe). Adherents would under no circumstances "serve" in the U.S. military, because they would consider it treasonous.

Table 7.3

Racial Composition of New Enlisted Recruits in 2006 and 2007

	2006 Percentage of Total U.S. Male Population, 18-24 Years Old	2006 Percentage of Total Recruits	2006 Recruit/ Population Ratio	2007 Percentage of Total Recruits	2007 Recruit/ Population Ration*
White	61.99%	65.32%	1.05	65.50%	1.06
Black or African American	11.87	12.34	1.04	12.82	1.06
Asian/Pacific Islander	3.49	3.31	0.95	3.25	0.93
Combination of two or more races	1.56	0.57	0.37	0.66	0.42
American Indian/ Alaska	0.73	21.6	2.96	1.96	2.68
Declined to specify race/ ethnicity		3.49		2.76	

Groups with recruit-to-population ration greater than 1.0 are overrepresented among enlisted recruits, and groups with rations less than 1.0 are underrepresented.

*Calculated using 2006 population estimates.

Source: Tim Kane, Who Bears the Burden? *Demographic Characteristics of U.S. Military Recruits Before and After 9/11*. Center for Data Analysis, CDA05-08, November 7, 2005. The Heritage Center for Data Analysis. Heritage Foundation calculations based on data from U.S. Department of Defense, Defense Manpower Data Center, Non-Prior Service Accessions, 2006-2007, and Steven Ruggles, Matthew Sobek, Trent Alexander, Catherine A. Fitch, Ronald Goeken, Patricia Kelly Hall, Miriam King, and Chad Ronnander, Integrated Public Use Microdata Series: Version 4.0, University of Minnesota, Minnesota Population Center, 2008, at http://usa.ipums.org/usa (July 21, 2008).

4. Environmental patriotism: similar to the first category, but allegiance is explicitly tied to all of creation and not simply human society.
5. Assimilative patriotism: the United States is perceived as the superior power and the tribal nation is subordinate.
6. Cooptive or colonized patriotism: adherents refuse to conceive of a separate tribal political consciousness that has merit and is deserving of allegiance.
7. Apatriotic: belief that patriotism is an irrelevant concept for Native Americans.[24]

An example of category 1 is found in the 1994 speech by Chief Irving Powless Jr. of the Onondaga Nation quoted at the beginning of this chapter. After questioning the validity of the 1924 General Indian Citizenship Act, Powless stated,

Table 7.4
U.S. Military Recruits By Race

Race	Population Percent	2003 Recruit Percent	2003 Army Percent	Recruit/Population Ratio	Army/Population Ration
American Indian/ Alaska Native	0.78	1.82	1.19	2.35	1.54
Asian	3.67	1.23	1.14	0.34	0.31
Black	11.33	14.99	16.25	1.32	1.44
Native Hawaiian/ Pacific Islander	0.13	0.42	0.45	3.30	3.53
White	77.44	75.79	78.50	0.98	1.01
Combination of two or more races	1.93	2.67	2.46	1.38	1.28
Other	4.73	–	–	–	–
Declined to Respond	–	3.08	2.18	–	–
Hispanic	12.11	11.50	10.74	0.95	0.89
Not Hispanic	87.89	84.64	82.65	0.96	0.94
Declined to Respond	–	3.87	6.61	–	–

Source: Tim Kane, Who Bears the Burden? Demographic Characteristics of U.S. Military Recruits Before and After 9/11. Center for Data Analysis, CDA05-08, November 7, 2005. The Heritage Foundation calculations are based on data from the U.S. Department of Defense, Office of the Undersecretary of Defense, October 1998-September 1999 Non-Prior Service (NPS) Enlisted Accessions, January 2003-September 2003 Enlisted Accessions, and U.S. Bureau of the Census, *United States Census 2000*, Summary File 1, at www.census.gov/Press Release/www/2001/sumfile 1.html (July 6, 2005).

[T]he Haudenosaunee [also known as the Iroquois Confederacy] have never accepted this law. We do not consider ourselves as citizens of the United States. This law is a violation of the treaties that we signed that prove that we are sovereign. Because we are a sovereign people the United States cannot make us citizens of their nation against our will.... I have never voted in any election of the United States nor do I intend to vote in any coming elections. Most of our people have never voted in your elections. A few have, but there [are] not that many who have moved in that direction.[25]

What Powless did not address was the fact that as a chief he is required to be very active in Onondaga and Iroquois Confederacy political struggles and he is compelled by the Iroquois Constitution to cast votes in matters affecting his own nation or those of the Confederacy. But Powless's views represent only one view of indigenous political reality, albeit one rooted in indigenous nationality.

Natives as American Voters: Ambivalence among the Assimilators

As Duffy's categories show, the subject of patriotism is far more complicated than many might imagine. In fact, a majority of Indians support tribal sovereignty, but

Photo 7.1
Lori Piestewa before being deployed from Ft. Bliss, Texas, on February 18, 2003. Piestewa was the first woman in the U.S. armed forces killed in the 2003 Iraq War and is the first native woman (Hopi) to die in combat while serving with the U.S. military.
Source: www.Army.mil

increasingly many of those Indians also believe that in order to protect their sovereign rights they must participate in the American electoral process.[26] This has been borne out by research conducted by the First American Education Project, which noted in a 2004 report on Indian voting that "overall, Native participation grew from a small amount in some places to tremendously in others."[27] This is also evidenced in Laughlin McDonald's recent study of American Indians' struggles for equal voting rights. He found that the average voter turnout during the 2000 elections for Buffalo, Dewey, Shannon, and Todd counties in South Dakota, driven predominately by Indian voters, was 42.7 percent. However, by the 2004 elections, voter turnout in those same counties increased to 65.2 percent. He attributed increased Indian political participation to many driving forces, including "business development, new wealth from casinos, the need to interact with nontribal governments, and obtainment of state and federal funds for health clinics, education improvements, water-reclamation projects, and cleanup of old mining areas."[28]

The political pragmatism of such participation in U.S. elections was evident in 2008 when Joe A. Garcia, president of the NCAI, declared that "increasing civic participation among American Indian and Alaska Native communities is imperative to protecting sovereignty and ensuring Native issues are addressed on every level of government."[29] While other Indian political topics have been ignored, the voting behavior of individual Indians has received some scholarly attention since Congress extended the franchise to Indians in 1924.

Of those Indians who have opted to exercise the franchise in county, municipal, state, or federal elections, their right to exercise this most fundamental of democratic liberties came later than it did for any other large group in the United States. This should not be surprising, since federal and state lawmakers have been wholly inconsistent in defining the meanings of citizenship for a multitude of groups, many of whom happened to be nonwhite or nonmale: women; Africans brought to the country enslaved and their descendants; indigenous nations (until 1924); other categories of involuntary immigrants (people of Mexican birth or identity who "became" American when the United States acquired Texas, New Mexico, and other territory after the Mexican War); "noncitizen nationals" who lived in possessions that never became states (Filipinos between 1898 and 1946, Puerto Ricans between 1900 and 1917, Virgin Islanders between 1917 and 1927, persons born in American Samoa now); voluntary immigrants from Asia and elsewhere, who for many years were ineligible for naturalization; refugees who can never return to their homelands; and finally "refugees uprooted by disruptions in which they have reason to believe the United States was complicit, for example, Vietnamese 'boat people.'"[30]

On the other hand, the denial of the franchise to Indians seems convoluted because, sporadically since at least the early nineteenth century, many federal policymakers have sought by various assimilative measures to bring Indians, whether willingly or not, into the American body politic. As Commissioner of Indian Affairs Thomas J. Morgan put it in 1891, in assessing the steps the government was using to bring the Indians to a "higher state of civilization,"

> The allotment of land, the restriction of the power of alienation, the compulsory education of their children, the destruction of the tribal organization, the bestowment of citizenship, the repression of heathenish and hurtful practices, the suppression of outbreaks, and punishment for lawlessness are among the things which belong unmistakably to the prerogatives of the National Government.[31]

In short, while most racial and ethnic groups and women faced a forced exclusion from the American social contract, Indians, from the 1880s, faced a forced inclusion into the American polity. However, it was an inconsistent and ambivalent inclusion at best. Most of the actions by federal policymakers from the nineteenth century to the 1970s were aimed at "Americanizing" and "civilizing" Indians. However, there were occasionally opposite actions by lawmakers and justices that insisted that Indians were "alien peoples" or were not quite up to or deserving of complete American citizenship.

Thus, with the adoption of the Fifteenth Amendment ("the right of citizens of the United States to vote shall not be denied or abridged by the United States or by any State on account of race, color, or previous condition of servitude") and Congress's enactment of the 1924 General Indian Citizenship Act (which read in part that "all non-citizen Indians born within the territorial limits of the United States . . . are hereby declared to be citizens of the United States"), it might appear that the matter of whether

Indians were entitled to vote in U.S. elections had been solved. Such was not the case, however.

First, tribal nations continued to exist as separate sovereign entities since the citizenship act only applied to individual Indians, not Indian nations. Second, some states denied the franchise to Indians who wanted to vote. States, which establish voting eligibility criteria, were well aware of the ongoing vitality of tribal sovereignty as evidenced by (1) treaty rights exempting tribal lands and members from most state regulations and taxation and (2) state constitutional disclaimer clauses prohibiting state governments from extending their jurisdiction or taxing authority over Indians or tribes inside Indian Country who hold lands in trust. While black Americans faced poll taxes, literacy requirements, gerrymandering, violence, at-large elections, and other devices that denied them the franchise, Indians, because of their extraconstitutional political status, faced some similar discriminatory measures but also encountered a variety of unique obstacles placed before them by state officials.

Daniel McCool, a political scientist, found that states have devised a number of strategies to keep Indians from voting. He grouped them in three categories: (1) constitutional ambiguity, (2) political and economic factors, and (3) cultural and racial discrimination.[32] Evidence of constitutional ambiguity is found in several states—Idaho, New Mexico, and Washington—that denied Indians the vote because of specific provisions in their constitutions regarding "Indians not taxed." Such Indians, according to the Idaho Constitution, could not vote or serve as jurors if they were considered to be nontaxable because they had not "severed their tribal relations and adopted the habits of civilization."[33] In Arizona, the franchise was denied to Indians until *Harrison v. Laveen* in 1948 on the specious grounds that they were "under guardianship." The pertinent clause in the Arizona Constitution read that "no person under guardianship, non compos mentis, or insane shall be qualified to vote in any election."

Political and economic factors have also been used to deny Indians the right to vote. In *Elk v. Wilkins,* the Supreme Court held that Indians maintained allegiance to their own "alien nations" and could thus not be considered loyal Americans. In Utah, Indians on reservations were denied voting privileges under an 1897 state law until 1956, when an opinion of the state attorney general stated that they were in fact "residents" of Utah. Later that year, the Utah Supreme Court in *Allen v. Merrell* (1956) upheld the attorney general's opinion by declaring that "allowing them [Indians] to vote might place substantial control of the county government and the expenditures of its funds in a group of citizens who, as a class, had an extremely limited interest in its function and very little responsibility in providing the financial support thereof."[34]

Finally, outright cultural and racial discrimination was sometimes used to deny Indians the right to vote. For example, as late as 1937 the state of Colorado denied Indians voting rights, claiming that they were not yet citizens. This action directly flouted the General Indian Citizenship Act of 1924. As the state's attorney general said in a letter to Superintendent Watson of the Ute Agency on November 24, 1936, "it is our opinion that until Congress enfranchises the Indian, he will not have the right to vote."[35]

And the state of North Carolina, in action comparable to what blacks experienced, discriminated against Indians under color of a provision of the state election law that declared that a person desiring to register must be able to read and write any section of the U.S. Constitution in the English language and must show this ability "to the satisfaction of the registrar." As the Cherokee Indian superintendent stated: "We have had Indian graduates of Carlisle, Haskell and other schools in instances much better educated than the registrar himself, turned down because they did not read or write to his satisfaction."[36]

While states no longer overtly disallow Indians the right to vote, and Congress has stepped in with the passage of the Voting Rights Act of 1965 (and amendments) to prohibit tests or other devices to disenfranchise racial minorities, the problem of voter dilution—"the impairment of the equal opportunity of minority voters to participate in the political process and to elect candidates of their choice"—continues to be a real concern for some tribes and their citizens. Annexation, at-large representation, and gerrymandering are three diluting devices states have used to weaken the vote of minority groups, including Indian nations.

In a 2007 book, Robinson, Olson, and McCool provide the first detailed analysis of the impact the Voting Rights Act has had on Indian voting patterns, and they evaluate the sixty-six cases Indians have filed based on the act as they have struggled to exercise the franchise in the face of state and county attempts to dilute their voting power. For Indian peoples, particularly in areas where the Indian population is sizable, vote dilution has been an ongoing problem. This is especially true in the following states: Arizona, Colorado, Nevada, New Mexico, Utah, Minnesota, Montana, Nebraska, North Dakota, and South Dakota. The two states with the most litigation involving Indian vote dilution are South Dakota and New Mexico, each with twelve cases. Impressively, of the sixty-six cases, Indian parties or their advocates have only lost four. The cases can be grouped into five categories: (1) the Indians' right to register, vote, and run for office are disallowed or diminished; (2) the Indians are not provided adequate minority language assistance; (3) the Indians challenge at-large electoral systems that dilute their vote; (4) the Indians file suit based on malapportionment and gerrymandering of districts; and (5) the Indians file suits based on procedural aspects.[37]

Recognizing that many states, counties, and cities continue to erect barriers to native voters, Congress renewed special provisions of the Voting Rights Act in 2006. Nonetheless, a recent study by the American Civil Liberties Union (ACLU) found that Indian voting rights continue to be challenged in these five areas. For example, voting dilution persists in Martin, South Dakota, a border town near the Pine Ridge and Rosebud reservations with a population of just over one thousand people, nearly 45 percent of which is composed of American Indians. The ACLU sued the city in 2002 on behalf of two Indian voters over their recently adopted redistricting plan. The city responded by changing its plan, but the new plan still fragmented the Indian community, giving white voters an overwhelming majority. The ACLU amended their complaint to address the new plan and the case went to trial. In 2005 the district court ruled against the plaintiffs, saying they failed to demonstrate that the majority voted as a block to defeat the minorities' preferred candidate. However, the Eighth Circuit reversed this decision on May 5, 2006. In 2007, on remand, the district court found that the city's redistricting plan diluted Indian voting, violating the Voting Rights Act.[38] When the city appealed this decision, a three-judge panel of the Eighth Circuit affirmed the district court's finding. However, they subsequently granted the city's petition for a rehearing. The full Eighth Circuit panel heard the case in September 2009, but their decision is still pending.[39]

There is, says Glenn A. Phelps, an ongoing constitutional tension regarding Indians as citizens and voters in American electoral politics that is unique to the tribal-federal relationship. The tension is this: "Claims of tribal sovereignty and immunity from state and local processes cannot, in principle, coexist with the responsibilities incumbent upon citizenship and suffrage in state and local governments."[40] This harkens back to one of the quandaries raised in chapter 2—Indians as citizens of separate nations, yet citizens of the state and federal government. The tension put another way is this: "Indians living within Indian Country are immune from state and local taxes and are largely immune from state and local laws. Yet they claim the right to vote for representatives who can levy taxes and make rules and regulations for non-Indians—taxes and rules from which reservation Indians themselves are immune."[41]

This status suits tribal citizens fine and is clearly rooted in the treaty and trust relationship. But some non-Indians take offense to this political arrangement and argue that it is a violation of the rule of law. It is a tension that persists.

Indians, Ideology, and Partisanship

Considering the scanty research record, it is impossible to arrive at anything more than general impressions of Indian political ideology or political behavior patterns in American elections. There is, unfortunately, even less data available on how Indians participate in tribal elections.[42] It is still worthwhile, however, to briefly discuss the available findings with the caveat that much more work must be done before we can accurately discuss these important topics.

One recent study on Indian party identification indicates that on the national level Indians, as individuals, do engage in some partisan politics. As table 7.5 shows, more Indians see themselves as Democrats, although a sizable number identify themselves as Republican. And interestingly, more Indians identify themselves as moderate and conservative than as liberal. This might explain how former Senator Ben Nighthorse Campbell (R-CO) made the switch from the Democratic Party to the Republican Party with relative ease during the 104th Congress. Campbell asserted that the core Republican principles of promoting less federal government control and championing the free-enterprise system were in keeping with tribal philosophies.

Green Party candidates Ralph Nader (president), a longtime consumer advocate, and Winona LaDuke (vice president), a member of the Mississippi Band of Anishinaabe of the White Earth Nation in Minnesota, in 1996 and again in 2000 seemed to energize a number of American Indians (and those on the left) who had grown disillusioned with the candidates and policies of the two major parties.[43]

LaDuke is known widely in Indian Country, in the environmental movement, and in the international community as a human rights activist. She has traveled and lectured extensively, both domestically and abroad, and has published fiction and nonfiction works on the rights of indigenous women and environmental racism.[44] The Green Party's 2000 political platform resonated with many aboriginal peoples as it emphasized and expressed support for tribal sovereignty, treaty rights, the development of sustainable energy supplies, and the breaching of dams to save wildlife and restore their habitats. It also contained what was termed the "seventh generation amendment," which was being touted as an amendment to the U.S. Constitution that declared that American citizens had the right to enjoy all renewable resources and that these would not be impaired for the future generations.[45]

In the 2004 federal elections, as described earlier, a nationally well-coordinated effort was made to "get out the Indian vote." Although the data are still being analyzed,

Table 7.5

American Indian Partisan Identification

Partisan Identification	1990-2004 (%)
Extremely liberal	1.93 (5)*
Liberal	13.13 (34)
Slightly liberal	9.65 (25)
Moderate	32.82 (85)
Slightly conservative	17.37 (45)
Conservative	19.31 (50)
Extremely Conservative	5.79 (15)
Total	100 (259)

Note: 127 respondents did not answer the question.

*Figures in parenthesis represent the number of respondents.

Source: Paula D. McClain and Joseph Stewart Jr., *"Can We All Get Along?" Racial and Ethnic Minorities in American Politics*, 5th ed. (Boulder, Colo.: Westview Press, 2009). © 2009 Paula McClain, Joseph Stewart Jr.. Reprinted by permission of Westview Press, a member of the Perseus Book Group. American National Election Studies Cumulative Data File (1948-2004). All respondents who identified as Native American in the 1990-2004 American National Election Studies were combined into a single file to obtain a sufficient sample size to identify partisan identification. These data do not allow for the tribal affiliation of the respondents.

it is clear that while many Native-preferred candidates—like Kerry for president—were unsuccessful, "party preference among Native voters remains consistent, [and] the overwhelming support of Native voters can be virtually guaranteed only when a candidate has a record of support for Native issues. Further, in such cases where a candidate has a consistent record of hostility towards issues of importance to Native voters a strong showing of electoral opposition from Native voters can almost be assured."[46]

A study of partisan preferences for Indian voters in Wisconsin, Minnesota, and North and South Dakota from 1982 to 1992 indicates a strong preference for Democrats.[47] An even stronger preference was indicated among Pueblo Indians, who in 1994 voted overwhelmingly Democratic—85 percent, "a one-sided level of support which parallels the strongest Democratic voting constituencies in the United States."[48] Table 7.6, which identifies Indian and Alaska Native state legislators, bears this out.

Navajos, on the other hand, over the last forty years or so "have shifted from Republican to Democratic and, during the Reagan years, slightly back to the Republican, at least in national elections."[49] However, in 2004, the Navajo Nation formally endorsed John Kerry for president, given his expressed support for Navajo sovereignty, treaty rights, and health care. At the state and local levels Navajos exhibit a strong Democratic preference.

Besides tribal-specific differences, there is recent evidence of generational differences as well. A survey developed by the Solidarity Foundation, an Indian research group, was sent to over one thousand Indian high school- and college-age students. Their responses were then compared with an equivalent sample of Indians over the age of thirty-five. The preliminary results indicate that "the coming generation is more inclined and better equipped than ever to assume leadership positions in their communities. The survey found that the Indian youth of today are more aware, more involved, and more concerned about Native issues than ever before."[50]

Table 7.6

American Indian and Alaska Native State Legislators, 2009

State	Body	Name	Tribe	Party	First Year in Office
Alaska	House	Richard Foster	Nome Eskimo	Democrat	1989
		Reggie Joule	Inuit	Democrat	1996
		Mary Nelson	Yupik	Democrat	1999
		Woodie Salmon	Chalkyitsik	Democrat	2004
		Bill Thomas Jr.	Chilkoot	Republican	2004
	Senate	Lyman Hoffman	Yupik	Democrat	1990
		Albert Kookesh	Tlingit	Democrat	1996
		Donald Olson	Inupiat	Democrat	2001
Arizona	House	Albert Torn	Navajo	Democrat	2005
		Chris Deschene	Navajo	Democrat	2009
	Senate	Albert Hale	Navajo	Democrat	2004
Colorado	House	Debbie Stafford	Lakota Sioux	Democrat	2002
	Senate	Suzanne Williams	Comanche	Democrat	1997
		Paula E. Sandavol	Yaqui	Democrat	2002
Kentucky	House	Reginald Meeks	Cherokee	Democrat	2001
Maine	House	Donald Soctomah	Passamaquoddy	Tribal Rep.	1999
		Wayne Mitchell	Penobscot	Tribal Rep.	2009
Maryland	House	Talmadge Branch	Tuscarora	Democrat	1995
Montana	House	Margaret Campbell	Assiniboine	Democrat	2004
		Shannon Augare	Blackfeet	Democrat	2007
		Douglas Cordier	Salish	Democrat	2007
		Tony Belcourt	Chippewa Cree	Democrat	2009
		Frosty Calf Boss Ribs		Democrat	2009
		Sharon Stewart-Peregoy	Crow	Democrat	2009
	Senate	Carol Juneau	Hidatsa Mandan	Democrat	1999
		Jonathan Windy Boy	Chippewa Cree	Democrat	2009
		Carolyn Pease Lopez	Crow	Democrat	2009
Nevada	House	John Oceguera	Walker River Paiute	Democrat	2000
New Mexico	House	Nick Salazar	Tewa	Democrat	1973
		James Madalena	Jemez Pueblo	Democrat	1985
		Ray Begaye	Navajo	Democrat	1999
		Teressa Zanetti		Republican	2002
	Senate	John Pinto	Navajo	Democrat	1977
		Lynda Lovejoy	Navajo	Democrat	1988
North Carolina	House	Ronnie Sutton	Lumbee	Democrat	1991
North Dakota	Senate	Richard Marcellais	Chippeqa	Democrat	2007
Oklahoma	House	Chris Benge	Cherokee	Republican	1999
		Lisa J. Billy	Chickasaw/Choctaw	Republican	2001
		Doug Cox	Creek	Republican	2005
		Rex Duncan	Choctaw	Republican	2005
		Larry Glen	Cherokee	Democrat	2005
		Shane Jett	Cherokee	Republican	2005
		Steve Martin	Cherokee	Republican	2005

(Continued)

Table 7.6

American Indian and Alaska Native State Legislators, 2009 (*Continued*)

State	Body	Name	Tribe	Party	First Year in Office
		Jerry McPeak	Creek	Democrat	2005
		Jerry Shoemake	Cherokee	Democrat	2005
		Danielle Sullivan	Choctaw	Republican	2005
		Paul Wesselhoft	Pottawatomie	Republican	2005
		Chuch Hoskin	Cherokee	Democrat	2007
		Fred Jordan	Cherokee	Republican	2007
		Ken Lutrell	Cherokee	Democrat	2007
		Al Macaffrey	Choctaw	Democrat	2007
		Skye McNeil	Creek	Republican	2007
		Anatasia Pittman	Seminole (Freed-man Member)	Democrat	2007
		T. W. Shannon	Chickasaw	Republican	2007
	Senate	Richard Lerblanc	Muscogee Creek	Democrat	2003
		Constance Johnson		Democart	2005
		Sean Burage	Choctaw	Democrat	2006
		John Sparks	Cherokee	Democrat	2006
		Brian Bingham	Creek	Republican	2007
Pennsylvania	House	Barbara M. Smith	Sac & Fox	Democrat	2006
South Dakota	House	Ed Iron Cloud III	Oglala Sioux	Democrat	2009
		Kevin Killer	Oglala Sioux	Democrat	2009
	Senate	Jim Bradford	Oglala Sioux	Republican	2009
Washington	House	Jeff Morris	Tsimshian	Democrat	1996
		John McCoy	Tulalip	Democrat	2002
	Senate	Claudia Kaufmann	Nez Perce	Democrat	2007
Wyoming	House	W. Patrick Goggles	Arapaho	Democrat	2004

From: Paula D. McClain and Joseph Stewart Jr., "*Can We All Get Along?*" *Racial and Ethnic Minorities in American Politics*, 5th ed. (Boulder, Colo.: Westview Press, 2010). *Sources*: National Caucus of Native American State Legislators, www.ncsl.org/programs/statetribe/native caucus.htm; INDN'S (Indigenous Democratic Network List, www.indnslist.org/elected officials.

As for partisan identification, the survey's results show that Indian youth are moving away from clear partisan affiliation, preferring to identify as independent or even as nonaffiliated. When asked the question, "With which political party do you most closely associate your own belief and values?" only 37 percent of those under twenty-six years of age replied that they identified as Democrat. This compared with 54 percent of those over twenty-six who identified as Democrat.

The survey does reveal, however, that the Republican Party is still not drawing Indians into the fold. Less than 5 percent of the respondents identified as Republican. Independents, on the other hand, captured the allegiance of 17 percent of the youth. And while less than 30 percent of the adults did not affiliate with a particular party, over 40 percent of the youth were unaffiliated. In fact, 48.3 percent of young Indian males said they were not attached to any political party.

Many tribes and their members, regardless of their views on partisanship, realize that state, county, and local politics are becoming increasingly important. In 2005, the Indigenous Democratic Network (INDN) List was formed. This grassroots political

Photo 7.2
Democratic presidential hopeful, Sen. Barack Obama is escorted to the stage by tribal members at a rally in Crow Agency, Montana.
Source: AP/WIDE WORLD PHOTOS

organization recruits and trains American Indians to run for political office. As McDonald notes, "In 2006, INDN's List supported twenty-six candidates from twelve states, representing twenty-one tribes."[51] By 2008, "twenty-two American Indians from sixteen tribes and eleven states . . . won their state and local contests."[52] And in 2009, there were sixty-two American Indians and Alaska Natives serving in seventeen state legislatures, a number that continues to expand every election year. Table 7.6 identifies these individuals.

With the growth in native voter turnout and their subsequent success in shaping elections in some areas, American Indians are increasingly seen as playing an expanding role in state and federal elections. This was evident in the attention Democratic presidential candidates paid to Indian Country in 2008. Senator Barack Obama visited the Crow Reservation in Montana in May and expressed his commitment to "empower Native America in the development of the national policy agenda."[53] Senator Hillary Clinton also visited a Montana reservation, the Flathead Indian Reservation, a week later. Obama and Clinton also campaigned on the Pine Ridge Reservation in South Dakota and the Wind River Indian Reservation in Wyoming.

Republican presidential candidate John McCain and Democratic presidential candidate Obama paid particular attention to indigenous issues and each outlined policy platforms for Indian Country. Obama received the lion's share of indigenous political support and was endorsed by over one hundred native leaders, seven tribal councils, and the Great Plains Tribal Chairman's Association representing sixteen native nations.[54] In a 2008 poll examining native voter preference in the presidential race, Obama led his opponent

McCain by eighty-three points. Doing well across all age ranges, Obama found his greatest support among native voters between ages 18 and 34. There was a greater variance in voter preference, however, when sampled by state. While Obama received a majority of the native vote, McCain and Obama had equal backing in Oklahoma, with each gaining 42 percent of the support from polled native voters (table 7.7). Obama appeared to secure the overwhelming support of native people for several reasons: first, he was a person of color; second, his many visits and policy enunciations articulated goals—support for tribal sovereignty and treaty rights—that comported with native nation values; third, he exuded a charisma and wielded unmatched oratorical skills that are highly prized in Indian Country; and finally, his abundant faith in the ideal of democracy and social progress reminded natives of the historic trust relationship forged generations ago. Native nations were thus optimistic that Obama would forge a national agenda that comported with the sovereignty, self-determination, and basic respect for native nations.

Native Voting Patterns

Data on native voting patterns (within tribal elections or in nontribal elections) remains scant at best. McCool has identified several reasons for this in addition to

Table 7.7

SURVEY OF NATIVE AMERICAN VOTERS NATIONWIDE LATE OCTOBER 2008

Native Vote Washington conducted a poll of 600 American Indian and Alaska Native voters from 30 states including Washington, Arizona, New Mexico, Montana, and Oklahoma. The poll examined voter preference in the presidential race between Democratic candidate Senator Barack Obama and Republican Senator John McCain.

If the election were being held today, would you vote for (or have already voted for):

	Obama	*McCain*	*Undecided/Other*
Overall	89%	6%	5%
Already Voted	95%	4%	1%
Men	91%	5%	4%
Women	87%	7%	6%
Ages 18-34	87%	7%	6%
Ages 35-54	89%	6%	5%
Ages 55+	90%	6%	4%
WA	94%	3%	2%
AZ	74%	14%	12%
NM	85%	13%	2%
OK	42%	42%	16%
MT	94%	2%	3%

www.nativevotewa.org

the ones already discussed. First, a sizable number of native peoples still live in geo-graphically remote areas of the country, thus making surveying difficult. Second, there are linguistic, technological, and cultural factors that make survey research difficult. For example, telephone surveys of Indians usually produce samples that favor urban Indians and other off-reservation Indians since those Indians tend to have phones and many reservation Indians still do not. Third, there is the added difficulty of separating Indians from non-Indians in aggregate polling data.[55]

Despite the paucity of Indian voting data, since 2003 the First American Education Project, under the leadership of Russ Lehman, has produced two studies that provide some early comparative survey data on the voting patterns of indigenous peoples in selected states. The project's 2005 study, "Native Vote 2004," looked at data for Okla-homa, Arizona, Minnesota, Montana, New Mexico, South Dakota, Washington, and Wisconsin. While noting that Indian registration and turnout were still lower than that of most of the country, "many Native communities saw increases of 50 percent to 150 percent in their turnout."[56] This research shows a "direct correlation between focused localized commitments to increasing participation rates in Native communities and the actual increases that result."[57] See table 7.8 for figures on selected tribal nations in Arizona. For each of the tribes, there was an increase in the turnout of those registered to vote.

With such a small percentage of the voting population, the question that begs to be asked is whether the Indians' vote or their election to office can make a difference in local, state, or federal politics. McCool says it can if two conditions are met: "First, the minority must bloc vote, and second, the race must be close."[58] It also helps if the tribe is able to frame the vote of a particular issue, like Proposition 5 (the gaming initiative in California), in such a way that melds with the public's positive construction of Indian cultural identity. In the western states (and in North Carolina), where a majority of Indians live, the Indian vote, as noted earlier, has on occasion made a real difference in certain state and federal elections, and has had some effect on policy.

For example, Robinson, Olson, and McCool conducted fifteen interviews with American Indian office holders in local government in 2004 and 2005. The office hold-ers were primarily county commissioners and school district officials. They asked each Indian official, "What impact do you think you have had on laws and regulations, the delivery of service, Indian people's access to local government, and Indian people's perceptions about local government?"[59] While seven of the elected officials expressed the view that they had made an impact on laws and regulations, five others said their presence had no impact. One commissioner bluntly stated: "I'm only one vote here, we get overrun on anything." With regard to their impact on delivery of services in their jurisdiction, however, the native officials were much more positive about the impact their presence was having.[60]

Conclusion

The subject of Indian political participation, or lack thereof, in non-Indian politi-cal affairs encompasses an extremely complicated set of historical, sociological, and political-legal processes. As a result of Indian gaming revenues, it promises to be an exceedingly volatile and unpredictable area because tribes continue to exist as dis-tinct sovereigns with, in many cases, fiercely loyal citizens; yet an increasing number

Table 7.8.
General Election Voter Turnout 2000, 2004—Arizona Indian Reservations

Tribe	Year	Registered Voters	Turnout as a Turnout	% of Those Registered
Navajo[1]	2000	56,326	27,736	49.24%
	2004	63,618	34,213	53.79%
Hopi[2]	2000	1,851	555	29.99%
	2004	2,075	905	43.63%
Tohono O'odham[3]	2000	3,964	2,236	56.43%
	2004	4,739	2,806	59.24%
Gila River[4]	2000	2,836	964	34.00%
	2004	3,166	1,504	47.51%
White Mountain[5]	2000	4,243	1,876	44.22%
	2004	4,865	2,442	50.20%
San Carlos[6]	2000	1,418	721	50.86%
	2004	1,735	1,012	58.34%
Colorado River Indian Tribes[7]	2000	1,414	757	53.56%
	2004	2,187	1,370	62.66%
Hualapai[8]	2000	365	184	50.43%
	2004	420	233	55.49%
Cocopah[9]	2000	2,089	1,010	48.35%
	2004	2,647	1,457	55.07%
Ft. McDowell[10]	2000	196	97	49.50%
	2004	355	274	77.22%
Havasupai[11]	2000	131	59	45.05%
	2004	102	57	55.90%
Salt River	2000	1,763	939	53.28%
	2004	2,444	1,475	60.39%

Source: Native Vote 2004: A National Survey and Analysis of Efforts to Increase the Native Vote in 2004 and the Results Achieved. www.first-americans.net/native%20votes%20Report%2004.pdf.
Notes:

[1]In 2004, the precincts located on the Navajo populations included: Apache (33), Navajo (18), and Coconino (20). There are slight differences in precincts between 2004 and 2000 due to redistricting.
[2]Precincts include: Keams Canyon, Oraibi, Polacca, and Toreva (Navajo County) and Moenkopi (Coconino County).
[3]Precincts include: Baboquivari, Chukut Kuk, Gu Achi, Gu Vo, Pisinemo, San Xavier, San Lucy, Schuk Toak, and Sells (Pima County), Sif Oidak (Pinal County), and Hickiwan (Maricopa County).
[4]Precincts include: Pee Posh, Komatke, and Lone Butte (Maricopa County) and Sacaton, Blackwater, Santan, and Casa Blanca (Pinal County).
[5]Precincts include: Cibecue, Hon Dah, Whiteriver #1, and Whiteriver #2 (Navajo County), McNary (Apache County), and Canyon Day and Carrizo (Gila County).
[6]Includes precincts 11 and 16 (Graham County).
[7]Precincts include: Parker One and La Pera (La Paz County).
[8]Includes Peach Springs (Mahave County).
[9]Includes Sommertown (Yuma County).
[10]Includes Ft. McDowell (Maricopa County).
[11]Includes Havasupai (Coconino County).

of American Indians and tribal governments themselves are becoming more actively engaged in local, state, and federal political matters.

How these seemingly contradictory forces will affect the future of intergovernmental relations is, of course, impossible to predict. What will become of tribal sovereignty if tribal participatory rates in non-Indian politics continue to escalate? Will federal forces set about to revive the terminationist sentiment of the 1950s and 1960s because of a perception that indigenous participation in non-Indian politics means that Indians have become so assimilated that their own governing structures and institutions are no longer necessary? How will tribes respond if this is the case? Suffice it to say, it is a state of affairs that promises to remain dynamic.

CHAPTER 8

Native Interest Group Activity and Activism

When AIM [the American Indian Movement] was founded on July 28, 1968, in Minneapolis, Minnesota, the living conditions we found ourselves in were deplorable. It wasn't that we didn't know there was racism in the cities. It was how racism forced us into squalid slum tenement buildings, closed doors to job opportunities, and fostered racist laws, jails, courts, and prisons. Beginning with our founding meeting, we immediately set out to bring about change in those institutions of public concern: housing, education, employment, welfare, and the courts.

—Dennis Banks, Anishinabe activist, 1994[1]

POLITICAL SCIENTISTS Paula McClain and Joe Stewart note that "interest groups that focus on issues of importance to Blacks, Latinos, Asians, and American Indians have been essential to the progress made toward the incorporation of these groups into the American political system."[2] While this statement is broadly accurate for most of the groups, the situation of indigenous nations is much more complicated, as we have shown throughout the text. For much of this nation's history, the general thrust of most racial and ethnic groups and their members has been to seek inclusion (to become constitutionally incorporated) into the American social contract; by contrast, the general thrust of most indigenous nations and their citizens (notwithstanding their American citizenship) has been to retain their political and cultural exclusion from absorption or incorporation in the American polity, although increasingly, as a result of the gaming phenomenon, American Indians are being economically incorporated on a scale never seen before.

Of course, the forces of American colonialism—including the imposition of Western religious beliefs, Western values, and Western property arrangements—have unabashedly sought to incorporate Indian lands, resources, and citizens, while sometimes exhibiting a measure of respect for Indian treaty rights, attempting to restore some tribal lands, and providing some protection for Indian religious beliefs and sacred sites.

These forces, combined with individual Indian free will, high out-marriage rates, the urbanization of Indians, and the near hegemony of the media and the corporate world, contribute mightily to the character of an indigenous America that is more diversified than ever before. Notwithstanding this increasing and seemingly inexorable diversification among indigenous peoples, the evidence still shows that maintaining and reaffirming Indian political, economic, and cultural identity is a central issue for most indigenous peoples most of the time. And this is true regardless of whether they are reservation-based or urban-based, full blood or mixed blood, recognized or non-recognized, exercising treaty rights or treatyless, practicing traditional spiritual beliefs or members of Christian sects. In a 1997 survey of Indian youth, more than 96 percent of those surveyed "identified themselves with their Indian nation, and more than 40 percent identified themselves solely with their Indian nationality. Only a little more than half of the youth identified themselves as American citizens."[3] Cornell developed a four-cell figure that graphically depicts some of the complexity facing Indian interest groups and their political goals (table 8.1). First, regarding orientation to organization, Indian interest groups interested in reformative goals do not seek fundamental change in the structure of intergovernmental relations. Their preference, rather, is for a "redistribution of services, resources, or rewards within that structure."[4] For example, these groups would support Indian preference in the Indian Bureau.

Groups pursuing transformative goals, on the other hand, seek a basic restructuring of intergovernmental relations. For example, they would most likely support the revival of the treaty relationship and the termination of the Congress's presumed plenary power over tribes. Second, regarding orientation to institutions of the larger society, there is the dichotomy of integration and segregative goals. Indian interest groups pursuing integrative goals, while seeking either reformative or transformative changes, generally "accept the appropriateness in the Indian setting of Euro-American economic and political institutions and, in general, the appropriateness of the dominant culture."[5] Groups pursuing segregative goals, by contrast, question the value and appropriateness of Euro-American cultural, economic, and political institutions for Indians and tend to see them as being "unresponsive to Indian needs, inimical to Indian interests, or threatening to the survival of culturally distinct Indian communities."[6]

Cornell, of course, rightly notes that the distinctions between the dichotomous pairings is a matter of degrees. When discussing the four combinations that are represented by cells A, B, C, and D, we see a wide range of fluid possibilities. Cell A depicts meager opposition to the status quo and little conflict between the various groups. Cell

Table 8.1
Indian Political Goals

		Orientation to Organization of Indian-White Relations	
		Reformative	*Transformative*
Orientation to	Integrative	A	B
Institutions of	Segregative	C	D
Larger Society			

Source: From *The Return of the Native* by Stephen Cornell © 1988. By permission of Oxford University Press, Inc.

B indicates serious opposition to the organization of intergroup relations but a positive orientation toward majority-group institutions. Cell C depicts much less opposition to the organization of intergroup relations but shows a negative orientation toward majority-group institutions. Finally, cell D indicates "substantial opposition to the status quo and substantial intergroup goal conflict."[7]

Types of Indian Political Mobilization

In pursuing their various goals, Indians have politically organized along five lines: (1) intratribal, (2) tribal, (3) intertribal coalitions and alliances, (4) alliances of like-minded individuals, and (5) extratribal coalitions and alliances.[8] Indians organize because individuals or tribes share common political, economic, or cultural goals and seek to influence public policy decisions that affect them and their constituents.

Intratribal

Intratribal political mobilization, which we only briefly describe because our focus is tribes in the intergovernmental matrix, occurs when segments of specific tribes, frustrated by the direction of tribal leadership, organize to challenge or confront the existing tribal power structure. For example, within the Navajo Nation a number of intratribal interest groups have formed over the years, bent on lobbying or pressing their government to create, or block, policies deemed important to the group's membership. A sample of these includes the Navajo Returned Students Association (organized in the early twentieth century to represent the needs and interests of Indian students educated at off-reservation boarding schools), Navajo Native American Church (organized in the 1940s to advocate for the rights of Church members during a time when the use of peyote, the sacrament of the Church's members, was banned by the tribal government), Diné Coalition (Navajo individuals opposed to coal gasification in the 1970s), and Diné Citizens Against Ruining the Environment (organized in 1988 to oppose the dumping of toxic waste and other environmental degradation of Navajo lands).

Tribal

This type of mobilization involves organization and action by members of a single tribe in pursuit of tribal-specific goals. To continue with our Navajo example, beginning in the 1870s and continuing through the early twentieth century, the Navajo Nation's leadership successfully lobbied the federal government to have sizable chunks of land added to their existing reservation during an era when explicit federal policy was aimed at dissolving reservations via the general allotment policy begun in 1887 and continuing through the early 1930s.[9]

Intertribal Coalitions and Alliances

This type of political mobilization involves members of multiple tribes acting on the basis of tribal affiliation in pursuit of common political or economic goals. Historical examples include the temporary coalition of the various Pueblo Nations in 1680

Photo 8.1
Iona Doc, right, and a coalition of other American Indian elders perform a ceremonial dance, December 14, 1995, in front of the federal building in Los Angeles, during a protest rally to stop Ward Valley, California, from becoming a radioactive dump site. The possible transfer of the federal land at Ward Valley to the state of California is part of the larger budget debate between Congress and the White House.
Source: AP/WIDE WORLD PHOTOS

to drive out the Spanish invaders and the efforts of Pontiac, an Ottawa Indian, in the 1760s to create an intertribal league to fend off the English invaders.

A third example came in the early nineteenth century, when Tecumseh and the Shawnee Prophet, Tenskwatawa, formed an alliance of a number of northeastern and midwestern tribes to try to halt and reverse the flow of Euro-Americans into their territories. A fourth example is the attempts by the Five Civilized Tribes from 1846 to 1886 to get the United States to provide their nations some kind of official status within the American constitutional framework. This culminated in a failed attempt in the late nineteenth century to organize a constitutionally incorporated Indian state, the State of Sequoyah.[10]

Contemporary examples of intertribal coalitions and alliances, both regional and national (some now defunct) include the United South and Eastern Tribes, Inc.; the Great Lakes Intertribal Council; the Intertribal Council of California; the Alaska Native Brotherhood and Sisterhood (ANB/S); the Coalition of Eastern Native Americans (CENA, defunct); the Northwest Indian Fisheries Commission; the Columbia River Intertribal Fish Commission; the National Congress of American Indians (NCAI); the National Tribal Chairmen's Association (NTCA, defunct); and the Council of Energy Resource Tribes (CERT).

Let us examine a few of these more closely. The Alaska Native Brotherhood and Sisterhood were founded in 1912 and 1915, respectively. The combined group was the first significant political and social intertribal organization in Alaska before statehood. Although in its early years it primarily was a self-help group and advocated for citizenship for natives, over time it came to play an active role in aboriginal rights. It has fought for native fishing rights and land claims, in particular. Although the leadership of both the brotherhood and the sisterhood have sought to portray ANB/S as a territory- or statewide organization, "for all practical purposes they were limited to southeast Alaska," and the membership consisted mostly of Tlingit and Haida Indians.[11]

The CENA was a regional intertribal interest group formed in the 1970s to advocate for the rights of eastern tribes, especially nonrecognized tribal groups. Its membership included the Mattaponi, Tunica-Biloxi, Lumbee, and Haliwa. The CENA emerged out of a conference centered on eastern Indian issues that had been organized by the Institute for the Development of Indian Law, one of the many Indian interest groups in the category of alliances of like-minded individuals.

But CENA, like other intertribal organizations, such as the Intertribal Council of Nevada and the Small Tribes Organization of Western Washington, generally lacked not only size and numbers, but bargaining resources and adequate funding. CENA engaged in brief flurries of organizational activity in the 1970s but did not survive that decade.

The NTCA, a national intertribal association of federally recognized tribal government leaders, was formed in 1971 with federal financial assistance. For a number of years, NTCA was one of the few Indian interest groups that gave direct input into federal Indian policymaking and administrative decisions. In a sense, this is appropriate, since Indian self-determination by definition requires direct Indian involvement and tribal governments are the elected bodies the federal government recognizes and financially supports.

However, as direct recipients of federal aid and largesse, the NTCA was open to charges of being beholden to federal administrators and not necessarily to their tribal constituencies.[12] Moreover, with NTCA dominating tribal input to the federal administration, other Indian interest groups were essentially ignored and sometimes oppressed. As Cornell argues, "by regarding those governments as the only legitimate representatives of Indian interests, the federal government effectively justifies ignoring political actions that bypass the tribal councils or their representatives."[13] In effect, organizations like NTCA served as buffers "against more hostile political actors and constituencies whose goals diverge more sharply from those of the larger society."[14]

The activist American Indian Movement (AIM) was the organization that NTCA was most nervous about. AIM is discussed later in this chapter. Importantly, although the NTCA opposed much of the early Indian activism of the 1960s and 1970s, by the end of that period, it was more supportive of activism, like the Longest Walk of 1978. Why the organizational change of heart? Because the "persistence of the Indian people had come to transform the government entity, and it became a viable reality."[15]

CERT, discussed in more detail in chapter 6, is a nonprofit Indian interest group founded in 1976 by the leaders of twenty-five tribes whose lands contained substantial nonrenewable resources: an estimated one third of the nation's low sulfur strippable coal, 40 percent of its privately owned uranium, 4 percent of the oil and natural gas, and substantial quantities of oil shale and geothermal resources. Peter MacDonald, former chairman of the Navajo Nation, touted CERT as an Indian version of OPEC. But OPEC is a conglomerate of independent nations, while tribes are economically interconnected and, until recently, economically dominated by the federal government via their geopolitical position. CERT today has an active American tribal membership of fifty-three nations. Four Canadian tribes are also members of CERT.

Finally, there is the NCAI, the oldest (founded in 1944), largest, and most representative intertribal interest group.[16] Its current membership includes approximately 250 indigenous entities and 1,500 individual Indians, since the organization was established as both a federated body and an individual membership organization. NCAI was organized primarily as a nonpartisan group to improve the status of Indians in the United States by focusing on legal aid, legislative action, education, and special training for Indians in the Bureau of Indian Affairs (BIA). It also published a newsletter, the NCAI Sentinel.

NCAI helped lead the fight to create the Indian Claims Commission in 1946, blunted the devastating termination policy initiated in the early 1950s, and worked to force recalcitrant states to grant Indians the right to vote in state and federal elections.[17]

But in the 1960s and 1970s more activist Indian interest groups like AIM and the National Indian Youth Council (NIYC) arose to challenge NCAI's politics as being out of touch with grassroots Indians' needs. Impatient with the pace of change and with the NCAI's political methods and composition, the younger Indians of AIM and NIYC were also acquainted with urban life, which had enlarged their understanding of Euro-American society.[18]

AIM, NIYC, organizations like CENA that supported nonrecognized tribes, and those organized for urban Indians like the National Urban Indian Council and American Indians United also were established to provide representation for those Indians not represented in NCAI. NCAI's influence waned also because the battle for Indian rights shifted to the federal courts. In the 1970s, legal interest groups became prominent. These included the Native American Rights Fund (NARF), organized in 1970; the Institute for the Development of Indian Law; and the Indian Law Resource Center. These groups were fairly successful by concentrating their efforts on promoting their policy goals through the courts.[19]

NCAI, because of its representativeness, remains the dominant voice for Indian tribes in the United States. It is "an important forum for tribal and intertribal Indian debates and concerns, its annual meetings help set the national Indian agenda for lobbying and litigation efforts, and its membership reflects the diversity of tribal Indian communities."[20] NCAI, however, is no longer interested solely in domestic indigenous issues. On July 20–23, 1999, after several years of planning, NCAI and its equivalent organization in Canada, the Assembly of First Nations, met for a four-day conference, "Uniting First Nations: Tecumseh's Vision," in Vancouver, British Columbia.

The joint meeting was held to strengthen the sovereignty and unity of North American Indian nations and to educate non-Indians about the distinctive nature of Indian governments. It was also concerned with creating opportunities for intertribal economic interchanges that would support the individual and collective capacities of the various First Nations.[21] The leaders forged a "Declaration of Kinship and Cooperation" to evidence their solidarity in regard to tribal sovereignty, spiritual practices, traditional knowledge, economic and social well-being, and promoting the rights of Indians to travel uninterrupted across the border separating Canada and the United States.[22]

In 2001, in the wake of a series of devastating U.S. Supreme Court decisions that reduced tribal governing authority over non-Indians inside Indian Country, the NCAI established the Sovereignty Protection Initiative. The goal of this initiative is to attempt to "halt or reverse the Supreme Court's erosion of tribal sovereignty" by working more closely with member tribes and the NARF and by being much more selective about which cases to take before the High Court.

Alliances of Like-Minded Indian Individuals (or Pan-Indian or Supratribal Organizations)

Pan-Indian political mobilization involves organizations and action "by individual Indians on the basis of Indianness and in pursuit of pan-Indian goals."[23] The very idea of "American Indians," a historical misnomer, now encapsulates a distinctly "Indian" identity that is distinct from one's tribal identity. Indeed, as Cornell describes it, "increasingly for large numbers of Indians, Indian identity—as distinct from tribal identity—has become a conscious and important basis of action and thought in its own right. A host of 'American Indian' and 'Native American' organizations testify to its salience, as do the numerous cooperative political efforts by Indian groups and organizations on behalf of both tribal and supratribal interests."[24]

Pan-Indian or supratribal interest groups generally espouse a political identity rather than a cultural identity and, importantly, are the result of Indian–non-Indian interaction. This was evident in the first such national Indian organization, the Society of American Indians (SAI), established in 1911. This organization was triggered by the experiences of Indian graduates of the federal government's boarding schools started in the latter half of the nineteenth century. At these schools, the explicit goal was the assimilation of Indians from many tribes by forced regimentation and inculcation of Western religious, property, and social values and norms.[25]

But as generations of Indians passed through the schools they learned about not only Western culture but other tribal cultures, religions, and values as well. At schools like Carlisle in Pennsylvania (the original federal Indian boarding school), Haskell in Kansas, and many others, "a variety of tribal backgrounds could be found and as Sioux began to learn about Yakima, as Apache worked and studied with Crows, and as other tribal peoples heard about the problems each tribe was having with the government, the Indian students began to understand that each tribe was subject to irrational and casual dealings by the government."[26]

Of the eighteen Indians who convened in Columbus, Ohio, in 1911 to plan the formation of a national organization to work for the improvement of all Indians, eleven were boarding-school graduates. SAI made virtually no effort to include in their membership traditional tribal Indians, and independent tribal governments were barely in existence, since they were in the transitional period. In effect, SAI, as a national body, stepped into a vacuum.

In its form, leadership, and aim, SAI was similar to the white reform organizations and the developing black movements of the Progressive Era. Its most dynamic leaders were largely middle class, well educated, "conscious of their attainments and responsibilities to those less favoured than themselves and proud of their respectability."[27] Generally, the objectives of the group were to encourage Indian leadership, promote self-help, and foster the assimilation of Indians while encouraging them to exhibit pride in their race.

Two issues crippled the organization and led to its demise in the early 1930s: the organization's conflicted position on the BIA—whether to reform it or abolish it—and the group's equally problematic position on traditional tribal religions and the Native American Church (NAC). Many of the society's members were Christian and supported neither the continuation of traditional religions nor the growing NAC religion, with its controversial sacramental use of peyote.[28] But the organization probably also failed because Indians were not quite prepared to genuinely step "beyond the confines of tribal existence to a conception of nationalism."[29]

SAI was followed by the National Council of American Indians in the 1920s and 1930s. This organization, founded by two former society members, Gertrude and R. T. Bonnin, included many other former SAI members as well. Although purporting to represent many tribes, in actuality the council was a small, struggling group held together by the faith and hard work of the Bonnins. It was interested in helping Indians secure the right to vote and assisting individual Indians with other grievances, and worked with some tribal nations. The letterhead of the council stationery proclaimed its goal: "Help Indians Help Themselves in Protecting Their Rights and Properties."[30] The organization produced a newsletter and worked closely with non-Indian reform organizations. Gertrude Bonnin knew and worked closely with John Collier in the 1920s and 1930s. But facing a plethora of difficulties, including lack of tribal support and adequate resources, it folded in the mid-1930s.

A confluence of events in the 1950s, 1960s, and 1970s led to a welter of pan-Indian interest groups operating on a number of levels: local, regional, national, and international. The confluence encompassed (1) the federal government's termination and relocation programs, (2) the civil rights movement, (3) university-trained Indian lawyers and professors, (4) the resurgence of powwows and other Indian cultural expressions that cut across tribal lines, and (5) the explosion of national Indian news media. The outgrowth of this conjuncture was a new generation of Indians who organized a variety of organizations aimed not at supporting restorative or integrative goals, but at transforming and segregating their constituencies.

A partial list of these interest organizations includes the NIYC (founded 1961), the Alaska Federation of Natives (1966), United Native Americans (1967), AIM (1968), Indians of All Tribes (1969), NARF (1970), the International Indian Treaty Council (IITC; 1974), Women of All Red Nations (1975), the Indian Law Resource Center (1977), and the Institute for the Development of Indian Law (1971). Several of these supratribal organizations are discussed in the following sections.

National Indian Youth Council

The NIYC was established in 1961 by a group of young Indians, many of whom were in college or were recent college graduates. It was established shortly after the conclusion of the Conference on American Indians in Chicago. One of the purposes of the Chicago conference, attended by academics and Indians, was to develop a policy statement to be presented to the Kennedy administration.[31] Throughout the 1960s NIYC engaged in numerous protests, demonstrations, and marches in an effort to protect Indian treaty, hunting, and fishing rights. NIYC was clearly influenced by and at times aligned with the black civil rights movement.[32]

Today, it is directed by a nine-member Indian board and continues to work to improve conditions for Indians in the areas of job training and placement, voter registration, and environmental issues, and has been involved in human rights issues for

Indians in Nicaragua. In 1984 it gained consultative status with the United Nations Economic and Social Council.[33] NIYC is the second-oldest national Indian organization.

American Indian Movement

AIM was established in Minneapolis, Minnesota, in 1968 by Dennis Banks, Clyde Bellecourt, Eddie Benton-Banai, and George Mitchell under the name Concerned Indian Americans (CIA).[34] But the CIA acronym proved unacceptable and the name "AIM" was quickly adopted. Russell Means joined later and became one of AIM's most charismatic and outspoken leaders.[35]

AIM emerged in and yet was independent of the civil rights cauldron of that era and had as its original purpose protecting the rights of urban Indians who had endured high levels of poverty, discrimination, and police brutality. AIM has been involved in a wide array of issues throughout its stormy history, including seeking economic independence for Indians, religious freedom, protection of Indian treaty rights, land restoration, environmental protection, indigenous education, and combating racism and stereotyping.[36]

AIM has been at the forefront of a number of well-publicized protests—the 1972 Trail of Broken Treaties in Washington, D.C., the 1973 occupation of Wounded Knee in South Dakota, and the 1978 "Longest Walk" from the West Coast to Washington, D.C. AIM's activities, along with the emergence of Indian self-determination and a number of legislative and litigative victories for Indians, generated a severe backlash among certain segments of non-Indian society, including the federal government. The U.S. government, in fact, engaged in a fourteen-year legal battle (1975–1988) in an effort to discredit, intimidate, and ultimately destroy the movement.[37]

By the late 1970s, many AIM leaders were in exile or prison, and the organization was under considerable pressure from law enforcement agencies like the Federal Bureau of Investigation and its parent agency, the Department of Justice, which were engaged in a counterintelligence program (COINTELPRO) against AIM. Because of these pressures and the resulting dissension among AIM's membership, the national leadership of the movement essentially disbanded.[38] In 1992, however, AIM was showing signs of an organizational revival, and a "summit" meeting of AIM chapters took place the following year in New Mexico.

However, some of the fissures that had developed between AIM's early leaders intensified and, by the mid-1990s, AIM had essentially fragmented into two major entities: the National American Indian Movement Inc., based in Minneapolis and headed by Clyde and Vernon Bellecourt, and the International Confederation of Autonomous AIM, under the leadership of Russell Means and Ward Churchill, and based in Denver.[39]

Controversy and contention continue to surround AIM, its leadership, and its legacy. In 2003, two former AIM members, Arlo Looking Cloud and John Graham, were indicted for the brutal murder of Anna Mae Pictou Aquash, an AIM activist, who was killed in 1975. And in 2005, Ward Churchill came under intense public and native scrutiny when it was publicized that he had written an article after the terrorist attacks of September 11, 2001, in which he had called some of the victims of the World Trade Center bombing "little Eichmann's."[40] Complicating Churchill's situation was that his cultural identity as an American Indian, long considered problematic by many in Indian Country, was openly called into question by an increasing number of Indian

Photo 8.2
American Indian Movement activist Russell Means, protesting Columbus Day celebrations on October 12, 1998, in Pueblo, Colorado. The protestors gathered to show their opposition to the hanging of a wreath on a statue of Chrisopher Columbus by Pueblo's Italian community. AIM is one of the oldest and most visible organizations working on behalf of Indian interests today. *Source*: AP/WIDE WORLD PHOTOS

and non-Indian writers and academics. Under investigation by the University of Colorado, Boulder, Churchill was found to have engaged in research misconduct and his employment was terminated in 2007. Churchill filed a lawsuit against the university for unlawful termination of employment and in 2009 a Denver jury found that Churchill had been wrongfully fired but awarded him only $1 in monetary compensation. Later, a district court judge vacated the monetary award and declined Churchill's request for reinstatement.

International Indian Treaty Council

The IITC, sometimes referred to as "AIM's international diplomatic arm," was organized in 1974 under the direction of Jimmie Durham. Designed as an advocacy and educational organization concerned with the struggles of indigenous peoples on a global scale, the IITC, which is recognized as a "Category II" nongovernmental organization in consultative status with the United Nations Economic and Social Council, has played a central role in placing the struggles of indigenous peoples before the world community. One commentator noted that IITC was formed explicitly to "international-ize the struggles of indigenous peoples by building links with other groups and raising issues of concern at international conferences and meetings."[41]

IITC had an important role in creating the United Nations Working Group on Indigenous Peoples in 1982, which led the way in putting together the United Nations Declaration of the Rights on Indigenous Peoples that was finally adopted in 2007. The IITC also attends international forums and provides delegations to the Commission on Human Rights, the Sub-Commission on Human Rights, the Sub-Commission on the Prevention of Discrimination and the Protection of Minorities, and others. It also has a program to train aboriginal peoples in the intricacies of the United Nations procedures and protocol.

Native American Rights Fund

Although American Indians have been going to federal courts seeking justice since 1831, it was not until the formation of NARF in 1970 that Indians had a national Indian interest law firm dedicated to the protection and enhancement of indigenous rights on major policy issues of a legal nature. NARF is careful in its selection of cases and chooses "those that will affect the greatest number of people and at the same time have a significant impact on Indian policy."[42] Importantly, NARF defends tribes who cannot afford the financial burden of obtaining justice in the courts. The Board of Directors has determined that NARF's legal resources should be concentrated in the five areas identified in the organization's mission statement: (1) preservation of tribal existence, (2) protection of tribal resources, (3) promotion of human rights, (4) accountability of governments, and (5) development of Indian law.[43]

NARF is governed by a volunteer board composed of twelve Indians from various tribes. It has a staff of about eleven attorneys, many of whom are Indian. They handle approximately fifty major cases at any given time. Since it established its headquarters in Boulder, Colorado, in 1971, NARF has helped tribes attain a measure of success in more than two hundred cases. Examples include protecting the inherent sovereignty of tribes; obtaining federal recognition for a number of Indian groups; assisting tribes in recovering land and water rights; helping Indians on matters involving religious freedom, including access to sacred sites, use of sacred objects, repatriation of human remains, the religious rights of Indian prisoners, and protecting the voting rights of Indians in several states.

NARF, like nearly all Indian interest groups, has received its share of criticism. Some have argued that it is essentially governed by "an elitist group of thirteen Indians" whose goals may not be in harmony with an Indian clientele.[44] Another criticism has been that NARF's use of federal funding and its founding with funds from the Ford Foundation affects its decisions on whether to select certain cases that might be controversial (e.g., eastern Indian land claims and federal recognition cases). However, others contend that this charge is largely without merit "since NARF attorneys have aggressively pursued a variety of basic legal issues for a wide number of Native American communities. They have rarely shied away from taking on states as well as federal agencies."[45]

Despite the criticism they have received, it is indisputable that NARF and the other interest groups discussed in this section have played a profound role in significantly improving the lives of tribal nations and individual Indians in a host of areas.

Extratribal Coalitions and Alliances

American Indian nations, because of their sovereign status as small nations with treaty-based rights, have historically not engaged in many permanent coalitions or alliances with non-native groups because the thrust of indigenous efforts—to retain their extra-constitutional and separate governmental status—is fundamentally different from that of all other groups and individuals. In the 1960s, however, this changed because of the civil rights movement. A small number of Indians did attend the March on Washington in 1963, but the lack of tribal participation was a clear reflection that the ideology of the civil rights movement at the time, was contrary to tribal interests. As Vine Deloria Jr. remarked, Indians were not willing to concede their treaty rights for the political equality allegedly promised by the civil rights activists.[46]

In 1964, however, some young college-educated urban Indians, like those active in the NIYC and the Survival of American Indians Association, did adopt some of the tactics and ideas of the civil rights movement when they held a "fish-in" in the Pacific Northwest to publicize the problems of the Puyallup and other tribes in their efforts to exercise their treaty right to fish. The tribes' efforts gained national attention, and celebrities like the comedian Dick Gregory and actor Marlon Brando joined in solidarity with the tribes.[47] These fish-ins, then, and the increasingly militant stance of many Indians, drew from the language and techniques of the Black Power activists in order to bring the attention of the mass media to the struggles of Indians.

The environmental movement that was emerging in this era was also an arena of some coalition-building. As Grace Thorpe, daughter of legendary athlete Jim Thorpe and president of the Native Environmental Coalition of Native Americans (NECONA), put it, "We must unite as people of the world to stop the nuclear industry that is dividing and contaminating us."[48] One of NECONA's organizational goals is to network with non-Indian environmentalists to develop grassroots resistance to the nuclear industry.

Other ad hoc extratribal coalitions have been formed as well. In 1981, when the United States was proposing the MX Mobile Missile System, a loose coalition of opponents included leaders of such indigenous organizations as the Council for a Livable World, the Great Basin MX Alliance, the Sagebrush Alliance of Nevada, and the Western Shoshone Sacred Lands Association.[49]

In 1998, the forty-two Indian member tribes of the InterTribal Bison Cooperative (ITBC), with a collective herd of over eight thousand bison, joined in an unsuccessful lawsuit, *Intertribal Bison Cooperative et al. v. Babbitt,* to enjoin the Department of the Interior over their bison control plan, made in agreement with the state of Montana, to slaughter some of Yellowstone National Park's bison herd.[50] The bison allegedly were a threat to the cattle herds of ranchers, who feared the buffalo might infect their herds with brucellosis, a bacterial disease that affects cattle and causes undulant fever in humans. ITBC's coalition partners included the Earth Justice Legal Defense Fund, the Greater Yellowstone Coalition, the Jackson Hole Alliance for Responsible Planning, Defenders of Wildlife, and the Gallatin Wildlife Association. In May 1999, the coalition partners appealed the court decision to the Ninth Circuit Court of Appeals, which affirmed the district court's ruling.[51]

And in 2000 the NCSL and the NCAI collaborated on a project to improve tribal-state relations in policymaking on important public policy issues. This timely project has led to the development of educational materials aimed at informing the members of both groups about the rights, status, and opportunities available when both sets of governments act in a spirit of cooperation.[52]

Indigenous Political Activism

Across the globe, indigenous peoples—including the tribal and First Nations of the Americas, the Aborigines of Australia, the Maori of New Zealand, the Saami of the Scandinavian countries, and the Ainu of Japan—began in the 1950s to make their voices heard in domestic (state) and international (United Nations) forums. Constituting what has come to be called the *Fourth World*—in other words, sharing political and economic marginalization with Third World countries but being denied the benefits of the international doctrine of self-determination that the First, Second, and Third World countries enjoyed—indigenous nations were demanding in a respectful manner that their historically deprived or underrecognized rights to inherent sovereignty, cultural autonomy, political self-determination, and economic self-sufficiency finally be accorded a measure of recognition by their host states and by the international community.[53]

Some real improvements have been made at the international level in recent years. In 2009, the United States became a member of the United Nations Human Rights Council (HRC). The United States will be reviewed in 2010 by the HRC's Universal Periodic Review (UPR) process. "Under the UPR all 192 UN member States (countries) are reviewed every four years to assess compliance with their obligations to respect and implement human rights for all."[54] In preparation, the U.S. State Department has arranged "listening sessions" across the country, two of which are specifically designated for indigenous peoples.

Although the International Decade of the World's Indigenous People, 1994–2004, ended without a ratified version of the Draft Declaration on the Rights of Indigenous People, in 2002 there was established in the Economic and Security Council a Permanent Forum on Indigenous issues that provides a place for aboriginal peoples to express their views and grievances about the manner in which they are being treated by their host states.[55] On September 13, 2007, the General Assembly adopted the Declaration on the Rights of Indigenous Peoples, outlining the rights of the world's estimated 370 million indigenous peoples. The Declaration, while not a legally-binding document, outlines standards for the treatment of indigenous peoples, including the recognition of the individual and collective rights of indigenous peoples to self-determination and to maintain and strengthen their distinct political, legal, economic, social, and cultural institutions. A total of 143 member states voted in favor of the Declaration, 11 abstained, and 4 voted against the Declaration. These four negative votes were cast by Australia, the United States, Canada, and New Zealand.

However, in recent years, three of these states have changed, or are in the process of changing, their position. Australia, for example, officially endorsed the Declaration in April 2009. And Canada's Governor General, Michaelle Jean, in March 2010, declared that Canada would take the necessary steps to grant "qualified recognition," though indigenous groups are pushing for unconditional recognition.[56] On April 19, 2010, New Zealand announced its support of the Declaration and one day later, U.S. Ambassador to the U.N. Susan Rice announced the United States had begun the process of reconsidering its position on the Declaration.[57] Interestingly, Maine's state legislature passed a 2008 Joint Resolution in support of the Declaration. Native nations are anxious to see whether the Obama administration will unconditionally support the Declaration's adoption.

Indigenous activism and resistance to colonizing European states and their derivative settler states date to when indigenous peoples' homelands were first invaded half a millennium ago. However, from the late 1950s to the late 1970s, an ad hoc and unpredicted merger of events, including the assertiveness of key indigenous personalities who used legal training and moral persuasion to influence state policymakers, an increasing awareness by the host states of the importance of human and civil rights in their multicultural and multiracial societies, and a sense that indigenous peoples had a depth of environmental knowledge that could be of benefit to the society at large[58] fueled a unique surge of activism that enabled indigenous peoples in the United States and elsewhere to, in some cases, begin to (re)gain access to lands, (re)claim some measure of ownership of natural resources, (re)assert their distinctive treaty rights (where they existed—the United States, Canada, and New Zealand), and partake of other benefits and privileges heretofore underprotected or in some cases flatly denied to them by their host states. For American Indians, whether urban or reservation based, this activism fueled a "more open and confident sense of identity."[59]

This section examines this unfolding of indigenous activism in the United States by examining the key actors, events, and processes that made it happen. And as we shall see, the Indian activist movement of this era was not fundamentally a part of the other racial or ethnic social movements (e.g., black civil rights), although it certainly benefited from those movements by adopting some of their symbols and other aspects, and by taking advantage of the changed political atmosphere to push through the Indian activists' agenda. In a greater sense, then, "the Indian movement is a continuing resistance which has its basic roots in the Indian experience of the last [five] centuries."[60]

Early Patterns of Indigenous Resistance

The history of indigenous political activism and resistance dates back to the earliest days of contact between tribal peoples and European explorers and settlers. Much of the conflict that arose centered on the inability or, in some instances, the unwillingness of the European and later the Euro-American governments to prevent their citizens from violating treaties or other pledges the states had made to the tribal nations.[61] The Indians' collective response to such violations, like the Great Pueblo Revolt of 1680,[62] "was likely not to be seen as protest but tended to be defined as 'war.'"[63]

There were, in these early days, at least two types of indigenous collective action, both taking the form of "revitalization movements": religious revitalization movements (RRMs) and social revitalization movements (SRMs). RRMs, of which there have been many, sought to provide "spiritual solutions to the conditions of economic marginalization, political repression, and major losses of territory, as well as the ability to carry on traditional life."[64] Among the more prominent of these movements were those of the Delaware Prophet (1760–1763), the Shawnee Prophet (1805–1811), and the Winnebago Prophet (1830); the Ghost Dance movement of 1870; and the more famous Ghost Dance movement in 1890. In each of these movements, a prophet relied on spiritual knowledge and reached out to an intertribal following, asserting that they must either fight the invading whites or "pray for a cataclysmic event that would restore the Indian nations to peace, plenty, and the life they had known before American or European intrusions."[65]

For example, the 1890 Ghost Dance was led by a Paiute Prophet, Wovoka, who promised that all Indians who joined the Ghost Dance Faith (which spread quickly among the Cheyenne, Arapaho, Sioux, Kiowa, Caddo, and Paiute) would see the return of dead warriors and the decimated buffalo herds. They would return to a new earth "where all tribes would live forever in peace and prosperity free of white people."[66] But local whites were fearful that the Indians, especially the Sioux, were intent on engaging in more warfare, and because of sensationalized press accounts that exacerbated these fears, the federal government responded by sending in heavily armed troops to break the strength of the dancers and their leaders.

One of the Sioux leaders was Sitting Bull, a Hunkpapa holy man who had embraced the new religion. He was assassinated by U.S. government–employed Indian police to defuse the Ghost Dance situation and be rid of a venerated leader. What then followed was one of the worst massacres in the history of Indian-white relations. George A. Custer's former regiment, the Seventh Cavalry, gathered 340 starving Lakota men, women, and children, led by Big Foot, at Wounded Knee Creek on the Pine Ridge Indian Reservation. While the Indians were being disarmed, gunfire erupted. When the shooting finally stopped, 146 Sioux lay dead on the frozen ground.[67] Many other Lakota were killed in the ensuing weeks, as federal and military officials sought to stamp out the last vestiges of Indian resistance to colonial rule. The U.S. government awarded thirty Congressional Medals of Honor to soldiers who participated in the Wounded Knee massacre. Although this carnage was a shattering blow to the Indians, Wovoka's Ghost Dance religion did not end; he, in fact, remained an influential holy person until his death in 1932.[68]

SRMs, a majority of which led to reformed religions, "also served to establish modified forms of community organization designed to better accommodate American-style agriculture, reservation land, and political restrictions."[69] Such movements included the Handsome Lake Church (1799–present), the Delaware Big House Religion (1760–1910), the Kickapoo Prophet (1830–1851), the Shaker Church (1881–present), and the official incorporation of the NAC (1918–present).

The Handsome Lake religion is based on the ideas of Handsome Lake (1735–1815), an Iroquois leader who had a series of visions in 1799 while he lay unconscious. His visions, which led to the development of what is called the Code of Handsome Lake, focused on abstinence, family values, and the perpetuation of Iroquois ceremonies, songs, and dances of thanksgiving. There are four general tenets in the code: (1) Ohnega (alcohol), the worst vice, was not to be consumed; (2) Otgo (witchcraft) was to be used only for healing and not for evil purposes; (3) Onohwet (love medicine), which "clouds the mind and sickens the body to the point of death," must no longer be used; and (4) the blessings of marriage, family, and children were to be fully appreciated and supported by the people.[70]

Handsome Lake preached this reformed faith from his home on the Allegheny River in Pennsylvania. It was truly a syncretic religion, since he encouraged his followers to learn the white man's ways by attending school. And while he preached the confession of sin, he also supported the perpetuation of traditional ceremonies and prayers like the Great Feather Dance, the Drum Dance, and the Sustenance Dance. This faith is still strong among the Iroquois today.

Besides these two broad types of revitalization movements, there were also the efforts of many individual tribes systematically fighting to have their treaty rights upheld. For instance, although the spirit of the Lakota had been temporarily crushed after the Wounded Knee massacre, tribal leaders, responding to the government's legally problematic dismantling of the Great Sioux Reservation into individual units and their subsequent allotment, began to file lawsuits in the 1890s in the U.S. Court of Claims. Tribes in the Pacific Northwest responded similarly to the threat of allotment.

In fact, "the pattern of resistance clearly shows that the thrust toward solving problems has been a religious-political appeal to a sense of values expected of a society and that the appeal has generally fallen on deaf ears."[71] And as we saw in the last chapter under the discussion of interest groups, "as the twentieth century began the movement of resistance took on a national aspect and the subsequent movements of this century have fluctuated between resistance on the tribal or reservation level and sporadic efforts to organize the tribes on a national basis."[72]

Contemporary Indian Activism

Indian resistance continued from the first decades of the twentieth century up to the explosion of activities in the 1960s. Most resistance and activism before the 1960s occurred at the individual tribal level and tended to focus on specific issues that threatened tribal lands, resources, or civil or treaty rights—Navajo livestock reduction in the 1930s and 1940s, Iroquois challenges to dams and other water projects in the 1940s through the 1960s, the Lumbee routing of the Ku Klux Klan in 1957, the fishing rights struggles of the Pacific Northwest tribes in the 1950s and 1960s.[73]

The successful fish-in movement involving tribes in Washington State (eventually the Indians judicially secured the right to one half of the harvestable salmon under their 1855 treaty) proved an outstanding training ground for Indian rights activists. "The fish-ins taught Indian activists two important goals: first, that the redress of tribal grievances could be pursued by an alliance of tribal and supratribal organizations and collective action, and, second, that attracting the attention of national media was crucial to obtaining judicial and legislative review."[74]

The first lesson has already been addressed. The second, however—the role of the media—has not, but it is important and warrants some attention. During the fish-ins, tribal and organizational leaders reached out and involved entertainment figures to help publicize their situation. When AIM was born in 1968, its leadership early on sought to manipulate the media to their advantage. While generally used with success, this tactic had serious costs. AIM's leadership "sometimes traded on America's fascination with the image of the male warrior" because AIM was "still bounded by their own vision of history and the biases of reporters and the public."[75]

The findings of a 1996 study that focused on the National Broadcasting Company's (NBC's) news coverage of AIM from 1968 to 1979 bears this out.[76] Timothy Baylor culled from the data five "media frames," or ways in which the media depicted AIM's goals and actions: militant, stereotype, treaty rights, civil rights, and factionalism. He found that 98 percent of NBC's evening coverage of AIM's activities was couched in either the militant or stereotype frames, although AIM's leadership sought to emphasize treaty rights and civil rights issues. In fact, "the Militant frame clearly dominated the nightly news segments. The operationalized Militant frame included any segment that labeled Indian protesters as 'militant' or where the focus was on violence and the breakdown of law and order."[77] The study concludes by describing the "dysfunctions of media attention," which presents "a distorted and incomplete picture of a movement's message and goals."[78]

The term *Red Power* has been attributed to Vine Deloria Jr., then the executive director of the NCAI, in a 1966 speech at the organization's annual meeting. Deloria, a Standing Rock Sioux, was one of a new group of Indians committed to transforming Indian-white relations by attempting to bridge the gulf between more radical organizations like the NIYC and established ones like the NCAI. He also believed that alliances between the various tribal and pan-Indian organizations, urban and reservation Indians, and eastern and western tribes would prove beneficial to Indian interests.[79]

The rise of tribal-based civil and treaty rights activism, the birth of a number of national Indian organizations (e.g., NIYC, AIM, the Indian Law Resource Center), the increasingly urban-based nature of the Indian population, the printing of powerful books like Vine Deloria's *Custer Died for Your Sins* in 1969, the influx of federal funds to Indians as poverty-stricken communities under the War on Poverty programs, and the broader civil rights developments all fueled a tribal and national indigenous political consciousness that led to a surge of Indian protest activity by the end of the 1960s. Figure 8.1 graphically charts the number of event days of protest from 1960 to 1980.

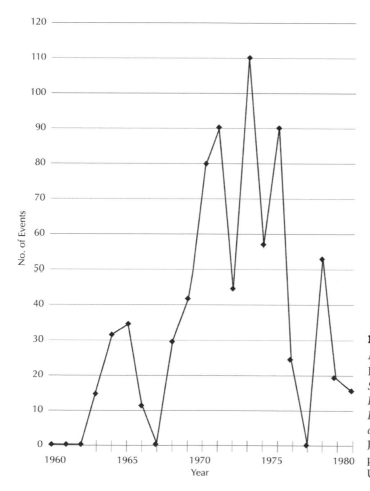

Figure 8.1
American Indian Protest Events, 1960-1980
Source: From *American Indian Ethnic Renewal: Red Power and the Resurgence of Identity and Culture* by Joane Nagel, © 1997. By permission of Oxford University Press, Inc.

A turning point in the level of activity was the 1969 takeover and occupation of Alcatraz Island near San Francisco. This event, for many commentators,[80] represents the launching point of the Red Power period, which ran from 1969 to 1978. This period marked a noticeable shift from tribally based protests to larger nationally organized events, spurred "by Indians from a variety of tribes sharing a common interest in Indian and tribal rights broadly conceived."[81] The activist political strategy focused on calling the federal government to account for its past and present misdeeds and omissions. And as Deloria showed, "treaty rights rather than eligibility and need became the criteria for protest and the idea was to play directly on whatever reservoir of cumulative guilt lay hidden in the public psyche."[82]

The underlying goals of the Indians of Alcatraz were to make the American public aware of the reality of their situation and by extension that of Indians throughout the land, and to assert the need for Indian self-determination.[83] The occupation certainly succeeded in realizing these goals, as the ensuing flurry of events, laws, court decisions, and policies attests. Some seventy-four Indian occupations and demonstrations followed in Alcatraz's wake. These included the Trail of Broken Treaties and the BIA takeover in 1972; Wounded Knee II in 1973; the takeover of the Alexian Brothers Roman Catholic novitiate in Gresham, Wisconsin, in 1975 by the Menominee Warrior Society with AIM support; and the Longest Walk, from San Francisco to Washington, D.C., in 1978, symbolizing the forced removal of Indians and protesting pending congressional bills aimed at terminating or dramatically reducing Indian treaty rights.

Two interesting observations can be made of this tumultuous period. First was the role of the traditional religious dimension of Indian life. This subject had previously caused division among Indian organizations, pitting Indian traditionalists, who favored retaining and exercising traditional knowledge and spiritual practices, against Indian Christians, who generally accepted assimilation to American religious, social, and economic values. But traditional religion became the most important aspect of many of these occupations and demonstrations "and signaled that despite several centuries of assimilationist thrust tribal identity was still a major factor."[84] Second, and related to the first observation, the Red Power movement helped educate and alter the consciousness of many Americans about Indians. The movement and its supporters stressed the fact that "Indians have cultures, traditions, history, and communities that they want to preserve—but that they also want equal justice, economic opportunity, access to education, and more accurate portrayal of Indians in the media and in history books."[85]

In effect, the indigenous political response posed a remarkable challenge to the existing nature of Indian-white relationships in several respects. First, the rise of nontribal groups like urban-based Indian organizations, larger intertribal organizations, and local communities not involved in the administrative structural relationship between the tribes and the BIA was a direct challenge to the existing political relationship because it bypassed the established system of power relations.

Second, the Indian response went further and openly attacked the structural relationship by filing court cases challenging congressional and BIA decision-making powers by reasserting land claims and treaty rights, by making their own recommendations for improving Indian status, and by reclaiming the right of self-determination. Third, Indians, by seeking to exercise self-determination, were basically rejecting the largely assimilationist orientation that had been the cornerstone of federal Indian policy for most of the previous two hundred years.[86]

The U.S. response to all this indigenous activity was, as one would expect, variegated. Generally, however, most responses to Indian activism can be grouped into four categories: (1) efforts to suppress and discredit the most radical elements of Indian resistance by engaging in a systematic campaign of surveillance, infiltration, and indictment (e.g., the government's COINTELPRO against AIM and its leadership); (2) anti-Indian activity and legislation aimed at offsetting or striking against Indian political and legal gains that at times upset white land titles or hunting and fishing industries (e.g., the introduction of bills to abrogate Indian treaties and weaken Indian rights in general); (3) symbolic reform in response to particular Indian demands (e.g., establishment of the American Indian Policy Review Commission in 1975, increasing Indian staffing at the BIA, and creating a new position, the assistant secretary of Indian affairs, to replace the commissioner of Indian affairs position); and (4) substantive measures to accommodate Indian concerns and demands (e.g., return of some traditional lands to certain tribes, like Blue Lake's return to the Taos Pueblo Indians in 1970, the Indian Self-Determination and Education Assistance Act of 1975, and the Indian Religious Freedom Act of 1978).[87]

During this critical period, and even extending back into the 1950s (and the Vocational Training Act of 1956), indigenous persons, organizations, and nations, fighting on multiple fronts, began to gain access to federal jobs, public works support, housing assistance, communication aid, and other federal support and services. Much of this federal assistance arrived in Indian Country because indigenous peoples were part of that large constituency known simply as "the poor."

As Congress declared on May 1, 1961, in passing the Area Redevelopment Act to "alleviate conditions of substantial and persistent unemployment and underemployment in certain economically distressed areas," the secretary of commerce was to designate as redevelopment areas "those areas (including Indian reservations) within the United States which are in need of such assistance."[88] Such laws were some of the first cases where Congress and the executive branch made tribes eligible for federal assistance on a basis similar to that of other governments. This precedent would be greatly expanded when Lyndon B. Johnson became president.[89]

Thus, when Johnson declared "War on Poverty" in 1964 and instituted a variety of social welfare programs, tribal leaders continued their fight to be included and committed federal lawmakers saw to it that tribal governments were made eligible for many of the programs authorized by Congress. The poverty war's most important agency was the Office of Economic Opportunity (OEO) (including Head Start, Community Action Programs, and Legal Services), and this body and the other programs unleashed as part of the Great Society represented "the first major instance in which Indian tribal governments had money and were not beholden for it to the Bureau of Indian Affairs."[90]

The distinctive issues confronting aboriginal peoples led to the establishment of Indian "desks" in the OEO and other agencies, like the Departments of Commerce, Housing and Urban Development, Agriculture, and Labor. These Indian desks meant that the funds were processed apart from the general programs, a recognition of the unique nature of tribes as governing, if poverty-stricken, bodies.[91]

These funds gave tribal governments opportunities to be somewhat more creative in their efforts to attack the social, economic, and legal problems their communities endured. For example, the Legal Services program provided tribal nations and individual Indians more access to legal counsel. The California Indian Legal Services program initiated a project that evolved to become the NARF, which, with additional funding from the Ford Foundation, became a leading Indian legal interest group, as discussed previously.[92] Navajo political leaders Peter McDonald and Peterson Zah, both of whom would become tribal chairs of the largest reservation, gained valuable work experience through OEO's Office of Navajo Economic Opportunity, which was established on the reservation in the 1960s.

As Philip Deloria states, "apart from the money, the most important byproduct of the Great Society—of which the Office of Economic Opportunity was the doyenne—for tribal self-determination was the notion that Indian tribes are or should be eligible for federal services other than those specially for Indians."[93]

President Johnson also, by way of executive order, created the National Council on Indian Opportunity in 1969. This body initially consisted of the secretaries of agriculture, commerce, housing and urban development, interior, and labor, and the head of the OEO, along with six prominent Indian members: Roger A. Jourdain, Wendell Chino, Cato Valandra, Raymond Nakai, William J. Hensley, and LaDonna Harris.[94] The organization, although it was initially chaired by Vice President Hubert Humphrey, had little impact on national Indian policy issues and expired by 1975. Nevertheless, for a time it did provide a national platform for Indian issues and served as a place where indigenous concerns could be articulated.[95]

Overall, one could make a plausible argument that the late 1960s and the 1970s entailed a significant shift in the political fortunes of American Indian nations, since "major legislation enacted after 1968 has, for the most part, incorporated the policy goals and preferences of Indian constituencies and groups."[96]

Ronald Reagan's 1980 election, however, reversed direction on Indian rights and implemented massive cutbacks in federal funding for tribes—cutbacks that, coincidentally, opened the door for Indian gaming operations to commence. In addition to these severe economic cutbacks, there was also a resurgence of states' rights, which meant that tribes and states would again challenge one another over many issues. Furthermore, Reagan's and Bush's appointments of many conservatives to the federal courts signaled that even the federal judiciary, which for a brief period in the 1970s had been a bastion of liberalism where tribes had been able to secure some fundamental protections and enforcement of their treaty rights, would no longer be as friendly an environment for tribes.

The 1990s through 2008, the Clinton and Bush years, provided a bizarre blend. Some tribes wielded great power through economic self-determination and political activism because of gaming revenues, while many others still languished in dire poverty, with low educational attainments, high suicide and alcoholism rates, and poor health. Even as tribes were exercising new political strength by forming new organizational alliances with other tribes to protect and enhance their economic base and political status, and even as they were more actively participating in local, state, and federal elections, they were confronted by internal and external constraints—federal and state court rulings, a conservative Congress, a fickle public, and emboldened state governments—that threatened to derail tribal efforts to become relatively self-sufficient sovereigns, alongside the state and federal governments.

It is still too early to tell what impact the Obama administration will have on Indian Country. While Obama has appointed a number of American Indians to his team and offered a muted apology, it is yet unclear whether his goals for federal-Indian relations will result in significant and long-term change.

Additionally, a number of non-Indian interest groups have recently formed, or been revived, which have as their objective the reduction or termination of tribal sovereignty, treaty rights, Indian gaming operations, and so forth. With sturdy-sounding names like the American Land Rights Association, Citizens Equal Rights Foundation (CERF), United Property Owners, and One Nation United (ONU), and with mission statements that include comments such as "Citizens Equal Rights Foundation was established to protect and support the constitutional rights of all people, both Indian and non-Indians,"[97] and "United Property Owners is a non-partisan, non-profit umbrella organization . . . who joined together in 1989 in a mutual effort to defend our constitutionally guaranteed civil liberties and property rights,"[98] one would think these organizations would support the principled position of tribal nations looking to exercise their treaty and constitutionally-based rights. Such is not the case, however. For example, the mission statement of the Citizens Equal Rights Alliance, which is connected to CERF, declares that "Federal Indian policy is unaccountable, destructive, racist and unconstitutional." ONU graphically declares that "it has become obvious that tax and regulatory inequities favor the tribes and threaten to thwart economic development efforts across our nation."[99]

In fact, these groups have been termed "hate groups" by a number of tribes and tribal organizations because their activities often include economic boycotts, spying, public ridicule, ethnic slurs, and threats of violence.[100]

Conclusion

Native nations and organized interest groups will continue their efforts to stabilize and improve their status by engaging in a variety of activist approaches as they continue into the new millennium. This will include (1) being more active in nontribal political systems so that Indians' unique needs will be represented; (2) being more selective about bringing lawsuits in state or federal courts because of the courts' current ideological bent; (3) continuing their efforts to educate their own people and the American public and policymakers about Indians' distinctive legal, political, and cultural rights; and (4) working to improve communications and facilitate better relations intertribally and intergovernmentally and to find a way for the wealthy gaming tribes to support and assist the less wealthy or nongaming tribes, both politically and economically.

Such efforts, while not guaranteed to produce success, will be in keeping with the adaptive and flexible activist tradition that has enabled Indian peoples to sustain themselves despite the oppressive odds they have faced throughout history.

CHAPTER 9

Native Peoples, Images, and the Media

The NCAA [National Collegiate Athletic Association] objects to institutions using racial/ethnic/national origin references in their intercollegiate athletic programs.... Several institutions have made changes that adhere to the core values of the NCAA Constitution pertaining to cultural diversity, ethical sportsmanship and nondiscrimination. We applaud that, and we will continue to monitor these institutions and others. All institutions are encouraged to promote these core values and take proactive steps at every NCAA event through institutional management to enhance the integrity of intercollegiate athletics related to these issues.

—NCAA Executive Committee, 2005[1]

THIS STATEMENT, issued by the National Collegiate Athletic Association's (NCAA) Executive Committee laid out the guidelines for use of American Indian "mascots" during postseason tournaments. While not prohibiting mascots entirely or forcing institutions to change their mascots, the new policy identified eighteen colleges and universities that continue to use imagery and references often deemed derogatory, including the University of Illinois–Champaign Fighting Illini, Catawba College Indians, and others, and declared that the NCAA, effective February 1, 2006, would prohibit colleges or universities with "hostile or abusive mascots, nicknames, or imagery" from hosting any championship events. Interestingly, within a month of this significant policy change the Florida State Seminoles, the Central Michigan Chippewas, and the Utah Utes were granted exemptions from the policy because of the firestorm of protests—some of it coming from tribes themselves—the policy had unleashed.

Nevertheless, the NCAA's partial ban of such mascots was hailed by many American Indians as a long overdue and respectful measure, but it also was derided by many non-Indians, including a number of school officials, who viewed it as a politically correct move. These disparate responses to the NCAA guidelines show the philosophical gulf that persists between, on one hand, the way American Indians perceive their

Photo 9.1

Photo 9.2

Photo 9.3

Many images of Indians in the media and throughout popular culutre are considered to be demeaning and culturally invasive by American Indians. Protests against offensive holiday celebrations, sports teams, and other affronts have increased over the years, and while some progress has been made, many problems persist.
Source: AP/WIDE WORLD PHOTOS

treatment and portrayal and, on the other, the attitude and behavior of a segment of the non-Indian population that maintains that they have the right to continue such characterizations.

Other American minorities have also endured demeaning images and stereotypes. African Americans struggled with the "Little Black Sambo" depiction, which was finally jettisoned in 1981, when Sambo's Restaurant declared bankruptcy; Mexican Americans had to endure the "Frito Bandito," a mascot used to sell corn chips, which because of complaints was discontinued in 1971; and Asian Americans have been stereotyped as the mysterious and evil "Fu Manchu," or as the assimilated "model minority." However, while product symbols like Aunt Jemima, Uncle Ben, and the Taco Bell Chihuahua persist, such negative images have "largely disappeared from the public landscape, owing to the growing political and market power of these groups."[2]

Indigenous peoples, however, remain subject to stereotypical and oftentimes denigrating images that are no longer tolerated by other minorities or the American public. The ongoing Washington Redskins trademark case is another clear example. In this lawsuit, Suzan Harjo, Vine Deloria, and others filed a suit with the U.S. Patent and Trademark Office, charging that the "Redskins" name was defamatory to American Indians. In 1999 the Trademark Trial and Appeal Board of the U.S. Department of Commerce unanimously ruled in the Indians' favor. The Washington Redskins organization appealed this decision, and in 2003 the U.S. District Court ruled in *Pro-Football, Inc., v. Harjo*[3] that the finding of disparagement was "not supported by substantial evidence and must be reversed" and that the case had been filed after an undue delay.

But in July 2005, the Court of Appeals found that the question of delay had been built on shaky premises and remanded the case back to the lower court for additional examination.[4] Suzan Harjo, the lead plaintiff, said she was "very pleased" with the appellate court's decision.[5] However, on remand, the U.S. District Court for D.C. found that the doctrine of laches was still applicable since the youngest plaintiff had turned eighteen almost eight years before the case was filed. In 2009, The U.S. Supreme Court declined to hear the appeal. As a result, the legal team arguing for the discontinuation of the Redskins name and logo is preparing to file a new suit with a younger generation of Indian activists between the ages of 18 and 24.

Indians and Indian interest groups like the National Congress of American Indians (NCAI), which has long condemned sports teams that use Indian names and images as "mascots," hope that the Harjo case and the NCAA's partial ban will persuade teams to drop offensive names in favor of nonoffensive names. A number of high schools, colleges, and universities have, in fact, changed their names because of Indian and non-Indian pressure—in 1969 Dartmouth College dropped the name "Indians" and adopted the phrase "Big Green"; in 1972 Indian students at Stanford University successfully petitioned and had the university drop its "Indian" name for the "Cardinal"; in 1995 St. Johns University changed its name from the "Redmen" to the "Red Storm"; and in 1998 Southern Nazarene University, a small Christian school in Bethany, Oklahoma, ended its use of the name "Redskins" and adopted instead the nickname "Crimson Storm."[6] After losing their appeal of the NCAA mascot ban and being placed on the list of schools prohibited from hosting postseason tournaments, the University of Illinois Board of Trustees in 2007 decided to retire the University's former mascot—Chief Illiniwek—in name, performance, and symbol. Similarly, the North Dakota Supreme Court in 2010 supported a Board of Higher Education decision to retire the University of North Dakota's Fighting Sioux nickname and logo, which will remain until the 2011–2012 school year.

Other schools and professional sports teams, however, persist in retaining names and logos that are considered demeaning and racist by many native people—the Cleveland Indians, the Atlanta Braves, the Kansas City Chiefs, the Florida Seminoles, and the Chicago Blackhawks, to name but a few. The appropriation of tribal names and symbols, and the depiction of Indians in stereotypical ways, is of course evident in other sectors of American society as well. Products like Land-O'-Lakes butter, which depicts an Indian "princess"; Red Man Chewing Tobacco; Calumet Baking Powder; and Mazola Corn Oil; and the names of numerous other products like vehicles (Mazda Navajo, Jeep Cherokee) and military equipment (Apache helicopter) serve to perpetuate stereotypical images of Native peoples that have developed over the last half-millennium.

The often stereotypical and sometimes prejudicial images projected in the media run the gamut. First, there are seemingly "positive" depictions of indigenous people as "noble savages" or as "enlightened savages," which portray Indians as friendly, courteous, natural environmentalists, hospitable to whites, and capable of full assimilation, though invariably poor and relatively defenseless. Many non-Indians considered Indians helpless victims because of European and Euro-American policies that devastated tribal nations by taking Indian lands and resources, and due to the natives' apparent inherent cultural and technological deficiencies. These largely benevolent stereotypes tended to emphasize the physical strength, manual dexterity, quiet (stoic) demeanor, and modest nature of Indians.

On the other side, of course, are "negative" stereotypical images like that of Indians as "bloodthirsty savages," of the "bad-Indian" who is violent toward all ages and genders, and is greedy, lecherous, filthy, and evil.[7] This characterization of Indians, which arose when Euro-American acquisitiveness for Indian property increased in the early 1600s, depicts Indians as heavily decorated with war paint, carrying tomahawks, and always ready to scalp innocent non-Indians. William Bradford, a leading Pilgrim in New England in 1620, provided one of the earliest descriptions of Indians as bloodthirsty savages. In describing the conditions confronting Pilgrim settlers, Bradford observed that the settlers were,

> in continual danger of the savage people, who are cruel, barbarous, and most treacherous, being most furious in their rage and merciless where overcome; not being content only to take away life, but delight to torment men in the most bloody manner that may be; flaying some alive with the shells of fishes, cutting off the members and joints of others by piecemeal and broiling on the coals, eat the collops of their flesh in their sight whilst they live, with other cruelties horrible to be related.[8]

Bradford's depiction of Indians as cannibalistic murderers practically denied them any human rights and led to many episodes of Indian dispossession and occasional efforts to exterminate particular tribal communities.

A contemporary example of the negative stereotype, or the "bad Indian," is the attitude of an increasing number of federal policymakers and the American public that Indians, largely because of gaming proceeds, have become extremely wealthy and are taking advantage of federal laws to enrich themselves at the expense of the American taxpayer.

A third conception of Indians also persists: that of the "tragic savage." This arose as the threat of American Indians to whites decreased in the late nineteenth century because of the ravages of diseases, reservation confinement, and warfare's toll. Having been rendered largely impotent in the eyes of whites, Indians appeared to be doomed to cultural and even physical extinction. If they lived, it was thought they would persist as drunken paupers, dependent entirely on federal largesse for their existence.

These images—noble or enlightened savage, bloodthirsty savage, or tragic savage—represent the result of dynamics of cultural encounters and actually "have very little to do with the real life situation of the people that the image is supposed to portray. They reveal more about the culture doing the portraying than the individuals supposedly being portrayed."[9]

A contemporary example of cultural appropriation and Indian stereotyping involves one of the more well-known tribes, the Rosebud Sioux, and one of the greatest

Sioux historical figures, Tasunke Witko, also known as Crazy Horse. He was a beloved leader and one of the most powerful warriors of the Oglala Lakota people, noted for their success in the Battle of the Little Big Horn in 1876, which resulted in the death of General George A. Custer and his soldiers.

Crazy Horse was killed in 1877 at Fort Robinson, Nebraska, by white soldiers. He was estimated to be thirty-six years old at the time of his death. He is remembered as a staunch Sioux nationalist who remained committed to his people throughout his short life. He never signed a treaty with the federal government, and he opposed the use of alcohol by his people.[10] Besides being revered by his own people and many other Indians, Crazy Horse has also inspired a host of developments among non-Indians. For instance, in 1948 a Boston-based sculptor, Korczak Ziolkowski, began carving a mountain in the Black Hills of South Dakota, which will eventually culminate in a mountain-sized statue of Crazy Horse. And in 1982 the U.S. Postal Service issued a stamp in Crazy Horse's honor.

By contrast, in 1992, the Hornell Brewing Company introduced "the Original Crazy Horse Malt Liquor," containing 5.9 percent alcohol. The product's bottle showed an Indian chief wearing a war bonnet, adorned by various "Indian" designs. The malt liquor label contained the following statement:

> The Black Hills of Dakota, steeped in the history of the American West, home of Proud Indian Nations. A land where imagination conjures up images of blue clad Pony Soldiers and magnificent Native American Warriors. A Land still rutted with wagon tracks of intrepid pioneers. A land where wailful winds whisper of Sitting Bull, Crazy Horse and Custer. A land of character, of bravery, of tradition. A land that truly speaks of the spirit that is America.[11]

There were immediate tribal and nationwide protests against the beer. The U.S. Congress in 1992 enacted legislation barring the use of Crazy Horse's name as a brand name for any alcoholic beverage.[12] The malt liquor's manufacturer, however, successfully challenged the federal law as violating the company's First Amendment rights.[13] Seth H. Big Crow Sr., one of Crazy Horse's many descendants, then filed a suit in the Rosebud Sioux Tribal Court, charging that the Hornell Brewing Company had illegally appropriated the commercial publicity value of Crazy Horse's name, had defamed the Crazy Horse estate, and had negligently and intentionally inflicted emotional distress on Crazy Horse's descendants and the Sioux People. The estate requested compensation in the form of tobacco, a horse, and blankets, but also sought monetary damages.

Hornell responded by arguing that they had not operated on the Rosebud Reservation and that, therefore, the tribal court lacked jurisdiction to hear the case. In October 1994, Tribal Judge Stanley E. Whiting upheld Hornell's contention and ruled that the court lacked personal jurisdiction over the breweries and subject-matter jurisdiction over the estate's claim. The Rosebud Sioux Supreme Court reversed the jurisdictional claim, holding that the plaintiffs had, in fact, been harmed on the reservation, thus bringing the matter under the tribe's jurisdiction. The Tribe's Supreme Court then remanded (sent back) the case to the tribal court for a prompt trial.

Hornell Breweries, anticipating a loss in tribal court, then filed suit in U.S. district court against the estate and the Rosebud Tribal Court, asserting that the tribal court lacked jurisdiction. The district court enjoined the tribal court from proceeding on the merits of the case. The tribal court and the Crazy Horse estate appealed this decision to the Eighth Circuit Court of Appeals, which held in 1998 that the tribal court did not have sovereign authority over the breweries, since the company's activities were conducted outside the reservation.

The federal court of appeals emphasized that its decision did not turn upon the merits of the claims made by Crazy Horse's heir. But the fact that a federal court found that the principles of Indian law prevented Crazy Horse's descendants from successfully challenging a brewery from exploiting the name of their ancestor, and one of the Sioux's most important leaders, to market a product known to cause great harm to native peoples had to be a disheartening blow not only to the Sioux but to all Indians.

Along with the persistence of these stereotypes is the equally problematic issue of "timelessness" in defining Indians. As the historian Robert Berkhofer shows, "in spite of centuries of contact [with white Europeans] and the changed conditions of Native American lives, whites still picture the 'real' Indian as the one before contact or during the early period of that contact," as the "aborigine he once was, or as they imagine he once was rather than as he is now."[14]

Indian peoples, in other words, are frequently depicted in the media as largely historical figures, and if they diverge from the way they are historically remembered—even when the historical depictions themselves are in error—they are viewed as less authentic. Thus, when the Makah went whale hunting in 1999 and did not use strictly "traditional" weapons and equipment, they were viewed as not being authentic Makah. Such a sense of abstract timelessness is rarely applied to non-Indian groups or minority communities.

Our focus in this chapter, however, is on the role of the mass media as they impact and are impacted by Native people.[15] The *mass media,* broadly defined, refers to the large-scale means of communicating information from one person or group to another. The mass media are typically divided into two types: print media (newspapers, journals, and magazines, which convey information through written words and pictures) and broadcast media (radio and television, which communicate information electronically through sounds and images). Also, there is an increasing reliance on what are called *group media,* which entail the use of facsimile images (faxes) or computers and their linkages on the Internet.[16]

As we saw briefly in our discussion of the American Indian Movement (AIM), the attitudes of federal policymakers are influenced by the mass media and harbor conflicting images of Indian people. These attitudes and images influence the types of laws, policies, and court decisions that emerge from governmental offices. In the remainder of this chapter, we discuss how non-Indian media portray Indians and how this affects Indian rights; then we address how Indian media portray their nations' issues and the relationship of Indians to the larger society.

Also, we discuss the related issues of freedom of speech and freedom of the press as they are being experienced by Indians. And we assess the way the Indian media operate, or are not allowed to operate, in Indian Country. Censorship by tribal governments remains a problem for Indian writers and correspondents.

Non-Indian Media and Images of Indians

Horace Greeley was editor of the *New York Tribune,* which was founded in 1841, and had long promoted western expansion. In 1859 he headed west to promote the building of the transcontinental railroad. As he traveled, he wrote a series of articles for the

Tribune, which by this time had a readership of nearly forty thousand. Greeley saw and met Indians from many tribes on his travels, including Delaware, Kiowa, Arapaho, Ottawa, Osage, Potawatomie, and Kickapoo. Greeley was a leading reformer and lifelong abolitionist, but his written accounts give a less flattering portrayal of Indians than one might expect.

"I have learned," said Greeley, "to appreciate better than hitherto . . . the dislike, aversion, contempt, wherewith Indians are usually regarded by their white neighbors, and have been since the days of the Puritans."[17] Indian nations, it appeared to Greeley and many other journalists of his time, had missed the march of progress, were essentially barbarians, and stood as obstacles to the "manifest destiny" of non-Indians.

Of course, Greeley's image of Indians as barbaric, savage, and degraded—the ignoble or bloodthirsty savage—contrasts with the earlier image of aboriginal peoples as "noble savages," and with the later image of Indians as the "tragic savage" or the "Vanishing Race." By the early twentieth century, as Indians' reservations were subdivided and of necessity Indians interacted with the whites who moved into the former Indian Country, there was a sense that when Indians lived in close proximity to whites they adopted white vices, like alcohol, but rarely adopted white virtues. The "tragic" Indian of this portrait—impoverished, alcoholic, and weakened—was no longer a threat but an object of pity.[18]

The Pueblos, Collier, and Tribal Regeneration

In the 1920s, the struggle of the Pueblo Indians of New Mexico—tribal nations who never waged war on the United States—helped to reshape the media's image of Indians. The Pueblo struggled to retain their lands in the face of intense pressure from local whites who wanted to gain ownership of Pueblo land through any means available. The Pueblo's land problems received the attention of John Collier, the future commissioner of Indian affairs, and several reform organizations like the American Indian Defense Association, which believed that Indians had been poorly treated and deserved better.

The Pueblo nations were romanticized in the press as "hard-working good Indians. They don't fight and never wanted to. . . . The Pueblos have very beautiful poetic dances. . . . Their children are beautiful. Their women are good mothers. . . . They are very religious, practically all of them good Catholics."[19] Because of the positive press generated during this land struggle, the Pueblo were able to fight off these specific challenges to their territory—although in 1906 they had lost ownership of Blue Lake and forty-eight thousand acres of surrounding land. This experience helped catapult John Collier into the commissionership in 1933, from which he was able to advocate for the return of a measure of tribal self-rule, which Congress eventually adopted in the 1934 passage of the Indian Reorganization Act.

Fighting Back: Indians and World War II

The end of World War II heralded a radical shift in federal Indian policy from cultural and political regeneration to federal cost-cutting measures and renewed attempts at assimilation. The goal of assimilation was thought to be warranted because an estimated twenty-five thousand Indian men served in World War II and several hundred Indian women worked as nurses or served in the Women's Auxiliary Service. The national media exploited the stereotype of Indians as superpatriots and especially skilled in the art of war. Secretary of the Interior Harold Ickes, in an article he wrote for *Colliers,* contended that Indians had particularly suitable attributes for fighting:

> Endurance, rhythm, a feeling for timing, co-ordination, sense perception, an uncanny ability to get over any sort of terrain at night, and better than all else, an enthusiasm for fighting. He [the Indian soldier] takes a rough job and makes a game of it.[20]

The image of Indians as the ideal and stoical warriors, patriotic and loyal to the American cause, prompted federal lawmakers after the war to assert that Indians desired to be freed from federal wardship and were fully prepared and anxious to be assimilated into postwar American society. The end result of the movement to "emancipate" the Indians was the radical termination and relocation policies of the 1950s, in which the United States unilaterally withdrew its support for a number of Indian nations. The twin policies of termination and relocation had dramatic and largely detrimental consequences for those terminated.[21]

For example, the Menominee, the first and largest tribe terminated, were alleged to be prosperous and already well along the path to being assimilated. A 1953 *Chicago Tribune* story proclaimed of the Menominee: "In wealth, they are second only to the Oklahoma oil-rich Indians. . . . The Menominee are industrious and thrifty, generally educated in the lower schools, quite a few in high school, and some in college. . . . About 95 percent of the Menominee are Catholic."[22] While the Menominee, because of their vast timber resources, were somewhat more prosperous than other tribes, they were ill-prepared for the radical termination of their sovereign political status and unconvinced it would be in their best interest. Nevertheless, their legal termination began in 1954, and within a short time the tribe's members were impoverished, were forced to sell tribal lands, and faced enormous political and cultural problems.[23] A massive lobbying campaign by the Menominee and other terminated tribes and their many supporters forced the government to restore the Menominee to recognized status in 1973.

Indigenous Activism and the Media: 1960s–1970s

The 1960s and 1970s represent a crucial period in not only American Indian policy history, but American society at large. The Vietnam War, the civil rights movement, the rise of environmental politics, and a concern for cultural diversity were issues animating this period. The media, of course, had become even more prominent in shaping the public's views of all these events, from the televised presidential debates between John Kennedy and Richard Nixon to the coverage of the Vietnam War and the protests at home against it. As John W. Sayer noted in his study on the Wounded Knee trials of AIM leaders Dennis Banks and Russell Means, "the American people were becoming dependent on media images to shape their attitudes and assumptions about the political and cultural changes taking place around them."[24]

From this maelstrom of change arose native activists intent on regaining long-denied rights to hunt and fish, reclaiming lost lands, and gaining status as "recognized" tribes. Even as the federal government attempted to use the media to further its agenda, so those groups and local movements clamoring for political and economic power attempted to exploit the media as well. The leaders of AIM, especially Russell Means, seemed particularly skilled at exploiting the media to gain political support, but also financial aid from volunteers and churches. But as effective as Indians were at using the media, they did this by acting in a way that sometimes reinforced the American public's fascination with the images of Indians, especially of Indian males as either "noble" or "ignoble" warriors. In the St. Paul–Minneapolis area, where much of this activism began and played out,

> the media portraits of the well-known male defendants [Banks and Means] and their equally famous male attorneys, William Kunstler and Mark Lane, drew on already fixed images of the white male militants of the sixties and the stereotypical Indian warrior of Hollywood films. These same images of masculinity were cultivated by the participants themselves and then accentuated in the media, reinforcing old stereotypes and at times overshadowing more important issues.[25]

As Sayer's account shows, AIM's leaders were regularly referred to in the media as "militants," "insurgents," "tall, graceful, bronzed," and "modern day Sitting Bulls." The media's characterization of Indian activists and Indian militancy in general appears to have had some effect on the Supreme Court's narrow construal of the tribal sovereignty doctrine in a major case in 1973, *McClanahan v. Arizona State Tax Commission*.[26] In this case the Court said that tribal sovereignty was to be understood merely as a "backdrop," not the defining principle, against which to read applicable treaties, statutes, and policies.

The 1980s–2000s

In basic respects, Indian nations emerged out of the 1970s with a renewed sense of the importance of their sovereignty. The U.S. government was generally supportive of tribal efforts to exercise a measure of political and economic self-determination, as evidenced by laws like the Indian Self-Determination and Education Assistance Act (1975) and the Indian Child Welfare Act (1978). But these and other legislative and judicial victories prompted a surge of anti-Indian sentiment that manifested itself in a number of bills designed to abrogate Indian rights and treaties. The media, of course, contributed discourse that fueled both positive and negative perceptions of Indian peoples.

The perpetuation of conflicting images continued unabated in the 1980s and 1990s, although the negative accounts still outweighed the positive depictions. Robert H. White, writing in the *New York Times* in 1990, said,

> [T]he only news to travel from Indian Country to the major media in 1990 has been news of disaster: a violent standoff between Mohawks and government officials in Quebec; fatal gun battles over casino gambling at the St. Regis reservation in New York State; the ignoble fall of Peter MacDonald from the helm of the Navajo Nation. America has been saturated with images of incompetent leadership and hare-brained business schemes.[27]

As Tim Johnson, executive editor of *Indian Country Today*, observed in 2005, "Indians have gone from the stereotypical impoverished noble savage to the stereotypical Mr. Money Bags. It's amazing how quickly we've been universally branded."[28]

Moreover, the dramatic increase in the number of gaming tribes contributed to a growing sense that virtually all Indians were reaping significant financial benefits, which prompted a new surge of federal anti-Indian legislation aimed at restricting the scope of Indian gaming and bills that would terminate or reduce federal entitlements to tribal governments.

A significant difference, however, was that an increasing number of Indian voices were being heard in both mainstream and Indian publications, and Indian journalists in particular were challenging the media when they thought the media's stories were inaccurate.[29] Indigenous peoples have also been proactive in shaping positive representations of themselves in non-Indian media. For example, First Nations, Inuit, and Metis garnered global attention when they came together to welcome visitors to the 2010 Olympic games in Vancouver, British Columbia. This was the first time that indigenous peoples were recognized by the International Olympic Committee as official host partners. First Nations also shaped the official logo and the game's three official mascots— Miga, Quatchi, and Sumi—each based in indigenous traditions.

Indigenous Media: Images of Themselves

Throughout history, indigenous peoples' primary means of communication has been oral transmission. And while the oral tradition remains present in tribal societies, Indian peoples since as early as the 1820s, but particularly since the 1970s, have been actively developing other media. Indians have formed their own professional association for journalists, established independent newspapers, and become active in filmmaking, and a number of tribal governments have established their own radio and television stations and become much more involved in telecommunications technology. Tribal governments and individual Indians have incorporated these and other modes of communication to advance the needs of their communities and to educate and enlighten their non-Indian neighbors.

Print Media

The earliest Indian-owned newspaper was the *Cherokee Phoenix,* begun in 1827 at New Echota, in the heart of the Cherokee Nation. As the first editor, Elias Boudinot, stated, "to attain a correct and complete knowledge of these people, there must be a vehicle of Indian intelligence. . . . [T]he columns of the Cherokee Phoenix will be filled, partly with English, and partly with Cherokee print; and all matter which is of common interest will be given in both languages in parallel columns."[30] The newspaper, however, was destroyed by white Georgians as the state, with federal support, forcibly evicted the majority of the Cherokee from their original homelands to the West as part of the Indian removal campaign.

Although Cherokees John Rollin Ridge, Charles Watie, and Colonel Elias Cornelius Boudinot (the son of Elias Boudinot) were active writers for various newspapers in the 1840s and 1850s, publishing by tribes and individual Indians was rare until nearly the end of the nineteenth century. Then came another push of native journalism, occurring mostly in Indian Territory (present-day Oklahoma), where the Cherokee, Choctaw, Creek, and Osage established newspapers. But the federal government's coercive assimilation plan, focused on the allotment and Christianization of Indians, weakened these efforts and Indian publishing went into a period of decline. Native journalism would not begin to recover until the conclusion of World War II.[31]

Nevertheless, a number of non-Indian newspapers, journals, and magazines, most of them controlled by publishers and editors who supported Indian assimilation, continued to operate in Indian Country between 1900 and World War II:

Adair Weekly Ledger (founded 1904), Oklahoma
Claremore State Herald (1905), Oklahoma
Winnebago Chieftain (1905), Nebraska
Quilete Independent (1908), Washington
Quilete Chieftain (1910), Washington
Odanah Star (1912), Wisconsin
Rossville Reporter (1913), Kansas
Martin Messenger (1914), South Dakota
Wassaja (1916), California
Alaska Fisherman (1923), Alaska
California Indian News (1935), California

World War II and the ensuing federal policies of Indian termination and relocation led to a new surge of periodical activity, fueled in part by the urbanization and pan-Indianism that emerged as a result of these policies. In 1947, the NCAI began publishing the *Bulletin* and urban Indians in Chicago and Seattle later began publishing newsletters: the *Chicago Warrior* in 1955 and the *Indian Center News* in 1960, respectively. More importantly from a sovereignty perspective, tribes began publishing newspapers: the *Ute Bulletin* (1950), the *Char-Kooska News* (1956), and the *Navajo Times* (1959).[32]

The greatest proliferation of Indian news media began in the halcyon days of Lyndon Johnson's Great Society and War on Poverty because of the availability of federal funds, which Indians used to initiate newspapers and newsletters. The continuing urbanization of Indians, the increasing number of Indian college graduates securing journalism degrees, and the strengthening of tribal self-determination aided this increase in publications. *Akwesasne Notes*, for example, was established in 1969 on the Mohawk Reservation and quickly gained both a national and a hemispheric reputation as an activist paper that supported the efforts of native peoples to regain their sovereignty, cultural identity, and enforcement of treaty rights. *Wassaja*, published by the American Indian Historical Society beginning in 1972, also had a national focus. The *Lakota Times* (1981), a weekly national Indian newspaper renamed *Indian Country Today* in 1992, and *News from Indian Country*, which was established in 1987 and is published twice a month, are the two largest Indian-owned newspapers.[33]

In 1971 a group of American Indian journalists meeting in Washington, D.C., established the American Indian Press Association. This organization sought to create an intertribal news bureau to gather and disseminate political, cultural, and economic information to reservation- and urban-based newspapers and publications throughout Indian Country.[34] The organization, which changed its name to the Native American Journalists Association (NAJA) in 1984, advocates freedom of information but has been firmly committed to preserving Indian culture and traditions and correcting the historical record about native peoples.

NAJA, which has its home office in Minneapolis, has open membership: individuals of all races may join. The organization also provides internships for Indian students who are interested in journalism as a career. Between 1995 and 1996 NAJA awarded thirty-one scholarships to Indian students. NAJA has always emphasized doing journalism with an indigenous perspective. That is, the members stress oral tradition, interviews, and literary material.[35]

Radio and Television

Radio and, to a lesser extent, television appear to be natural media for indigenous peoples, since they involve the oral and visual transmission of knowledge, and since tribal peoples rely on storytelling to carry on tradition, to educate, and to entertain. In fact, John Collier, the commissioner of Indian affairs in the 1930s and 1940s, was well aware of the Indians' oral traditions and he had funds set aside for radio broadcasts in Alaska villages and supported a national program designed to enlighten and inform Americans about Indian peoples, their unique history, and current Indian affairs.[36]

Native nations, however, did not become involved in the use or ownership of radio or television until the 1970s. The first radio stations began in Alaska in the wake of the Alaska Native Claims Settlement Act (ANCSA) of 1971. One of the major developments under ANCSA involved the creation of thirteen regional Native corporations to manage the cash and lands conveyed under the act. Three public radio stations, two Native and one non-Native, were started to keep Alaska's Natives informed about the political, legal, economic, and cultural issues affecting their lands and rights. The stations also employed a reporter to keep track of the state legislature's activities.

Other native nations followed suit and by the mid-1990s twenty-six tribal public radio stations (e.g., KNNB, White Mountain Apache; WYDH, Poarch Band Creek; KSUT, Southern Ute; and KCIE, Jicarilla Apache) and one tribally controlled commercial radio station were serving tribal peoples across the United States and Canada.[37]

The Navajo Nation owns the lone commercial station, KTNN (AM radio), a fifty-thousand-watt station operating in Window Rock, Arizona. KTNN's first broadcast was on September 3, 1985. The station is designed to entertain, inform, and educate the Navajo people and their many visitors. KTNN broadcasts in both the Navajo and English languages and reaches a wide Southwestern audience. Televisions are still relatively uncommon on the reservation and the tribal newspaper is read by less than one tenth of the 172,000-member nation. Many Navajo, however, own radios at home and listen in their vehicles. As Tom James, a Navajo speaker, said, "I like KTNN because most of the time it is in our language, and the announcers tell us what is going on. . . . I always make sure there is a radio beside me. It's my only source of news information."[38] Navajo candidates for tribal office, and local, state, and national office seekers, also take advantage of the relatively low cost of radio advertising and the wide audience KTNN reaches.

There is only one tribally controlled television station in the United States: the Navajo Nation's NNTV-5, airing out of Window Rock. In addition, an educational licensed station, KRSC TV-35, operates at Rogers State College in Claremore, Oklahoma. This is a partnership enterprise of six tribes in northeastern Oklahoma.

As a result of a $6 million donation by the San Manuel Band of Serrano Mission Indians, KVCR Television will launch the nations' first twenty-four hour Native television channel, planned to reach airwave in the spring of 2011.[39]

A few native nations, with a sense for the important role that Hollywood plays on the public's knowledge of Indians, are gingerly stepping forward and are forging alliances with some well-known actors or are partnering on other projects. For example, in 2003, the Oneida Indian Nation of New York State; Sonny Skyhawk, an Indian producer in Los Angeles; and NBC Sports joined hands and developed "The World of American Dance," the first Indian-financed documentary to be aired nationally. And in 2005, Rick Schroder, who most recently appeared on the television drama *NYPD Blue,* convinced twelve tribes to donate about $1 million for a film that he directed, *Black Cloud,* about a Diné boxer who earns a spot on the U.S. Olympic team.[40]

A very important organization, Native American Public Telecommunications (NAPT)—formerly the Native American Public Broadcasting Consortium—was founded in 1978. This organization seeks to "inform, educate and encourage the awareness of tribal histories, cultures, languages, opportunities and aspirations through the fullest participation of American Indians and Alaska Natives in creating and employing all forms of educational and public telecommunications programs and services, thereby supporting tribal sovereignty."[41]

NAPT has cataloged over 250 entries and original works—books, videos, films, and so on—by its contributors and members for tribal educational, cultural, and arts development programs. The organization's multiple missions include producing telecommunication programs for all media, including television and radio; providing training opportunities for American Indians and Alaska Natives; promoting the increase and control of information technologies; and building partnerships with tribal governments and Indian organizations.

New Media (Cable TV, Fax, E-mail, and Internet)

As the information age envelops all in its path, indigenous peoples find that they, too, are becoming involved, by choice and by necessity. Indian casinos are marketing some of their services online, and many tribal governments have become dependent on fax machines, cellular phones, and e-mail transmissions, and have established their own websites. But native peoples still lag behind other Americans in their use of technology.

While 94 percent of American homes—both urban and rural—have telephones, only about 56 percent of Indian families living in rural areas or on reservations have phones.[42] A major reason for the lack of phones is the high cost to establish phone service, which can range from $200 to more than $3000. In reaction to this, President Clinton announced on April 16, 2000, that he and William E. Kennard, chairman of the Federal Communications Commission, had developed a plan to provide basic telephone service to some three hundred thousand Indian households, each for $1 a month.[43]

Some tribes have formed their own communications companies to improve service to their constituencies, including the Cheyenne River Sioux (Telephone Authority), Ft. Mohave (Ft. Mohave Telecommunications, Inc.), Gila River (Gila River Telecommunications, Inc.), and Tohono O'odham (Tohono O'odham Utility Authority).

In 1997, a group of tribally owned telecommunications companies formed the National Tribal Telecommunication Alliance, a consortium that seeks to improve communications capabilities within their communities. In November 2009 the

Native Public Media (NPM) gathered data on technology use access and adoption in Indian Country. NPM, whose mission is "to promote healthy, engaged, independent Native communities by strengthening and expanding Native American media capacity and by empowering a strong, proud Native American voice," found that native peoples are increasingly utilizing technology to interact, communicate, and gain knowledge and skills. They concluded that "[d]espite a lack of access, higher prices for broadband and often non-existent infrastructure, leaders in these communities have developed a vision and built self-sufficient networks and community technology centers to connect and strengthen their Native communities."[44] The NPM report states that the success of tribal projects focused on technology require strong leadership, planning commitment from tribal leaders, and community participation.

Noting the barriers native nations face in accessing technology, the NPM report makes eight policy recommendations: (1) implement strategic initiative targeting tribal communications development, (2) create a tribal broadband plan, (3) create effectual consultation and coordination with tribal governments, (4) reform the Universal Service Fund and their delivery of broadband support, (5) increase Internet access in Indian country, (6) remove funding barriers facing tribal applications for technology support available through the American Reinvestment and Recovery Act, (7) increase federal funding and education, and (8) increase research and analysis of American Indian access to and use of technology.[45]

Of course, Indian and non-Indian individuals, organizations, and tribal governments have established many websites that seek to address the informational needs of Indians and the public, but technology issues are still largely unexplored in Indian Country. See appendix H for a list of sites one may consult to gain insights into the political, legal, cultural, and economic issues confronting Indian people.

Indians in Non-Indian Media

Although there has historically been significant tension between the Indian media and the non-Indian media, the most recent generation has witnessed some real improvements in this relationship. One of the positive outgrowths of the civil rights era of the 1960s was that newspapers and television stations were pressed to hire more minority writers and correspondents. Tanna Beebe, a member of the Cowlitz and Quinault Tribe of Washington State, was one of the first Indians hired by a non-Indian–owned television station, KIRO-TV in Seattle, in the early 1970s.

However, for Beebe it was not a smooth transition from her prior position as communications coordinator for a California Indian organization to working in a large urban newsroom. Beebe said, "It was different. Big-time different. I was raised by my grandmother, and I was taught that asking questions was rude. It was a sign of bad breeding. I wanted to write, but asking questions was distasteful."[46] Beebe was a role model for Hattie Kauffman, a Nez Percé who in 1987 became the first American Indian hired by a national network when she went to work for ABC's *Good Morning America*. In 1990, Kauffman joined CBS's *This Morning* (now *The Early Show*), where she is a national correspondent. Kauffman is a four-time Emmy winner.[47]

The deadly hantavirus epidemic that struck in New Mexico in 1993, initially claiming the lives of several Navajo, attracted the attention of the public and particularly of Indian journalists and reporters. According to Mark Trahant, over a dozen Indian reporters from tribal, state, and national media descended on the area to cover this deadly outbreak.[48]

While the number of American Indian journalists has improved in the 2000s, comparatively there are still far too few in America's newsrooms. In 2005 there were some 54,100 professional journalists. But according to the American Society of Newspaper Editors, only 295 were American Indian.[49]

Native Nations and Freedom of Speech

The media clearly play an important and varied role in articulating the needs and issues confronting Indian peoples, while also acting to perpetuate stereotypical and demeaning images of Indians. This last section focuses on the manner in which the native media operate, or are not allowed to operate, in Indian Country.

Native journalists and broadcasters are confronted by a very different political and legal climate than are non-Indian reporters operating outside Indian Country. The fundamental difference is that while most of the mass media in the United States are privately owned (although they must cope with some government regulation), most of the mass media in Indian Country are owned and rigorously controlled by the tribal governing bodies. This means that while the First Amendment prohibits Congress from abridging the freedom of the press, Indian journalists working for tribally owned newspapers are sometimes denied fundamental First Amendment protection.[50]

The First Amendment is unavailable to tribal journalists because Indians stand in an entirely different constitutional position with regard to their tribal government than they do with regard to the federal or state governments. The differences arise because of the existence and meaning of tribal sovereignty. As a result, it is unclear whether censorship of Indian media by tribal politicians, who are in a sense the publishers, violates federal or tribal law.

However, tribal governments are exempt from having to comply with such laws as the Freedom of Information Act of 1967, which gives citizens the right to inspect unprotected government documents. One act that appears to extend a measure of freedom to tribal journalists is the 1968 Indian Civil Rights Act. That act imposed on tribal governments certain modified versions of most of the U.S. Bill of Rights. The pertinent section for this discussion is the following:

> No Indian tribe in exercising powers of self-government shall (1) make or enforce any law prohibiting the free exercise of religion, or abridging the freedom of speech, *or of the press*, or the right of the people peaceably to assemble and to petition for a redress of grievances" (emphasis added).[51]

Moreover, between 1852 and 1980 sixty-four tribes adopted written constitutions that contain explicit provisions recognizing freedom of the press.[52] Today that number has increased, but a number of indigenous groups still lack organic laws containing free speech language.[53]

Despite the clarity of these provisions, the experience of many journalists working for tribally owned media is that "free-press guarantees provide little or no protection because tribal governments view their newspaper staffs as employees wholly answerable to tribal governments."[54] The many free press problems encountered by tribal newspapers include politically motivated firings before or shortly after tribal elections, cutting off or selective reduction of publication funds, being forced to hire unqualified editors or reporters who are political supporters of tribal government officials, firings as a result of the publication of unflattering news stories or editorials, the banning of journalists from tribal government meetings, restriction of press access to particular tribal government documents, and occasional death threats over published stories.[55] Some examples follow.

Example 1: In October 2003, Lori Edmo-Suppah, an award-winning native journalist and the managing editor of the *Sho-Ban News,* the weekly tribal newspaper of the Shoshone-Bannock people, was fired for "gross insubordination" for allowing details of a tribal council meeting proceeding to be reported. The paper was also temporarily shut down.

Example 2: In August 2004, Tex Hall, the tribal chairman of the Three Affiliated Tribes (Mandan, Hidatsa, and Arikara), issued a memorandum threatening to fire any tribal employee who disclosed any tribal affairs to the press unless the information was first approved through his public relations office.[56]

Example 3: In March 2005, in the wake of the mass killing on the Red Lake Reservation in Minnesota, a number of journalists from around the nation and the world were frequently denied opportunities to interview tribal employees or tribal members about the killings. Some family members of the shooting victims were critical of these restrictions.[57]

Example 4: In June 1998, Fredrick Lane, the editor of the Lummi Nation's tribal newspaper, *Squol Quol,* was fired by the Tribal Business Committee for printing a letter by a county councilwoman, Marlene Dawson, to U.S. Senator Slade Gorton in which she said that federally financed Lummi schools were "incubators of racism."[58] Lane had been told not to run the letter because, according to the tribal chairman, the council was trying to improve its relationship with the county and federal governments.

Example 5: In July 1997, the entire staff of the Cherokee Nation government's bimonthly newspaper, the *Cherokee Nation,* was laid off after the newspaper ran stories covering allegations of wrongdoing by the nation's chief, Joe Byrd.

Example 6: In October 1997, a journalist for the weekly Minnesota-based *Native American Press/Ojibwe News* was arrested on trespassing charges by tribal law enforcement officers while attending a meeting regarding a controversial land sale among Minnesota Chippewa Tribes.

Example 7: In February 1998, Tom Arviso, editor of the *Navajo Times* in Window Rock, Arizona, endured two attempts by President Albert Hale's administration to have him removed because of the paper's investigation of alleged financial mismanagement by Hale. Mark Trahant, editor of the paper in the 1980s, had not been as lucky; he and his staff were summarily fired by the Navajo chairman, Peter MacDonald, after MacDonald's reelection in the fall of 1987.

Because of the tribal governments' increasing abuses of free speech, NAJA declared 1998 "The Year of Promoting Free Expression in Native America." NAJA's goal for the year was to educate tribal members and mainstream Americans about the difficult job faced by tribal journalists. As Paul DeMain, NAJA past president and editor and co-owner of *News from Indian Country,* one of the few independent Indian papers, put it, "It's very traumatic because people tend to lose their jobs for reporting things that tribal leaders would rather not see in print."[59]

There is no easy solution to this situation. Tribal governments will no doubt continue to insist that as owners they have a fundamental right to decide what will be printed or broadcast. As one tribal chairwoman said, "We believe, of course, in freedom of the press, but I have stated publicly that we have to have this censorship . . . in certain stories that involve confidentiality."[60] In this case, "confidentiality" could mean sensitive contractual negotiations between the tribal government and, say, a state over how gaming proceeds would be divided; or it could mean hiring decisions of key personnel.

Tribal journalists, however, are in the business of reporting the newsworthy developments within their geographical sphere, even those developments that portray the tribal government—their owner—in an unfavorable light. As DeMain stated, "What [tribal council members] don't realize is that the press exists to serve the people, not to simply serve the tribal chairman. It's the responsibility of the press to report on actions good and bad."[61]

NAJA, in an effort to bridge this wide gulf, has proposed a "free-press plan" that includes engaging tribal government leaders in dialogue with tribal media in an effort to find common ground. It is far too early to predict how this process will unfold, but as tribal governments continue to mature, freedom of speech and press must be at the forefront of this maturation. But since kinship, blood, and clan affiliations still suffuse many reservations' politics, such freedoms will not be easily achieved or sustained. As one commentator noted: "Reservations are basically one big family. These jobs [media] are handed out by relatives with the promise of publishing within certain parameters: not to publish negative things about the tribe."[62]

Still, some tribes have recognized the importance of a free press. For example, in 2003, the Navajo Nation's Economic Development Committee enacted a resolution that supported the request by the tribe's weekly paper, *The Navajo Times,* to become a private enterprise.[63]

Conclusion

The mass media occupy a crucial role in any democracy, including tribal democracies, and have important effects on public opinion. In the case of Indian nations, the media are viewed with deep suspicion because of their past and present role in perpetuating Indian stereotypes; yet there is a realization that the media—both tribally owned and non-Indian owned—are essential to breaking down those same stereotypes and contributing to the broader education of the masses.

The media promise to remain in a position of significant influence regarding how Americans perceive Indian people nationally and how tribes perceive themselves vis-à-vis their own issues locally. While gaming tribes have become increasingly adept at using their resources to influence the public and policymakers at all levels of government, especially on issues that might directly impinge on gaming revenues, they are also channeling some of their moneys toward the purchase, production, and control of various forms of mass media and the new media. There is ongoing tension, however, between tribal ownership of media and the freedom of Indian and non-Indian media to report on tribal politics.

CHAPTER 10

Indigenous Nations and the American Political System

To Navajos, the concept of sovereignty is simple. It means being independent and standing on one's own feet. Whether an individual, a family, a community, or a nation, one wants to stand on one's own. To build an independent nation, its individual members need to stand on their own feet, dependent on no one to survive or thrive.

—President Joe Shirley Jr., Navajo Nation, 2010[1]

IN THE PREVIOUS nine chapters we have sought to present a comprehensive and structural analysis of how indigenous peoples, as nations and as individuals, politically operate within the borders of Indian Country and in the context of state and federal politics. Our analysis covered a number of interrelated topics. First, we identified the nature and powers of tribal nations. Second, we assessed the structural and perceptual ambivalence tribes face when confronted by non-Indian legal and political institutions. Third, we described the history, organization, and evolution of native governing institutions and identified and addressed the plethora of issues they face—both internally and externally—in their daily operations. We then examined the major players who animate native and intergovernmental politics, and we also provided an analysis of federal Indian political history.

Next, we provided commentary on the serious socioeconomic issues indigenous peoples face, with special emphasis on the new directions Indian gaming revenues are allowing tribes to take. We then analyzed the ways indigenous peoples participate or choose not to participate in both indigenous and nonindigenous politics. In that same chapter, we also examined the particular strategies Indians have employed to guarantee their right to participate in American politics and discussed Indians' efforts at the same time to support their extraconstitutional status by exercising their sovereign decision not to participate. In the last two chapters, we addressed indigenous activism and interest group activity and analyzed and described the critical role that imagery and the media play in both elevating the rights of Indians and perpetuating stereotypical characterizations of native people.

One of the key findings of this study, although certainly not an original discovery, is that while American Indian peoples were at one time fully independent polities and exercised unbridled self-determination in all spheres—economic, cultural, and political—the arrival of European nations and the subsequent birth and expansion of the United States brought catastrophic changes to aboriginal peoples in every sphere. Tribal nations have been in a state of recovery since the precolonial era and struggle mightily with their status as the original sovereigns whose power, lands, and resources have faced nearly constant exploitation and constraints not imposed on any other polity in the United States.

Hence, while the major goal of this book is to describe and explain indigenous government and politics, of necessity it has also described and explained other relationships as well. Thus, it discussed intragroup dynamics, intertribal relations, tribal-state affairs, and, of course, tribal-federal politics.

Public policy may be defined as what governments do or do not do, why they do it, and what difference government's actions make, or more broadly, as a general plan of action adopted by a government to solve a problem, counter a threat, or pursue an objective. Under this definition, policies emanating from the federal government that involve Indian people, federal Indian policy, may be defined as a course of action or inaction pursued by the U.S. government and adopted as expedient in its relations with the indigenous peoples of North America. By *expedient,* we mean policy that is considered by government to be advantageous or advisable under the particular circumstances or during a specific time span.

It is most assuredly federal Indian policy and not simply Indian policy, because by and large natives have not set the policy. They have usually reacted to or had to endure given policies (removal, reservations, allotments, termination), although indigenous peoples were seldom the passive recipients of federal mandates that have sometimes been depicted. One can argue with a measure of veracity that the 1988 Tribal Self-Governance Act, as policy, was at least inspired by, if not established by, native nations. But native self-governance is only one of a group of policy issues that affect and are affected by tribes and Indians in the areas of politics, law, cultural rights, property and natural resources, and intergovernmental relations, among others.

Moreover, as described in chapter 2, indigenous peoples' lives and resources are frequently governed not only by political and economic expediency, but also by fundamental ambivalence. It is an ambivalence exacerbated by the complex interrelationship of federal and state governments; the Bureau of Indian Affairs (BIA) and other agencies; corporate America; interest groups; the media; tribal, local, national, and occasionally international crises; political parties; and the amorphous entity known simply as *the public.* The inherent diversity of 565 indigenous entities does not, of course, bring clarity to the situation, and the fact that a majority of native individuals now live off-reservation further complicates matters, because the BIA has never clearly asserted whether the government's trust responsibility extends to nonreservation Indians.

All of these factors are muddied even more by the fact that Indian treaties and the trust relationship have moral and ethical dimensions because in an obvious sense they entail a pledge of U.S. national honor. The combination of these distinct yet related rights and responsibilities leads to, on one hand, acceptance of the legal and moral claim by Indians against the federal government and, on the other hand, the reality that Indian tribes remain semi-independent political entities with the right to exercise inherent sovereign powers in the areas of commerce, property use, and governing authority.[2]

Factor in the treble citizenship aspect and the situation is even less clear. In addition to these convoluted realities, the application of federal Indian policy and law oftentimes depends on the images and perceptions of Indians that the public, presidential administration, Congress, and Supreme Court maintain. Indians are therefore,

> wholly at the mercy of forces and personalities beyond their control, and this fact alone distinguishes them from all other American minority groups. No constitutional protections exist for American Indians insofar as they wish to emphasize their ethnic identity. By the same token, federal law recognizes in American Indians certain rights and privileges that it cannot recognize in other minority groups.[3]

Other minority groups also struggle to gain and, increasingly (e.g., with affirmative action) must fight to retain hard-fought civil, political, and economic rights. American Indians, because of their preexisting sovereign status, have faced the additional difficulty of a federal government that, beginning in the 1880s, asserted that it had plenary (read *absolute*) authority over Indian governments, resources, and rights. Thus, federally recognized tribes are far more vulnerable than any other group in the United States because of the virtually absolute federal power that may be exercised at any time.

Even Indians in their individual capacity as American citizens are still not entitled to the full protection by the U.S. Constitution of their tribally based rights, since that document and its amendments still do not apply to tribes. The leading Supreme Court case on this crucial point is *Talton v. Mayes* (1896; printed in full in appendix B). In this decision, the Court was asked to rule on an appeal by a Cherokee citizen who claimed rights under the Constitution's Fifth Amendment in seeking to overturn a murder conviction by the Cherokee Supreme Court. While acknowledging that Congress had the right to determine how the Cherokee Nation exercised its rights, the Court ruled that this did not mean that Cherokee powers arose from or were limited by the U.S. Constitution.

As Justice White said, "It follows that as the powers of local self government enjoyed by the Cherokee Nation existed prior to the Constitution, they are not operated upon by the Fifth Amendment, which, as we have said, had for its sole object to control the powers conferred by the Constitution on the National Government."[4] Ironically, Talton was handed down the same day as *Plessy v. Ferguson,* which established the infamous "separate but equal" doctrine and sanctioned state "Jim Crow" laws for African Americans. *Plessy,* of course, was overturned in 1954 by *Brown v. Board of Education.* Since then the members of other racial and ethnic minorities have also slowly been brought under the U.S. Constitution and afforded its general protections from discrimination and unequal treatment.

However, the *Talton* precedent, recognizing the extraconstitutional status of American Indian tribes, remains the law. The 1968 Indian Civil Rights Act did impose key portions of the Bill of Rights, in statutory form, on tribal governments in their relations with reservation residents, but tribes are still immune from the reach of the federal Constitution. Important in this light is the fact that there is still no limitation on the power of Congress to enact legislation regarding tribal nations. Indigenous nations may, for example, be legally terminated, as a number were in the 1950s and 1960s. Other racial, ethnic, or gender groups need not fear such "termination," and states certainly could not be legally quashed by the federal government.

In this sense, the historical nature of distinctive aboriginal rights works to both advantage and disadvantage native nations. They may be advantaged in the sense that their existence in the Americas before European arrival and their treaty and trust relationships with Europeans and the United States accord them a sovereign status and specific legal, political, and property rights that other racial and ethnic groups do not enjoy. But tribes are disadvantaged because other less positive laws, doctrines, and policies also emerged during the historical era when foreigners—including the United States—presumed that they were superior peoples with the inherent right to disenfranchise, disempower, and dispossess indigenous peoples.

Such an attitude of superiority ushered in the perspectives that the federal government had plenary power over Indians, that native peoples were and remain wards of the government, and others. The question then becomes why the federal government and American society has not been willing to jettison those doctrines, values, and laws that are obviously rooted in prejudicial and racist discourse toward Indians, when much progress has been made in expunging similar discourse regarding African Americans, Asian Americans, women, and other groups.[5]

With this in mind it should be obvious why consistency, much less clarity, is difficult to achieve for indigenous peoples in politics, law, and policy. First, the political issues and barriers confronting urban Indians are significantly different from those confronting reservation-based Indians, who face issues different from those faced by Alaska Natives and Native Hawaiians, who face issues different from those faced by state-recognized tribal members. And when we factor in a need to clarify the meaning and scope of tribal sovereignty and tribal government's power in relation to non-Indians within their borders, understand the important status of Indian treaty rights, arrive at a workable definition of the trust relationship, or make an effort to articulate what federalism literally looks like with native nations included as legitimate political participants, we see that there are no easy answers, and that these topics beg for focused attention by the citizens and leaders of each of the three sovereigns.

As native nations and federal and state governments move ahead in the new millennium, the three parties and their interconnected constituencies must find a way to arrive at a set of definitions of fundamental doctrines of law and policy and develop flexible political and economic arrangements that will enable the leaders of tribes and the federal government to display genuine respect for the legal and moral pledges each sovereign has made to the other. For the U.S. and state governments, this means arriving at a clear understanding of the treaty and trust relationship with tribes that is an accurate reflection of the historical events, including the diplomatic record evidenced by the multitude of treaties and agreements negotiated between the parties, and each party agreeing to cede certain powers or resources while also pledging to respect the remaining rights and resources of their treaty partners.

In the Kansas Indians case (1866), in which the state of Kansas sought to tax individually allotted Indian lands in violation of a treaty, the Supreme Court reminded the state that the federal government was in charge of U.S. policy toward tribes. The Court reaffirmed the nation-to-nation relationship and outlined the legitimate conditions under which changes to treaties might take place:

> While the general government has a superintendency care over their [the Shawnee Tribe's] interests, and continues to treat with them as a nation, the State of Kansas is estopped from denying their title to it. She [Kansas] accepted this status when she accepted the act admitting her into the Union. Conferring rights and privileges on these Indians cannot affect their situation, which can only be changed by treaty stipulation, or a voluntary abandonment of their tribal organization. As long as the United States recognizes their national character they are under the protection of treaties and the laws of Congress, and their property is withdrawn from the operation of State laws. [6]

As is evident in this passage, the United States, as one of its treaty stipulations, often agreed to act as the tribes' protector from all enemies, foreign and domestic. The federal government should therefore be willing to adjust its domestic law, and require of the states and inspire in its non-Indian citizens public policies and political behavior that will ensure that the political, economic, and cultural rights of Indian nations as extraconstitutional yet treaty- and trust-connected sovereigns be respected. The fact that American Indians are also now American citizens should only serve to amplify the recognition that their rights, both as Americans and as members of distinctive tribal nations, should be duly protected.

Vine Deloria Jr., one of the most important chroniclers of indigenous political, legal, and religious experience, noted that Indian life, particularly the experience of reservation-based tribal peoples, "has only the slightest resemblance to the conditions of three decades ago, and the current situation has elements of hope and portents of disaster."[7] Native peoples are, on one hand, entering their most dynamic political, social, and economic period in over half a century because of positive changes in federal Indian policy (e.g., self-determination and self-governance policies); the revival or modification of tribal traditions, customs, and languages; and the lucrative gaming operations which are providing some tribes with previously unimagined wealth and a measure of political clout.

Yet paradoxically, indigenous groups are simultaneously facing a multipronged assault aimed at the extinction or reduction of some of their sovereign rights (e.g., attacks on tribal sovereign immunity) and at constraining their economic development (e.g., federal and state efforts to reign in or extract more from Indian gaming). The assault force consists of anti-Indian state and federal lawmakers, conservative federal judges and justices, and an ambivalent public, which at times seems supportive of tribal cultural and economic regenerative attempts, yet is willing to support or at least benignly accept efforts by their own lawmakers that are focused on reducing or ending unique aboriginal rights. In sum, while a few native nations have become real players in the larger American political and economic systems, most tribal rights are based on pillars made not of constitutional granite, but of treaty and trust-soaked sand which can be washed away at the whim of lawmakers or judicial activists.

While the Obama administration has set a tone for tribal consultation, the legislative and judicial branches of the federal government continue to pose threats to tribal sovereignty. While native peoples have been successful in gaining inclusion in national policy items such as economic development and health care, congressional legislation such as the Native American Government Reorganization Act curtails indigenous sovereignty. Furthermore, the United States Supreme Court continues to hand down decisions that severely constrain tribes' ability to exercise their sovereignty. In *Plains Commerce Bank v. Long Family Land and Cattle Co.* (2008), the Court recognized that tribal courts wield sovereign authority, but found that this authority does not extend over non-Indians or non-Indian businesses even when those individuals are engaging in consensual transactions with indigenous peoples or Native corporations.

A year later the Supreme Court held, in *Carcieri v. Salazar*, that the secretary of the interior lacked authority to take land into trust for the Narrangansett Tribe because they were not federally recognized when the Indian Reorganization Act (IRA) of 1934, which contains provisions for placing land in trust, was enacted. This same year the High Court, in *Hawaii v. Office of Hawaiian Affairs*, held that while Congress acknowledged and apologized for the United States' role in the overthrow of the Kingdom of Hawaii in 1893, the Apology Resolution and Native Hawaiian pending claims to lands held in public trust could not strip Hawaii of its sovereign authority to sell, transfer, or exchange these lands.

The Supreme Court justices in these recent cases display an ignorance, almost a hostility, toward indigenous peoples that mirrors attitudes displayed over a century ago, at the height of late-nineteenth-century assimilation policies. These decisions have left native nations apprehensive about whether they can look to the Supreme Court for any recognition or even basic support of tribal sovereignty.

In the remainder of this closing chapter, we discuss some of the major external and internal issues confronting native peoples that have a direct bearing on their political, economic, and cultural aspirations.

External Issues and Recommendations

Congress should step forward and issue a number of clear-cut directives. First, it should disavow the doctrine of discovery (defined as vesting absolute or superior land title in the U.S. over the aboriginal land rights of native peoples) and the use of the plenary power doctrine (defined as absolute and unlimited) as violating the limitations imposed by the U.S. Constitution and the bilateral treaty relationship. Second, it should remind the federal courts that Congress alone has the power to "regulate trade with Indian tribes," and that it is not the business of the Supreme Court to explicitly or implicitly override U.S. treaty commitments to tribes, which it has done in cases like *South Dakota v. Bourland* (1993), in which Justice Clarence Thomas said that Congress had implicitly abrogated a provision of the Fort Laramie Treaty of 1868, although the general judicial rule is that Congress must act unequivocally when it seeks to abrogate treaties.[8]

Third, the Congress, under its exclusive authority authorized in the commerce clause, should act to remind state governments that they are without constitutional authority to interfere in internal tribal affairs absent express congressional action and tribal consent. This is a direct result of the doctrine of tribal sovereignty, the Constitution's supremacy and treaty clauses, and the disclaimer clauses found in most western state constitutions and enabling acts. This action would bring real clarity to the current ambiguous state of tribal-state affairs.

Fourth, the treaty-making process should be revived since, despite the grant of American citizenship to individual Indians, native nations still find that there is no protection for their sovereign rights under the Constitution. Absent a formal treaty-making procedure, there "are no checks and balances available that would prevent any branch of government from doing whatever it wanted with Indians and their lands and rights."[9] Until such time as the treaty process is restarted, American Indians, as extra-constitutional sovereigns, will lack any consistent protection of their rights, since only as individuals do Indians receive any measure of constitutional protection, although even individual Indians have learned that their basic constitutional rights may also be abridged by the federal government. This was the case in *Employment Division v. Smith* (1990), in which the Supreme Court held that the First Amendment was not sufficient to protect the traditional religious rights of two Indians who belonged to the Native American Church, which uses peyote sacramentally.[10] Revival of the treaty-making process would help ensure that native sovereignty was accorded the integrity and respect it deserves.

Finally, the United States should emphatically and unconditionally embrace the United Nations Declaration on the Rights of Indigenous Peoples, which affirms the rights of indigenous peoples to maintain and strengthen their own institutions, cultures, and traditions and to pursue their development in keeping with their own needs and aspirations.

Internal Issues and Recommendations

Serious internal issues continue to bedevil native governments, although considering what they have endured at the hands of the federal government, tribal governments do a remarkable job of meeting the basic needs of most of their citizens most of the time. That said, a major issue is deepening tribal political fragmentation or factionalism, which appears to be eroding the collective nature of a number of indigenous communities. Over the past forty years there have been a growing number of intratribal conflicts, some of which have resulted in virtual civil war within some tribes. First, there was the eruption of the Wounded Knee conflict in 1973, which focused in part on the conflict pitting Tribal Chairman Richard Wilson and his supporters in and around the town of Pine Ridge, South Dakota, against a segment of more traditional, treaty-oriented tribal people supported by many young Oglala and the American Indian Movement.[11]

Second was a dispute in Navajo country, pitting then Tribal Chairman Peter MacDonald and his supporters against a large segment of opposition political leaders and their supporters, who alleged that the MacDonald regime was corrupt and had mismanaged tribal and federal funds.[12] Third, a conflict erupted on the Akwesasne Mohawk Reservation in 1990 that led to the killing of two young Mohawks by other Mohawks in a deep struggle over the direction the nation should go politically and economically.[13]

Fourth, gaming revenues have fueled an upsurge in the number of tribal governments that have acted to "banish" or legally "disenroll" certain members or, in some cases, large groups of individuals or specific families. Gaming revenues are not the only reason banishments are occurring at a heightened pace—criminal activity is another factor—but they are the leading factor. This issue poses grave difficulties for native peoples, not only in their efforts to retain a cohesive cultural identity, but it may play a role leading to federal lawmakers getting more directly involved in tribal membership decisions if those lawmakers feel that tribal officials are violating the civil liberties of individual Indians who are not only tribal citizens but state and federal citizens as well.

But why does this political division seem so prominent now? Is it an outgrowth of mostly contemporary phenomena like gaming, of conflicts over issues like tribal membership, of decisions regarding what kinds of economic development are permissible (e.g., should tribal lands be used to "host" radioactive waste?), or does it have deeper historical roots? The answer is that both contemporary issues and history play a part in divisions that exist among all tribes, although the degree of this tension varies from tribe to tribe. The major historical factor sparking tension within tribes is their colonization and the great losses of property, identity, and human life caused by that process. And according to Robert Porter, colonialism is perpetuated by the reliance of many tribes on the Anglo-American legal system, which, by encouraging adversarial proceedings, serves to exacerbate, not resolve, intratribal disputes.[14]

Whatever its source, such tension is causing severe damage within a number of tribal nations. Tribal political fragmentation affects more than just the tribes' members. In the case of the Lumbee of North Carolina, several segments have broken off to form their own groups, like the Hatteras Tuscarora, Cherokee of Robeson and Adjoining Counties, and the Eastern Carolina Tuscarora. These political cleavages have contributed in no small measure to the tribes' inability to gain federal recognition (the BIA historically questioned their Indianness because of this apparent lack of cultural and political cohesion) and have caused tension between Lumbee and tribes like the Eastern Cherokee of North Carolina, who resent the appropriation of their tribal name by some segments of Indians formerly known as Lumbee.[15]

Another issue of real political importance for many native nations is the need for structural reform of governing institutions. Such reform has been suggested to provide a greater degree of political representation for Indian constituents and because it may lead to greater political and economic stability for tribal governments as they seek to gain recognition and to attract investors into Indian Country. A majority of tribes have governing institutions that trace back to John Collier and the period of the IRA of 1934, which authorized tribes who adopted the measure to develop constitutional governments. Since that time, the Indian population has increased greatly "and this rapid increase in population of both reservations and tribal membership has caused many problems not anticipated by the people who adopted tribal constitutions a half century ago."[16]

For some tribes, like the Oglala Lakota of Pine Ridge or the Northern Cheyenne of Montana, the problem is the constitutional structure itself, with members of the populations and sometimes the tribal council itself not always accepting the tribal constitution as "their" fundamental law. This lack of acceptance stems, in part, from the fact that many tribal leaders and their constituencies have viewed the IRA constitutions as hastily drawn and forcibly imposed documents.

This sense of colonial imposition was and is, of course, reinforced by the particular actions of the BIA personnel with the secretary of the interior "functioning as a reviewing body, interpreting a constitution and telling a tribe whether or not a certain action can be taken, or determining if the tribe's amendment can be added to its constitution. As a result, a tribe comes to see its constitution as the federal government's document, not its own."[17]

But increasingly, tribal leaders are engaging in structural government reform to incorporate distinctive, traditional values that they believe are essential in the reform process. For example, the San Carlos Apache of Arizona have recently set about restructuring their constitution in an effort to improve conditions on the reservation. Their steps have included removing the clause authorizing the BIA to approve of constitutional amendments, enlarging the number of tribal council delegates to increase political representation, and creating separate branches of government.[18]

The Comanche Tribe of Oklahoma in the early 1990s initiated tribal-wide discussions in an effort to incorporate traditional Comanche values into a revised constitutional government, since it appeared that the IRA constitutional model was a source of tension within the community.

Two related reform suggestions have also been made: some form of separation and limitation of powers and the expansion of the size of the tribal legislative branch. Separation of powers is considered crucial since all societies must find ways to prevent those who wield legitimate power from abusing that power or accruing too much power to themselves or their office. As Cornell and Kalt found in their multitribal study, "[T]oo often, for example, those with claims against either the tribe as a whole or other tribal members can appeal only to the tribal council. Without constitutional checks and balances, such as an independent judiciary of some sort, tribal politicians are in a position to turn authority into personal power or gain."[19] Tribal courts, in fact, occupy a crucial role in tribal restructuring since they are the branch specifically anointed to administer justice for the tribe, its members, and other aggrieved parties.

An expanded tribal council membership would ensure greater representation for tribal citizens, strengthen the tribe's sense of nationhood by enabling it to perform more legislative functions, be less easily intimidated by the BIA, and strengthen the separation of powers by more clearly distinguishing the legislative from the executive branch.[20]

Conversely, at least one indigenous people, the Navajo Nation, moved in the opposite direction when the nation's citizens voted overwhelmingly to reduce the size of their council from eighty-eight members to twenty-four, and to grant their president line-item veto authority.

Two other issues, with both internal and external dimensions, are also deeply troubling for tribal nations. First, of all racial and ethnic groups in the United States, American Indians have the highest intergroup marriage rate (marriage between persons of different races), at over 50 percent, according to a recent study.[21] By comparison, whites intermarry less than 5 percent of the time, while the figure for African Americans is less than 10 percent. Such a high rate of intergroup marriage for Indians raises profound questions about the future meaning of tribal sovereignty and how tribes will define their citizenry, and will almost surely have an impact on the trust relationship.

Finally, while crime rates are falling dramatically across much of America, in Indian Country the opposite is occurring. Alcohol-related crimes, gang activity, sexual exploitation of American Indian women and girls, and interracial crimes are rampant and threaten to engulf tribal judicial systems already understaffed, undertrained, and underfunded. In the most comprehensive report yet on crime in Indian Country, the Justice Department announced that their findings reveal a disturbing picture of victimization of American Indians and Alaska Natives. The rate of violent crimes estimated from self-reported victimization for American Indians is well above that of other U.S. racial or ethnic groups and is more than twice the national average. This disparity in the rates of exposure to violence affecting American Indians occurs across age groups, housing locations, and gender.

Of this violence, the most disturbing data from a tribal perspective is that the suicide rate—especially among Indian youth—continues to rise, although it has declined for the general population. The rate of teen suicide among native youth is three times the national average, although in some states the rate can be as high as eight times that of other racial and ethnic groups. On the Red Lake Reservation (central Minnesota) alone, in 2004 there were sixty-nine attempted suicides by young people.[22]

Conclusion

The issues confronting indigenous nations in the United States are myriad and the challenges are enormous. But the larger problems of forced removal, reservation confinement, cultural genocide, and termination have been confronted and surmounted before. And there are indications that as difficult as conditions appear at the present, from both internal and external perspectives, tribal nations are working hard to find ways to make the necessary adjustments to keep their peoples, their remaining lands and resources, and their cultures moving forward.

Hence we find that solutions to the four complicated political, economic, and geographic quandaries identified in the beginning of this text have not yet been found. First, native nations, as governing bodies, still face the conflicting tasks of providing social services for their constituents but also operating profitable and competitive businesses. Second, indigenous peoples do have the right and the desire to exercise self-determination, but the federal government often defines its trust responsibility to tribes in a paternalistic manner that contradicts tribal self-determination.

Third, Indians are tribal citizens, but they also are entitled to the rights accorded them as state and federal citizens. Finally, tribal governments represent separate nations inhabiting territorial units where the U.S. Constitution is still largely inapplicable; but over time and as a result of the unpredictable mixture of human evolution, federal policies, and intermarriage some Indian reservations have become home to a majority of non-Indians over whom tribal governments have a variable measure of jurisdiction.

The first quandary is one native governments continue to struggle with. Some native nations have had their burden eased somewhat because of gaming revenues, but the issue of constitutional reform is an ongoing problem for many tribes and crises erupt frequently in Indian Country as the level of corruption in tribal government appears to be on the rise.[23] Quandary two also remains problematic. Even as First Nations have reclaimed some of their long dormant and stymied powers of self-governance, they continue to be confronted by an agency, the BIA, that seeks to retain a powerful measure of control over the decision-making authority of tribes. The BIA's response to the trust fund scandal exemplifies its desire to retain this control, in the face of compelling evidence that many tribal nations are in a better position to administer their own funds through direct relations with Congress.

Quandary three also continues to cause Indians and non-Indians great difficulties. Individual Indians, enfranchised by federal law in 1924 and gradually extended the franchise by states, still find that their political, property, and civil rights may be diminished or ended by federal or state action, especially when the rights being expressed or exercised—say, the right to practice a traditional religious ceremony—are determined to be in conflict with the desires of a state or federal agency. Non-Indians are sometimes troubled by what they perceive are "extra" rights and benefits that tribal members enjoy.

An example is when Indians are exercising an off-reservation treaty right to hunt or fish that conflicts with the state's hunting and fishing regulations. Another example involves the issue of taxation, with tribal members being exempt from many state and some federal taxes, an exemption that confuses non-Indians who are unaware of the historical or legal basis for such exemptions. The lack of educational curriculum materials explaining why tribal members enjoy these and other rights and exemptions is a fundamental issue that begs for greater attention.

Finally, quandary four centers around the scope of tribal government powers over non-Indians. Historically, tribes often had criminal and civil jurisdiction over non-Indians who ventured into their lands. Over time, however, various treaties, federal policies, and court cases have sought to reduce the amount of jurisdiction tribal courts may exercise over non-Indians. Tribes have resisted such diminishments of their inherent powers, but many now concede that while they lack criminal jurisdiction over non-Indians, they should retain civil jurisdiction over non-member Indians and non-Indians. Tribal jurisdiction over non-member Indians was strongly reaffirmed in the 2004 Lara decision, but civil jurisdiction over non-Indians has been severely constrained by recent court cases, despite spirited resistance by native nations.[24]

The persistence of these quandaries evidences the strength and vitality, yet precariousness of indigenous peoples, the nations within states, who struggle to retain and wield political, economic, and cultural sovereignty in an insecure political world.

1778 Delaware–U.S. Treaty

TREATY WITH THE DELAWARE INDIANS, 1778

Articles of agreement and confederation, made and entered into by Andrew and Thomas Lewis, Esquires, Commissioners for, and in Behalf of the United States of North-America of the one Part, and Capt. White Eyes, Capt. John Kill Buck, Junior, and Capt. Pipe, Deputies and Chief Men of the Delaware Nation of the other Part.

Article I

That all offences or acts of hostilities by one, or either of the contracting parties against the other, be mutually forgiven, and buried in the depth of oblivion, never more to be had in remembrance.

Article II

That a perpetual peace and friendship shall from henceforth take place, and subsist between the contracting parties aforesaid, through all succeeding generations: and if either of the parties are engaged in a just and necessary war with any other nation or nations, that then each shall assist the other in due proportion to their abilities, till their enemies are brought to reasonable terms of accommodation: and that if either of them shall discover any hostile designs forming against the other, they shall give the earliest notice thereof, that timeous measures may be taken to prevent their ill effect.

Article III

And whereas the United States are engaged in a just and necessary war, in defence and support of life, liberty and independence, against the King of England and his adherents, and as said King is yet possessed of several posts and forts on the lakes and other places, the reduction of which is of great importance to the peace and security of the contracting parties, and as the most practicable way for the troops of the United

States to some of the posts and forts is by passing through the country of the Delaware nation, the aforesaid deputies, on behalf of themselves and their nation, do hereby stipulate and agree to give a free passage through their country to the troops aforesaid, and the same to conduct by the nearest and best ways to the posts, forts, or towns of the enemies of the United States, affording to said troops such supplies of corn, meat, horses, or whatever may be in their power for the accommodation of such troops, on the commanding officers, &c. paying, or engageing to pay, the full value of whatever they can supply them with. And the said deputies, on the behalf of their nation, engage to join the troops of the United States aforesaid, with such a number of their best and most expert warriors as they can spare, consistent with their own safety, and act in concert with them; and for the better security of the old men, women and children of the aforesaid nation, whilst their warriors are engaged against the common enemy, it is agreed on the part of the United States, that a fort of sufficient strength and capacity be built at the expense of the said States, with such assistance as it may be in the power of the said Delaware Nation to give, in the most convenient place, and advantageous situation, as shall be agreed on by the commanding officer of the troops aforesaid, with the advice and concurrence of the deputies of the aforesaid Delaware Nation, which fort shall be garrisoned by such a number of the troops of the United States, as the commanding officer can spare for the present, and hereafter by such numbers, as the wise men of the United States in council, shall think most conducive to the common good.

Article IV

For the better security of the peace and friendship now entered into by the contracting parties, against all infractions of the same by the citizens of either party, to the prejudice of the other, neither party shall proceed to the infliction of punishments on the citizens of the other, otherwise than by securing the offender or offenders by imprisonment, or any other competent means, till a fair and impartial trial can be had by judges or juries of both parties, as near as can be to the laws, customs and usages of the contracting parties and natural justice: The mode of such trials to be hereafter fixed by the wise men of the United States in Congress assembled, with the assistance of such deputies of the Delaware nation, as may be appointed to act in concert with them in adjusting this matter to their mutual liking. And it is further agreed between the parties aforesaid, that neither shall entertain or give countenance to the enemies of the other, or protect in their respective states, criminal fugitives, servants or slaves, but the same to apprehend, and secure and deliver to the State or States, to which such enemies, criminals, servants or slaves respectively belong.

Article V

Whereas the confederation entered into by the Delaware nation and the United States, renders the first dependent on the latter for all the articles of clothing, utensils and implements of war, and it is judged not only reasonable, but indispensably necessary, that the aforesaid Nation be supplied with such articles from time to time, as far as the United States may have it in their power, by a well-regulated trade, under the conduct of an intelligent, candid agent, with an adequate salary, one more influenced by the love of his country, and a constant attention to the duties of his department by promoting the common interest, than the sinister purposes of converting and binding all the duties of his office to his private emolument: Convinced of the necessity of such measures, the Commissioners of the United States, at the earnest solicitation of the deputies aforesaid, have engaged in behalf of the United States, that such a trade shall be afforded said nation, conducted on such principles of mutual interest as the wisdom of the United States in Congress assembled shall think most conducive to adopt for their mutual convenience.

Article VI

Whereas the enemies of the United States have endeavored, by every artifice in their power, to possess the Indians in general with an opinion, that it is the design of the States aforesaid, to extirpate the Indians and take possession of their country: to obviate such false suggestion, the United States do engage to guarantee to the aforesaid nation of Delawares, and their heirs, all their territorial rights in the fullest and most ample manner, as it hath been bounded by former treaties, as long as they the said Delaware nation shall abide by, and hold fast the chain of friendship now entered into. And it is further agreed on between the contracting parties should it for the future be found conducive for the mutual interest of both parties to invite any other tribes who have been friends to the interest of the United States, to join the present confederation, and to form a state whereof the Delaware nation shall be the head, and have a representation in Congress: Provided, nothing contained in this article to be considered as conclusive until it meets with the approbation of Congress. And it is also the intent and meaning of this article, that no protection or countenance shall be afforded to any who are at present our enemies, by which they might escape the punishment they deserve.

In Witness whereof, the parties have hereunto interchangeably set their hands and seals, at Fort Pitt, September seventeenth, anno Domini one thousand seven hundred and seventy-eight.

Andrew Lewis,
Thomas Lewis,
White Eyes, his x mark,
The Pipe, his x mark

In presence of—

Lach'n McIntosh, brigadier-general, commander of the Western Department.
Daniel Brodhead, colonel Eighth Pennsylvania Regiment,
W. Crawford, colonel,
John Campbell,
John Stephenson,
John Gibson, colonel Thirteenth Virginia Regiment,
A. Graham, brigade major,
Lach. McIntosh, jr., major brigade,
Benjamin Mills,
Joseph L. Finley, captain Eighth Pennsylvania Regiment,
John Finley, captain Eighth Pennsylvania Regiment.

Source: 7 Stat., 13–15.

Talton v. Mayes (1896)

TALTON v. MAYES
SUPREME COURT OF THE UNITED STATES
163 U.S. 376; 16 S. Ct. 986; 1896 U.S. LEXIS 2276; 41 L. Ed. 196
Argued April 16, 17, 1896.
May 18, 1896, Decided
APPEAL FROM THE CIRCUIT COURT OF THE UNITED STATES
FOR THE WESTERN DISTRICT OF ARKANSAS.

On February 15, 1893, a petition for habeas corpus was filed in the District Court of the United States for the Western District of Arkansas, setting forth that the plaintiff therein (who is the appellant here) was, on the 31st day of December, 1892, convicted, on a charge of murder, in a special Supreme Court of the Cherokee nation, Coowees-koowee District, and sentenced to be hanged on February 28, 1893, and that petitioner was then held, awaiting the time of execution, in the national jail at Tahlequah, Indian Territory, by Wash. Mayes, high sheriff of the Cherokee nation. It was further alleged that the petitioner was deprived of his liberty without due process of law; that he was in confinement in contravention to the Constitution and laws of the United States, and also in violation of the constitution and laws of the Cherokee nation. These contentions rested upon the averment that the indictment under which he had been tried and convicted was void because returned by a body consisting of five grand jurors, which was not only an insufficient number to constitute a grand jury under the Constitution and laws of the United States, but also was wholly inadequate to compose such jury under the laws of the Cherokee nation, which, it was alleged, provided for a grand jury of thirteen, of which number a majority was necessary to find an indictment. The petitioner, moreover, averred that he had not been tried by a fair and impartial jury, and that many gross irregularities and errors to his prejudice had been committed on the trial. The district judge issued the writ, which was duly served upon the high sheriff, who produced the body of the petitioner and made return setting up the conviction and sentence as justifying the detention of the prisoner. Incorporated in the return was a transcript of the proceedings in the Cherokee court had upon the indictment and trial of the petitioner. In the copy of the indictment contained in the original transcript, filed in this court, it was recited that the indictment was found by the grand jury on the 1st day of December, 1892, while the offence therein stated was alleged to have been committed "on or about the 3rd day of December, 1892." The evidence contained in the transcript, however, showed that the offence was committed on November 3, 1892, and in a supplement to the transcript, filed in this court, it appears that said date was given in the indictment. No motion or demurrer or other attack upon the sufficiency of the indictment was made upon the trial in the Cherokee court based upon the ground that the offence was stated in the indictment to have been committed on a date subsequent to the finding of the indictment, nor is there any specification of error of that character contained in the petition for the allowance of the writ of habeas corpus. After hearing, the district judge discharged the writ and remanded the petitioner to the custody of the sheriff, and from this judgment the appeal now under consideration was allowed.

SYLLABUS: The crime of murder committed by one Cherokee Indian upon the person of another within the jurisdiction of the Cherokee nation is not an offence against the United States, but an offence against the local laws of the Cherokee nation; and the statutes of the United States which provide for an indictment by a grand jury, and the number of persons who shall constitute such a body, have no application.

The Fifth Amendment to the Constitution does not apply to local legislation of the Cherokee nation, so as to require all prosecutions for offences committed against the laws of that nation to be initiated by a grand jury in accordance with the provisions of that amendment.

The question whether a statute of the Cherokee nation which was not repugnant to the Constitution of the United States or in conflict with any treaty or law of the United States had been repealed by another statute of that nation, and the determination of what was the existing law of the Cherokee nation as to the constitution of the grand jury, is solely a matter within the jurisdiction of the courts of that nation, and the decision of such a question in itself necessarily involves no infraction of the Constitution of the United States.

COUNSEL: Mr. Leonidas D. Yarrell for appellant. Mr. Elijah V. Brookshire and Mr. Benjamin T. Duval were on his brief.

Mr. R. C. Garland for appellee. Mr. A. H. Garland and Mr. William M. Cravens were on his brief.

OPINION BY: WHITE

OPINION: Mr. JUSTICE WHITE, after stating the case, delivered the opinion of the court.

Prior to May, 1892, a law enacted by the legislature of the Cherokee nation made it the duty of the judges of the Circuit and District Courts of the nation, fourteen days before the commencement of the first regular term of said courts, to furnish to the sheriff a list of the names of five persons, who should be summoned by the sheriff to act as grand jurors for that district during the year. The first regular term of the courts named commenced on the second Monday in May. On November 28, 1892, a law was enacted providing for the summoning and empaneling of a grand jury of thirteen, the names of the persons to compose such jury to be furnished to the sheriff, as under the previous law, fourteen days before the commencement of the regular term of the Circuit and District Courts. There was no express repeal of the provisions of the prior law. Under the terms of the act of November 28, 1892, a grand jury could not have been empaneled before the term beginning on the second Monday of May, 1893. The indictment in question was returned in December, 1892, by a grand jury consisting of five persons, which grand jury had been empaneled under the prior law, to serve during the year 1892. The right of the appellant to the relief which he seeks must exist, if at all, by virtue of section 753 of the Revised Statutes of the United States, which is as follows:

> The writ of habeas corpus shall in no case extend to a prisoner in jail, unless where he is in custody under or by color of the authority of the United States, or is committed for trial before some court thereof, or is in custody for an act done or omitted in pursuance of a law of the United States, or of an order, process or decree of a court or judge thereof, or is in custody in violation of the Constitution or of a law or treaty of the United States; or, being a subject or citizen of a foreign State, and domiciled therein, is in custody for an act done or omitted under any alleged right, title, authority, privilege, protection or exemption claimed under the commission, or order, or sanction of any foreign State, or under color thereof, the validity and effect whereof depend upon the law of nations; or unless it is necessary to bring the prisoner into court to testify.

Appellant and the person he was charged with having murdered were both Cherokee Indians, and the crime was committed within the Cherokee territory.

To bring himself within the statute, the appellant asserts, 1st, that the grand jury, consisting only of five persons, was not a grand jury within the contemplation of the Fifth Amendment to the Constitution, which it is asserted is operative upon the Cherokee nation in the exercise of its legislative authority as to purely local matters; 2d, that the indictment by a grand jury thus constituted was not due process of law within the intendment of the Fourteenth Amendment; 3d, even if the law of the Cherokee nation providing for a grand jury of five was valid under the Constitution of the United States such law had been repealed, and was not therefore in existence at the time the indictment was found. A decision as to the merits of these contentions involves a consideration of the relation of the Cherokee nation to the United States, and of the operation of the constitutional provisions relied on upon the purely local legislation of that nation.

By treaties and statutes of the United States the right of the Cherokee nation to exist as an autonomous body, subject always to the paramount authority of the United States, has been recognized. And from this fact there has consequently been conceded to exist in that nation power to make laws defining offences and providing for the trial and punishment of those who violate them when the offences are committed by one member of the tribe against another one of its members within the territory of the nation.

Thus, by the fifth article of the treaty of 1835, 7 Stat. 478, 481, it is provided:

> The United States hereby covenant and agree that the lands ceded to the Cherokee nation in the foregoing article shall, in no future time without their consent, be included within the territorial limits or jurisdiction of any State or Territory.

But they shall secure to the Cherokee nation the right by their national councils to make and carry into effect all such laws as they may deem necessary for the government and protection of the persons and property within their own country belonging to their people or such persons as have connected themselves with them: Provided always that they shall not be inconsistent with the Constitution of the United States and such acts of Congress as have been or may be passed regulating trade and intercourse with the Indians; and also, that they shall not be considered as extending to such citizens and army of the United States as may travel or reside in the Indian country by permission according to the laws and regulations established by the government of the same.

This guarantee of self government was reaffirmed in the treaty of 1868, 14 Stat. 799, 803, the thirteenth article of which reads as follows:

Article XIII. The Cherokees also agree that a court or courts may be established by the United States in said territory, with such jurisdiction and organized in such manner as may be prescribed by law: Provided, That the judicial tribunals of the nation shall be allowed to retain exclusive jurisdiction in all civil and criminal cases arising within their country in which members of the nation, by nativity or adoption, shall be the only parties, or where the cause of action shall arise in the Cherokee nation, except as otherwise provided in this treaty.

So, also, in "An act to provide a temporary government for the Territory of Oklahoma, to enlarge the jurisdiction of the United States court in the Indian Territory, and for other purposes," approved May 2, 1890, c. 182, 26 Stat. 81, it was provided, in section 30, as follows: "That the judicial tribunals of the Indian nations shall retain exclusive jurisdiction in all civil and criminal cases arising in the country in which members of the nation by nativity or by adoption shall be the only parties; and as to all such cases the laws of the State of Arkansas extended over and put in force in said Indian Territory by this act shall not apply."

And section 31 of the last mentioned act closes with the following paragraph:

The Constitution of the United States and all general laws of the United States which prohibit crimes and misdemeanors in any place within the sole and exclusive jurisdiction of the United States except in the District of Columbia, and all laws relating to national banking associations, shall have the same force and effect in the Indian Territory as elsewhere in the United States; but nothing in this act shall be so construed as to deprive any of the courts of the civilized nations of exclusive jurisdiction over all cases arising wherein members of said nations, whether by treaty, blood or adoption, are the sole parties, nor so as to interfere with the right and powers of said civilized nations to punish said members for violation of the statutes and laws enacted by their national councils where such laws are not contrary to the treaties and laws of the United States.

The crime of murder committed by one Cherokee Indian upon the person of another within the jurisdiction of the Cherokee nation is, therefore, clearly not an offence against the United States, but an offence against the local laws of the Cherokee nation. Necessarily, the statutes of the United States which provide for an indictment by a grand jury, and the number of persons who shall constitute such a body, have no application, for such statutes relate only, if not otherwise specially provided, to grand juries empaneled for the courts of and under the laws of the United States.

The question, therefore, is, does the Fifth Amendment to the Constitution apply to the local legislation of the Cherokee nation so as to require all prosecutions for offences committed against the laws of that nation to be initiated by a grand jury organized in accordance with the provisions of that amendment. The solution of this question involves an inquiry as to the nature and origin of the power of local government exercised by the Cherokee nation and recognized to exist in it by the treaties and statutes above referred to. Since the case of *Barron v. Baltimore*, 7 Pet. 243, it has been settled that the Fifth Amendment to the Constitution of the United States is a limitation only upon the powers of the General Government, that is, that the amendment operates solely on the Constitution itself by qualifying the powers of the National Government which the Constitution called into being. To quote the language of Chief Justice Marshall, this amendment is limitative of the "powers granted in the instrument itself and not of distinct governments framed by different persons and for different purposes. If these propositions be correct, the Fifth Amendment must be understood as restraining the power of the General Government, not as applicable to the States." The cases in this court which have sanctioned this view are too well recognized to render it necessary to do more than merely refer to them. *Fox v. Ohio*, 5 How. 410, 424; *Withers v. Buckley*, 20 How. 84; *Twitchell v. The Commonwealth*, 7 Wall. 321; *Edwards v. Elliott*, 21 Wall. 532, 557; *Person v. Yewdall*, 95 U.S. 294, 296; *Davis v. Texas*, 139 U.S. 651.

The case in this regard therefore depends upon whether the powers of local government exercised by the Cherokee nation are Federal powers created by and springing from the Constitution of the United States, and hence controlled by the Fifth Amendment to that Constitution, or whether they are local powers not created by the Constitution, although subject to its general provisions and the paramount authority of Congress. The repeated adjudications of this court have long since answered the former question in the negative. In *Cherokee Nation v. Georgia*, 5 Pet. 1, which involved the right of the Cherokee nation to maintain an original bill in this court as a foreign State, which was ruled adversely to that right, speaking through Mr. Chief Justice Marshall, this court said (p. 16):

> Is the Cherokee nation a foreign State in the sense in which that term is used in the Constitution?
>
> The counsel for the plaintiffs have maintained the affirmative of this proposition with great earnestness and ability. So much of the argument as was intended to prove the character of the Cherokees as a State, as a distinct political society, separated from others, capable of managing its own affairs and governing itself, has, in the opinion of a majority of the judges, been completely successful. They have been uniformly treated as a State from the settlement of our country. The numerous treaties made with them by the United States recognize them as a people capable of maintaining the relations of peace and war, of being responsible in their political character for any violation of their engagements or for any aggression committed on the citizens of the United States by any individual of their community. Laws have been enacted in the spirit of these treaties. The acts of our

government plainly recognize the Cherokee nation as a State, and the courts are bound by those acts.

It cannot be doubted, as said in *Worcester v. The State of Georgia,* 6 Pet. 515, 559, that prior to the formation of the Constitution treaties were made with the Cherokee tribes by which their autonomous existence was recognized. And in that case Chief Justice Marshall also said (p. 559):

> The Indian nations had always been considered as distinct, independent political communities, retaining their original natural rights. . . . The very term "nation," so generally applied to them, means a "people distinct from others." The Constitution, by declaring treaties already made, as well as those to be made, to be the supreme law of the land, has adopted and sanctioned the previous treaties with the Indian nations, and consequently admits their rank among those powers who are capable of making treaties.

In reviewing the whole subject in *Kagama v. United States,* 118 U.S. 375, this court said (p. 381):

> With the Indians themselves these relations are equally difficult to define. They were, and always have been, regarded as having a semi-independent position when they preserved their tribal relations; not as States, not as nations, not as possessed of the full attributes of sovereignty, but as a separate people with the power of regulating their internal and social relations, and thus far not brought under the laws of the Union, or of the State within whose limits they resided.

True it is that in many adjudications of this court the fact has been fully recognized, that although possessed of these attributes of local self government, when exercising their tribal functions, all such rights are subject to the supreme legislative authority of the United States. *Cherokee Nation v. Kansas Railway Co.,* 135 U.S. 641, where the cases are fully reviewed. But the existence of the right in Congress to regulate the manner in which the local powers of the Cherokee nation shall be exercised does not render such local powers Federal powers arising from and created by the Constitution of the United States. It follows that as the powers of local self government enjoyed by the Cherokee nation existed prior to the Constitution, they are not operated upon by the Fifth Amendment, which, as we have said, had for its sole object to control the powers conferred by the Constitution on the National Government. The fact that the Indian tribes are subject to the dominant authority of Congress, and that their powers of local self government are also operated upon and restrained by the general provisions of the Constitution of the United States, completely answers the argument of inconvenience which was pressed in the discussion at bar. The claim that the finding of an indictment by a grand jury of less than thirteen violates the due process clause of the Fourteenth Amendment is conclusively answered by *Hurtado v. California,* 110 U.S. 516, and *McNulty v. California,* 149 U.S. 645. The question whether a statute of the Cherokee nation which was not repugnant to the Constitution of the United States or in conflict with any treaty or law of the United States had been repealed by another statute of that nation, and the determination of what was the existing law of the Cherokee nation as to the constitution of the grand jury, were solely matters within the jurisdiction of the courts of that nation, and the decision of such a question in itself necessarily involves no infraction of the Constitution of the United States. Such has been the decision of this court with reference to similar contentions arising upon an indictment and conviction in a state court. In re *Duncan*, 139 U.S. 449. The ruling in that case is equally applicable to the contentions in this particular arising from the record before us.

The counsel for the appellant has very properly abandoned any claim to relief because of alleged errors occurring subsequent to the finding of the indictment. As to the point raised in reference to the date of the commission of the offence as stated in the indictment, the record as corrected shows that the error in question did not exist. It is, therefore, unnecessary to notice the argument based upon the assumption that the indictment charged the offence to have been committed subsequent to the finding of the true bill.

The judgment is

Affirmed.

MR. JUSTICE HARLAN dissented.

Constitution and Bylaws of the Pueblo of Santa Clara, New Mexico

CONSTITUTION AND BYLAWS OF THE PUEBLO OF SANTA CLARA, NEW MEXICO
Approved: December 20, 1935

Preamble

We the people of Santa Clara pueblo, in order to establish justice, promote the common welfare and preserve the advantages of self-government, do ordain and establish this constitution.

Article I—Jurisdiction

This constitution shall apply within the exterior boundaries of Santa Clara pueblo grant and to such other lands as are now or may in the future be under the jurisdiction of the pueblo of Santa Clara. This constitution shall apply to and be for the benefit of all persons who are members of the pueblo of Santa Clara.

Article II—Membership

Sec. 1. Conditions of membership.—The membership of the Santa Clara pueblo shall consist as follows:

(a) All persons of Indian blood whose names appear on the census roll of the Santa Clara pueblo as of November 1, 1935 provided that, within one year from the adoption and approval of this constitution corrections may be made in the said roll by the pueblo council with the approval of the Secretary of the Interior.
(b) All persons born of parents both of whom are members of the Santa Clara pueblo.

(c) All children of mixed marriages between members of the Santa Clara pueblo and nonmembers. Provided such children have been recognized and adopted by the council.
(d) All persons naturalized as members of the pueblo.

Sec. 2. Naturalization.—Indians from other pueblos or reservations who marry a member of Santa Clara pueblo may become members of the pueblo, with the assent of the council, by naturalization. To do this they must (1) go before the pueblo council and renounce allegiance to their tribe and declare intention of becoming members of the Santa Clara pueblo. They shall swear that from that date on they will not receive any benefits from their people, except through inheritance. (2) A year later they shall go before the pueblo council again, swear allegiance to the pueblo of Santa Clara and receive membership papers; provided, they have kept their promise from the time of their first appearance before the pueblo council.

Article III—Organization of the Pueblo Council

Sec. 1. Officers.—The governing power of the pueblo of Santa Clara shall be vested in the pueblo council which shall consist of the following officers:

Officers:	Number
Governor	1
Lieutenant Governor	1
Representatives	8
Secretary	1
Treasurer	1
Interpreter	1
Sheriff	1

and such other officers as the council may recognize or appoint.

Sec. 2. Election of Governor, Lieutenant Governor, secretary, treasurer, interpreter, and sheriff.—On the first Saturday of each year an election shall be held within the pueblo of Santa Clara, at which a Governor, Lieutenant Governor, secretary, treasurer, interpreter, and sheriff shall be elected by secret ballot to serve for the ensuing year.

Sec. 3. Who may vote.—Every member of the pueblo of Santa Clara who is of sane mind and over 18 years of age, may vote at any election. Any member who is absent from the pueblo on the date of any election shall have the right to vote by mail under such rules as may be prescribed by the pueblo council.

Sec. 4. Candidates.—Candidates for Governor, Lieutenant Governor, secretary, treasurer, interpreter, and sheriff shall be nominated at least fifteen (15) days before the date upon which each election is to be held. Nominations for the first election shall be made by the recognized parties now existing within the pueblo. Thereafter, nominations shall be made in a manner prescribed by the council of the pueblo.

Sec. 5. Representatives.—Two representatives shall be appointed to the pueblo council upon the date of the first election, for a term of 1 year by each of the four recognized parties now existing within the pueblo, and in all future elections eight representatives shall be chosen in a manner to be prescribed by the council.

Sec. 6. Manner of elections.—All nominations for office and elections shall be made and held in a manner prescribed by the council of the pueblo.

Article IV—The Pueblo Council and Its Powers

Sec. 1. Legislative power.—The legislative power shall be vested in the pueblo council, and the said power shall be exercised in accordance with, and not in conflict with, the constitution or any laws of the United States of America.

The pueblo council shall have the following rights and powers:

1. To employ legal counsel, the choice of counsel and fixing of fees to be subject to the approval of the Secretary of the Interior.
2. To prevent the sale, disposition, lease, or encumbrance of pueblo lands, interests in lands, or other tribal assets.
3. To negotiate, with the Federal, State, and local governments and with the councils and governing authorities of other pueblos or Indian tribes.
4. To advise the Secretary of the Interior with regard to all appropriation estimates or Federal projects for the benefit of the pueblo prior to the submission of such estimates to the Bureau of the Budget and to Congress.
5. To enact ordinances, not inconsistent with the constitution and bylaws of the pueblo, for the maintenance of law and order within the pueblo and for the punishment of members, and the exclusion of nonmembers violating any such ordinances, for the raising of revenue and the appropriation of available funds for pueblo purposes, for the regulation of trade, inheritance, land-holding, and private dealings in land within the pueblo, for the guidance of the officers of the pueblo in all their duties, and generally for the protection of the welfare of the pueblo and for the execution of all other powers vested in the pueblo by existing law: Provided, That any ordinance which affects persons who are not members of the pueblo shall not take effect until it has been approved by the Secretary of the Interior or some officer designated by him.
6. To delegate any of the foregoing powers to appropriate officers of the pueblo, reserving the right to review any action taken by virtue of such delegated power.

Sec. 2. Judicial Power.—The pueblo council shall also adjudicate all matters coming before it over which it has jurisdiction. In all controversies coming before the pueblo council, the council shall have the right to examine all witnesses, and ascertain full details of the controversy, and after the matter shall have been sufficiently commented upon by the interested parties, the council shall retire to a private place to make a decision. All of the members of the council except the Governor and the Lieutenant Governor shall have the right to vote upon a decision, and a majority shall rule. In the event of a tie, the Governor shall have the right to cast a vote, thereby breaking the tie. It shall be the duty of the Governor and the Lieutenant Governor to express to the other members of the pueblo council their views regarding the case before a vote is taken.

Sec. 3. Common law of pueblo.—With respect to all matters not covered by the written constitution, bylaws, and ordinances of the pueblo of Santa Clara, nor by those laws of the United States of America which are applicable to the pueblo of Santa Clara, the customs and usages of the pueblo, civil, and criminal, as interpreted by the council, shall have the force of law.

Article V—The Governor, His Powers and Duties

The Governor shall be the executive head of the pueblo government. It shall be his duty to enforce the laws of the pueblo, civil and criminal, written and unwritten. If any person considers that any ruling of the Governor is unjust, he shall have the right to demand through any representative of the pueblo council or directly to the pueblo council that the matter be brought before the pueblo council for adjudication at the next meeting of said officers.

In all community work the Governor shall be the sole overseer unless he is unavoidably absent, in which event the Lieutenant Governor shall have the same rights and duties as the Governor.

Article VI—Vacancies and Impeachments

Sec. 1. Vacancies.—Should any vacancy occur in any of the offices or any member of the council, the council shall, by a majority vote, have the right to name a successor for the said office, except that in the event the office of Governor becomes vacant for any reason, then and in that event the Lieutenant Governor shall thereupon become the Governor with all duties and powers of the said office, and further, that the successor to any pueblo representative appointed by a particular group shall be chosen by the same group.

Sec. 2. Impeachment.—Any officer charged with grave offenses may be tried before the other members of the council. The manner of conducting impeachments shall be prescribed by the council. The council shall act as the trial court and if they decide, by a two-thirds vote, to remove the accused member from office he will be removed.

Article VII—Land

Sec. 1. Pueblo title.—Title to all lands of the pueblo, whether assigned to the use of individuals or withheld for the common use of the members of the pueblo, shall forever remain in the pueblo itself and not in the individual members thereof. All the members of the pueblo are declared to have an equal right to make beneficial use, in accordance with ordinances of the council, of any land of the pueblo not heretofore or hereafter assigned to individual members.

For the purpose of this article the word "member" shall be defined by the council.

Sec. 2. Individual rights of possession.—The right of full possession shall be guaranteed to every member of the pueblo, holding lands assigned to him by the Pueblo Council, for cultivation or other purposes: Provided, That no member holding said lands shall sell or will same to an alien. All lands assigned to individuals of the pueblo must be completely fenced within three years. Any violation of the above provision shall be sufficient cause for the council to dispossess him of said land. He shall have the right, however, to rent to a pueblo member or with the approval of the council, to an alien, all lands under his possession, for a term not to exceed two years. He shall have the right to sell his interest in said lands to any other member of the pueblo after his assignment has been finally approved, subject to such regulations as the council may prescribe.

Sec. 3. Council to have power of granting assignments.—When any member of the pueblo desires a piece of unimproved pueblo land, he shall select his land, and then make his application for same to the council of the pueblo. If the council decides to grant him the land, or any part thereof, they shall mark out the boundaries of same. The grantee shall thereafter have full possession of said land, unless the council shall, in accordance with the constitution, bylaws, and ordinances of the pueblo, dispossess him of the same.

Sec. 4. Prior assignments recognized.—All assignments of land heretofore made by the pueblo authorities are hereby recognized and confirmed.

Article VIII—Amendments

No amendments or changes shall be made in the constitution or bylaws of the pueblo except by a decision of the general pueblo. At the request of the council the Secretary of the Interior shall submit any proposed amendment to the said constitution or bylaws to a vote of the people. If such amendment is approved by a majority of the qualified voters of the pueblo, 21 years old or over, voting at an election in which at least 30 percent of those entitled to vote shall vote, it shall be submitted to the Secretary of the Interior, and if he shall approve the same it shall become effective.

BYLAWS OF THE PUEBLO OF SANTA CLARA, NEW MEXICO

Article I—Duties of Officers

Sec. 1. Governor.—The Governor shall be in full charge of all meetings of the pueblo council. It shall be his duty to see that perfect order is preserved in every respect. In the discussion of all business but one person shall be allowed to speak at a time, and the Governor shall have the right to set a time limit upon speakers. When any member of the pueblo council or any other person desires to speak at a meeting of the pueblo council, such person shall first ask permission of the Governor to do so before proceeding. It shall be the duty of the Governor to see that all business presented to the council within any month be disposed of, if possible, before the beginning of the next month.

Sec. 2. Lieutenant Governor.—The Lieutenant Governor shall be next in rank to the Governor. In case of the death, resignation, absence, impeachment, or other disability of the Governor, the Lieutenant Governor shall become Governor or act as Governor during such disability or absence. As long as the Governor is at the pueblo holding office, the Lieutenant Governor shall have the power only of a representative in the council, except as otherwise provided in the constitution and bylaws of the pueblo.

Sec. 3. Representatives.—Representatives shall represent their people in the pueblo council. They shall bring before the council at every meeting the matters that their people want brought before the council and such other matters as each representative believes should be presented to the council. Such matters may originate with any member of the pueblo or may originate with the representative himself.

Sec. 4. Secretary.—The secretary shall keep a record of all council proceedings and all business authorized or transacted by the council. At the beginning of each regular meeting he shall call the roll of councilmen and all specially summoned persons expected to be present. He shall then read the minutes of the previous meeting and the officers shall then decide as to whether they should be approved as they stand, and all persons present shall have the right to suggest corrections. After the minutes of the previous meeting have been accepted, the secretary will then mark them approved. The secretary shall attend to all official correspondence as directed by the pueblo council and the Governor.

Sec. 5. Treasurer.—It shall be the duty of the treasurer to receive all money due to the pueblo and to give a receipt for the same. He shall deposit the pueblo money in a bank which should be approved by the pueblo council. He shall keep a record in his books of all moneys received and paid out. Moneys of the pueblo shall be paid by check signed by the treasurer and countersigned by the Governor. No moneys shall be paid out unless the same shall have been authorized to be expended by the council and vouchers for same shall have been signed by the Governor and the secretary. At each regular meeting of the pueblo council, the treasurer shall present to them a statement of receipts and disbursements made by him since the last regular meeting and he shall submit to the pueblo council at each regular meeting all of his books and a statement of the financial condition of the pueblo funds.

Sec. 6. Interpreter.—The interpreter shall translate from the Tewa language into the English language or from English into the Tewa language whenever directed to do so by the pueblo council. He shall also assist the secretary with the official correspondence of the pueblo.

Sec. 7. Sheriff.—It shall be the duty of the sheriff to assist the Governor in keeping law and order in the pueblo. He shall maintain order at all meetings, also in the village and on the pueblo lands. He shall report on disorders to the council. He shall have authority to stop trouble immediately wherever he finds it, without special authorization from the Governor. In case of disputes or difficulties, the sheriff shall bring the parties in controversy before the council for a decision. He shall bring before the council for punishment all violators of the laws of the pueblo. He shall serve notices or summons upon all persons required to be present before the council in criminal or civil proceedings.

Article II—Qualifications of Office

Sec. 1. Qualifications of Governor and Lieutenant Governor.—The Governor and the Lieutenant governor must be at least twenty-five (25) years of age and shall not be over sixty-five (65) years of age. They must be members of the pueblo of Santa Clara and be residents of said pueblo at the time of their election. They must be able to speak the Tewa language fluently and also be able to speak either the English or Spanish languages well enough to be understood.

Sec. 2. Qualifications of representatives.—Representatives must be at least twenty-five (25) years of age. They must be members of the pueblo of Santa Clara and residents thereof at the time of their selection. They must be able to speak the Tewa language fluently.

Sec. 3. Qualifications of secretary, treasurer, and sheriff.—The secretary, treasurer, and sheriff must be not less than twenty-five (25) years of age and not over sixty-five (65) years of age. They must be members of the pueblo of Santa Clara and residents thereof at the time of their election. They must be able to speak the Tewa language fluently and speak, read, and write the English language, and it will be preferable to have those who can also understand the Spanish language.

Sec. 4. Qualifications of the Interpreter.—The interpreter shall be not less than twenty-five (25) years of age, and not over sixty-five (65) years of age, and must be a member of the pueblo of Santa Clara and a resident thereof at the time of his election. He must be able to speak the Tewa language fluently and to translate the said language into English and Spanish and the English and Spanish languages into the Tewa language.

Article III—Conduct of Council Meetings

Sec. 1. Regular meetings.—Regular meetings of the pueblo council shall be held at least once a month, at such time and place as shall be fixed by the council and special meetings shall be held at such times and places as shall be fixed by the council. No action shall be taken by the council at any meeting unless at least a majority of the members are present.

Sec. 2. Attendance of council members.—Every member of the pueblo council shall be required to be present at each regular monthly meeting and at each special meeting of the Pueblo council unless it should be impossible for such member to be there, in which event said member shall notify the Governor of his inability to attend, giving reasons therefor. The Governor will then refer the matter to the pueblo council who, if the reasons given are found to be justifiable, shall excuse the absence of the said member. In the event that members of the council receive compensation for their services from the pueblo funds, an unexcused absence shall be punished by a fine to be fixed by the pueblo council.

Sec. 3. Matters of general interest to pueblo.—In all matters in which all of the people of the pueblo of Santa Clara are interested, the pueblo council shall cause the sheriff to notify all members of the pueblo of the time and place at which such business is to be transacted. At least three days' notice of such general meeting of the pueblo council shall be given in such manner as shall be prescribed by the bylaws of the pueblo. If any member of the pueblo wants a special meeting for all the people in the pueblo, he will first get permission from the pueblo council through a representative or through the Governor.

Sec. 4. Special Meetings on grievances.—If any member of the pueblo of Santa Clara has any grievance against any other member of the said pueblo which cannot await settlement at the regular pueblo council meeting, he shall report the same to the Governor who, if he deems that the case requires speedy attention, shall call a special meeting of the council at such time and place as the Governor shall fix, to pass upon the said matter.

Sec. 5. Advice of counsel.—If any cause cannot be fully understood by the pueblo council, the pueblo council may consult the special attorney for the Pueblo Indians and ask for his advice.

Article IV—Personal Liberties

Sec. 1. Private rights of each member of the pueblo.—Each member of the pueblo of Santa Clara shall be assured his private rights as a citizen of the United States, and no attempt shall be made by the officers of the pueblo to enforce any order upon him depriving him of said rights.

Sec. 2. Preference to Relatives.—Preference to relatives shall not be given by Council members under any circumstances. If they clearly show preference they will be exposing themselves to impeachment.

Sec. 3. Old members of the pueblo.—All members of the pueblo who have completed their 75th year shall not be compelled to work on community work (pueblo cleaning, fencing, etc.), and ditch work. If, however, they of their own accord attend to community work they will be free to work as they please.

Retired members will not, however, be able to fill the places of sons who are of working age and not justified in refusing to serve on community work and ditch work.

Article V—Intoxication

Any person showing signs of intoxication will not be allowed to take part in a council meeting. Council members who attend meetings while intoxicated or who have missed a meeting because of intoxication will face a charge of impeachment.

All liquor charges will be decided by the pueblo council and fines will be made by the council when cases come up before the council.

Article VI—Stock

From March 1 to November 1 of each year it shall be the duty of all members of the pueblo to report all loose animals found in cultivated fields of the pueblo to the Governor. The Governor will then notify the owners. If they do not remove the animals from the fields at once, they will be subject to a fine. The fine will be made according to the amount of damage done. If the Governor cannot by himself settle a question like this he will be free to bring the case before the pueblo council.

Article VII—Ratification

This constitution and bylaws, when ratified by a majority vote of the members of the pueblo over twenty-one years of age at a special election, called by the Secretary of the Interior, in which at least thirty percent (30%) of the eligible voters shall vote, shall be submitted to the Secretary of the Interior for his approval and shall be effective from the date of such approval. The constitution and bylaws of the pueblo may thereafter be amended or revoked in the manner provided under article VII of the constitution.

CERTIFICATION OF ADOPTION
Pursuant to an order, approved November 23, 1935, by the Secretary of the Interior, the attached constitution and by-laws was submitted for ratification to the Indians of the Santa Clara Pueblo and was on December 14, 1935, duly adopted by a vote of 145 for and 8 against, in an election in which over 30 percent of those entitled to vote cast their ballots, in accordance with section 16 of the Indian Reorganization Act of June 18, 1934 (48 Stat. 984), as amended by the act of June 15, 1935 (Pub., No. 147, 74th Cong.).

Patrici Gutierrez, Chairman of the Election Board.
Cleto Tafoya, Secretary of the Election Board
Nestor Naranjo
John Naranjo
Anastacio Naranjo
Agapito Naranjo

Jose G. Naranjo
Joseph Filario Tafoya
S.D. Aberle, Superintendent in charge of the United Pueblos Agency

I, Harold L. Ickes, the Secretary of the Interior of the United States of America, by virtue of the authority granted me by the act of June 18, 1934 (48 Stat. 984), as amended, do hereby approve of the attached constitution and bylaws of the pueblo of Santa Clara.

All rules and regulations heretofore promulgated by the Interior Department or by the Office of Indian Affairs, so far as they may be incompatible with any of the provisions of said constitution or by-laws are hereby declared inapplicable to the pueblo of Santa Clara.

All officers and employees of the Interior Department are ordered to abide by the provisions of the said constitution and by-laws.

Approval recommended December 18, 1935.

John Collier, Commissioner of Indian Affairs.

Harold L. Ickes, Secretary of the Interior

Washington, D.C., December 20, 1935.

Source: Department of the Interior, Constitution and Bylaws of the Pueblo of Santa Clara New Mexico (Washington, D.C.: Government Printing Office, 1936).

Memorandum for the Heads of Executive Departments and Agencies

SUBJECT: Tribal Consultation

The United States has a unique legal and political relationship with Indian tribal governments, established through and confirmed by the Constitution of the United States, treaties, statutes, executive orders, and judicial decisions. In recognition of that special relationship, pursuant to Executive Order 13175 of November 6, 2000, executive departments and agencies (agencies) are charged with engaging in regular and meaningful consultation and collaboration with tribal officials in the development of Federal policies that have tribal implications, and are responsible for strengthening the government-to-government relationship between the United States and Indian tribes.

History has shown that failure to include the voices of tribal officials in formulating policy affecting their communities has all too often led to undesirable and, at times, devastating and tragic results. By contrast, meaningful dialogue between Federal officials and tribal officials has greatly improved Federal policy toward Indian tribes. Consultation is a critical ingredient of a sound and productive Federal-tribal relationship.

My Administration is committed to regular and meaningful consultation and collaboration with tribal officials in policy decisions that have tribal implications including, as an initial step, through complete and consistent implementation of Executive Order 13175. Accordingly, I hereby direct each agency head to submit to the Director of the Office of Management and Budget (OMB), within 90 days after the date of this memorandum, a detailed plan of actions the agency will take to implement the policies and directives of Executive Order 13175. This plan shall be developed after consultation by the agency with Indian tribes and tribal officials as defined in Executive Order 13175. I also direct each agency head to submit to the Director of the OMB, within 270 days after the date of this memorandum, and annually thereafter, a progress report on the status of each action included in its plan together with any proposed updates to its plan.

Each agency's plan and subsequent reports shall designate an appropriate official to coordinate implementation of the plan and preparation of progress reports required by this memorandum. The Assistant to the President for Domestic Policy and the Director of the OMB shall review agency plans and subsequent reports for consistency with the policies and the directives of Executive Order 13175.

In addition, the Director of the OMB, in coordination with the Assistant to the President for Domestic Policy, shall submit to me, within 1 year from the date of this memorandum, a report on the implementation of Executive Order 13175 across the executive branch based on the review of agency plans and progress reports. Recommendations for improving the plans and making the tribal consultation process more effective, if any, should be included in this report.

The terms "Indian tribe," and "policies that have tribal implications" as used in this memorandum are as defined in Executive Order 13175.

The Director of the OMB is hereby authorized and directed to publish this memorandum in the Federal Register. This memorandum is not intended to, and does not, create any right of benefit, substantive or procedural, enforceable at law or in equity by any party against the United States, its departments, agencies, or entities, its officers, employees, or agents, or any other person. Executive departments and agencies shall carry out the provisions of this memorandum to the extent permitted by law and consistent with their statutory and regulatory authorities and their enforcement mechanisms.

BARACK OBAMA
THE WHITE HOUSE
Washington, November 5, 2009

Source: Presidential Documents, *Federal Register,* Vol. 74, No. 215, Monday, November 9, 2009. FR Doc. E9-27142.

Major Congressional Law Affecting Indians

- An Act to Provide for the Government of the Territory Northwest of the River Ohio, 1 Stat. 50 (August 7, 1789).
- An Act to Regulate Trade and Intercourse with the Indian Tribes, 1 Stat. 137 (July 22, 1790).
- An Act for Establishing Trading Houses with the Indian Tribes, 1 Stat. 452 (April 18, 1796).
- An Act Making Provision for the Civilization of the Indian Tribes Adjoining the Frontier Settlements, 3 Stat. 516 (March 3, 1819).
- An Act to Abolish the United States' Trading Establishment with the Indian Tribes, 3 Stat. 679 (May 6, 1822).
- An Act to Provide for an Exchange of Lands with the Indians Residing in any of the States or Territories, and for their Removal West of the River Mississippi, 4 Stat. 411 (May 28, 1830).
- An Act to Provide for the Appointment of a Commissioner of Indian Affairs, and for other Purposes, 4 Stat. 564 (July 9, 1832).
- An Act to Regulate Trade and Intercourse with the Indian Tribes, and to Preserve Peace on the Frontiers, 4 Stat. 729 (June 30, 1834).
- An Act to Provide for the Organization of the Department of Indian Affairs, 4 Stat. 735 (June 30, 1834).
- An Act Making Appropriations for the Current and Contingent Expenses of the Indian Department, and for Fulfilling Treaty Stipulations with Various Indian Tribes, 16 Stat. 544 (March 3, 1871). Note: contained the rider that effectively ended the original treaty-making process between Indian nations and the United States.
- An Act Making Appropriations for the Current and Contingent Expenses of the Indian Department, and for Fulfilling Treaty Stipulations with Various Indian Tribes, 23 Stat. 362 (March 3, 1885). Note: contained a rider that gave the federal government criminal jurisdiction over seven major crimes in Indian Country.

- An Act to Provide for the Allotment of Lands in Severalty to Indians on the Various Reservations, 24 Stat. 388 (February 8, 1887).
- An Act to Amend and Further Extend the Benefits of the Act Approved February 8, 1887, 26 Stat. 794 (February 28, 1891).
- An Act to Provide for the Adjudication and Payment of Claims Arising from Indian Depredations, 26 Stat. 851 (March 3, 1891).
- An Act for the Protection of the People of the Indian Territory, 30 Stat. 495 (June 28, 1898). Note: legally dismembered the sovereign status of the Five Civilized Tribes of Indian Territory.
- An Act to Amend Section Six of an Act Approved February 8, 1887, entitled "An Act to Provide for the Allotment of Lands in Severalty to Indians, . . ." 34 Stat. 182 (May 8, 1906).
- An Act Providing for the Allotment and Distribution of Indian Tribal Funds, 34 Stat. 1221 (March 2, 1907).
- An Act Authorizing Certain Tribes of Indians to Submit Claims to the Court of Claims, 41 Stat. 623 (May 26, 1920).
- An Act Authorizing Appropriations and Expenditures for the Administration of Indian Affairs, 42 Stat. 208 (November 2, 1921).
- An Act to Authorize the Secretary of the Interior to Issue Certificates of Citizenship to Indians, 43 Stat. 253 (June 2, 1924).
- An Act to Authorize the Secretary of the Interior to Adjust Reimbursable Debts of Indians and Tribes of Indians, 47 Stat. 564 (July 1, 1932).
- An Act Authorizing the Secretary of the Interior to Arrange with States or Territories for the Education, Medical Attention, Relief of Distress, and Social Welfare of Indians, 48 Stat. 596 (April 16, 1934). Note: popularly known as the Johnson-O'Malley Act.
- An Act to Conserve and Develop Indian Lands and Resources; to Extend to Indians the Right to Form Business and Other Organizations; to Establish a Credit System for Indians; to Grant Certain Rights of Home Rule to Indians; to Provide for Vocational Education for Indians, 48 Stat. 984 (June 18, 1934). Note: popularly known as the Indian Reorganization Act.
- An Act to Facilitate and Simplify the Administration of Indian Affairs, 60 Stat. 939 (August 8, 1946). Note: popularly known as the Indian Delegation Act.
- An Act to Create an Indian Claims Commission, to Provide for the Powers, Duties, and Functions thereof, 60 Stat. 250 (August 13, 1946).
- An Act to Codify and Enact into Positive Law Title 4 of the United States Code, entitled "Flag and Seal, Seat of Government, and the States," 61 Stat. 641, 645 (July 30, 1947). Note: contained a provision, section 109, popularly known as the Buck Act, which exempted Indians from certain taxes.
- An Act Making Appropriations for the Departments of State, Justice, Commerce, and the Judiciary, 66 Stat. 549, 560 (July 10, 1952). Note: included a provision, section 208, popularly known as the McCarran Amendment, involving water rights adjudications.
- A House Concurrent Resolution, 67 Stat. B132 (August 1, 1953). Note: popularly known as the Termination Resolution, which inaugurated the policy to "end their [Indian tribes'] status as wards of the United States, and to grant them all of the rights and prerogatives pertaining to American citizenship."

- An Act to Eliminate Certain Discriminatory Legislation against Indians in the United States, 67 Stat. 586 (August 15,1953). Note: repealed many of the Indian liquor laws that had been in place for generations.
- An Act to Confer Jurisdiction on the States of California, Minnesota, Nebraska, Oregon, and Wisconsin, with Respect to Criminal Offenses and Civil Causes of Action Committed or Arising on Indian Reservations within Such States, 67 Stat. 588 (August 15, 1953). Note: popularly known as Public Law 280.
- An Act to Provide for a Per Capita Distribution of Menominee Tribal Funds and Authorize the Withdrawal of the Menominee Tribe from Federal Jurisdiction, 68 Stat. 250 (June 17, 1954). Note: popularly known as the Menominee Termination Act.
- An Act Relative to Employment for Certain Adult Indians on or Near Indian Reservations, 70 Stat. 986 (August 3, 1956). Note: popularly known as the Vocational Training Act.
- An Act to Amend the Judicial Code to Permit Indian Tribes to Maintain Civil Actions in Federal District Courts without Regard to the $10,000 Limitation, 80 Stat. 880 (October 10, 1966).
- An Act to Prescribe Penalties for Certain Acts of Violence or Intimidation, and for Other Purposes, 82 Stat. 73, 77 (April 11, 1968). Note: under title II, "Rights of Indians," this act is popularly known as the Indian Civil Rights Act.
- An Act to Provide for the Settlement of Certain Land Claims of Alaska Natives, 85 Stat. 688 (December 18, 1971). Note: popularly known as the Alaska Native Claims Settlement Act.
- An Act to Repeal the Act Terminating Federal Supervision over the Property and Members of the Menominee Indian Tribe of Wisconsin, . . . 87 Stat. 770 (December 22, 1973). Note: popularly known as the Menominee Restoration Act.
- An Act to Provide for Financing the Economic Development of Indians and Indian Organizations, 88 Stat. 77 (April 12, 1974). Note: popularly known as the Indian Financing Act.
- An Act to Provide for Maximum Indian Participation in the Government and Education of the Indian People, 88 Stat. 2203 (January 4, 1975). Note: popularly known as the Indian Self-Determination and Education Assistance Act.
- A Joint Resolution Establishing the Policy for American Indian Religious Freedom, 92 Stat. 469 (August 11, 1978). Note: popularly known as the American Indian Religious Freedom Act.
- An Act to Establish Standards for the Placement of Indian Children in Foster or Adoptive Homes, to Prevent the Breakup of Indian Families, 92 Stat. 3069 (November 8, 1978). Note: popularly known as the Indian Child Welfare Act.
- An Act to Provide for the Settlement of Land Claims of Indians, Indian Nations and Tribes and Bands of Indians in the State of Maine, Including the Passamaquoddy Tribe, the Penobscot Nation, and the Houlton Band of Maliseet Indians, 94 Stat. 1785 (October 10, 1980). Note: popularly known as the Maine Indian Claims Settlement Act.
- An Act to Authorize the Purchase, Sale, and Exchange of Lands by Indian Tribes and by the Devils Lake Sioux Tribe of the Devils Lake Sioux Reservation of North Dakota Specifically, and for Other Purposes, 96 Stat. 2515, 2517 (January 12, 1983). Note: included a title II, the "Indian Land Consolidation Act."

- An Act to Settle Certain Claims of the Mashantucket Pequot Indians, 97 Stat. 851 (October 18, 1983). Note: popularly known as the Mashantucket Pequot Indian Claims Settlement Act.
- An Act Entitled the Indian Self-Determination and Education Assistance Act Amendments of 1988, 102 Stat. 2285 (October 5, 1988). Note: popularly known as the Indian Self-Determination and Education Assistance Act Amendments of 1988.
- An Act to Regulate Gaming on Indian Lands, 102 Stat. 2467 (October 17, 1988). Note: popularly known as the Indian Gaming Regulatory Act.
- An Act to Establish Procedures for Review of Tribal Constitutions and Bylaws or Amendments Thereto Pursuant to the Act of June 18, 1934, 102 Stat. 2938 (November 1, 1988).
- An Act to Provide for the Protection of Native American Graves, and for Other Purposes, 104 Stat. 3048 (November 16, 1990). Note: popularly known as the Native American Graves Protection and Repatriation Act.
- An Act to Assist the Development of Tribal Judicial Systems, and for Other Purposes, 107 Stat. 2004 (December 3, 1993). Note: popularly known as the Indian Tribal Justice Act.
- An Act to Amend the American Indian Religious Freedom Act to Provide for the Traditional Use of Peyote by Indians for Religious Purposes, 108 Stat. 3125 (October 6, 1994). Note: popularly known as the American Indian Religious Freedom Act Amendments of 1994.
- An Act to Reform the Management of Indian Trust Funds, and for Other Purposes, 108 Stat. 4239 (October 25 1994). Note: popularly known as the American Indian Trust Fund Management Reform Act of 1994.
- An Act to Specify the Terms of Contracts Entered into by the United States and Indian Tribal Organizations under the Indian Self-Determination and Education Assistance Act and to Provide for Tribal Self-Governance, and for Other Purposes, 108 Stat. 4250 (October 25, 1994). Note: popularly known as the Indian Self-Governance Act of 1994.
- An Act to Provide Federal Assistance for Indian Tribes in a Manner That Recognizes the Right of Tribal Self-Governance, and for Other Purposes, 110 Stat. 4016 (October 26, 1996). Note: popularly known as the Native American Housing Assistance and Self-Determination Act of 1996.
- An Act to Reduce the Fractionated Ownership of Indian Lands and for Other Purposes, 114 Stat. 1991 (November 7, 2000). Note: popularly known as the Indian Land Consolidation Act Amendments of 2000.
- An Act to Amend the Indian Land Consolidation Act to Improve Provisions Relating to Probate of Trust and Restricted Land, and for Other Purposes, 118 Stat. 1773 (October 27, 2004). Note: popularly known as the American Indian Probate Reform Act of 2004.
- An Act to Amend the Native American Programs Act of 1974 to Provide for the Revitalization of Native American Languages, 120 Stat. 2705 (December 14, 2006). Note: popularly known as the Esther Martinez Native American Languages Preservation Act of 2006.
- An Act to Reauthorize the Program of the Secretary of Housing and Urban Development for Loan Guarantees for Indian Housing, 121 Stat. 229 (June 18, 2007).

Note: popularly known as the Native American Home Ownership Opportunity Act of 2007.

- An Act to Reauthorize the Programs for Housing Assistance for Native Americans, 122 Stat. 4319 (October 14, 2008). Note: popularly known as the Native American Housing Assistance and Self-determination Reauthorization Act of 2008.
- An Act to Require the Issuance of Medals to recognize the Dedication and Valor of Native American Code Talkers, 122 Stat. 4774 (October 15, 2008). Note: popularly known as the Code Talkers Recognition Act of 2008.
- An Act to Repeal Section 10 (f) of Public Law 93-531, commonly known as the 'Bennett Freeze,' 123 Stat. 1611 (May 8, 2009). Note: popularly known as the Bennett Freeze Repeal Act of 2009.
- An Act to protect Indian arts and crafts, and for other purposes. 124 Stat. 2258 Slip Copy (July 29, 2010). Note: popularly known as the Tribal Law and Order Act of 2010.

Selected Internet Resources

THIS IS A SELECTED list of Internet resources that should prove useful to those interested in gaining more insight into indigenous political and economic issues. Neither the author nor the publisher can verify that all the information on these various sites is accurate. A number of tribes have their own home pages and readers are encouraged to visit their sites for information relevant to specific tribal nations.

American Indian Data

www.census.gov/population/www/socdemo/race/indian.html
This site provides statistical and tabular data on Indian reservation housing, social and economic characteristics of Indians, and so forth, drawn from the 1990 U.S. Census.

American Indian Policy Center

www.airpi.org
This organization's mission is to provide policymakers and the public with accurate information on American Indian political and legal issues. It includes links to forums, research articles, and news.

Bureau of Indian Affairs

www.bia.gov/
This is the official site of the BIA, provided by the Department of the Interior. It provides important information on federally recognized tribes and valuable data on many topics. A current list of federally recognized tribes and tribal directories can be accessed from their document library.

Index of Native American Organizations on the Internet

www.hanksville.org/NAresources/indices/NAorg.html
This site provides a list, with links, to over one hundred Indian organizations, including tribes, interest groups, and cultural associations.

Index of Native American Resources on the Internet

www.hanksville.org/NAresources/
This site provides links to a large number of Indian resources, including culture, language, and education pages.

Indian Country Today Online

www.indiancountrytoday.com/
This is the largest Indian newspaper in the United States.

National Congress of American Indians

www.ncai.org/
This is the home page of the largest intertribal organization in the United States.

National Indian Gaming Association

www.indiangaming.org/
This site provides useful publications, reports, and resources pertaining to American Indian gaming. AIGA's website also provides information on training, employment, and network opportunities.

Native American Documents Project

www2.csusm.edu/nadp/
This home page provides data and published reports from the Commission of Indian Affairs and the Board of Indian Commissioners for 1871, allotment data from 1870, and information on the Rogue River War and Siletz Reservation.

Native American/Educational/Environmental/Resources

www.usa.gov/Government/Tribal.shtml
This home page provides comprehensive links to environmental, legal, cultural, and educational pages as well as employment and economic development opportunities. Also provides links to national tribal organizations, regional tribal councils, and Tribal nation websites.

Native American Rights Fund

www.narf.org/
The Native American Rights Fund (NARF) is a nonprofit organization that provides legal representation and assistance to native nations. This site contains important updates on judicial decisions and congressional legislation pertaining to native nations and peoples.

Notes

Notes to Preface

1. See Anne M. McCulloch, "Perspectives on Native Americans in Political Science," *Teaching Political Science: Politics in Perspective* 16, no. 3 (1989): 93–98.

2. Franke Wilmer, Michael E. Melody, and Margaret Maier Murdock, "Including Native American Perspectives in the Political Science Curriculum," *P.S.: Political Science & Politics* 27, no. 2 (June 1994): 269–76.

Notes to Introduction

1. Rob Capriccioso, "White House Announces Nation-to-Nation Conference," *Indian Country Today,* October 16, 2009.

2. The White House, Office of the Press Secretary, "Remarks by the President During the Opening of the Tribal Nations Conference and Interactive Discussion with Tribal Leaders," Department of Interior, Washington, D.C.

3. Rob Capriccioso, "Living history: 'One Who Helps People throughout the Land' Elected 44th President, Native Voters Played a Big Role." *Indian Country Today,* November 12, 2008, p. 5.

4. Staff and wire reports, "Obama Promises Native Americans Place on Agenda," *USA Today,* November 5, 2009.

5. Steven Argue, "Abortion Banned on Pine Ridge, Cecilia Fire Thunder Removed From Presidency," June 15, 2006. Retrieved November 19, 2009, from www.indybay.org/newsitems/2006/06/15/18280789.php?show_comments=1.

6. Argue, "Abortion Banned."

7. Aguilar, "The Power of Thunder," *AlterNet,* April 4, 2006. Retrieved from http://www.alternet.org/story/34314.

8. Aguilar, "The Power of Thunder"; "We the People: American Indians and Alaska Natives in the United States" Census 2000 Special Reports. Issued February 2006. U.S. Department of Commerce.

9. Aguilar, "The Power of Thunder."

10. Jodi Rave, "Fire Thunder under Fire," *Rapid City Journal,* July 29, 2006.

11. Bruce Duthu, *American Indians and the Law* (New York: Penguin, 2008), 144.

12. Monica Davey, "As Tribal Leaders, Women Still Fight Old Views," *New York Times*, February 4, 2006, p. A1, A9.

13. Treaty with the Makah, January 21, 1855, 12 U.S. Statutes at Large (hereafter, Stat.) 939.

14. Charlotte Cote, "Post(?)-Colonial Discourse and the Re-invention of the Indian as Savage: Makah/Nuuchahnulth Whaling in the 20th Century." Paper presented at the annual American Studies Association conference, Montreal, October 28–November 1, 1999, 4.

15. Sam Howe Verhovek, "After the Hunt, Bitter Protest and Salty Blubber," *New York Times*, May 19, 1999, 14(N).

16. Alex Tizon, "Recent Makah Whale Hunt Spurs Racist Comments Against Indians," *Seattle Times*, May 30, 1999, 24.

17. Wayne Johnson, "Harvest from the Sea," *New York Times*, May 21, 1999, 27(N).

18. *Metcalf v. Doloy*, 214 F.3d 1135.

19. *Anderson v. Evans*, 314 F.3d 1006.

20. *Anderson v. Evans*, 350 F.3d 815.

21. *Anderson v. Evans*, 371 F.3d 475.

22. *Seattle Times* Staff, "Makah Tribal Member in Illegal Whale Hunt Issues Statement," *Seattle Times*, September 14, 2007.

23. J. Patrick Coolican, "Tribe Wants to Keep Whaling Despite Losing Court Appeal," *Seattle Times*, December 2, 2003, B1.

24. *Seminole v. United States*, 316 U.S. 286, 296-97 (1942).

25. Statement of Judge Royce C. Lamberth in *Cobell v. Babbitt*, 37 F. Supp. 2d 6, 99–100 (1999) in concluding his opinion holding the secretaries of interior and justice in contempt of court for their failure to produce the court-ordered records involving the Indian trust fund accounts.

26. Timothy Egan, "Poor Indians on Rich Land Fight a U.S. Maze," *New York Times*, March 9, 1999, A20.

27. Egan, "Poor Indians," A20.

28. John E. Echohawk, "Testimony before the United States Senate Committee on Indian Affairs," Executive Director, Native American Rights Fund, March 29, 2007.

29. Charlie Savage, "U.S. Will Settle Indian Lawsuit For $3.4 Billion," *New York Times*, December 9, 2009, p. A1.

30. Echohawk, "Testimony."

31. *Cobell v. Babbitt*, 39 F. Supp. 2d 6, 15 (1999).

32. Timothy Egan, "Indians Win Round in Fight on Trust Funds," *New York Times*, February 23, 1999, A1.

33. Egan, "Indians Win Round," A1.

34. *New York Times*, "Citing Government's Failure, Judge to Oversee Indian Accounts," December 22, 1999, A18.

35. John Files, "For 4th Time, Judge Seeks to Shield Indian Data," *New York Times*, October 22, 2005, p. A22.

36. John Files, "Indian Fund Investigator Angrily Quits," *New York Times*, April 7, 2004, A16.

37. Files, "Indian Fund," A16.

38. 2005 WL 1618744.

39. 2005 WL 1618744.

40. Charlie Savage, "U.S. Will Settle Indian Lawsuit For $3.4 Billion," *New York Times*, December 9, 2009, p. A4.

41. "Statement of the President on the Settlement of Cobell Class-Action Lawsuit on Indian Trust Management." Retrieved from www.whitehouse.gov/the-press-office/statement-president-settlement-cobell-class-action-lawsuit-indian-trust-management.

42. Statement of Ken Salazar, Secretary of the Interior, on proposed settlement of *Cobell v. Salazar* before the Committee on Indian Affairs United States Senate, December 17, 2009. Retrieved from indian.senate.gov/public/_files/KenSalazartestimony.pdf.

43. Charlie Savage, "U.S. Will Settle Indian Lawsuit For $3.4 Billion," *New York Times,* December 9, 2009, p. A4

44. Justice William Brennan in a dissenting opinion in *Lyng v. Northwest Indian Cemetery Protective Association,* 485 U.S. 439, 460 (1988).

45. Executive Order No. 13007, "Indian Sacred Sites," *Federal Register* 61, no. 104 (24 May 1996).

46. *Bear Lodge v. Babbitt,* 2 F. Supp. 2d 1448, 1452 (1998).

47. *Bear Lodge v. Babbitt,* D.C. No. 96-CV-063-D (1999).

48. H.R. 2419-366, section 8104

49. *Navajo Nation v. U.S. Forest Service,* 535 F.3d 1058

50. Libertad, "Supreme Court Affirms Tribes Have No Religious Rights," June 17, 2009. Retrieved January 10, 2010, from http://arizona.indymedia.org/news/2009/06/74502.php.

Notes to Chapter 1

1. U.S. Congress, *American Indian Policy Review Commission: Final Report,* vol. 1 (Washington, D.C.: Government Printing Office, 1977), 3.

2. See, e.g., Haunani-Kay Trask, *From a Native Daughter: Colonialism and Sovereignty in Hawai'i* (Monroe: Common Courage, 1993); Roger MacPherson Furrer, ed., *He Alo á He Alo (Face to Face): Hawaiian Voices on Sovereignty* (Honolulu: American Friends Service Committee-Hawai'i, 1993).

3. 528 U.S. 495 (2000).

4. "Native Hawaiian Reconciliation Draft Report Released," www.justice.gov/opa/pr/2000/August/494otj.htm.

5. J. Khaulani Kauanui, "Kauanui: Understanding Both Versions of the Akaka Bill," *Indian Country Today,* January 15, 2010.

6. Dean E. Murphy, "Bill Giving Native Hawaiian Sovereignty Is Too Much for Some, Too Little for Others," *New York Times,* July 17, 2005, 12.

7. J. Kehaulani Kauanui, "Precarious Positions: Native Hawaiian and U.S. Federal Recognition," *The Contemporary Pacific,* 17, no. 1 (2005): 2.

8. Vine Deloria Jr., "The American Indian Image in North America," *Encyclopedia of Indians of the Americas,* vol. 1 (St. Clair Shores, Mich.: Scholarly Press, 1974), 43.

9. Paula D. McClain and Joseph Stewart Jr., "Can We All Get Along?" *Racial and Ethnic Minorities in American Politics,* 4th ed. (Boulder, Colo.: Westview, 2006), 6, citing John Higham, *Strangers in the Land: Patterns of American Nativism, 1860–1925* (Westport, Conn.: Greenwood, 1963).

10. 180 U.S. 261 (1901).

11. Felix S. Cohen, *Handbook of Federal Indian Law,* reprint ed. (Albuquerque: University of New Mexico Press, 1972), 268.

12. Jack Utter, *American Indians: Answers to Today's Questions* (Lake Ann, Mich.: National Woodlands, 1993), 30–31.

13. William Quinn Jr., "Federal Acknowledgment of American Indian Tribes? The Historical Development of a Legal Concept," *American Journal of Legal History* 34 (October 1990): 331–63.

14. 56 Federal Register 47, 325 (1991).

15. 25 Code of Federal Regulations 83.7 (a)–(g) (1991).

16. 25 U.S.C. chapter 1, section 1, 961.

17. 25 U.S.C. chapter 1, 962.

18. William W. Quinn Jr., "Federal Acknowledgment of American Indian Tribes: Authority, Judicial Interposition, and 25 C.F.R. Sec. 83," *American Indian Law Review* 17 (Fall 1992): 48.

19. Quinn, "Federal Acknowledgment of American Indian Tribes," 52.

20. Felix Cohen, "The Erosion of Indian Rights, 1950–1953: A Case Study in Bureaucracy," *Yale Law Journal* 62 (February 1953): 352.

21. Letter from Carol A. Bacon, acting director of the Office of Tribal Services, Bureau of Indian Affairs, 3 December 1991. The author has a copy of the letter.

22. 108 Stat., 709.

23. See U.S. Congress, House, "A Bill to Provide for Administrative Procedures to Extend Federal Recognition to Certain Indian Groups, and for Other Purposes," 105th Cong., 2d sess., 1998, H. Rept. 1154. As of this writing—May 1999—none of these bills has become law.

24. Ellen Barry, "Agency Willing to Relinquish Power to Recognize Tribes," *Boston Globe,* May 26, 2000, B1.

25. Government Accounting Office, *Indian Issues: Timeliness of the Tribal Recognition Process Has Improved, but It Will Take Years to Clear the Existing Backlog of Petitions,* GAO-05-347T, February 10, 2005 (Washington, D.C.: GAO), 9.

26. 118 U.S. 948 (1998).

27. See, e.g., Trask, *From a Native Daughter,* and Anaya, "The Native Hawaiian People," 309.

28. Allogan Slagle, "Unfinished Justice: Completing the Restoration and Acknowledgment of California Indian Tribes," *American Indian Journal* 13, no. 4 (Fall 1989): 325–45.

29. William W. Quinn Jr., "The Southeast Syndrome: Notes on Indian Descendant Recruitment Organizations and Their Perceptions of Native American Culture," *American Indian Quarterly* 14, no. 2 (Spring 1990): 147–54.

30. Jackie J. Kim, "The Indian Federal Recognition Procedures Act of 1995: A Congressional Solution to an Administrative Morass," *The Administrative Law Journal of the American University* 9, no. 3 (Fall 1995): 899–932.

31. See "Office of Federal Acknowledgment," www.bia.gov/WhoWeAre/AS-IA/OFA/index .htm, for statistical details of the acknowledgment project's efforts.

32. Bureau of Indian Affairs, "State Summary of Acknowledgment Cases." Retrieved June 15, 2010, from www.bia.gov/idc/groups/public/documents/text/idc-001217.pdf.

33. Bureau of Indian Affairs, "State Summary."

34. Donald Fixico, *Termination and Relocation: Federal Indian Policy, 1945–1960* (Albuquerque: University of New Mexico Press, 1986).

35. 67 Stat., B132.

36. 110 Stat., 130.

37. N.C. Public Laws, 1953, chapter 874, p. 747.

38. 70 Stat., 254.

39. David E. Wilkins, "Breaking into the Intergovernmental Matrix: The Lumbee Tribe's Efforts to Secure Federal Acknowledgment," *Publius: The Journal of Federalism* 23 (Fall 1993): 123–42.

40. McClain and Stewart, "Can We All Get Along?" 7.

41. Bart Vogel, "Who Is an Indian in Federal Indian Law?" in *Studies in American Indian Law,* ed. Ralph Johnson (Pullman: Washington State University, 1970), 53.

42. C. Matthew Snipp, *American Indians: The First of This Land* (New York: Russell Sage Foundation, 1989), 34.

43. Snipp, *American Indians,* 33.

44. Cohen, *Handbook,* 2.

45. Cohen, *Handbook,* 2.

46. 29 Stat., 321.

47. Abdul G. Kahn, *Report on the Indian Definition Study* (Washington, D.C.: Department of Education, 1980).

48. Kahn, *Report on the Indian Definition Study,* 56.

49. Joane Nagel, *American Indian Ethnic Renewal: Red Power and the Resurgence of Identity and Culture* (New York: Oxford University Press, 1996), 243.

50. There is finally an increasing body of literature addressing the subject of blood quantum and its effect on Native identity and the political status of tribal nations. See, for example, Miller's *Invisible Indigenes,* chapter 5; Erik M. Zissu, *Blood Matters: The Five Civilized Tribes and the Search for Unity in the Twentieth Century* (NY: Routledge, 2001); Circe Sturm, *Blood Politics: Race, Culture, and Identity in the Cherokee Nation of Oklahoma* (Berkeley: University of California Press, 2002); and Eva Marie Garroute, *Real Indians: Identity and the Survival of Native America* (Berkeley: University of California Press, 2003), especially chapter 2.

51. Leilani Clark, "Inner Circle Outcasts: Disenrollemt from American Indian Tribes Is on the Rise in California, and the Pomo Are No Different. Is It Simple Genealogy or Is It Simple Greed?" *News and Culture in the North Bay,* June 10, 2009.

52. Brian Stackes, "Planned Bureau of Indian Affairs Regulations Stir Concerns Among Tribal Leaders," *Indian Country Today,* August 18, 2000, 1.

53. Russell Thornton, "Tribal Membership Requirements and the Demography of 'Old' and 'New' Native Americans," in *Changing Numbers, Changing Needs: American Indian Demography and Public Health,* ed. Gary D. Sandefur, Ronald R. Rindfuss, and Barney Cohen (Washington, D.C.: National Academy Press, 1996), 110–11.

54. See, e.g., Vine Deloria Jr. and Raymond J. DeMallie, comp., *Documents of American Indian Diplomacy: Treaties, Agreements, and Conventions, 1775–1979,* 2 vols. (Norman: University of Oklahoma Press, 1999); and Robert A. Williams Jr., *Linking Arms Together: American Indian Treaty Visions of Law and Peace, 1600–1800* (New York: Oxford University Press, 1997).

55. 16 Stat., 566.

56. 7 Stat., 391.

57. 7 Stat., 391.

58. Cesare Marino, "Reservations," in *Native America in the Twentieth Century: An Encyclopedia,* ed. Mary B. Davis (New York: Garland, 1996), 544–56.

59. Elinor Langer, "Special Issue: Famous are the Flowers: Hawaiian Resistance Then- and Now," *The Nation* (April 28, 2008), 15–30.

60. *Hawaii et. al., v. Office of Hawaiian Affairs, et. al.* 129 S. Ct. 1436 (2009).

61. Joint Resolution to Acknowledge the 100th Anniversary of the January 17, 1893, Overthrow of the Kingdom of Hawaii (Apology Resolution), Pub. L. No. 103-150, 107 Stat. 1510.

62. *Hawaii et. al., v. Office of Hawaiian Affairs, et. al.* 129 S. Ct. 1436 (2009).

63. Vine Deloria Jr. and Clifford M. Lytle, *American Indians, American Justice* (Austin: University of Texas Press, 1983), 58.

64. Deloria and Lytle, *American Indians,* 58.

65. *Osage Nation v. Irby* (Oklahoma Tax Commission) 10th Circ. No. 09-5050 (2010).

66. See Robert F. Heizer, *The Destruction of California Indians* (Lincoln: University of Nebraska Press, 1993) for a first-rate account of what these nations experienced from 1847 to 1865.

67. Title 18, U.S. Code, section 1151.

68. Matthew Snipp, "American Indians," in Susan B. Carter, Scott Sigmund Gartner, Michael R. Haines, Alan L. Olmstead, Richard Sutch, and Gavin Wright, editors, *Historical Statistics of the United States: Millennial Edition* (Online Version) (New York: Cambridge University Press, 2006).

69. www.census.gov/main/www/cen2000.

70. Russell Thornton, *American Indian Holocaust and Survival: A Population History Since 1492* (Norman: University of Oklahoma Press, 1987).

71. "Overview of Race and Hispanic Origin," Census 2000 Brief Issued March 2001, by Elizabeth M. Greico and Rachel C. Cassidy. www.census.gov/c2kbr01-1.pdf.

72. American Indian and Alaska Native Heritage Month: November 2009," www.census.gov/newsroom/releases/archives/facts_for_features_special_editions/cb09-ff20.html

73. Russell Thornton, "What the Census Doesn't Count," *New York Times,* March 23, 2001, A21.

74. C. Matthew Snipp, "The Size and Distribution of the American Indian Population: Fertility, Mortality, Migration, and Residence," in *Changing Numbers, Changing Needs: American*

Indian Demography and Public Health, ed. Gary D. Sandefur, Ronald R. Rindfuss, and Barney Cohen (Washington, D.C.: National Academy Press, 1996), 42–43.

75. "American Indian and Alaska Heritage Month. November 2009," www.census.gov/ newsroom/releases/archives/facts_for_features_special_editions/cb09-ff20.html.

76. Snipp, *American Indians: The First of This Land,* 171.

77. Snipp, *American Indians: The First of This Land,* 165.

78. Lawrence H. Fuchs, *The American Kaleidoscope* (Hanover, N.H.: Wesleyan University Press, 1990), 329.

79. Gale Courey Toensing, "NCAI Launches 'Indian Country Counts' Census Campaign," *Indian Country Today,* 29, no. 20 (October 21, 2009).

Notes to Chapter 2

1. Milner S. Ball, "Constitution, Court, Indian Tribes," *American Bar Foundation Research Journal* 1 (1987): 1–139.

2. Bonnie Tsui, *New York Times,* August 23, 2009.

3. Sarah Wheaton, *New York Times,* August 27, 2009.

4. Emily Jones, *Star Tribune,* May 1, 2009.

5. Danny Hakim, *New York Times,* September 25, 2009.

6. Charlie Savage, *New York Times,* December 9, 2009.

7. See Vine Deloria Jr., *Red Earth, White Lies* (Boulder, Colo.: Fulcrum, 1996) for a critical, indigenous analysis of the Bering Strait theory and tribal responses to such scientific speculation.

8. Jeanette Wolfley and Susan Johnson, "Tribal Sovereignty," National Council of State Legislatures, Denver, CO, and Washington, DC, 1996.

9. See Vine Deloria Jr. and Raymond J. DeMallie's recent two-volume study, *Documents of American Indian Diplomacy: Treaties, Agreements, and Conventions, 1775–1979* (Norman: University of Oklahoma Press, 1999) for an outstanding treatment of this diverse diplomatic record.

10. See David E. Wilkins, "Convoluted Essence: Indian Rights and the Federal Trust Doctrine," *Native Americas* XIX, no. 1 (Spring 1997): 24–31 for an analysis of the conflicting federal definitions. And see David E. Wilkins, "'With the Greatest Respect and Fidelity': A Cherokee Vision of the 'Trust' Doctrine," *The Social Science Journal* 34, no. 4 (1997): 495–510 for a discussion of one tribe's views on what "trust" means to them. The U.S. Supreme Court in two companion but contradictory cases, *United States v. White Mountain Apache Tribe,* 537 U.S. 465 (2003) and *United States v. Navajo Nation,* 537 U.S. 488 (2003), showed how difficult it is to arrive at a consistent definition of what the trust relationship is. In White Mountain the court held that the Department of Interior had a fiduciary—a trust—duty to maintain a former military post, Fort Apache, that had been given to the tribe. But in *Navajo Nation* the same court said that the federal government had not violated its trust duties to the Navajo people by acting in a coal company's interest rather than the interest of the tribe.

11. Memorandum of November 5, 2009—Tribal Consultation, *Federal Register,* Vol. 74, No. 215, Monday, November 9, 2009.

12. Vine Deloria Jr., "The Distinctive Status of Indian Rights," in *The Plains Indians of the Twentieth Century,* ed. Peter Iverson (Norman: University of Oklahoma Press, 1985), 241.

13. However, the United States has asserted that it wields "plenary power" over Puerto Rico, a commonwealth, as well. See Nell Jessup Newton, "Federal Power over Indians: Its Sources, Scope, and Limitations," *University of Pennsylvania Law Review* 132 (1984): 195–288; Laurence M. Hauptman, "Congress, Plenary Power, and the American Indian, 1870–1992," in *Exiled in the Land of the Free,* ed. Oren Lyons and John Mohawk (Santa Fe, N.Mex.: Clear Light, 1992), 318–36; and David E. Wilkins, "The U.S. Supreme Court's Explication of 'Federal Plenary Power':

An Analysis of Case Law Affecting Tribal Sovereignty, 1886–1914," *American Indian Quarterly* 18, no. 3 (Winter 1994): 349–68.

14. 124 S. Ct. 1628 (2004).

15. 124 S. Ct. 1634 (2004).

16. Deloria, "Distinctive Status," 240.

17. *Johnson v. McIntosh,* 21 U.S. (8 Wheat.) 543 (1823).

18. *Tee-Hit-Ton v. United States,* 348 U.S. 273 (1955).

19. *United States v. Antelope,* 430 U.S. 641 (1977).

20. In the 1950s and 1960s Congress enacted several "termination" laws in which the government divested itself of its legal obligations and moral responsibilities to certain tribes and in effect denied the right of those tribes to legally exist in the eyes of the federal government.

21. Ralph W. Johnson and E. Susan Crystal, "Indians and Equal Protection," *Washington Law Review* 54 (1979).

22. Wolfley and Johnson, "Tribal Sovereignty," 3.

23. Sam Deloria, "Introduction," in *Indian Tribal Sovereignty and Treaty Rights* (Albuquerque, N.Mex.: La Confluencia, 1978), s23.

24. See David E. Wilkins and Tsianina Lomawaima, *Uneven Ground: American Indian Sovereignty and Federal Law* (Norman: University of Oklahoma Press, 2001): Chapter 6, "'No Reasonable Plea': Disclaimers in Tribal-State Relations," discusses these important clauses in detail.

25. 7 Stat., 156.

26. 25 Stat., 392.

27. 41 Stat., 350.

28. 3 Stat., 516.

29. 60 U.S. (19 How.) 393, 404–5 (1857).

30. Senate Committee on the Judiciary, *Report to the Senate on the Effect of the Fourteenth Amendment to the Constitution upon the Indian Tribes of the Country,* 41st Cong., 3d sess., 1870, S. Rept. 268, 11.

31. House, Commissioner of Indian Affairs, Annual Report 42d Cong., 3d sess, 1872, H. Exec. Doc. 1, 400.

32. 112 U.S. 94, 99 (1884).

33. *Seventh Annual Report of the Board of Indian Commissioners for the Year 1875* (Washington, D.C.: Government Printing Office, 1876), 13–14.

34. Felix S. Cohen, *Handbook of Indian Law,* reprint ed. (Albuquerque: University of New Mexico Press, 1972), 154, quoting from Senator Orville H. Platte.

35. 26 Stat., 81, 99–100.

36. Vine Deloria Jr. and Clifford M. Lytle, *American Indians, American Justice* (Austin: University of Texas Press, 1983), 220.

37. U.S. Supreme Court. Records and Briefs. Transcript of Record. *The United States v. Fred Nice.* Brief for the United States by Solicitor General John W. Davis, November 1915, 22.

38. 241 U.S. 591 (1916).

39. 241 U.S. 591, 598 (1916).

40. 41 Stat., 350.

41. 43 Stat., 253.

42. See Franke Wilmer, *The Indigenous Voice in World Politics* (Newbury Park, Calif.: Sage, 1993), for an excellent treatment of the persistent efforts of indigenous peoples, both in the United States and in other nation-states, to gain full admittance before the United Nations as separately recognized sovereign entities.

43. U.S. Attorney General Hugh Swinton Legare, as quoted in House, *Commissioner of Indian Affairs Annual Report,* 32d Cong., 1st sess. (1851), H. Exec. Doc. 2, 274.

44. Senate, *Report on the Effect of the Fourteenth Amendment,* 10.

45. Deloria, "Introduction," s24.

46. *Talton v. Mayes,* 163 U.S. 376, 384 (1896).

47. *Lyng v. Northwest Indian Cemetery Protective Association,* 485 U.S. 439 (1988) and *Employment Division, Dept. of Human Resources v. Smith,* 494 U.S. 872 (1990).

48. See *Groundhog v. Keeler,* 442 F. 2d 674 (1971).

49. *Worcester v. Georgia,* 31 U.S. (6 Pet.) 515 (1832).

50. *Cherokee Nation v. Georgia,* 30 U.S. (5 Pet.) 1 (1831).

51. See, e.g., Ex Parte Crow Dog, 109 U.S. 556 (1883), *Merrion v. Jicarilla Apache Tribe,* 455 U.S. 130 (1982), and *United States v. Lara,* 124 S. Ct. 1628 (2004).

52. *Oliphant v. Suquamish,* 435 U.S. 191 (1978).

53. *Seminole v. United States,* 316 U.S. 286 (1942).

54. *United States v. Kagama,* 118 U.S. 375, 383–84 (1886).

55. *Elk v. Wilkins,* 112 U.S. 94, 100 (1884).

56. *Cherokee Tobacco,* 78 U.S. (11 Wall.) 616 (1871).

57. *Perrin v. United States,* 232 U.S. 478 (1914).

58. *Lone Wolf v. Hitchcock,* 187 U.S. 553 (1903).

59. *Worcester v. Georgia,* 31 U.S. (6 Pet.) 515 (1832).

60. The Supreme Court has rendered several recent decisions that ominously point in this direction: see, e.g., *Nevada v. Hicks* (2001), *Inyo County v. Paiute-Shoshone Indians of Bishop Community of Bishop Colony* (2003), and *City of Sherrill, New York v. Oneida Indian Nation of New York* (2005). Two recent articles also discuss this disturbing and constitutionally problematic change of direction in favor of states' rights over indigenous sovereignty: David H. Getches, "Beyond Indian Law: The Rehnquist Court's Pursuit of States' Rights, Color-Blind Justice and Mainstream Values," *Minnesota Law Review,* vol. 86, no. 2 (December 2001): 267–362; and David E. Wilkins and Keith Richotte, "The Rehnquist Court and Indigenous Rights: The Expedited Diminution of Native Powers of Governance," *Publius: The Journal of Federalism,* vol. 33, no. 3 (Summer 2003): 83–110.

61. For instance, the doctrine of discovery is sometimes seen as a preemptive legal principle that limited the rights of competing European states and the United States and merely provided the "discovering" state with the exclusive right to purchase such lands as the tribes were willing to sell; but sometimes discovery is treated as a principle that irrefutably vested legal ownership of America in the discovering states, thereby permanently diminishing the land rights of tribes to the status of an occupant—a tenant if you will—with a lesser beneficial title and no power to sell.

62. Phillip S. Deloria, "The Era of Indian Self-Determination: An Overview," in *Indian Self-Rule,* ed. Ken Philp (Salt Lake City, Utah: Howe Brothers, 1986).

63. Vine Deloria Jr., "'Reserving to Themselves': Treaties and the Powers of Indian Tribes," *Arizona Law Review* 38 (Fall 1996), 978.

64. Robert H. White, *Tribal Assets: The Rebirth of Native America* (New York: Henry Holt, 1991).

65. David E. Wilkins, "Modernization, Colonialism, Dependency: How Appropriate Are These Models for Providing an Explanation of North American Indian 'Underdevelopment'"? *Ethnic and Racial Studies* 16, no. 3 (July 1993): 390–419. And see the U.S. Commission on Civil Rights, *A Quiet Crisis: Federal Funding and Unmet Needs in Indian Country* (Washington, D.C.: Government Printing Office, 2003).

66. Deloria, "Indian Self-Determination," 193.

67. Deloria, "Indian Self-Determination," 193.

68. Deloria, "Indian Self-Determination," 193.

69. Deloria, "Indian Self-Determination," 193.

Notes to Chapter 3

1. "A Visiting Englishman, 1765," in *Introduction to Tribal Government,* ed. Michael Hansen (Yerington, Nev.: Yerington Paiute Tribe, 1985), 20.

2. Franke Wilmer, Michael E. Melody, and Margaret Maier Murdock, "Including Native American Perspectives in the Political Science Curriculum," *PS: Political Science & Politics* 27, no. 2 (June 1994): 272.

3. Thanks to Robert B. Porter, whose work contributed to our understanding of these categories. See his article, "Strengthening Tribal Sovereignty Through Government Reform: What Are the Issues?" *Kansas Journal of Law and Public Policy* 7 (1997).

4. U.S. Congress. *American Indian Policy Review Commission: Report on Tribal Government* (Washington, D.C.: Government Printing Office, 1976), 28.

5. Vine Deloria Jr., *Red Earth, White Lies: Native Americans and the Myth of Scientific Fact* (New York: Scribner, 1995), 97.

6. U.S. Commission on Civil Rights, *Indian Tribes: A Continuing Quest for Survival* (Washington, D.C.: Government Printing Office, 1981), 15.

7. As Deloria put it, even the acknowledged dean of American Bering Strait scholars, William Laughlin, provides little concrete evidence of an Indian migration. Laughlin says, "Conditions in the interior [of Alaska] were severe, and likely only a few of its inhabitants found their way into North America; these wanderers probably became the ancestors of American Indians." But as Deloria notes, "Notice that Laughlin does not say for certain that any of these inhabitants crossed the Bering Strait—he only says it was 'likely' that a few people did. We get no evidence at all that any Paleo-Indians were within a thousand miles of Alaska during this time. No sites, trails, or signs of habitation are cited" (Deloria, *Red Earth, White Lies*, 87).

8. James Wilson, *The Earth Shall Weep: A History of Native America* (New York: Atlantic Monthly Press, 1998), 21.

9. James Wilson, *The Original Americans: U.S. Indians, Minority Rights Group Report no. 31* (London: Benjamin Franklin House, 1976), 11–12.

10. Franke Wilmer, *The Indigenous Voice in World Politics* (Newbury Park, Calif.: Sage, 1993), 67.

11. Robert A. Williams Jr., *Linking Arms Together: American Indian Treaty Visions of Law and Peace, 1600–1800* (New York: Oxford University Press, 1997), 31.

12. Vine Deloria Jr. and Clifford M. Lytle, *American Indians, American Justice* (Austin: University of Texas Press, 1983), 82.

13. Deloria and Lytle, *American Indians*, 82–83.

14. Sharon O'Brien, *American Indian Tribal Governments* (Norman: University of Oklahoma Press, 1989), 17.

15. Arthur C. Parker, "The Constitution of the Five Nations," *New York State Museum Bulletin* 184 (1916): 7–158.

16. Felix S. Cohen, *Handbook of Federal Indian Law*, reprint ed. (Albuquerque: University of New Mexico Press, 1972; originally published 1942), 128.

17. O'Brien, *American Indian Tribal*, 18.

18. Donald A. Grinde, "Iroquois Political Theory and the Roots of American Democracy," in *Exiled in the Land of the Free: Democracy, Indian Nations, and the U.S. Constitution*, ed. Oren Lyons and John Mohawk (Santa Fe, N.Mex.: Clear Light, 1992), 238.

19. Deloria and Lytle, *American Indians*, 88.

20. Grinde, "Iroquois Political Theory," 239.

21. Grinde, "Iroquois Political Theory," 242.

22. See, e.g., Bruce E. Johansen, *Forgotten Founders: How the American Indian Helped Shape Democracy* (Boston, Mass.: The Harvard Common Press, 1982); Donald A. Grinde Jr. and Bruce E. Johansen, *Exemplar of Liberty: Native America and the Evolution of Democracy* (Los Angeles, Calif.: American Indian Studies Center, 1991); and Lyons and Mohawk, *Exiled in the Land* (1992).

23. Vine Deloria Jr., "Anthros, Indians, and Planetary Reality," in *Indians and Anthropologists: Vine Deloria, Jr., and the Critique of Anthropology*, ed. Thomas Biolsi and Larry J. Zimmerman (Tucson: University of Arizona Press, 1997), 217. But see also Jerry D. Stubben, "The Indigenous Influence Theory of American Democracy," *Social Science Quarterly* 81, no. 3 (September 2000):

716–31. Stubben did an analysis of much of the extant literature and concluded that "indigenous societies influenced European and American societies and the democratic theories and institutions derived by these societies during the sixteenth to eighteenth centuries, not to the high degree promoted by Grinde, Johansen, and others, but not to the very limited degree that Payne, Levy, and Tooker espouse" (727–28).

24. James J. Lopach, Margery Hunter Brown, and Richmond L. Clow, *Tribal Government Today: Politics on Montana Indian Reservation* (Boulder, Colo.: Westview, 1990), 177.

25. Phillip Wearne, *Return of the Indian: Conquest and Revival in the Americas* (Philadelphia: Temple University Press, 1996), 50.

26. See, e.g., Jack Weatherford, *Indian Givers: How the Indians of the Americas Transformed the World* (New York: Fawcett Columbine, 1988) and Vine Deloria Jr., *Indian Education in America* (Boulder, Colo.: American Indian Science and Engineering Society, 1991).

27. Wearne, *Return of the Indian,* 52.

28. O'Brien, *American Indian Tribal,* 14.

29. Tom Holm, "Indian Concepts of Authority and the Crisis in Tribal Government," *Social Science Journal* 19, no. 3 (July 1982): 60.

30. See Laura F. Klein and Lillian A. Ackerman, eds., *Women and Power in Native North America* (Norman: University of Oklahoma Press, 1995); Patricia Albers and Beatrice Medicine, eds, *The Hidden Half* (Washington, D.C.: University Press of America, 1983); M. Annette Jaimes and Theresa Halsey, "American Indian Women: At the Center of Indigenous Resistance in North America," in M. Annette Jaimes, ed, *The State of Native America* (Boston: South End Press, 1992), 311–44.

31. See, e.g., Wilma Mankiller, *Mankiller: A Chief and Her People* (New York: St. Martin's Press, 1993); and see the chapters in pt. 5, "Tribal Governance/Gender," in *Readings in American Indian Law: Recalling the Rhythms of Survival* (Philadelphia: Temple University Press, 1998), 205–75.

32. See, e.g., Jo-Anne Fisk, "Native Women in Reserve Politics: Strategies and Struggles," *Journal of Legal Pluralism and Unofficial Law* 30 (1990): 121–37 and Bruce Miller, "Contemporary Tribal Codes and Gender Issues," *American Indian Culture and Research Journal* 18, no. 2 (1992): 43–74.

33. Correspondence from Dr. Jerry Stubben, January 18, 2001.

34. Deloria and Lytle, *American Indians,* 89.

35. Jack Utter, *American Indians: Answers to Today's Questions* (Lake Ann, Mich.: National Woodlands, 1993), 165–66.

36. Stephen Cornell, *The Return of the Native: American Indian Political Resurgence* (New York: Oxford University Press, 1988), 81.

37. Porter, "Strengthening Tribal Sovereignty," 75.

38. Bertha P. Dalton, *American Indians of the Southwest* (Albuquerque: University of New Mexico Press, 1983), 9.

39. Thomas D. Hall, *Social Change in the Southwest, 1350–1880* (Lawrence: University Press of Kansas, 1989), 238.

40. Hall, *Social Change,* 233.

41. Reginald G. Fisher, "An Outline of Pueblo Government," in *So Live the Works of Men,* ed. Donald D. Brand and Fred E. Harvey (Albuquerque: University of New Mexico Press, 1939), 147.

42. O'Brien, *American Indian Tribal Government,* 171.

43. Fisher, "An Outline," 156.

44. Cohen, *Handbook of Federal Indian Law,* 128.

45. Cohen, *Handbook of Federal Indian Law,* 129; note 59. This note gives a complete list of the tribes with constitutions.

46. *Civilized* was a term developed by whites to describe the remarkable social, educational, economic, and political changes made by these nations after their coerced removal from the Southeast to western lands.

47. See, e.g., Grant Foreman, *The Five Civilized Tribes* (Norman: University of Oklahoma Press, 1934); Angie Debo, *And Still the Waters Run: The Betrayal of the Five Civilized Tribes*

(Norman: University of Oklahoma Press, 1940); and Duane Champagne, *Social Order and Political Change: Constitutional Governments Among the Cherokee, the Choctaw, the Chickasaw, and the Creek* (Stanford, Calif.: Stanford University Press, 1992).

48. Jill Norgren, *The Cherokee Cases: The Confrontation of Law and Politics* (New York: McGraw-Hill, 1996), 16.

49. Norgren, *The Cherokee Cases,* 17.

50. Norgren, *The Cherokee Cases,* 18.

51. Norgren, *The Cherokee Cases,* 33.

52. Grant Foreman, *Indian Removal: The Emigration of the Five Civilized Tribes of Indians* (Norman: University of Oklahoma Press, 1932).

53. Duane H. King, "Cherokee," in *Native America in the Twentieth Century: An Encyclopedia,* ed. Mary B. Davis (New York: Garland, 1996), 97.

54. Norgren, *The Cherokee Cases,* 144.

55. Deloria and Lytle, *American Indians,* 92.

56. 34 Stat. 822.

57. Deloria and Lytle, *American Indians,* 93.

58. David E. Wilkins, *The Navajo Political Experience* (Tsaile, Ariz.: Diné College Press, 1999), chapter 9.

59. Robert W. Young, *A Political History of the Navajo Tribe* (Tsaile, Ariz.: Navajo Community College Press, 1978), 66.

60. Lopach et al., *Tribal Government Today,* 7.

61. Lopach et al., *Tribal Government Today,* 42.

62. 47 Stat. 564.

63. 47 Stat. 1568.

64. 48 Stat. 596.

65. 48 Stat. 647.

66. 48 Stat. 787.

67. 48 Stat. 984.

68. Cohen, *Handbook of Federal Indian Law,* 84.

69. Deloria and Lytle, *American Indians,* 100.

70. Vine Deloria Jr. and Clifford M. Lytle, *The Nations Within: Past and Future of American Indian Sovereignty* (New York: Pantheon, 1984), 171.

71. Deloria and Lytle, *The Nations Within,* 172. Emphasis added.

72. Deloria and Lytle, *American Indians,* 101.

73. Elmer Rusco, *A Fateful Time: The Background and Legislative History of the Indian Reorganization Act* (Reno: University of Nevada Press, 2000): xii-xiii.

74. See, e.g., Felix S. Cohen's *On the Drafting of Tribal Constitutions,* ed. David E. Wilkins (Norman: University of Oklahoma Press, 2006); and Eric D. LeMont,ed., *American Indian Constitutional Reform and the Rebuilding of Native Nations* (Austin: University of Texas Press, 2006).

75. Lopach et al., *Tribal Government Today,* 21.

76. Deloria and Lytle, *American Indians,* 102.

77. Mamie L. Mizen, *Federal Facilities for Indians: Tribal Relations with the Federal Government* (Washington, D.C.: Government Printing Office, 1967), viii–ix.

78. Mizen, *Federal Facilities for Indians,* 216.

79. Mizen, *Federal Facilities for Indians,* x.

80. George Pierre Castile, *To Show Heart: Native American Self-Determination and Federal Indian Policy, 1960–1975* (Tucson: University of Arizona Press, 1998).

81. Philip S. Deloria, "The Era of Indian Self-Determination: An Overview," in *Indian Self-Rule: First-Hand Accounts of Indian-White Relations from Roosevelt to Reagan,* ed. Kenneth R. Philp (Salt Lake City, Utah: Howe Brothers, 1986), 196.

82. 75 Stat. 47, 50.

83. *Colliflower v. Garland,* 342 F. 2d 369 (1965).

84. Petra T. Shattuck and Jill Norgren, *Partial Justice: Federal Indian Law in a Liberal Constitutional System* (Providence, R.I.: Berg, 1993), 169.

85. Peter Iverson, *The Navajo Nation* (Albuquerque: University of New Mexico Press, 1981), 95–100.

86. *Dodge v. Nakai*, 298 F. Supp. 26, 31 (1969).

87. Deloria, "The Era of Indian Self-Determination," 198.

88. Deloria and Lytle, *American Indians*, 103.

89. William C. Canby Jr., *American Indian Law*, 3rd ed. (St. Paul, Minn.: West Group), 61.

90. Cohen, *Handbook of Federal Indian Law*, 130.

91. Department of the Interior, *Opinions of the Solicitor: Indian Affairs* (Washington, D.C.: Government Printing Office, 1946), 447.

92. Arlene Hirschfelder and Martha Kreipe de Montaño, *The Native American Almanac: A Portrait of Native America Today* (New York: Prentice Hall, 1993), 74–75.

93. Lopach et al., *Tribal Government Today*, 110.

94. Wilkins, *Navajo Political Experience*, 130–31.

95. Lopach et al., *Tribal Government Today*, 67.

96. This section is drawn from Canby, *American Indian Law*, 62–65.

97. See, e.g., *Means v. Wilson*, 522 F. 2d 833 (1975); *Daly v. United States*, 483 F. 2d 700 (1973); and *White Eagle v. One Feather*, 478 F. 2d 1311 (1973).

98. Howard Meredith, *Modern American Indian Tribal Government and Politics* (Tsaile, Ariz.: Navajo Community College Press, 1993), 52.

99. Frank Pommersheim, *Broken Ground and Flowing Waters: An Introductory Text with Materials on Rosebud Sioux Tribal Government* (Rosebud, S.Dak.: Sinte Gleska College Press, 1977), 19.

100. Canby, *American Indian Law*, 62.

101. Hansen, *Introduction to Tribal Government*, 68.

102. O'Brien, *American Indian Tribal Government*, 133.

103. Stephen L. Pevar, *The Rights of Indians as Tribes: The Basic ACLU Guide to Indian and Tribal Rights*, 2nd ed. (Carbondale: Southern Illinois University Press, 1992), 98, quoting from *Sage v. Lodge Grass School District No. 27*, 13 *Indian Law Reporter*, 6035–6040, Crow Court of Appeals (1986).

104. Deloria and Lytle, *American Indians*, 109.

105. James Bradley Thayer, "A People Without Law," *Atlantic Monthly* 48 (October 1891), 540–51, and (November 1891), 676–87.

106. Sharon O'Brien, "Tribal Governments," in *Native America*, ed. Davis, 653.

107. Deloria and Lytle, *American Indians*, 110.

108. See, e.g., Karl Llewellyn and E. A. Hoebel, *The Cheyenne Way: Conflict and Case Law in Primitive Jurisprudence* (Norman: University of Oklahoma Press, 1941).

109. Pevar, *The Rights of Indians*, 96.

110. Deloria and Lytle, *American Indians*, 152.

111. William T. Hagan, *Indian Police and Judges: Experiments in Acculturation and Control* (New Haven, Conn.: Yale University Press, 1966).

112. 35 Fed. 575 (D.C. Ore.).

113. Frank Pommersheim, *Braid of Feathers: American Indian Law and Contemporary Tribal Life* (Berkeley: University of California Press, 1995), 63.

114. Pommersheim, *Braid of Feathers*, 65.

115. Nell Jessup Newton, "Tribal Court Praxis: One Year in the Life of Twenty Indian Tribal Courts," *American Indian Law Review* 22 (1998): 291.

116. Newton, "Tribal Court Praxis," 291.

117. Newton, "Tribal Court Praxis," 293.

118. Canby, *American Indian Law*, 64.

119. Vincent C. Milani, "The Right to Counsel in Native American Tribal Courts: Tribal Sovereignty and Congressional Control," *American Criminal Law Review* 31, no. 4 (Summer 1994): 1279–1301.

120. Department of Justice. Bureau of Justice Statistics. Steven W. Perry, *American Indians and Crime* (Washington, D.C.: Office of Justice Programs, December 2004).

121. Deloria and Lytle, *American Indians,* 137–38.

122. Deloria and Lytle, *American Indians,* 136.

123. Rosita Worl, "Indian-White Relations in Alaska," in *Encyclopedia of North American Indians: Native American History, Culture, and Life from Paleo-Indians to the Present,* ed. Frederick E. Hoxie (Boston: Houghton Mifflin, 1996), 274.

124. 48 Stat. 984.

125. 49 Stat. 1250.

126. Cohen, *Handbook of Federal Indian Law,* 404.

127. Worl, "Indian-White Relations in Alaska," 276.

128. 85 Stat. 688.

129. Stephen Colt, "Alaska Native Regional Corporations," in *Native America,* ed. Davis, 13.

130. Colt, "Alaska Native Regional," 13.

131. Worl, "Indian-White Relations in Alaska," 276.

132. Donald C. Mitchell, *Sold American: The Study of Alaska Natives and Their Land, 1867–1959* (Hanover, N.H.: University Press of New England, 1997), 10.

133. Mitchell, *Sold American,* 11.

134. Pevar, *The Rights of Indians,* 255.

135. See Thomas R. Berger, *Village Journey: The Report of the Alaska Native Review Commission* (New York: Hill and Wang, 1985), chapter 7, "Recommendations."

136. 59 Federal Register 9280, 9286–87 (1994).

137. www.indianz.com/news/archives/002193.asp (October 27, 2003).

138. David C. Mass, "Alaska Native Claims Settlement Act," in *Native America,* ed. Davis, 13.

139. O'Brien, *American Indian Tribal Governments,* chapter 11, "The Powers of Tribal Governments."

140. Lopach et al., *Tribal Government Today,* 181.

141. Lopach et al., *Tribal Government Today,* 181.

142. The Kikmongwi is the "village chief"; all the villagers are his children. He is a life-appointed individual who makes decisions regarding traditional religion. Hopi Dictionary Project, Hopi Dictionary/Hopiikwa Lavàytutuveni: *A Hopi English Dictionary of the Third Mesa Dialect* (Tucson: University of Arizona Press, 1997), 141.

143. Peggy Berryhill, "Hopi Potskwaniat: The Hopi Pathway to the Future," *Native Americas* 15, no. 1 (Spring 1998): 32.

144. Porter, "Strengthening Tribal Sovereignty," 8.

145. Stephen Cornell and Joseph Kalt, eds. *What Can Tribes Do? Strategies and Institutions in American Indian Economic Development* (Los Angeles: American Indian Studies Center, University of California, 1992), 18.

146. Deloria and Lytle, *The Nations Within,* 246.

147. Deloria and Lytle, *American Indians,* 109.

148. Porter, "Strengthening Tribal Sovereignty," 77.

Notes to Chapter 4

1. John Echohawk, "We Are Sovereign People," in *Surviving in Two Worlds: Contemporary Native American Voices,* ed. Lois Crozier-Hogle and Darryl Babe Wilson (Austin: University of Texas Press, 1997), 69.

2. 31 U.S. (6 Pet.) 515 (1832).

3. 517 U.S. 44 (1996).

4. See, e.g., Dorothy V. Jones, *License for Empire: Colonialism by Treaty in Early America* (Chicago: University of Chicago Press, 1982).

5. Raymond DeMallie, "American Indian Treaty-Making: Motives and Meanings," *American Indian Journal* 3 (January 1977).

6. Vine Deloria Jr. "The Application of the Constitution to American Indians," in *Exiled in the Land of the Free,* ed. Oren Lyons and John Mohawk (Santa Fe, N.Mex.: Clear Light, 1992), 284.

7. Deloria, "The Application," 284.

8. Felix S. Cohen, *Handbook of Federal Indian Law,* reprint ed. (Albuquerque: University of New Mexico Press, 1972), 91.

9. Cohen, *Handbook,* note 18, quoting from House Report No. 474, Commissioner of Indian Affairs, 23rd Cong., 1st sess., May 20, 1834.

10. Francis Paul Prucha, *American Indian Policy in the Formative Years: The Indian Trade and Intercourse Acts, 1790–1834* (Lincoln: University of Nebraska Press, 1962).

11. See, e.g., "The Civilization Fund Act," 3 Stat. 516.

12. See, e.g., "An Act to Provide for the Punishment of Crimes and Offenses Committed Within the Indian Boundaries," 3 Stat. 383.

13. In fact, beginning in the 1880s, Congress delegated much of its constitutional authority to oversee and administer Indian affairs to administrative officials. This has, in some instances, been even more disastrous for Indians because tribes have discovered that their sovereign as well as their political and property rights are often subject to the whims of federal bureaucrats. Compounding this, the federal courts typically acquiesce to the decisions of executive officials and infrequently overturn their decisions.

14. David J. Vogler, *The Politics of Congress,* 4th ed. (Boston: Allyn and Bacon, 1983), chapter 4.

15. Richard S. Jones, *American Indian Policy: Background, Nature, History, Current Issues, Future Trends. Congressional Research Report 87-227 GOV* (Washington, D.C.: Government Printing Office, 1987), 79.

16. Vine Deloria Jr., "Congress in Its Wisdom: The Course of Indian Legislation," in *The Aggressions of Civilization,* ed. Sandra L. Cadwalader and Vine Deloria Jr. (Philadelphia: Temple University Press, 1984), 106.

17. Deloria, "Congress in Its Wisdom," 106.

18. 16 Stat. 544, 566.

19. Cohen, *Handbook,* 67.

20. Deloria, "Congress in Its Wisdom," 107.

21. Russel Barsh and James Y. Henderson, *The Road: Indian Tribes and Political Liberty* (Berkeley: University of California Press, 1980), 222.

22. 60 Stat. 812.

23. Jones, *American Indian Policy,* 81.

24. Senate Select Committee on Indian Affairs, *History, Jurisdiction, and Summary of Legislative Activities, 1981–1982,* 97th Cong., 2nd sess. (1983), S. Doc. 1.

25. U.S. Congress, *American Indian Policy Review Commission, Final Report* (Washington, D.C.: Government Printing Office, 1977), iii.

26. U.S. Congress, *Final Report,* 24.

27. U.S. Congress, *Final Report,* 295.

28. U.S. Congress, *Final Report,* 295.

29. Congressional Record, 98th Cong., 2nd sess., June 6, 1984, S6669.

30. Jones, *American Indian Policy,* 84.

31. *Congressional Quarterly Weekly* 51, no. 2 (January 9, 1993): 67.

32. Interview with Bob Holmes, August 31, 1998.

33. Senate, *Budget Views and Estimates for Fiscal Year 1991,* 101st Cong., 2nd sess. (1990), 1.

34. Vogler, *The Politics of Congress,* 160.

35. S. Lyman Tyler, *A History of Indian Policy* (Washington, D.C.: Government Printing Office, 1973), 8.

36. 94 Stat. 1785.

37. See, e.g., William T. Hagan, "To Correct Certain Evils: The Indian Land Claims Cases," in *Iroquois Land Claims,* ed. Christopher Vecsey and William A. Starna (Syracuse, N.Y.: Syracuse University Press, 1988), 17–30.

38. Senate, *Budget Views,* 1.

39. 14 Stat. 492, 514.

40. Lloyd Burton, *American Indian Water Rights and the Limits of Law* (Lawrence: University Press of Kansas, 1991), x.

41. Burton, *American Indian Water,* 39–40.

42. See Daniel McCool, *Native Waters: Contemporary Indian Water Settlements and the Second Treaty Era* (Tucson: University of Arizona Press, 2002).

43. George McCoy, "Mental Health," in *Native America in the Twentieth Century: An Encyclopedia,* ed. Mary B. Davis (New York: Garland, 1996), 330–34.

44. Jack F. Trope and Walter R. Echo-Hawk, "The Native American Graves Protection and Repatriation Act: Background and Legislative History," *Arizona State Law Journal* 24 (1992): 39.

45. David E. Wilkins, "GOP Must Recall Its Obligations to Tribes," *Arizona Daily Star,* 19 June 1995, A11.

46. W. Ron Allen, "Gorton's Lost Crusade," *Native America* 17, no. 3 (Fall 2000): 32–33.

47. Tim Egan, "Backlash Growing as Indians Make a Stand for Sovereignty," *New York Times,* March 9, 1998, A16.

48. Senate Committee on Indian Affairs, *Hearing on Tribal Sovereign Immunity,* 104th Cong., 2nd sess., September 24, 1996, 1.

49. Jerry Gray, "Senate Shelves Proposals to Restrict Indian Legal Protection," *New York Times,* September 17, 1997, A20.

50. Daniel K. Inouye, foreword to *Documents of American Indian Diplomacy: Treaties, Agreements, and Conventions, 1775–1979,* 2 vols., ed. Vine Deloria Jr. and Raymond J. DeMallie (Norman: University of Oklahoma Press, 1999), ix.

51. Letter to Chairman Kent Conrad and Ranking Member Judd Gregg from Byron Dorgan (Chairman) and John Barrasso (Vice Chairman), United States Senate Committee on Indian Affairs, Re: FY 2010 Funding For Native American Programs (13 March 2009), 3.

52. Rob Capriccioso, "Health Care Reform Signed into Law," *Indian Country Today* (March 26, 2010).

53. Letter to Chairman Kent Conrad and Ranking Member Judd Gregg from Byron Dorgan (Chairman) and John Barrasso (Vice Chairman), United States Senate Committee on Indian Affairs, Re: FY 2010 Funding For Native American Programs (13 March 2009), 7.

54. Letter to Chairman Kent Conrad and Ranking Member Judd Gregg from Byron Dorgan (Chairman) and John Barrasso (Vice Chairman), United States Senate Committee on Indian Affairs, Re: FY 2010 Funding For Native American Programs (13 March 2009), 14.

55. Lummi Nation Self-Governance Communication and Education Project, *Self-Governance: A New Partnership* (Bellingham, Wash.: Lummi Nation, 1995).

56. Deloria, "The Application of the Constitution," 285.

57. The May 10, 1911, agreement between the United States and the Wiminuche Band of Southern Ute is printed in Deloria and DeMallie, *Documents of Diplomacy,* 504–505.

58. The New American State Papers: *Indian Affairs,* vol. 4, Northwest (Wilmington, Del.: Scholarly Resources, Inc., 1972), 24–26.

59. Weekly Compilation of Presidential Documents, May 9, 1994, vol. 30, no. 18, 941.

60. U.S. Commission on Civil Rights, "Redefining Rights in America: The Civil Rights Record of the George W. Bush Administration, 2001–2004," www.law.umaryland.edu/marshall/uscrr/documents/cr12r24.pdf.

61. See www.democracynow.org/2004/8/10/bush_on_native_american_issues-tribal, for transcript of this interview.

62. Jim Adams, "'Grave Concerns' Over Roberts Nomination," *Indian Country Today,* July 29, 2005.

63. David H. DeJong, *Promises of the Past: A History of Indian Education* (Golden, Colo.: North American Press, 1993), 190.

64. Vine Deloria Jr. and David E. Wilkins, *Tribes, Treaties, and Constitutional Tribulations* (Austin: University of Texas Press, 1999), 41.

65. Deloria and Wilkins, *Tribes, Treaties,* 40.

66. As an example of opportunism, whether planned or not, on December 29, 2000, Assistant Secretary of the Interior Kevin Gover ruled favorably for the Wisconsin Menominee in their effort to construct a casino in Kenosha, Wisconsin. Five days later, on January 3, Gover stepped down as head of the bureau and accepted a position with the Washington, D.C., law and lobbying firm of Steptoe and Johnson, which had been courting the Menominee for their business for nearly a year, while Gover was considering the tribe's bid for what will become the Midwest's largest casino. Gover maintained that he had not known that the law firm was seeking the tribe's business at the same time it was pursuing him as an employee, and had he been aware of this he would have disqualified himself from ruling on the tribe's request (Pat Doyle, "Ex-BIA Chief's New Job Raises Revolving-Door Question," *Minnesota Star Tribune,* January 21, 2001, A21).

67. *Wolsey v. Chapman,* 101 U.S. 755, 769 (1879).

68. 48 Stat. 984, 986.

69. Jerry D. Stubben, "Indian Preference: Racial Discrimination or a Political Right?" in *American Indian Policy: Self-Governance and Economic Development,* ed. Lyman H. Letgers and Fremont J. Lyden (Westport, Conn.: Greenwood, 1993), 107.

70. 417 U.S. 535 (1974).

71. *Rice v. Cayetano,* 528 U.S. 495 (2000).

72. Vine Deloria Jr., *Custer Died for Your Sins: An Indian Manifesto,* reprint ed. (Norman: University of Oklahoma Press, 1988; originally published in 1969), 130.

73. Indian Self-Determination Act Amendments of 1994, 108 Stat. 4250, 4270.

74. U.S. Commission on Civil Rights, "A Quiet Crisis: Federal Funding and Unmet Needs in Indian Country" (July 2003): 10. Retrieved June 15, 2010, from www.usccr.gov/pubs/na0703/na0204.pdf.

75. U.S. Commission on Civil Rights, 12.

76. National Academy of Public Administration, *A Study of Management and Administration: The Bureau of Indian Affairs, August 1999* (Washington, D.C.: Native American Public Administration, 1999), 21.

77. See Robert McCarthy, "The Bureau of Indian Affairs and the Federal Trust Obligation to American Indians," *Brigham Young University Journal of Public Law,* vol. 19 (2004) for a broad examination of the BIA.

78. William C. Canby Jr., *American Indian Law,* 3rd ed. (St. Paul, Minn.: West Group, 1998), 54.

79. Canby, *American Indian Law,* 49.

80. Canby, *American Indian Law,* 50.

81. "Remarks of Kevin Gover, Assistant Secretary-Indian Affairs, Department of the Interior at the Ceremony Acknowledging the 175th Anniversary of the Establishment of the Bureau of Indian Affairs, September 8, 2000," www.tahtonka.com/apology.html.

82. Rob Capriccioso, "A Sorry Saga: Obama Signs Native American Apology Resolution; Fails to Draw Attention to It," *Indian Country Today,* January 13, 2010.

83. Rob Capriccioso, "A Sorry Saga: Obama Signs Native American Apology Resolution; Fails to Draw Attention to It," *Indian Country Today,* January 13, 2010.

84. Rob Calpriccioso, "Brownback Offers Obama Political Cover on Native Apology," *Indian Country Today,* January 29, 2010.

85. Robert McCarthy, "The Bureau of Indian Affairs and the Federal Trust Obligation to American Indians," *Brigham Young University Journal of Public Law,* vol. 19 (2004): 159.

86. See, e.g., Charles S. Wilkinson, *American Indians, Time, and the Law* (New Haven, Conn.: Yale University Press, 1987).

87. See, e.g., Karl J. Kramer, "The Most Dangerous Branch: An Institutional Approach to Understanding the Role of the Judiciary in American Indian Jurisdictional Determination," *Wisconsin Law Review* 5–6 (1986): 989–1038.

88. See, e.g., David E. Wilkins, *American Indian Sovereignty and the U.S. Supreme Court: The Masking of Justice* (Austin: University of Texas Press, 1997).

89. Matthew Fletcher, "Sotomayor Could Make a Difference," *Indian Country Today,* August 14, 2009.

90. Tracy Labin, "We Stand United Before the Court: The Tribal Supreme Court Project," *New England Law Review* 37, no. 3 (Spring 2003): 696.

91. *Native American Church v. Navajo Tribal Council,* 272 F. 2d 131 (1959).

92. Earl S. Mackey and Philip S. Deloria, *State-Tribal Agreements: A Comprehensive Study* (Commission on State-Tribal Relations, 1981), 1.

93. James B. Reed and Judy A. Zelio, *States and Tribes: Building New Traditions* (Denver, CO: National Council of State Legislatures, 1995): v.

94. Susan Johnson, Jeanne Kaufman, John Dossett, and Sarah Hicks, *Government to Government: Understanding State and Tribal Governments* (Denver, Colo.: National Conference of State Legislatures, 2000).

95. Johnson, Kaufman, Dossett, and Hicks, *Government to Government,* vi.

96. Melissa Savage, *Traffic Safety on Tribal Lands* (Denver, Colo.: National Conference of State Legislatures, October 2004): 1.

97. Savage, *Traffic Safety,* 8-9.

98. See, e.g., Article 3 of the Treaty with the Nisqualli, Puyallup, etc., December 26, 1854 (10 Stat. 1132).

99. See ftp://ftp.halcyon.com/pub/FWDP/Americas/env_mou.txt for a copy of the memorandum of understanding. See also Northwest Indian Fisheries Commission, Comprehensive Tribal Fisheries Management, *A Holistic Approach: A Report from the Treaty Indian Tribes of Western Washington* (Olympia, Wash.: Northwest Indian Fisheries Commission, n.d.).

100. Northwest Indian Fisheries Commission Home Page. Retrieved June 15, 2010, from www.nwifc.gov.

101. It is simultaneously charged with "managing all Indian Affairs" but is also charged with helping tribes become "self-determined," an apparent irreconcilability.

Notes to Chapter 5

1. U.S. Commissioner of Indian Affairs, *Annual Report,* Thomas J. Morgan (Washington, D.C.: Government Printing Office, 1889) as quoted in Francis Paul Prucha, ed., *Documents of United States Indian Policy,* 2nd ed. (Lincoln: University of Nebraska Press, 1990), 177.

2. Presidential Documents, Federal REgister, vol. 74, no. 215, Monday, November 9, 2009. FR Doc. E9-27142.

3. See also Janet A. McDonnell, *The Dispossession of the American Indian, 1887–1934* (Bloomington: Indiana University Press, 1991); Vine Deloria Jr. and Clifford M. Lytle, *The Nations Within: The Past and Future of American Indian Sovereignty* (New York: Pantheon, 1984); Vine Deloria Jr., *American Indian Policy in the Twentieth Century* (Norman: University of Oklahoma Press, 1985); Kenneth R. Philp, ed., *First Hand Accounts of Indian-White Relations: From Roosevelt to Reagan* (Salt Lake City, Utah: Howe Brothers, 1986); Peter Iverson, *"We Are Still Here:" American Indians in the Twentieth Century* (Wheeling, Ill.: Harlan

Davidson, 1998); and George Pierre Castile, *To Show Heart: Native American Self-Determination and Federal Indian Policy, 1960–1975* (Tucson: University of Arizona Press, 1998).

4. We rely heavily on the excellent historical summary found in Franke Wilmer, *The Indigenous Voice in World Politics* (Newbury Park, Calif.: Sage, 1993).

5. Wilmer, *Indigenous Voice*, 73.

6. Francis Paul Prucha, *American Indian Policy in the Formative Years: The Indian Trade and Intercourse Acts, 1790–1834* (Lincoln: University of Nebraska Press, 1962), 2.

7. 4 Stat. 411.

8. See, e.g., the Treaty of Dancing Rabbit Creek with the Choctaw Nation, 7 Stat. 330.

9. William C. Canby Jr., *American Indian Law*, 3rd ed. (St. Paul, Minn.: West Group, 1998), 17.

10. Vine Deloria Jr. and Clifford M. Lytle, *American Indians, American Justice* (Austin: University of Texas Press, 1983), 33.

11. Deloria and Lytle, *American Indians*, 33.

12. Deloria and Lytle, *American Indians*, 7.

13. U.S. Commissioner of Indian Affairs, Francis A. Walker, *Annual Report* (Washington, D.C.: Government Printing Office, 1872), 399–400.

14. Henry M. Teller, "Debate in the Senate on Land in Severalty," in *Americanizing the American Indians: Writings by the "Friends of the Indian" 1880–1900*, ed. Francis Paul Prucha (Lincoln: University of Nebraska Press, 1973), 139.

15. Vine Deloria Jr. and David E. Wilkins, *Tribes, Treaties, and Constitutional Tribulations* (Austin: University of Texas Press, 1999), 101.

16. Wilmer, *Indigenous Voice*, 82.

17. 24 Stat. 388.

18. James Wilson, *The Original Americans: U.S. Indians, Minority Rights Group Report no. 31* (London: Benjamin Franklin House, 1976), 18–19.

19. Vine Deloria, "Indian Affairs, 1973: Hebrews 13:8," in *Spirit and Reason: The Vine Deloria, Jr., Reader*, ed. Barbara Deloria, Kristen Foehner, and Sam Scinta (Golden, Colo.: Fulcrum, 1999), 191.

20. McDonnell, *The Dispossession of the American Indian*, 10.

21. Wilson, *The Original Americans*, 19.

22. Deloria and Lytle, *The Nations Within*, 256–57.

23. Lewis Meriam, *The Problem of Indian Administration* (Baltimore: Johns Hopkins University Press, 1928), 41.

24. Deloria and Lytle, *The Nations Within*, 44.

25. Deloria and Lytle, *The Nations Within*, 45.

26. Deloria and Lytle, *The Nations Within*, 46–47.

27. 48 Stat. 984.

28. Deloria and Lytle, *American Indians*, 14.

29. Deloria and Lytle, *American Indians*, 14.

30. Wilmer, *Indigenous Voice*, 85.

31. See Russel Barsh and James Youngblood Henderson, *The Road: Indian Tribes and Political Liberty* (Berkeley: University of California Press, 1980), chapter 10, "The Triumph of the Doctrine of Plenary Power, 1934–1968," for a good discussion of this critical period.

32. 67 Stat. B132.

33. Donald L. Fixico, *Termination and Relocation: Federal Indian Policy, 1945–1960* (Albuquerque: University of New Mexico Press, 1986), 181.

34. Charles F. Wilkinson and Eric R. Biggs, "The Evolution of the Termination Policy," *American Indian Law Review* 5 (Summer 1977): 92–93.

35. 82 Stat. 77.

36. Samuel R. Cook, "Self-Determination without Termination: Richard Nixon's Indian Policy Revisited," *Native American Studies* 12, no. 1 (1998): 1–11.

37. Dale Risling et al., *Self-Governance—A New Partnership* (Bellingham, Wash.: Lummi Nation Self-Governance Communication and Education Project, 1995), 4.

38. 485 U.S. 439 (1988).

39. 485 U.S. 99 (1988).

40. White House Press Release, "In Historic Meeting with American Indian and Alaska Native Tribal Leaders," www.the peoplespaths.net/history/premes/html. Accessed on August 3, 2010.

41. See, e.g., *Cotton Petroleum Corporation v. New Mexico*, 490 U.S. 163 (1989); *Brendale v. Confederated Tribes and Bands of the Yakima Indian Nation*, 492 U.S. 408 (1989); *County of Yakima v. Confederated Tribes and Bands of the Yakima Indian Nation*, 502 U.S. 251 (1992); *Seminole Tribe of Florida v. Florida*, 517 U.S. 44 (1996); and *Strate v. A-1 Contractors*, 520 U.S. 438 (1997).

Notes to Chapter 6

1. Marjane Ambler, *Breaking the Iron Bonds: Indian Control of Energy Development* (Lawrence: University Press of Kansas, 1990), 2; David D. Kirkpatrick, "Senecas See Comeback Over Sale of Cigarettes," *The New York Times* (March 6, 2010): A12.

2. U.S. Commission on Civil Rights, "A Quiet Crisis," ix.

3. Patricia M. Barnes, Patricia F. Adams, and Eve Powell-Griner, "Health Characteristics of the American Indian or Alaska Native Adult Population: United States, 2004–2008," *National Health Statistics Reports*, no. 20 (March 9, 2010).

4. U.S. Commission on Civil Rights, "A Quiet Crisis," x.

5. National American Indian Housing Council, "Indian Housing Fact Sheet," www.naihc .net/news/index.asp?bid=6316.

6. Gary Anders and Duane Champagne, "U.S. Indian Reservation Economic Development," in *The Native North American Almanac: A Reference Work on Native North Americans in the United States and Canada*, ed. Duane Champagne (Detroit: Gale Research, 1994), 926.

7. See, e.g., Robert H. White, *Tribal Assets: The Rebirth of Native America* (New York: Henry Holt, 1990); and Stephen Cornell and Joseph Kalt, eds., *What Can Tribes Do? Strategies and Institutions in American Indian Economic Development* (Los Angeles: American Indian Studies Center, 1992).

8. Michael Lawson, "Heirship: The Indian Amoeba," reprinted in U.S. Senate, Hearing S.2480 and S.2663 before the Senate Select Committee on Indian Affairs, 98th Cong., 2d sess., "To Amend the Indian Land Consolidation Act of 1983" (Washington, D.C.: Government Printing Office, 1984), 85.

9. Lawson, "Heirship," 85–86.

10. Vine Deloria Jr. and Clifford M. Lytle, *The Nations Within: The Past and Future of American Indian Sovereignty* (New York: Pantheon, 1984), 257.

11. U.S. Congress, *American Indian Policy Review Commission: Final Report* (Washington, D.C.: Government Printing Office, 1977), 311.

12. 481 U.S. 704 (1987).

13. 117 U.S. 727 (1997).

14. See Michelle M. Lindo, "Youpee v. Babbitt: The Indian Land Inheritance Problem Revisited," *American Indian Law Review* 22 (1997): 223–49.

15. 114 Stat. 1991 (November 7, 2000); 118 Stat. 1773 (October 27, 2004).

16. National Opinion Research Center, "Gambling Impact and Behavior Study: Report to the National Gambling Impact Study Commission," www.norc.uchicago.edu, 12.

17. National Indian Gaming Association, "An Analysis of the Economic Impact of Indian Gaming in 2004" (Washington, D.C.: 2004), 14.

18. Peter Iverson, *"We Are Still Here:" American Indians in the Twentieth Century* (Wheeling, Ill.: Harlan Davidson, 1998), 191.

19. "Executive Summary: The Economics of Indian Gaming," *National Indian Gaming Association* (2008). Retrieved March 29, 2010, from www.indiangaming.org/info/pr/press-releases-2009/NIGA_08_Econ_Impact_Report.pdf.

20. See W. Dale Mason, *Indian Gaming: Tribal Sovereignty and American Politics* (Norman: University of Oklahoma Press, 2000) for a good discussion of the gaming act, how and why gaming arose in Indian Country in New Mexico and Oklahoma, and how the tribes in those states have been affected by state and national policy.

21. 102 Stat. 2467.

22. "The Harvard Project on American Indian Economic Development." Retrieved June 15, 2010, from www.ksg.harvard.edu/hpaied.

23. Fox Butterfield, "Indian Casino Revenues Grow to Sizable Segment of Industry," *New York Times,* June 16, 2005, A18.

24. Shakopee Mdewakanton Sioux Community 2008 Donation Report

25. Adrian Sainz, "Seminole Tribe to Buy Hard Rock," *Star Tribune,* December 8, 2006, D3.

26. Edward Walsh, "States Try to Rein in Tribal Gaming Boom," *Washington Post*, April 12, 1998, A9.

27. Thaddieus W. Conner and William A. Taggart, "A Research Note on the Impact of the Economic Recession on Indian Gaming in Connecticut," *Indigenous Policy Journal* 20, no. 3, 1–14.

28. Anne M. McCulloch, "The Politics of Indian Gaming: Tribe/State Relations and American Federalism," *Publius: The Journal of Federalism* 24, no. 3: 108–9.

29. Stephen Cornell, Joseph Kalt, Matthew Kreps, and Jonathan Taylor, American Indian Gaming Policy and Its Socioeconomic Effects: A Report to the National Gambling Impact Study Commission (Cambridge, MA: Economics Resource Group, 1998).

30. Minnesota Planning, *High Stakes: Gambling in Minnesota* (St. Paul: Minnesota Planning, 1992), 17.

31. Cornell et al., *American Indian Gaming,* 76–77.

32. Chris Wood, "Gunfire and Gambling," *Maclean's* 103 (May 7, 1990): 22.

33. David W. Chen and Charlie LeDuff, "With Growth in Gambling, Casinos Create Bitter Divisions Among Indians," *New York Times,* October 28, 2001, A21.

34. Haudenosaunee Statement on High Stakes Gambling, April 2005. Author has copy of this statement.

35. "Comment: The Secretary of the Interior as Referee: The States, the Indian Nations, and How Gambling Led to the Illegality of the Secretary of the Interiors Regulations in 25 C.F.R. 291" Rebecca S. Linder-Cornelius, Spring 2001, 84 Marquette Law Review 685.

36. John M. Broder, "As Schwarzenegger Tries to Slow it, Gambling Grows," *New York Times,* October 10, 2004, 18.

37. Kevin Bruyneel, "The Colonizer Demands its 'Fair Share,' and More: Contemporary American Anti-Tribalism from Arnold Schwarzenegger to the Extreme Right," *New Political Science* 28, no. 3, 299.

38. Rob Capriccioso, "New York Times Muddies Perceptions of Indian Gaming," *Indian Country Today* 28, no. 19 (October 15, 2008), 2.

39. Fox Butterfield, "Indians' Wish List: Big-City Sites for Casinos," *New York Times,* April 8, 2005, A1, A20.

40. Joanna Kakissis, "Congress Considers Indian Casino Tax," *Star Tribune,* September 20, 1995, 9A.

41. Steven Light and Kathryn Rand, *Indian Gaming and Tribal Sovereignty: The Casino Compromise* (Lawrence: University Press of Kansas, 2005), 9.

42. Cornell et al., *American Indian Gaming,* 38.

43. Senate, Final Report of the Special Committee, 105.

44. Vine Deloria Jr., "Congress in Its Wisdom: The Course of Indian Legislation," in *The Aggressions of Civilization,* ed. Sandra L. Cadwalader and Vine Deloria Jr. (Philadelphia: Temple University Press, 1984), 119.

45. U.S. Congress, *American Indian Policy Review Commission: Final Report* (Washington, D.C.: Government Printing Office, 1977), 314.

46. "Indian Farmers File Bias Suit against U.S.," *New York Times,* November 25, 1999, A21.

47. C. Matthew Snipp, "Public Policy Impacts and American Indian Economic Development," in *Public Policy Impacts on American Indian Economic Development,* ed. C. Matthew Snipp (Albuquerque, N.Mex.: Native American Studies, 1988), 5.

48. See, e.g., Peter Iverson, *When Indians Became Cowboys: Native Peoples and Cattle Ranching in the American West* (Norman: University of Oklahoma Press, 1994) for a solid treatment of this little-known topic.

49. Jo Ann DiGiulio, "The Evolution of Arizona Tribal Economies (1850–Present)," in *American Indian Relationships in a Modern Arizona Economy,* ed. Malcolm Merrill (Phoenix: Arizona Town Hall, 1994), 51.

50. "Ak-Chin Tribal Enterprises." Retrieved June 15, 2010, from www.ak-chin.nsn.us/enterprises.html.

51. Ambler, *Breaking the Iron Bonds,* 29.

52. Department of the Interior, *Report of the Task Force on Indian Economic Development* (Washington, D.C.: Government Printing Office, 1986), 99.

53. David E. Wilkins, *The Navajo Political Experience* (Tsaile, Ariz.: Diné College Press, 1999), 162–63.

54. Ambler, *Breaking the Iron Bonds,* 50. And see Tanis C. Thorne's *The World's Richest Indian: The Scandal over Jackson Barnett's Oil Fortune* (New York: Oxford University Press, 2003).

55. Ambler, *Breaking the Iron Bonds,* 50.

56. Russel L. Barsh, "Indian Resources and the National Economy: Business Cycles and Policy Cycles," in *Native Americans and Public Policy,* ed. Fremont J. Lyden and Lyman H. Legters (Pittsburgh: University of Pittsburgh Press, 1992), 207.

57. U.S. Congress, *American Indian Policy Review Commission,* 339.

58. Donald L. Fixico, *The Invasion of Indian Country in the Twentieth Century: American Capitalism and Tribal Natural Resources* (Niwot, Colo.: University Press of Colorado, 1998), 160.

59. Ambler, *Breaking the Iron Bonds,* 93.

60. 455 U.S. 130.

61. 490 U.S. 163.

62. James B. Reed and Judy A. Zelio, eds., *States and Tribes: Building New Traditions* (Denver: National Conference of States Legislatures, 1995).

63. Fixico, *The Invasion of Indian Country,* 171.

64. Jim Robbins, "Sale of Carbon Credits Helping Land-Rich, but Cash-Poor, Tribes," *New York Times,* May 8, 2007, D3.

65. *United States v. Cook,* 86 (19 Wall.) 591.

66. Snipp, "Public Policy," 7.

67. Senate, *Final Report of the Special Committee,* 135.

68. Department of the Interior, *Report of the Task Force,* 109.

69. Department of the Interior, *Report of the Task Force,* 139.

70. Richmond Clow, "Natural Resource Management," in *Native America in the Twentieth Century: An Encyclopedia,* ed. Mary B. Davis (New York: Garland, 1996), 378.

71. Matthew B. Krepps, "Can Tribes Manage Their Own Resources? The 638 Program and American Indian Forestry," in *What Can Tribes Do? Strategies and Institutions in American Indian Economic Development,* ed. Stephen Cornell and Joseph P. Kalt (Los Angeles: American Indian Studies Center, 1992), 179–204.

72. Reed and Zelio, *States and Tribes,* 60.

73. Susan Guyette, *Planning for Balanced Development: A Guide for Native American and Rural Communities* (Santa Fe, N.Mex.: Clear Light, 1996), 171.

74. Department of the Interior, *Report of the Task Force,* 74.

75. Department of the Interior, *Report of the Task Force,* 79.

76. "About" (mission statement). Retrieved June 15, 2010, from http://aianta.org/.

77. Reed and Zelio, *States and Tribes,* 33.

78. Andrea Wilkins, *Economic Development in Tribal Reservation and Rural Communities* (Denver, Colo.: National Council of State Legislatures, 2004): 9.

79. "Press Release: Secretary Salazar, Governors Kulongoski and Schwarzenegger Announce Agreement on Klamath River Basin Restoration." Retrieved June 15, 2010, from www.doi.gov/news/pressreleases/2010_02_18_release.cfm.

80. Gary Anders and Duane Champagne, "U.S. Indian Reservation Economic Development," in *The Native North American Almanac: A Reference Work on Native North Americans in the United States and Canada* (Detroit: Gale Research, 1994), 934.

81. Deloria and Lytle, *The Nations Within,* 259.

Notes to Chapter 7

1. Speech by Chief Irving Powless Jr. of the Onondaga Nation, delivered October 26, 1994, 13.

2. James Dao, "Indians' New Money Buys Lobbying Power," *New York Times,* February 9, 1998, B1.

3. Russ Lehman, "The Emerging Role of Native Americans in the American Electoral Process" (Evergreen State College, First American Education Project, January 2003): 9.

4. Jack McNeel, "Native Vote Is Big in Montana," *Indian Country Today,* November 17, 2006.

5. Open Secrets Home Page. Retrieved June 15, 2010, from www.opensecrets.org.

6. "Indian Tribes Exempt from New Limits on Campaign Gifts," *New York Times,* March 18, 2003, A22.

7. "Indian Tribes Exempt."

8. Daniel McCool, "Indian Voting," in *American Indian Policy in the Twentieth Century,* ed. Vine Deloria Jr. (Norman: University of Oklahoma Press, 1985), 118.

9. McCool, "Indian Voting," 7.

10. Kerry Young, "American Indians Exercise Political Clout," *CQ Today Online News,* December 2, 2009. Retrieved February 9, 2010, from www.cqpolitics.com/wmspage.cfm?parm1=5.

11. Timothy Egan, "Senate Measures Would Deal Blow to Indian Rights," *New York Times,* August 27, 1997, A1.

12. *Agua Caliente Band of Cahuilla Indians v. The Superior Court of Sacramento County,* 148 P. 3d 1126 (2006).

13. *Agua Caliente Band of Cahuilla Indians v. The Superior Court of Sacramento County,* 148 P. 3d 1126 (2006).

14. Nancy Vogel, "Tribe Drops Fight Against Donation Disclosure Effort," *Los Angeles Times,* July 14, 2007.

15. See Robert B. Porter, "The Demise of the Ongwehoweh and the Rise of the Native American: Redressing the Genocidal Act of Forcing American Citizenship upon Indigenous People," *Harvard BlackLetter Law Journal* 5 (Spring 1999): 107–83, for a spirited discussion about the potential impact of American citizenship on indigenous peoples and questions raised about the import of indigenous participation in nonindigenous political affairs.

16. See Doug George-Kanentiio, "U.S. Interference in Native American Affairs Created the Land Claims Crisis," *Herald-American,* February 21, 1999, D7.

17. David H. Getches, Charles F. Wilkinson, and Robert A. Williams Jr., *Cases and Materials on Federal Indian Law,* 4th ed. (St. Paul, Minn.: West Group, 1998), 1.

18. Getches et al., *Cases and Materials,* 1.

19. Anne M. McCulloch, "Perspective on Native Americans in Political Science," *Teaching Political Science: Politics in Perspective* 16, no. 3 (Spring 1989): 93.

20. United States Department of Defense. (n.d.). "20th Century Warriors: Native American Participation in the United States Military," *American Indian Heritage Month*. Retrieved January 10, 2010, from www.defense.gov/specials/nativeamerican01/warrior.html.

21. "The Way of the Warrior," VisionMaker Video. See www.wpt.org/wayofthewarrior.

22. "The Way of the Warrior."

23. Pat Flannery and Betty Reid "Profile: Lori Piestewa," *Arizona Republic*, April 20, 2003; Osha Gray Davidson, "A Wrong Turn in the Desert," *Rolling Stone*, May 27, 2004.

24. Diane Duffy, "An Attitudinal Study of Native American Patriotism." Paper presented at the meeting of the International Society for Political Psychology Scientific Services, Krakow, Poland, July 22, 1997, 7.

25. Speech by Chief Irving Powless Jr. to the University of Buffalo Law School, March 21, 1998.

26. Valerie Taliman, "Native Nations and the Politics of 2000," *Native Americas* 17, no. 3: 10.

27. Russ Lehman and Alyssa Macy, "Native Vote 2004: A National Survey and Analysis of Efforts to Increase the Native Vote in 2004 and the Results Achieved." Retrieved from www.nativevotemn.org/news/NativeVote2004NationalReport.pdf.

28. Laughlin McDonald, *American Indians and the Fight for Equal Voting Rights* (Norman: University of Oklahoma Press, 2010), 301

29. Michael Drudge, "American Indian Vote Will Be a Factor in Several Swing States: Electoral Clout of America's Indigenous Peoples a Fairly New Phenomenon," August 18, 2008. Retrieved February 2, 2010, from www.america.gov/st/usg-english/2008/August/20080828074 932mnietsua0.2280237.html.

30. Linda K. Kerber, "The Meanings of Citizenship," *The Journal of American History* (December 1997): 836.

31. U.S. Commissioner of Indian Affairs, *Sixteenth Annual Report* (Washington, D.C.: Government Printing Office, 1891), 6.

32. McCool, "Indian Voting," 106. And see Jennifer Robinson, Susan Olson, and Daniel McCool, *"I'm Indian and I Vote": American Indians, the Voting Rights Act, and the Right to Vote* (Cambridge: Cambridge University Press, 2006).

33. See Nathan R. Margold, "Suffrage-Discrimination against Indians," August 13, 1937, in *Opinions of the Solicitors of the Department of the Interior Relating to Indian Affairs, 1917–1974*, vol. 1 (Washington, D.C.: Government Printing Office 1974), 778.

34. 6 Utah 2d 32, 39 (1956).

35. Margold, "Suffrage," 778.

36. Margold, "Suffrage," 779.

37. Robinson, Olson, McCool, *"I'm Indian and I Vote,"* 87.

38. "Voting Rights in Indian Country: A Special Report of the Voting Rights Project of the American Civil Liberties Union," American Civil Liberties Union (ACLU) September 2009. Retrieved from www.aclu.org/pdfs/votingrights/indiancountryreport.pdf.

39. ACLU Voting Rights Project, Annual Report (January 1, 2009–December 31, 2009). Retrieved February 2, 2010, from www.aclu.org/files/assets/vrp_annualreport_2009.pdf.

40. Glenn A. Phelps, "Mr. Gerry Goes to Arizona: Electoral Geography and Voting Rights," *American Indian Culture and Research Journal*, vol. 15, no. 2 (1991).

41. Phelps, "Mr. Gerry," 70.

42. But see Delmer Lonowski, "A Return to Tradition: Proportional Representation in Tribal Government," *American Indian Culture and Research Journal* 18, no. 1 (1994): 147–63; James J. Lopach, Margery Hunter Brown, and Richmond L. Clow, *Tribal Government Today: Politics on Montana Indian Reservations* (Boulder, Colo.: Westview, 1990); and David E. Wilkins, *The Navajo Political Experience* (Tsaile, Ariz.: Diné College Press, 1999).

43. Liz Hill, "The Green and the Red," *Native Americas* 17, no. 3 (Fall 2000): 18–25.

44. See Winona LaDuke, *Last Standing Woman* (Stillwater, Minn.: Voyageur, 1997) and *All Our Relations: Native Struggles for Land and Life* (Boston: South End Press, 1999).

45. See Ralph Nader and Winona LaDuke, "Green Party Native American Platform," paid political advertisement in *News from Indian Country* 14, no. 16 (late August 2000).

46. Lehman and Macy, "Native Vote 2004," 5.

47. Steven J. Doherty, "Native American Voting Behavior." Paper presented at the Midwest Political Science Association Annual Meeting, Chicago, 1994, cited in Paula D. McClain and Joseph Stewart Jr., *"Can We All Get Along?" Racial and Ethnic Minorities in American Politics,* 2nd ed. (Boulder, Colo.: Westview, 1998), 78.

48. Ursula J. Richards and David Soherr-Hadwiger, "Kivas, Casinos, and Campaigns: Effects of Casino Participation in New Mexico," paper presented at the 1996 Western Political Science Association, San Francisco, CA.

49. McClain and Stewart, *"Can We All Get Along?"* 78.

50. Alexander Ewen, "Generation X in Indian Country," *Native Americas* (Winter 1997): 24–29.

51. McDonald, *American Indians and the Fight for Equal Voting Rights,* 301.

52. McDonald, *American Indians,* 307.

53. Barack Obama, "Obama: A Full Partnership with Indian Country," *Indian Country Today,* October 14, 2008.

54. Gale Courey Toensing, "Obama's Support Is Widespread in Indian Country," *Indian Country Today,* October 17, 2008.

55. McCool, "Indian Voting," 118.

56. McCool, "Indian Voting," 7.

57. McCool, "Indian Voting," 7.

58. McCool, "Indian Voting," 129.

59. Robinson, Olson, and McCool, *"I'm Indian and I Vote,"* 249.

60. Robinson, Olson, and McCool, *"I'm Indian and I Vote,"* 254.

Notes to Chapter 8

1. Dennis Banks, foreword to *Native America: Portrait of the Peoples,* by Duane Champagne (Detroit: Visible Ink, 1994), xii.

2. Paula D. McClain and Joseph Stewart Jr., *"Can We All Get Along?" Racial and Ethnic Minorities in American Politics,* 2nd ed. (Boulder, Colo.: Westview, 1998), 88.

3. Alexander Ewen, "Generation X in Indian Country," *Native Americas* (Winter 1997): 25.

4. Stephen Cornell, *The Return of the Native: American Indian Political Resurgence* (New York: Oxford University Press, 1988), 152.

5. Cornell, *The Return of the Native,* 153.

6. Cornell, *The Return of the Native,* 153.

7. Cornell, *The Return of the Native,* 153.

8. See Joane Nagel, "The Political Mobilization of Native Americans," *Social Science Journal* 19, no. 3 (July 1982): 37–45, whose formulation of Indian interest activity is as follows: tribal, pantribal, and pan-Indian.

9. J. Lee Correll and Alfred Dehiya, *Anatomy of the Navajo Indian Reservation: How it Grew* (Window Rock, Ariz.: Navajo Times Publishing Company, 1972).

10. Angie Debo, *And Still the Waters Run: The Betrayal of the Five Civilized Tribes* (Princeton, N.J.: Princeton University Press, 1940, reprint, Norman: University of Oklahoma Press, 1989), 162–64.

11. Stephen Haycox, "Alaska Native Brotherhood/Sisterhood," in *Native America in the Twentieth Century: An Encyclopedia,* ed. Mary B. Davis (New York: Garland, 1996), 9–10.

12. Cornell, *The Return of the Native,* 205.

13. Cornell, *The Return of the Native,* 206.

14. Cornell, *The Return of the Native,* 206.

15. Roxanne Dunbar Ortiz, "Trail of Broken Treaties," in *Native America,* ed. Davis, 645.

16. See Thomas W. Cowger, *The National Congress of American Indians: The Founding Years* (Lincoln: University of Nebraska Press, 1999), which provides an assessment of the early years of this important organization.

17. N. B. Johnson, "The National Congress of American Indians," *Chronicles of Oklahoma* 30 (1952): 143.

18. Christine Bolt, *American Indian Policy and American Reform: Case Studies of the Campaign to Assimilate the American Indians* (Boston: Allen & Unwin, 1987), 300.

19. Vine Deloria Jr. and Clifford M. Lytle, *American Indians, American Justice* (Austin: University of Texas Press, 1983), 155–60.

20. Joane Nagel, *American Indian Ethnic Renewal: Red Power and the Resurgence of Identity and Culture* (New York: Oxford University Press), 117.

21. See "A Report on Indian Issues," *NCAI Sentinel* (Summer 1999): 1–3.

22. "Declaration of Kinship and Cooperation Among the Indigenous Peoples and Nations of North America."

23. Joane Nagel, "Political Mobilization," 38.

24. Cornell, *The Return of the Native,* 107.

25. Tsianina Lomawaima, *They Called It Prairie Light* (Lincoln: University of Nebraska Press, 1994).

26. Vine Deloria Jr., *The Indian Affair* (New York: Friendship, 1974), 43.

27. Bolt, *American Indian Policy,* 288.

28. Deloria, *The Indian Affair,* 45.

29. Vine Deloria Jr., "The Rise and Fall of the First Indian Movement," *Historian* 33, no. 4 (August 1971): 661.

30. Hazel W. Hertzberg, *The Search for an American Indian Identity: Modern Pan-Indian Movements* (Syracuse, N.Y.: Syracuse University Press, 1971), 207.

31. James Anaya, "National Indian Youth Council," in *Native America,* ed. Davis, 373.

32. Hertzberg, *The Search,* 292.

33. Anaya, "National Indian Youth," 374.

34. Rachel Bonney, "The Role of AIM Leaders in Indian Nationalism," *American Indian Quarterly* 3 (1977): 209–24.

35. See Russell Means with Marvin J. Wolf, *Where White Men Fear to Tread: The Autobiography of Russell Means* (New York: St. Martin's Press, 1995).

36. See Sandra K. Baringer, "Indian Activism and the AIM: A Bibliographical Essay," *American Indian Culture and Research Journal* 21, no. 4 (1997): 217–50.

37. See, e.g., Kenneth S. Stern, *Loud Hawk: The United States versus the American Indian Movement* (Norman: University of Oklahoma Press, 1994) and John William Sayer, *Ghost Dancing the Law: The Wounded Knee Trials* (Cambridge, Mass.: Harvard University Press, 1997).

38. Ward Churchill, "The Bloody Wake of Alcatraz," *American Indian Culture and Research Journal* 18, no. 4 (1994): 253–300.

39. See *News from Indian Country, Aquash Special Edition* (1999), which contains articles analyzing the ongoing conflict between the movement's leaders.

40. John Gravois, "Investigation Begets Investigation in the Wake of Ward Churchill," *Chronicle of Higher Education,* 51, no. 32 (April 15, 2005): A10.

41. Julian Burger, *Report from the Frontier: The State of the World's Indigenous People* (London: Zed, 1987), 58, as cited in Franke Wilmer, *The Indigenous Voice in World Politics* (Newbury Park, Calif.: Sage, 1993), 18. Wilmer's book is part of an expanding literature that examines the situation and struggles of indigenous peoples in a global context. Other works include Vine Deloria Jr., *Behind the Trail of Broken Treaties: An Indian Declaration of Independence* (New York: Delacorte, 1974, reprint, Austin: University of Texas Press, 1985); Thomas R. Berger, *A Long and*

Terrible Shadow: White Values, Native Rights in the Americas: 1492–1992 (Seattle: University of Washington Press, 1991); S. James Anaya, "Indigenous Rights Norms in Contemporary International Law," *Arizona Journal of International and Comparative Law* 8, no. 2 (February 1991): 1–39; and Richard J. Perry, *From Time Immemorial: Indigenous Peoples and State Systems* (Austin: University of Texas Press, 1996).

42. Deloria and Lytle, *American Indians,* 156.

43. "Our Mission" Native American Rights Fund, www.narf.org/about/mission.html.

44. Deloria and Lytle, *American Indians,* 158.

45. Laurence M. Hauptman, *Tribes & Tribulations: Misconceptions about American Indians and Their Histories* (Albuquerque: University of New Mexico Press, 1995), 122.

46. Vine Deloria Jr., *Behind the Trail,* 23.

47. Commission on Civil Rights, *Indian Tribes: A Continuing Quest for Survival* (Washington, D.C.: Government Printing Office, 1981), 67.

48. "Nuclear-Free Future Award," www.nuclear-free.com/english.res.htm.

49. Richard Halloran, "Opposition to MX Missile Gaining Strength in Capitol," *New York Times,* March 9, 1981, 16(N).

50. 5 F. Supp. 2d 1135 (D. Mont. 1988).

51. 175 F. 3d 1149 (1999).

52. Sia Davis and Aura Kannegis, *Improving State-Tribal Relations: An Introduction* (Denver, Colo.: National Council of State Legislatures, 2004): 1.

53. Wilmer, *The Indigenous Voice,* 5–6; S. James Anaya, *Indigenous Peoples in International Law* (New York: Oxford University Press, 1996).

54. The United Nations Universal Periodic Review, www.treatycouncil.org/PDFs/UPR_021910WEB.pdf.

55. See S. James Anaya, *Indigenous Peoples in International Law,* 2nd ed. (New York: Oxford University Press, 2004): 219–20.

56. Gale Courey Toensing, "Canada Promises 'Qualified Recognition' of UN Declaration," *Indian Country Today,* March 19, 2010.

57. Patrick Worsnip, "U.S. to Review Stance on U.N. Indigenous Rights Text," *Washington Post,* April 20, 2010; Edith M. Lederer, "New Zealand Backs Indigenous Rights, US to Review," *Buffalo News,* April 20, 2010.

58. See, e.g., Boutros Boutros-Ghali, foreword to *Voice of Indigenous Peoples,* ed. Alexander Ewen, 9–15 (Santa Fe, N.Mex.: Clear Light, 1994).

59. Troy Johnson, Joane Nagel, and Duane Champagne, eds., *American Indian Activism: Alcatraz to the Longest Walk* (Urbana: University of Illinois Press, 1997), 9.

60. Deloria, *The Indian Affair,* 47.

61. Deloria, *The Indian Affair,* 39.

62. Edward H. Spicer, *Cycles of Conquest* (Tucson: University of Arizona Press, 1962), 162–64.

63. Nagel, *American Indian Ethnic Renewal,* 159.

64. Johnson et al., *American Indian Activism,* 10.

65. Johnson et al., *American Indian Activism,* 11.

66. Sayer, *Ghost Dancing the Law,* 20.

67. Sayer, *Ghost Dancing the Law,* 21.

68. Frederick Hoxie, ed., *Encyclopedia of North American Indians* (Boston: Houghton Mifflin, 1996), 223.

69. Johnson et al., *American Indian Activism,* 11.

70. Ted Montour, "Handsome Lake," in *The Encyclopedia of North American Indians,* ed. Hoxie, 230–31.

71. Deloria, *The Indian Affair,* 43.

72. Deloria, *The Indian Affair,* 43.

73. Nagel, *American Indian Ethnic Renewal,* 160–62.

74. Nagel, *American Indian Ethnic Renewal,* 162.

75. Sayer, *Ghost Dancing the Law,* 10.

76. Timothy Baylor, "Media Framing of Movement Protest: The Case of American Indian Protest," *Social Science Journal* 33, no. 3 (1996): 241–55.

77. Baylor, "Media Framing," 244.

78. Baylor, "Media Framing," 251.

79. Vine Deloria Jr., *Custer Died for Your Sins: An Indian Manifesto* (New York: Macmillan, 1969, reprint, Norman: University of Oklahoma Press, 1988), 248.

80. See, e.g., Peter Blue Cloud, ed., *Alcatraz Is Not an Island* (Berkeley, Calif.: Wingbow Press, 1972); Adam Fortunate Eagle, *Alcatraz! Alcatraz!: The Indian Occupation of 1969–1971* (Berkeley, Calif.: Heyday Books, 1992); and Troy Johnson, *The Occupation of Alcatraz Island: Indian Self-Determination & the Rise of Indian Activism* (Urbana: University of Illinois Press, 1996).

81. Nagel, *American Indian Ethnic Renewal,* 164.

82. Vine Deloria Jr., "American Indians," in *Multiculturalism in the United States: A Comparative Guide to Acculturation and Ethnicity* (New York: Greenwood, 1992), 45.

83. Johnson et al., *American Indian Activism,* 32.

84. Deloria, *The Indian Affair,* 46.

85. Johnson et al., *American Indian Activism,* 38.

86. Cornell, *The Return of the Native,* 194.

87. Cornell, *The Return of the Native,* 202.

88. 75 Stat. 47, 49.

89. Philip S. Deloria, "The Era of Indian Self-Determination: An Overview," in *Indian Self-Rule,* ed. Kenneth R. Philp (Salt Lake City, Utah: Howe Brothers, 1986), 194.

90. Deloria, "The Era of Indian Self-Determination," 196.

91. George Pierre Castile, *To Show Heart: Native American Self-Determination and Federal Indian Policy, 1960–1975* (Tucson: University of Arizona Press, 1998), 29.

92. Peter Iverson, *"We Are Still Here": American Indians in the Twentieth Century* (Wheeling, Ill.: Harlan Davidson, 1998), 144.

93. Deloria, "The Era of Indian Self-Determination," 198.

94. Castile, *To Show Heart,* 70.

95. Castile, *To Show Heart,* 86.

96. Emma R. Gross, *Contemporary Federal Policy Toward American Indians* (Westport, Conn.: Greenwood, 1989), 107.

97. Citizens Equal Rights Commissions Home Page. Retrieved June 15, 2010, from www.citizensalliance.org/main/index.htm.

98. "Anti-American-Indian Organization," www.honornation.org/AntiIndian.htm.

99. Ibid.

100. Robert Taylor, "'Hate Group' member seeks GOP nod," *Indian Country Today,* February 27, 2002.

Notes to Chapter 9

1. www2.ncaa.org/page.

2. Nell Jessup Newton, "Symposium Rules of the Game. Sovereignty and the Native American Nation: Memory and Misrepresentation: Representing Crazy Horse," *Connecticut Law Review* 27 (Summer 1995): 1006–7.

3. 284 F. Supp. 2d 96 (D.D.C. 2003).

4. *Pro-Football, Inc., v. Harjo*, No. 03-7162.

5. Philip Burnham, "Harjo Appeal Given Boost," *Indian Country Today*, July 22, 2005.

6. www.ncai.org/indianissues/AntiDefemationandMascots/antidef.htm.

7. See, e.g., Robert F. Berkhofer Jr., *The White Man's Indian: Images of the American Indian from Columbus to the Present* (New York: Vintage Books, 1978), and Michael K. Green, "Images of Native Americans in Advertising: Some Moral Issues," *Journal of Business Ethics* 12 (1993): 155–62.

8. Richard Slotkin, *Regeneration through Violence: The Mythology of the American Frontier, 1600–1860* (Middlewood, Conn.: Wesleyan University Press, 1973), 38.

9. Michael K. Green, "Cultural Identities: Challenges for the Twenty-First Century," in *Issues in Native American Cultural Identity*, ed. Michael K. Green (New York: Peter Lang, 1995), 9.

10. See Mari Sandoz, *Crazy Horse: The Strong Man of the Oglala* (Lincoln: University of Nebraska Press, 1961).

11. *Hornell Brewing Co. v. The Rosebud Sioux Tribal Court*, 133 F.3d 1087, 1090.

12. 106 Stat. 1729. See Nell Jessup Newton, "Symposium Rules of the Game: Sovereignty and the Native American Nation: Memory and Misrepresentation: Representing Crazy Horse," *Connecticut Law Review* 27 (Summer 1995): 1003–54 for an account of the this legal conflict before its final resolution.

13. *Hornell Brewing Co. v. Brady*, 819 F. Supp. 1227 (1993).

14. Berkhofer, *The White Man's*, 28–29.

15. See, e.g., James E. Murphy and Sharon M. Murphy, *Let My People Know: American Indian Journalism, 1828–1978* (Norman: University of Oklahoma Press, 1981) and Mark N. Trahant, *Pictures of Our Nobler Selves: A History of Native American Contributions to News Media* (Nashville, Tenn.: Freedom Forum First Amendment Center, 1995) for a general overview of this subject matter.

16. Kenneth Janda, Jeffrey M. Berry, and Jerry Goldman, *The Challenge of Democracy: Government in America*, 5th ed. (Boston: Houghton Mifflin, 1997), 175.

17. John M. Coward, *The Newspaper Indian: Native American Identity in the Press, 1820–1890* (Urbana: University of Illinois Press, 1999), 2.

18. Mary Ann Weston, *Native America in the News: Images of Indians in the Twentieth Century Press* (Westport, Conn.: Greenwood, 1996), 11.

19. Weston, Native America in the News, 24.

20. Tom Holm, *Strong Hearts, Wounded Souls: Native American Veterans of the Vietnam War* (Austin: University of Texas Press, 1996).

21. Weston, *Native America in the News*, 94–95.

22. Weston, *Native America in the News*, 109.

23. See, e.g., Nicholas C. Peroff, *Menominee Drums: Tribal Termination and Restoration, 1954–1977* (Norman: University of Oklahoma Press, 1982).

24. John W. Sayer, *Ghost Dancing the Law: The Wounded Knee Trials* (Cambridge, Mass.: Harvard University Press, 1997), 223.

25. Sayer, *Ghost Dancing the Law*, 11.

26. 441 U.S. 164 (1973).

27. Weston, *Native America in the News*, 157–58.

28. James Ulmer, "Indians Investing, but Carefully, in Hollywood," *New York Times*, April 25, 2005, C7.

29. See, e.g., National Conference of Christians and Jews, *The American Indian and the Media* (Minneapolis: Lerner, 1991).

30. Trahant, Pictures of Our Nobler Selves, 3.

31. Daniel F. Birchfield Jr., "Periodicals," in *Native America in the Twentieth Century*, ed. Mary B. Davis (New York: Garland, 1996), 444.

32. Birchfield, "Periodicals," 445.

33. Arlene Hirschfelder and Martha Kreipe de Montano, *The Native American Almanac: A Portrait of Native America Today* (New York: Prentice Hall, 1993), 193.

34. Hanay Geiogomah, "American Indian Tribes in the Media Age," in *Native America: Portrait of the Peoples* (Detroit, Mich.: Visible Ink Press, 1994), 702.

35. Telephone interview with Theresa Lumbar, NAJA, 28 January 2000. See also Candy Hamilton, "Recruiting Native Journalists: The New Storytellers," *Winds of Change* 11, no. 2 (Spring 1996): 32–36, and NAJA's website at http://www.naja.com.

36. Trahant, *Pictures of Our Nobler Selves*, 21.

37. See, www.wco.com/~berryhp/stations.html for a list of the Native radio stations as of 1996. Also see Matthew L. Jones, "Radio & Television," in *Native America in the Twentieth Century*, ed. Davis, 533.

38. Trahant, *Pictures of Our Nobler Selves*, 22.

39. *Indian Country Today*, vol. 3, no. 8. Wednesday, July 28, 2010.

40. Ulmer, "Indians Investing," C7.

41. www.nativetelecom.org/org/mission.html.

42. Madonna P. Yawakie, "Building Telecommunication Capacity in Indian Country," *Winds of Change* 12, no. 4 (1997): 44.

43. "Low-Cost Phone Service Is Proposed for Indians," *New York Times*, April 17, 2000, A15.

44. Traci L. Morris, and Sascha D. Meinrath, "New Media, Technology and Internet Use in Indian Country: Quantitative and Qualitative Analyses," *Native Public Media*, November 2009, 4.

45. Traci L. Morris, and Sascha D. Meinrath, "New Media, Technology and Internet Use in Indian Country: Quantitative and Qualitative Analyses," *Native Public Media*, November 2009.

46. Trahant, *Pictures of Our Nobler Selves*, 25.

47. Susan King, "Hattie Kauffman: Consuming Job," *Los Angeles Times*, August 11, 1991, 10.

48. Trahant, *Pictures of Our Nobler Selves*, 28.

49. Margaret Holt, "Spreading News Among Indians Making Progress," *Chicago Tribune*, May 15, 2005, Section 2, 3.

50. Karen Lincoln Michel, "Repression on the Reservation," *Columbia Journalism Review* (November/December 1998): 48.

51. 82 Stat. 77.

52. Richard LaCourse, "A Native Press Primer," in Michel, "Repression on the Reservation," 51.

53. John Johnson, "A Navajo Newspaper Tests the Boundaries," *Los Angeles Times*, 19 October 1997, 1.

54. Michel, "Repression on the Reservation," 48.

55. LaCourse, "A Native Press Primer," in Michel, "Repression on the Reservation," 51.

56. Jodi Rave, "Tribal Chairman Putting Stranglehold on Journalists," *Lincoln Journal Star*, August 15, 2004, D8.

57. Emily Schmall, "Welcome to Red Lake," *Salon.com*, March 26, 2005.

58. Charles LeDuff, "Tribal Leaders Dismiss American Indian Editor," *New York Times*, July 6, 1998, 5.

59. Michel, "Repression on the Reservation," 49.

60. Mark Fitzgerald, "How Free Is the Native American Press? United '94 Panelists Discuss Censorship That Still Exists Today," *Editor & Publisher*, September 10, 1994, 13.

61. LeDuff, "American Indian Newspapers," 15.

62. LeDuff, "Tribal Leaders Dismiss American Indian Editor," 5.

63. Robert Capriccioso, "Native Press Unchained," *American Indian Report*, vol. xx, no. 5 (Falmouth Institute, May 2004): web.lexis-nexis.com/universe/printdoc, 6.

Notes to Chapter 10

1. "President Shirley's Statement for Navajo Nation Sovereignty Day," *Navajo-Hopi Observer*, April 28, 2010, p. 1.

2. Vine Deloria Jr., "American Indians," in *Multiculturalism in the United States: A Comparative Guide to Acculturation and Ethnicity,* ed. John D. Buenker and Lorman A. Ratner (New York: Greenwood, 1992), 34.

3. Deloria, "American Indians," 34.

4. 163 U.S. 376, 384 (1896).

5. Thanks to one of our anonymous reviewers for suggesting we discuss this important comparison.

6. 72 U.S. (5 Wall.) 737, 757 (1866).

7. Vine Deloria Jr., "The Reservation Continues," *National Forum* 71, no. 2 (Spring 1991): 10.

8. 508 U.S. 679 (1993).

9. Vine Deloria Jr. and David E. Wilkins, *Tribes, Treaties, and Constitutional Tribulations* (Austin: University of Texas Press, 1999), 70.

10. 494 U.S. 872 (1990).

11. See, e.g., Vine Deloria Jr., *Behind the Trail of Broken Treaties: An Indian Declaration of Independence* (New York: Delta Books, 1974) for good analysis of this pivotal event.

12. See, e.g., David E. Wilkins, *The Navajo Political Experience* (Tsaile, Ariz.: Diné College Press, 1999), 92–95, for a discussion of the conflict and the political reform that occurred in this dispute's aftermath.

13. See, e.g., David E. Wilkins, "Internal Tribal Fragmentation: An Examination of a Normative Model of Democratic Decision-Making," *Akwe:kon Journal* 9, no. 3 (Fall 1992): 33–39; and see Gerald R. Alfred, *Heeding the Voices of Our Ancestors: Kahnawake Mohawk Politics and the Rise of Native Nationalism* (Toronto: Oxford University Press, 1995).

14. See, e.g., Robert B. Porter, "Strengthening Tribal Sovereignty Through Peacemaking: How the Anglo-American Legal Tradition Destroys Indigenous Societies," *Columbia Human Rights Law Review* 28 (Winter 1997): 235.

15. David E. Wilkins, "Breaking into the Intergovernmental Matrix: The Lumbee Tribe's Efforts to Secure Federal Acknowledgment," *Publius: The Journal of Federalism* 23, no. 4 (Fall 1993): 123–42.

16. Vine Deloria Jr. and Clifford M. Lytle, *The Nations Within: The Past and Future of American Indian Sovereignty* (New York: Pantheon, 1984), 246.

17. James J. Lopach, Margery Hunter Brown, and Richmond L. Clow, *Tribal Government Today: Politics on Montana Indian Reservations,* revised ed. (Niwot: University Press of Colorado, 1998), 198.

18. Robert B. Porter, "Strengthening Tribal Sovereignty through Government Reform: What Are the Issues," *Kansas Journal of Law and Public Policy* 7 (Winter 1997): 72.

19. Stephen Cornell and Joseph P. Kalt, "Reloading the Dice: Improving the Chances for Economic Development on American Indian Reservations," in *What Can Tribes Do? Strategies and Institutions in American Indian Economic Development,* ed. Stephen Cornell and Joseph P. Kalt (Los Angeles: American Indian Studies Center, 1992), 25.

20. Deloria and Lytle, *The Nations Within,* 247.

21. Council of Economic Advisers, *Changing America: Indicators of Social and Economic Well-Being by Race and Hispanic Origin* (Washington, D.C.: Government Printing Office, 1998).

22. Department of Justice, *American Indians and Crime: 1999–2002* (Washington, D.C.: Bureau of Justice Statistics, 2004), iii.

23. See Porter, "Strengthening Tribal Sovereignty," 72–105; Ian Wilson Record, "Broken Government," *Native Americas* 16, no. 1 (Spring 1999): 10–17; Lois Ramano, "A Nation Divided: The

Cherokee Government in Crisis: And Tribal Leaders Say Chief Joe Byrd Is to Blame," *Washington Post*, July 17, 1997, B1.

24. See, e.g., *Duro v. Reina,* 495 U.S. 676 (1990) and *Strate v. A-1 Contractors,* 520 U.S. 438 (1997); *Montana v. Crow Tribe of Indians,* 523 U.S. 696 (1998); *Alaska v. Native Village of Venetie Tribal Government,* 522 U.S. 520 (1998); *Nevada v. Hicks,* 533 U.S. 353 (2001); *Atkinson Trading Co. v. Shirley,* 532 U.S. 645 (2001); and *City of Sherrill v. Oneida Indian Nation of New York,* 2005 WL 701058 (2005).

Glossary

Allotment policy   (established by the General Allotment, or Dawes, Act) Federal Indian policy initiated in 1887 to break up tribal governments, abolish Indian reservations by the allotment of communally held reservation lands to individual Indians for private ownership, and force Indians to assimilate into Euro-American society.

Blood quantum   An administrative measure of Indian ancestry, whether defined by a tribal government, Congress, or various federal agencies, in which, for example, a person considered to be a "full-blooded" Navajo is alleged to be entirely descended from Navajo ancestors; one-half blood quantum typically denotes someone who has a non-Indian parent and a "full-blooded" parent.

Bureau of Indian Affairs (BIA)   A federal agency established in 1824 and moved to the Department of the Interior in 1849. Originally, BIA personnel served as a diplomatic corps responsible for overseeing trade and other relations with Indian tribes. By the 1860s, however, the BIA had evolved into the lead colonizing agent for the federal government and dominated virtually every aspect of tribal life within reservations. Today, the BIA is more involved in advocating programs focused on tribal educational, social, economic, and cultural self-determination, although it has not entirely separated itself from its more paternalistic history.

Colonialism   The policy and practice of a strong power extending its control territorially, materially, and psychologically over a weaker nation or people. It is often thought of as an attribute of the late-nineteenth-century imperialists who conquered large tracts of the globe. And it is usually used pejoratively to denote an unwarranted sense of racial superiority and the set of attitudes, beliefs, and practices that sprang from this sense.

Discovery, doctrine of   This doctrine was first fully articulated in U.S. law in the seminal Supreme Court case *Johnson v. McIntosh* in 1823. The Court held that European explorers' "discovery" of land occupied by Indian tribes gave the discovering European nation (and the United States as successor) "an exclusive right to extinguish the Indian titles of occupancy, either by purchase or conquest." This meant that the "discovering" nation had preempted other European powers' involvement with the tribes in a

307

particular geographic area. More importantly, as interpreted by Western policymakers and legal scholars, this doctrine effectively excluded Indian tribes from direct participation as national entities in the process of international community development.

Domestic dependent nation   Phrase coined by Chief Justice John Marshall in the 1831 case *Cherokee Nation v. Georgia* to describe the status of tribal nations vis-à-vis the federal government. The Court concluded that tribes lacked foreign national status because they were in the United States and were not "states" within the meaning of the U.S. Constitution, but still had a significant degree of internal jurisdictional autonomy as "domestic dependent nations."

Extraconstitutional   Outside the constitutional framework. Tribes were preexisting and original sovereigns and did not participate in the creation of the U.S. Constitution, which focused on the establishment of the federal government and the relationship between the central government and the constituent states. Thus, tribal sovereign rights do not arise from and are not protected by the Constitution's provisions. The Indian Civil Rights Act of 1968 modified the relationship slightly because portions of the Constitution's first ten amendments, for the first time, were made applicable to tribal governments in their treatment of persons (Indian and non-Indian) within tribal jurisdiction.

Federally recognized tribes   Indian tribes recognized by the federal government as self-governing entities with whom the United States maintains a government-to-government political relationship. This relationship may be established by treaty or agreement, congressional legislation, executive order action, judicial ruling, or the secretary of the interior's decision. Recognized tribes are eligible for special services and benefits designated solely for such tribes (e.g., BIA programs, Indian Health Services), but they also benefit by and are subject to the federal government's trust doctrine and plenary power.

Fee-simple ownership   An estate in land of which the inheritor has unqualified ownership and sole power of disposition.

Five Civilized Tribes   A term coined by whites for the remarkable social, educational, economic, and political progress made by the Cherokee, Choctaw, Chickasaw, Seminole, and Creek Indians after their forced removal from the Southeast to lands west of the Mississippi during the Indian removal era of the 1830s and 1840s.

Fourth World   Spiritual/legal construct developed in the 1970s to distinguish indigenous peoples from nation-states in the Third World, the Second World, and the First World. Third-World nations are decolonized nation-states struggling to industrialize, generally along free-market lines and usually according to a Western majoritarian and pluralistic form of democracy; these nations tend to be distinguished by having been colonized, and later decolonized, by First World, Western, nations. Second-World nation-states are now part of the Commonwealth of Independent States and other eastern European countries that historically shared an experience as socialistic states with totalitarian governments; these nations now tend to be industrialized, restructuring for free-market operation, and in the process of democratizing. First World nations were the first polities to organize politically as nation-states; organize economically to create surplus agricultural capacity, which was followed by industrialization; and then develop democratic governments. These polities tend to exhibit free-market industrialization and political democratization. Franke Wilmer says indigenous peoples constitute a Fourth World "delineated by yet a fourth way of viewing world politics, a fourth path of historical experience bringing them into contact with the world system, and by which they are now becoming players in world politics." While the Third and Fourth Worlds share a history of colonialism and marginalization, Fourth-World peoples are a "step beyond in that they have not yet benefitted from the international principle of self-determination that both the Third World and now Second World nation-states enjoy."

Fractionated heirship   The status of Indian lands that arose because of the General Allotment Act, its amendments, and various allotting agreements. Although the Allotment Act authorized Indians to devise their interests in trust or restricted land through a will, as a practical matter a great deal of the land passed to Indian heirs through intestate succession, thus dividing ownership among all surviving heirs. There are approximately twelve million acres of allotted trust or restricted land, most of which is in multiple ownership. About half the allotted land in "heirship status" is owned by six or more heirs. The consequences of this fractionation of Indian allotments are (1) a complex mix of title interests to individual tracts of land, (2) limitations on the ability of individual owners to dispose of their interests in the land, (3) the devaluation of individual interests because of the inability to convey full title without consent of all of the heirs, (4) the loss of control of rental of the property to the BIA because of the inability to secure agreement among all of the heirs or even to locate heirs, (5) tribal members' loss of their interests in individual tracts to non-Indian or nonmember Indians, and (6) the inability to control the conduct of individual heirs with respect to the property due to the inapplicability of laws against trespass or conversion to persons owning any undivided interest in property.

Guardianship/wardship   The legally specious, and now largely defunct, characterization of the political relationship between tribes and the federal government often attributed to Chief Justice John Marshall in his 1831 ruling *Cherokee Nation v. Georgia,* in which he asserted that Indian tribes were not foreign nations but "domestic dependent nations," each of whose relationship to the United States "resembled that of a ward to a guardian." As the federal government's allotment and assimilation campaign exploded in the 1880s, Marshall's analogy of Indian wardship to federal guardians became reified in the minds of federal policymakers and BIA officials, who popularized the phrase and relied on it to justify any number of federal activities (e.g., suppression of Indian religious freedom, forced allotment of Indian lands, abrogation of Indian treaty rights) designed to hasten the assimilation of Indian people into mainstream American society. Despite the federal government's reliance on the phrase, Indian wardship and federal guardianship remained an illusion that was unsupported by legal authority and lacked tribal consent.

Indian Civil Rights Act (ICRA)   Passed in 1968, the ICRA was the first congressional legislation to impose many of the provisions of the U.S. Bill of Rights on the actions of tribal governments with regard to reservation residents; set out a model code for courts of Indian offenses; and required states to secure tribal consent before assuming legal jurisdiction in Indian Country under P.L. 280.

Indian Country   Broadly, it is country within which Indian laws and customs and federal laws relating to Indians are generally applicable. But it is also defined as all the land under the supervision and protection of the U.S. government that has been set aside primarily for the use of Indians. This includes all Indian reservations and any other areas (e.g., all other Indian communities, including the various Pueblos and Indian lands in Oklahoma, and individual allotments still held in trust by the federal government) under federal jurisdiction and designated for Indian use. And according to some courts, it also includes privately held non-Indian lands within the boundaries of Indian reservations, rights of way (including federal and state highways), and any additional lands tribes acquire.

Indian removal   Federal policy enacted in 1830 and lasting into the 1850s which authorized the president to negotiate with a majority of eastern (and other) tribes for their relocation to lands west of the Mississippi River.

Indian Reorganization Act   Also known as the Wheeler-Howard Act, this 1934 congressional measure is considered to be the most important piece of Indian legislation enacted in the twentieth century. Largely the brainchild of Commissioner of Indian Affairs John Collier, the IRA provided, for those tribes that adopted it, an end to the devastating allotment policy, the purchase of new lands to offset some of those lost through allotment, a measure of economic restoration, cultural regeneration, and the opportunity for tribes to adopt constitutionally based governments.

Indigenous   The United Nations Working Group on Indigenous Populations defines *indigenous populations* as those "composed of the existing descendants of peoples who inhabited the present territory of a country wholly or partially at the time when persons of a different culture or ethnic origin arrived there from other parts of the world, overcame them, and by conquest, settlement or other means, reduced them to a non-dominant or colonial situation; who today live more in conformity with their particular social, economic and cultural customs and traditions than with the institutions of the country of which they now form a part, under a State structure which incorporates mainly the national, social and cultural characteristics of other segments of the population which are dominant."

Interest group activities   The actions of organized associations of individuals who share the same views on a particular issue or set of issues and attempt to influence related government policies.

Kinship   One of the most hotly contested aspects of Indian culture, given the complexity and diversity evident throughout Indian Country. Most Indians believe that kinship provides a social structure of cooperation and nonviolence that is also a means of maintaining political alliances and economic interaction for their societies. Kinship systems, although varied, tend to determine the social position of the individual in a given society. Kinship ties also determine lines of descent, whether through the male (patrilineal) or the female (matrilineal), or through males and females.

Mass media   All means of communication with the public, including television, newspapers, magazines, radio, books, recordings, motion pictures, and the Internet.

Nation   A social group that shares a common ideology, common institutions and customs, and a sense of homogeneity; controls a territory viewed as a national homeland; and has a belief in a common ancestry. A prerequisite of nationhood is an awareness or belief that one's own group is unique in a most vital sense; therefore, the essence of a nation is not tangible but psychological, a matter of attitude rather than of fact. A nation may constitute part of a state, be coterminous with a state, or extend beyond the borders of a single state.

Pan-Indian   Involving more than one tribe. Typically used in reference to organizations, activities, goals, and culture relevant to all Indian tribes.

Partisan identification   The attachment a group or an individual feels to a particular political party. It measures direction toward a particular party and intensity of support. Party identification is usually a good predictor of voting behavior.

Plenary power   Complete in all aspects or essentials. In federal Indian policy and law, this term has three distinct meanings: (1) exclusive (i.e., that Congress, under the commerce clause, is vested with sole authority to conduct the federal government's affairs with Indian tribes); (2) preemptive (i.e., that Congress may enact legislation that effectively precludes state government's acting in Indian-related matters); and (3) unlimited or absolute, a judicially created definition that maintains that the federal government has virtually boundless authority and jurisdiction over Indian tribes, their lands, and their resources.

Rancheria   Spanish term applied to small Indian reservations in California.

Red Power   Indian militancy and pan-Indianism in the 1960s and 1970s.

Reformative goals   Indian tribes and organizations that seek incremental or moderate change in the basic structure of Indian–non-Indian relations through redistribution of services, resources, and rewards in that structure are said to be pursuing reformative goals, since they seek to improve Indian status within the existing framework of relations.

Religious revitalization movements   Indian social movements inspired by religious figures (e.g., the Shawnee Prophet or the Ghost Dance of 1870 and 1890).

Reservation   Tract of land owned by a tribe or tribes and held in trust status by the federal government for the Indians' benefit. Reservations have been created by treaty, statute, executive order, judicial decision, or order of the secretary of the interior. While many reservations were originally viewed as penal colonies or as enclaves where Indians would eventually learn to be "civilized," since the Indian Reorganization period of the 1930s they have come to be understood as the remaining homeland of tribal nations, where tribal law prevails. They are largely exempt from state jurisdiction, with exceptions.

Rider   A provision that may have no relation to the basic subject matter of the bill it is riding on. Riders become law if the bills in which they are included become law. Riders on appropriation bills are outstanding examples, though technically they are banned. The U.S. House of Representatives, unlike the Senate, has a strict germaneness rule; thus riders are usually Senate devices.

Social revitalization movements   Indian social movements designed to enable Indian tribes to accommodate the tremendous changes they were enduring in the wake of American expansionism (e.g., the Handsome Lake Church, the Kickapoo Prophet, the Shaker Church, and the Native American Church).

Sovereignty   A Western concept, both complex and contested, central to modern political thought. Its importance is bound up with specifying the essential character of the territorial state. Implicit in the discussions about the term since Bodin, Machiavelli, and Hobbes is the conviction that the state is the ultimate arbiter of its own fate in relation to the outside world. Each state is "sovereign" in international society, a law unto itself. However, absolute sovereignty no longer exists for any modern state because of international interdependence and the interpenetration of domestic and international politics, the mobility and globalization of capital and information, and the rising influence of transnational social movements and organizations. Sovereignty in modern times more accurately connotes legal competence: the power of a culturally and territorially distinct group of people to develop institutional arrangements that both protect and limit personal freedoms by social control.

Termination policy   Federal Indian policy from approximately 1953 to the mid-1960s that legislatively severed federal benefits and support services to certain tribes, bands, and California *rancherias* and forced the dissolution of their reservations. This policy was exemplified by House Concurrent Resolution No. 108 in 1953, Public Law 280, which conferred upon several designated states full criminal and some civil jurisdiction over Indian reservations, and by relocation, a federal policy focused on the relocation of Indians from rural and reservation areas to urban areas.

Transformative goals   Indian tribes or organizations that favor a fundamental restructuring of current Indian–non-Indian relations (e.g., calls to restart the treaty relationship or end congressional plenary power) are said to support transformative goals, since they desire to dramatically restructure or transform the structure of the relationship.

Treaty   A formal agreement, compact, or contract between two or more sovereign nations that creates legal rights and duties for the contracting parties. A treaty is not only a law but also a contract between two or more nations and must, if possible, be construed so as to give full force and effect to all its parts. Treaties can be bilateral (involving two nations) or multilateral and can deal with single or multiple issues. Indian treaties are of the same dignity as international treaties, but because of the unique political relationship that unfolded between tribes and the United States, the federal courts have created several so-called canons of construction to protect Indian rights. These serve to distinguish Indian treaties from those the United States negotiates with foreign nations in three ways: (1) a cardinal rule in the interpretation of Indian treaties is that ambiguities in treaty language are to be resolved in favor of the Indians; (2) since the wording of treaties was designed to be understood by the Indians, who often could not read and were not skilled in the technical language often used in treaties, doubtful clauses are to be resolved in a nontechnical way, as the Indians would have understood the language; and (3) treaties are to be liberally construed to favor Indians. These three legal doctrines have been enforced inconsistently by the courts, the Congress, and the executive branch; for example, the courts have also ruled repeatedly that Congress in exercising its plenary power may unilaterally abrogate Indian treaty provisions without tribal consent.

Tribal sovereignty   The spiritual, moral, and dynamic cultural force within a given tribal community empowering the group toward political, economic, and, most important, cultural integrity, and toward maturity in the group's relationships with its own members, with other peoples and their governments, and with the environment.

Tribe   A community or combination of communities that occupy a common territory, share a political ideology, and are related by kinship, traditions, and language.

Trust doctrine   Also known as the *trust relationship,* broadly entails the unique legal and moral duty of the federal government to assist Indian tribes in the protection of their lands, resources, and cultural heritage. The federal government, many courts have maintained, is to be held to the highest standards of good faith and honesty in its dealings with Indian peoples and their rights and resources. Nevertheless, since the trust doctrine is not explicitly constitutionally based, it is not enforceable against Congress, although it has occasionally proven a potent source of rights against the executive branch. Importantly, the trust doctrine, which is also referred to as a *trustee-beneficiary relationship* (with the federal government serving as the trustee and the tribes as the beneficiary) is not synonymous with the so-called guardian-ward relationship that was said to exist between tribes and the United States from the 1860s to the 1930s.

Suggested Readings

THE FOLLOWING is a short list of books and articles for further reading on the subjects addressed in each chapter. We have limited our suggestions to classic works and more recent studies that provide broad coverage of the subjects examined.

Introduction

Mohawk, John C. *Utopian Legacies: A History of Conquest and Oppression in the Western World.* Santa Fe, N.Mex.: Clear Light, 2000.

Sullivan, Robert. *A Whale Hunt: How a Native-American Village Did What No One Thought It Could.* New York: Simon & Schuster, 2002.

Chapter 1:
A Tour of Native Peoples and Native Lands

Champagne, Duane. *Native America: Portrait of the Peoples.* Detroit: Visible Ink, 1994.

Davis, Mary B., ed. *Native America in the Twentieth Century: An Encyclopedia.* New York: Garland, 1996.

Harvard Project on American Indian Economic Development. *The State of Native Nations: Conditions Under U.S. Policies of Self-Determination.* New York: Oxford University Press, 2008.

Paredes, J. Anthony, ed. *Indians of the Southeastern United States in the Late 20th Century.* Tuscaloosa: University of Alabama Press, 1992.

Snipp, C. Matthew, comp. *American Indians: The First of This Land.* New York: Russell Sage Foundation, 1989.

Sutton, Imre, ed. *Irredeemable America: The Indians' Estate and Land Claims.* Albuquerque: University of New Mexico Press, 1985.

Waldman, Carl. *Atlas of the North American Indian.* Revised ed. New York: Checkmark, 2000.

Chapter 2:
Indigenous Peoples Are Nations, Not Minorities

Barsh, Russel L., and James Youngblood Henderson. *The Road: Indian Tribes and Political Liberty.* Berkeley: University of California Press, 1980.

Carrillo, Jo, ed. *Readings in American Indian Law: Recalling the Rhythm of Survival.* Philadelphia: Temple University Press, 1998.

Cohen, Felix S. *Handbook of Federal Indian Law.* 1942. Reprint, Albuquerque: University of New Mexico Press, 1972.

Deloria, Vine, Jr. *Behind the Trail of Broken Treaties: An Indian Declaration of Independence.* 1974. Reprint, Austin: University of Texas Press, 1985.

———. ed. *American Indian Policy in the Twentieth Century.* Norman: University of Oklahoma Press, 1985.

Deloria, Vine, Jr., and Raymond J. DeMallie, comps. *Documents of American Indian Diplomacy: Treaties, Agreements, and Conventions, 1775–1979.* 2 vols. Norman: University of Oklahoma Press, 1999.

Deloria, Vine, Jr., and David E. Wilkins. *Tribes, Treaties, and Constitutional Tribulations.* Austin: University of Texas Press, 1999.

Duthu, N. Bruce. *American Indians and the Law.* New York: Viking Penguin, 2008.

Harding, Sidney. *Crow Dog's Case: American Indian Sovereignty, Tribal Law, and United States Law in the Nineteenth Century.* New York: Cambridge University Press, 1994.

Lyons, Oren, and John Mohawk, eds. *Exiled in the Land of the Free: Democracy, Indian Nations, and the U.S. Constitution.* Santa Fe, N.Mex.: Clear Light, 1992.

Wilkins, David, and K. Tsianina Lomawaima. *Uneven Ground: American Indian Sovereignty and Federal Law.* Norman: University of Oklahoma Press, 2001.

Chapter 3:
Indigenous Governments: Past, Present, and Future

Alfred, Gerald R. *Heeding the Voices of Our Ancestors: Kahnawake Mohawk Politics and the Rise of Native Nationalism.* Toronto: Oxford University Press, 1995.

Austin, Raymond D. *Navajo Courts and Navajo Common Law: A Tradition of Tribal Self-Governance.* Minneapolis: University of Minnesota Press, 2009.

Cohen, Felix S. (edited by David Wilkins). *On the Drafting of Tribal Constitutions.* Norman: University of Oklahoma Press, 2007.

Debo, Angie. *And Still the Waters Run: The Betrayal of the Five Civilized Tribes.* Princeton, N.J.: Princeton University Press, 1940.

Deloria, Vine, Jr., and Clifford M. Lytle. *American Indians, American Justice.* Austin: University of Texas Press, 1983.

Fowler, Loretta. *Arapahoe Politics, 1851–1978: Symbols in Crises of Authority.* Lincoln: University of Nebraska Press, 1982.

Lemont, Eric, ed. *American Indian Constitutional Reform and the Rebuilding of Native Nations.* Austin: University of Texas Press, 2006.

Lopach, James J., Margery Hunter Brown, and Richmond L. Clow. *Tribal Government Today: Politics on Montana Indian Reservations.* Revised ed. Niwot: University Press of Colorado, 1998.

O'Brien, Sharon. *American Indian Tribal Governments.* Norman: University of Oklahoma Press, 1989.

Wilkins, David. *Documents of Native American Political Development, 1500s–1933.* New York: Oxford University Press, 2009.

Chapter 4:
Actors in Native Politics

Cramer, Renée Ann. *Cash, Color, and Colonialism: The Politics of Tribal Acknowledgment.* Norman: University of Oklahoma Press, 2005.

Deloria, Vine, Jr. "Congress in Its Wisdom: The Course of Indian Legislation." In *The Aggressions of Civilization,* ed. Sandra L. Cadwalader and Vine Deloria Jr., 106–30. Philadelphia: Temple University Press, 1984.

Vine, Jr., Deloria, and David E. Wilkins, *Tribes, Treaties, and Constitutional Tribulations.* Austin: University of Texas Press, 1999.

Kvasnicka, Robert M., and Herman J. Viola, eds. *The Commissioners of Indian Affairs, 1824–1977.* Lincoln: University of Nebraska Press, 1979.

Reed, James B., and Judy A. Zelio, eds. *States and Tribes: Building New Traditions.* Denver, Colo.: National Conference of State Legislatures, 1995.

Taylor, Theodore W. *The Bureau of Indian Affairs.* Boulder, Colo.: Westview, 1984.

Wilkins, David E. *American Indian Sovereignty and the U.S. Supreme Court: The Masking of Justice.* Austin: University of Texas Press, 1997.

Chapter 5:
A History of Federal Indian Policy

Calloway, Colin G. *The American Revolution in Indian Country: Crisis and Diversity in Native American Communities.* New York: Cambridge University Press, 1995.

Iverson, Peter, ed. *The Plains Indians of the Twentieth Century.* Norman: University of Oklahoma Press, 1985.

Lobo, Susan, and Kurt Peters. *American Indians and the Urban Experience.* Walnut Creek, Calif.: Altamira Press, 2001.

Prucha, Francis Paul. *The Great Father: The United States Government and the American Indians.* 2 vols. Lincoln: University of Nebraska Press, 1984. Abridged ed. Lincoln: University of Nebraska Press, 1986.

Williams, Robert A., Jr. *Linking Arms Together: American Indian Treaty Visions of Law and Peace, 1600–1800.* New York: Oxford University Press, 1997.

Chapter 6:
Tribal Political Economy

Cattelino, Jessica R., *High Stakes: Florida Seminole Gaming and Sovereignty.* Durham, N.C.: Duke University Press, 2008.

Hosmer, Brian C. *American Indians in the Marketplace: Persistence and Innovation among the Menominees and Metlakatlans, 1870–1920.* Lawrence: University Press of Kansas, 1999.

Mason, W. Dale. *Indian Gaming: Tribal Sovereignty and American Politics.* Norman: University of Oklahoma Press, 2000.

McCool, Daniel. *Command of the Waters: Iron Triangles, Federal Water Development, and Indian Water.* Tucson: University of Arizona Press, 1994.

Shurts, John. *Indian Reserved Water Rights: The Winters Doctrine in Its Social and Legal Context, 1880s–1930s.* Norman: University of Oklahoma Press, 2000.

Thorne, Tanis C. *The World's Richest Indian: The Scandal over Jackson Barnett's Oil Fortune.* New York: Oxford University Press, 2003.

White, Richard. *The Roots of Dependency: Subsistence, Environment, and Social Change among the Choctaws, Pawnees, and Navajos.* Lincoln: University of Nebraska Press, 1983.

Chapter 7:
Indian Political Participation:
Patriotism, Suffrage, and Partisanship

Cornell, Stephen. *The Return of the Native: American Indian Political Resurgence.* New York: Oxford University Press, 1988.

Hertzberg, Hazel W. *The Search for an American Indian Identity.* Syracuse, N.Y.: Syracuse University Press, 1971.

Krouse, Susan Applegate. *North American Indians in the Great War.* Lincoln: University of Nebraska Press, 2009.

McCool, Daniel, Susan S. Olson, and Jennifer L. Robinson. *Native Vote: American Indians, the Voting Rights Act, and the Right to Vote.* New York, Cambridge University Press, 2007.

McDonald, Laughlin. *American Indians and the Fight for Equal Voting Rights.* Norman: University of Oklahoma Press, 2010.

Nagel, Joane. *American Indian Ethnic Renewal: Red Power and the Resurgence of Identity and Culture.* New York: Oxford University Press, 1996.

Chapter 8:
Indian Interest Group Activity and Activism

Cobb, Daniel. *Native Activism in Cold War America: The Struggle for Sovereignty.* Lawrence: University Press of Kansas, 2008.

Deloria, Vine, Jr. *Custer Died for Your Sins: An Indian Manifesto.* 1969. Reprint, Norman: University of Oklahoma Press, 1988.

Johnson, Troy R. *The Occupation of Alcatraz Island: Indian Self-Determination and the Rise of Indian Activism.* Urbana: University of Illinois Press, 1996.

Pertusati, Linda. *In Defense of Mohawk Land: Ethnopolitical Conflict in Native North America.* Albany: State University of New York Press, 1997.

Thorpe, Dagmar. *People of the Seventh Fire: Returning Lifeways of Native America.* Ithaca, N.Y.: Akwe:kon Press, 1996.

Wilmer, Franke. *The Indigenous Voice in World Politics.* Newbury Park, Calif.: Sage, 1993.

Chapter 9:
Native Peoples, Images, and the Media

Murphy, James E., and Sharon M. Murphy. *Let My People Know: American Indian Journalism, 1828–1978.* Norman: University of Oklahoma Press, 1981.

Spindel, Carol. *Dancing at Halftime: Sports and the Controversy over American Indian Mascots.* New York: New York University Press, 2000.

Stedman, Raymond William. *Shadows of the Indian: Stereotypes in American Culture.* Norman: University of Oklahoma Press, 1982.

Trahant, Mark N. *Pictures of Our Nobler Selves: A History of Native American Contributions to News Media.* Nashville, Tenn.: Freedom Forum First Amendment Center, 1995.

Chapter 10:
Indigenous Nations and the American Political System

Alfred, Taiaiake. *Peace, Power, Righteousness: An Indigenous Manifesto.* 2nd ed. Toronto: Oxford University Press, 2009.

Cook-Lynn, Elizabeth. *Anti-Indianism in Modern America: A Voice from Tatekeya's Earth.* Urbana: University of Illinois Press, 2001.

Deloria, Vine, Jr., and Clifford M. Lytle. *The Nations Within: The Past and Future of American Indian Sovereignty.* New York: Pantheon, 1984.

Grounds, Richard, George E. Tinker, and David E. Wilkins, eds. *Native Voices: American Indian Identity and Resistance.* Lawrence: University Press of Kansas, 2003.

Jemison, G. Peter, and Anna M. Schein, eds. *Treaty of Canandaigua: 200 Years of Treaty Relations between the Iroquois Confederacy and the United States.* Santa Fe, N.Mex.: Clear Light, 2000.

Case Index

Subject Index

Aboriginal Peoples (as term), 1

Abourezk, James, 90

Absentee Shawnee, 59

absolute power, 37–38, 72, 111, 231, 234, 311, 349

acculturation, 75, 127–28

Acoma Pueblo, 57, 157,

activism, xxx, xl, 66, 90, 202, 229; contemporary, 204–9; media 218–19; termination 131

Adair Weekly Ledger, 221

Adams, John, 125

administrative tasks, 93

affirmative action, 105, 106, 129, 231

age, xxxiii, 30, 66, 71, 73, 78, 104, 136, 180, 182, 184, 237, 254, 258, 260

agreements, xxx, xxxvi, 15, 48, 68, 94, 98, 128, 140, 147; on natural resources, 160, 163, 200; Reagan/Bush and, 102; TFW, xii, 119

agriculture, 62, 106, 138, 152–55, 203, 207

Ak-Chin Reservation, 155

Akaka bill. *See* Native Hawaiian Government Reorganization Bill

Akaka, Daniel K., 2

Akwesasne Mohawk Reservation, 148, 235

Akwesasne Notes, 221

Alaska Act, 64

Alaska Federation of Natives, 80, 196

Alaska Fisherman, 221

Alaska Native Brotherhood and Sisterhood (ANB/S), xi, 192–93

Alaska Native Claims Settlement Act (ANCSA), xi, xxi, xxii, xxiii, 7, 78–79, 80

Alaska Natives, xvii, xxii, xxiii, xl, 4, 7, 15, 17, 25–29, 64, 78–80, 93, 98, 99, 102, 105, 106, 134, 136, 159, 173, 174, 176, 182, 183, 184, 232, 237, 267; Congress, and, 79, 80; defined, 1, 7; education of, 133; government of, 23, 52, 69, 78–80; identification as, 26, 27, 29, 30; IRA and 64, 78–79; media and, 221–23; recognition of, 80; reservation for, xxiii, 20, 30

Alaska Statehood Act, 79

Albany Plan, 54, 55

Alcatraz Island, xxi, 206

alcohol: 109, 117, 148, 217; casinos banning, 148; Crazy Horse and, 214–15; crime and, 78, 237; Handsome Lake religion and, 203

alcoholism, 94, 98, 136; gaming and, 208

Aleuts, 1, 15, 78

Alexian Brothers Roman Catholic novitiate, 206

Allen, W. Ron, 17

alliances, xix, xx, xxxi, 34, 38, 54, 122, 191, 204–5, 209, 223, 224; extratribal, 200–1; intertribal, 191–95; intratribal, 191; supratribal (pan-Indian) 195–99, 204–5

allotment, xxxii, 24, 26, 44, 47, 48, 49, 61, 62, 65, 76, 94, 114, 127–28, 138, 152, 155, 171, 176, 191, 220, 230, 266, 272, 307, 309, 310; BIA and, 48, 105, 138, 139, 154; citizenship and, 42, 44, 127; end of, 63, 101, 129; Indian courts and, 76, 204; land claims and, 204; land consolidation and, 128, 138–41; Teller, Henry, and, 126

Ambler, Marjane, 135, 155

About the Authors

David E. Wilkins is a citizen of the Lumbee Nation and holds the McKnight Presidential Professorship in American Indian Studies at the University of Minnesota. He has adjunct appointments in political science, law, and American studies. He earned his PhD in political science from the University of North Carolina–Chapel Hill in December 1990.

Wilkins is the author or editor of thirteen books, including *Documents of Native American Political Development: 1533 to 1933* (2009) and *On the Drafting of Tribal Constitutions* (2006). His articles have appeared in a range of social science, law, history, and ethnic studies journals.

Heidi Kiiwetinepinesiik Stark (Turtle Mountain Ojibwe) is assistant professor of American Indian Studies at the University of Minnesota–Duluth. She earned her PhD in American studies from the University of Minnesota in 2008. She is currently revising her dissertation into a book that explores Anishinaabe treaty relations and U.S./Canadian state formation.